PARTY FOOD

PARTY FOOD

SMALL & SAVORY

BARBARA KAFKA

Photography by
Tom Eckerle

William Morrow and Company, Inc.
NEW YORK

Library of Congress Cataloging-in-Publication Data

Kafka, Barbara.
Party food / Barbara Kafka.
p.   cm.
Includes index.
ISBN 0–688–11184–X
1. Cookery.   2. Entertaining.   I. Title.
TX652.K28   1992
641.5′68—dc20   91–45725
CIP

Printed in the United States of America

First Edition

1 2 3 4 5 6 7 8 9 10

BOOK DESIGN BY MICHELLE WIENER

To all my guests,

particularly my family —

Ernie

Nicole

Michael

Richard

and

my parents

ACKNOWLEDGMENTS

While I have tested the recipes and eaten all the foods in this book, and some of them are very idiosyncratic indeed, it is no doubt true that in this book I am more indebted to cooks throughout the world and time than I am in any other book I have done. I did not invent meze or even stuffed grape leaves. Over the many years that I have been learning about food and cooking, I have read literally thousands of cookbooks and eaten at hundreds of restaurants in many parts of the world. All have contributed to my knowledge, my sense of flavor and form. I thank them all.

Where there is an immediately proximate source for a recipe, I have tried to credit it. In a general way, I have learned a great deal from the work of Barbara Tropp, Paula Wolfert and Nicole Routhier. This book does not lay any claim to authenticity ("This is exactly the way the Berbers of this tiny wadi make this recipe"). Instead, I remember flavors and ideas and then I try to create recipes that seem to work in my very contemporary kitchen, pleasing my palate and using methods not feasible for desert nomads but for me, and I hope for the reader.

There is one important exception. I am not a Chinese cook. Thanks to Jeffrey Steingarten of *Vogue* I had the special opportunity to work with Wei Ming, a fine chef who worked for Wellington Koo, in the home of Frances Tang. He taught me to make and form the doughs on pages 253–255 and 258–259. I must take responsibility for the descriptions and fillings.

I'm a rather loyal person. I've had the same husband for thirty-seven years and the same editor since 1980. My husband's interest in good food, fabulous palate, and patience with odd meals—all nibbles—odd working hours and preoccupation have been essential to my ability to work. My editor, Ann Bramson, has had faith in what must have seemed at times the most peculiar of my ideas, has loyally tried new cooking methods and new recipes with enthusiasm and has made my books better than they deserved to be. Maybe I just have had the luck of the draw.

With this book, there are two new creative forces in my life, Tom Eckerle and his charming family and Michelle Wiener. His photographs have given me realizations of my visions. She, new baby and all, has carefully crafted this book so that design, style and information meet seamlessly.

While most of the photographs have been taken either in Vermont or New York, at home, my guardian angels, Leo Lerman and Gray Foy, permitted me to derange their exquisite dining room and collections to take the photographs on pages 20 and 266.

This book would have been impossible without the work of many people in my kitchen and office. First of all, there is Lee Ann Cox, who has learned so much and helped so much. Anna Brandenburger has gone back to London and Chris Styler has returned to being a chef: but when they could, they were pleasures and aides. Esti Marpet manages me with the help over the last years, at various times, of Nancy Messing, Leanne Mella and Sydney Watts.

I have been gifted with a publisher, Al Marchioni, who has given me rope, money and friendship; Lisa Queen, who moves heaven and earth to place me in happy homes; a copy editor—and having been one for many years I know how difficult and important the work is—Toni Rachiele, of great tact. Ann's assistant, Sarah Guralnik; Lisa's assistant, Imen Budhai; and sub-rights manager, Michelle Corallo, have put up with an anxious author's endless phone calls.

While in that commercial vein, I want to thank the magazine editors who seem to like and buy my work. No cookbook author can live by books alone, and "I'm still here" thanks to Gail Zweigenthal at *Gourmet,* Eric Asimov, Penelope Green and Angela Dodson (with a bow to Carol Shaw) at *The New York Times,* Sharon Storrier-Lyneham and June McCallum at *Australian Vogue Entertaining* and Warren Picower and Malachy Duffy at *Food & Wine.* I thank Julian Shuckburgh, who first brought my books to Great Britain, and Drew Smith, who published me as long as he could at *Taste.*

I am lucky enough to have friends in many parts of the world. Some of them cannot boil water although they are usually good eaters, but with many I have a history of reciprocity: I cook for you, you cook for me. It's not a formal debt-paying thing but rather a sharing. Friends are why I learned to cook and sometimes how as well. The briefest of lists would include Brigitte de Saussure, Jeanette Leroy and Paul Haim, Helen Frankenthaler, Paul Levy, Corby Kummer (who also makes a good reader's suggestions) and Ann Bramson.

CONTENTS

All recipes underlined in green are vegetarian

All recipes underlined in gold are nonvegetarian

Nothing says cocktail party in all
its period elegance better than a
martini. Let guests mix their own.

"WHAT A SWELL PARTY THIS IS"

If you have seen a *Thin Man* movie on late-night television, you may have been as struck as I was by the dinner jackets, the constant martinis with their silver shaker and the impeccable servants who glide in behind the romping dog, Asta (beloved of constructors of crossword puzzles). While I admire the lighthearted charm and elegance, and wonder how they escaped being sozzled—yes, the dog too—I am also clear that no party of mine, cocktail or otherwise, resembles this high-toned fantasy.

In my teens, when cocktail parties were in flower, I was terrible at them. I think I became a food person because it was always easier for me to help dish up, pass and clean up than to circulate without an excuse for obtruding myself into the conversations of strangers. I have recovered and find that I can attend with pleasure informal parties without assigned seats, a longish way of saying "something like a cocktail party." The difference between today and the past is less emphasis on liquor—even an absence sometimes—and a much greater range of times of day and occasions when this kind of party fits in.

It's an informal, less demanding and relatively less expensive way of entertaining than dinner parties. Dogs and children fit in better. It can be brunch, lunch, a picnic, a barbecue, a few people sitting around of an evening, a little something before going out to dinner, a little something after theater or a concert, a supply of satisfying foods during the football game, a midafternoon selection of poolside nibbles, a gallery reception, a store opening, an office reception, a wedding reception, a baby shower, a holiday party, a graduation party, a paying-the-social-obligations party or even a full-scale cocktail party. It's a newer way of entertaining and we all do it.

The question is how to give one with a minimum of frazzling of oneself and one's guests combined with maximum pleasure. We must escape the thirties and forties image of the palmy movie days and the even older, Victorian norms of entertainment, leaving the silver trays in the closet along with the lace napkins. The silent butler—not a person but a hinge-topped silver box on a handle—can come out of the closet for the disposal of toothpicks. Fortunately, it seems to be less needed today for picking up cigarette butts. Guests never seemed to be without a cigarette in those old movies, even in love scenes; I used to wonder if they could act without one.

the food

"The world is so full of a number of things,
I'm sure we should all be as happy as kings."
—R.L.S.

I suppose "in the best of all possible worlds" we could feed everybody caviar if we

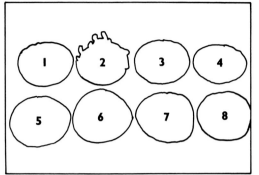

A *tray party is a nice and easy way to entertain. Find an attractive tray with sides. Arrange in it, matching or not, as many bowls as you have foods. Fill the bowls and deliver the tray to your guests. As this is probably a small party, you may want to put out bread-and-butter plates and salad forks for added elegance. If not, everything can be eaten from fingers or toothpicks. A Middle Eastern assortment could feature* **1** *Sesame Curried Almonds (page 50),* **2** *Cumin Carrots (page 70),* **3** *Moroccan Spiced Olives (page 53);* **4** *Chickpea Dip (page 16),* **5** *Spicy Middle Eastern Tomato Sauce (page 27),* **6** *miniature pitas (store-bought) or Fried Bread Puffs (page 125);* **7** *Fried Kibbeh (page 277) and/or Koftah (page 278) and* **8** *Cumin Mushrooms (page 70). The tomato sauce serves as a universal dunk. Try this with other assortments. Look in the Index under Greek or Italian, for instance, and see what you might use.*

wanted, have time to make a gross of canapés or filled pastries if we thought they were the most desirable thing and have help to serve and help to cook. Well, my world isn't like that, and I don't think there are many of us who have such options.

Not all parties require that we work our fingers to the bone. Many foods can be bought in jars, in cans or by the slice. You can buy a party without buying a caterer. You can go to delicatessens and take-out counters and scan specialty shops and supermarket shelves for good things in cans and jars and cull mail order catalogues. In each chapter, I have a Ready-Mades section discussing those perfectly valid short cuts, sometimes with a hint or two for doctoring what you buy to improve its flavor or a garnish that gussies. You can keep the makings of a party on the shelf or in the refrigerator or freezer so that you are unfazed by unexpected guests. Taste around until you find the products most acceptable to you.

Even so, we may need to or want to cook, and most of this book is filled with recipes. Choose a single spiced nut from Veggie Good (pages 48–53) or a full panoply of lavish goodies selected from all parts of the book.

This is not a menu book, a lifestyle book or a party book, although I hope you will have many wonderful parties based on it, that they will have a strong style—your own—with perhaps a few hints from me and that you will come up with an ever-changing assortment of menus. One of the nicest ways to use the book is to have something on hand, something you

have made that fits a dozen uses. The Sun-Dried Tomato Dip (page 8), for example, keeps virtually indefinitely in the refrigerator. One day it is put out in a crock surrounded by good bread, or it forms a layer of a Hero Sandwich (page 130), or spoonfuls are dropped on the ends of endive leaves as a more formal hors d'oeuvre, or it goes on pasta as a sauce at dinner, or the last of it goes in a little bowl to fill out A Tray Party. Small pastries can go in the freezer to be heated as needed. What you pick to have on hand will depend on what you like to cook and what you like to eat.

The book is arranged to use as you will. After all, how often do you want to give exactly the party I plan or the one you gave last month? You want a dip, look at Chapter 1; need a pâté, see Chapter 4; one fried food, see Chapter 7 and so on. Multiply or divide recipes based on the number of guests and the number of foods. As few as six people will need a lot of guacamole, salsa and chips if that's all there is. The same amount may be enough for fifteen when you add empanadas and slices of hard sausage.

All the inspiration in the world won't get you through to the end without a menu. The world has many models for groups of informal foods to be eaten at festive gatherings, although they are mainly consumed while seated around a table. Meze, the Greek assortment of nibbles of food to be eaten while sipping ouzo (page 203), comes to mind, along with the Russian zakouski with vodka (page 41) and the Chinese tea lunch. There are menus for and photographs of some of these traditional parties studded throughout the book.

We seem, however, to live in a more mix-and-match world, and there is nothing wrong in combining foods from different traditions and mixing in newly devised dishes. The important thing is to balance flavors, hot and cold, to vary cooking techniques so that the work is spread out throughout the kitchen and over time, and to have the food fit your tastes, your abilities and the kind of party you want to give. Again, there are parties of this sort in the book, or ideas that you really can trim (usually eliminating dishes) or modify to taste.

Before we get to the menu or indeed to be happy at our parties, we have to figure out what they are and what we are doing. Often,

we are not inviting people ahead and making a serious party; instead, we are simply welcoming a few friends. A quick raid on kitchen cabinets, freezer and refrigerator if we have been provident will solve the problem. Even these rushed, informal moments can be made a little special with one homemade dip (pages 8–13) and a single sliced raw vegetable. When it's in season, consider sliced bulb fennel; it's very quick, along with Creamy Asian Dip (page 13) or Walnut Dip (page 16).

Throughout the book I have tried to provide planning help by explaining how far ahead a recipe can be done, how things can be frozen and/or reheated and how many of a given kind of item you will need for a party.

A *simple version of the Italian canapé Crostini (page 131).*

Planning a big party? Make a shopping list and a preparation plan. It may start weeks before the actual event. You may bake and freeze a focaccia or two and then make spiced olives two weeks ahead and pâtés a week ahead of time, right through the more accelerated schedule of the last few days—finding where you hid the baskets, bowls and trays after the last party, calling for ice, checking the glasses and finishing the cooking. The day of the party should be for setting things out and reheating.

If children are included, try something on a bun that's less likely to slip from small hands and create sticky fingers. Miniature

Grill these ingredients and make these foods—1 Chicken Saté (page 272); 2 ramps and 3 portobello mushrooms for grilling; 4 Grilled Flank Steak (page 273) for thin slicing and putting on 5 Bruschette (page 131), along with 6 mustard and 7 baby eggplants, scored, oiled and ready for grilling (page 82). 8 Sliced tomatoes with basil are nice on plates or to put on open sandwiches with the meat. Accompany with 9 olive oil and vinegar for the tomatoes and for the things to be grilled.

Hamburgers (page 279) and Fishburgers (page 187) are favorites. My children were placated with tea sandwiches (page 118), which always seemed festive to them and didn't do too much damage.

the guests

Even before thinking of food, you need to think about your guests, your style and the number of extra hands you can count on: How many guests? How formal the party? Any help? Sometimes, "How many?" is easily answered by counting and ending up with, say, ten. Alternatively, you may be giving a really big party—a pay-everybody-back party or a wedding party. Then the number is usually defined by the space available. It is easy to be seduced by informality and the hope that "everybody won't arrive at the same time" into adding just a few more names to the list. Remember: It is extremely uncomfortable to be crammed into a space where it is impossible to move and hard to breathe, where water starts trickling down one's back and it is almost impossible for guests to get to the food and drinks. Such overcrowding may seem cozy to teenagers, which just shows my age.

There is some leeway if the weather is nice and there is an outdoors into which the guests can spill—not too likely in a sixteenth-floor city apartment. Even with a garden, it can rain or your tulips could get thoroughly trampled.

Vodka, aquavit and Champagne have developed a ritual of glasses for their service.

Formality can be determined by imagining the outfit on your ideal guest: blue jeans, white shirt and sneakers; an Ascot train and garden party hat; straight-from-the-office suit garnished with briefcase; slinky gown and black tie (not on the same guest); cocktail dress or tennis, croquet and South of France whites. Yes, this is a bit tongue-in-cheek, but a scenario helps you with the party plan.

You're not the only one who needs to know what is planned. Guests will be more comfortable if they know what to expect from a party. You can find a way to put it in the invitation—written or phoned. Written invitations are a lot better when inviting more than twenty. Remember the written word? It has not died. Large parties can use printed, fill-in-the-blanks invitations, but try to keep the coy firmly in check. Very formal events such as weddings can have engraved invitations. (While I am at it, I put in a plea for flowers sent well before the party, the thank-you notes sent soon after.)

Keep lists for acceptances and refusals, and if you have exceptionally absent-minded or rude friends and the party is rather formal, send reminder notes ten days before the party. Tell people when the party will be over as well as when it will begin; what the dress level will be ("We're all wearing jeans"; "I hope it will be very gala"; "Black tie" or "I think everybody will just be wearing stuff from the office"). You can be more specific ("It's an informal cocktail party"; "A few of us are going to sit around, drink beer, eat and watch the game"; "We're having a brunch to meet Mary's new friend"; "I thought we all

deserved a gala party after the work we've put into this project"; "Drop in—it's very informal"; "Be sure to bring the kids"). If you expect the party to stretch on into a full meal, give your guests a clue.

Have an answer prepared for "Can I bring Harry and Maude? They're spending the weekend." A simple "No," while tempting, is probably not enough. If it is a large informal party, you may want to say yes. If you are already overcrowded, say so, trying to sound more regretful than harried. You do not owe an invitee extra invitations.

the help

For most of us this means the members of the family or friends we can press-gang into service. If I can have one professional helper, I will choose a cleaner-upper. I can cope with beforehand and cooking and even stoking the guests, but I get tired by vacuuming time. An absence of help means no canapés—i.e., everything must go on a bowl or platter in ample quantities (not too much refilling) and require a minimum of passing. This leads to one buffet or a series of mini-buffets. In the one-buffet plan, everything looks much like a dinner party except that the food is in small pieces that need no cutting and no plates or forks. You may need some service forks and knives for spreading mustard or sauces on bread. This avoids the death of the hosts from overwork.

Mini-buffets are simply the same foods spread in small groups around the party space. The piroshki, sour cream, smoked salmon and blini go on one table; the chickpea dip and sliced vegetables go on another, and the spiced nuts and olives are set around the room in myriad small bowls. The food can vary from place to place or be the same. The mini-buffet system keeps the guests from crushing one another to death as does making two widely separated bars. Still, the herd instinct may defeat your best plans.

The next helper I would have at a big party would be a bartender. It keeps things much neater.

Summer memories of perfect picnics are provided by Deviled Eggs (page 88).

the stuff

Small parties don't require any special stuff; use what you have. One big party probably means borrowing or renting what you need. If big parties occur a few times a year, you may want to gradually acquire some larger pots, serving platters, bowls and spoons, et cetera.

Down the Hatch (pages 291–305) will tell you all about glasses, ice and places to keep it, pitchers, stirrers, mixers, fruit juices,

wine, liquor and anything else that has to do with serving the liquid part of the meal.

Napkins there must be in quantity. I have a small drawer crammed with tiny scraps of embroidered, printed or otherwise embellished bits of cloth that were cocktail napkins in more formal days. I no longer use them except in the most extraordinary circumstance: the Queen is coming (get real) or my fifth-grade teacher is paying a visit (residual panic). It's not just the washing and ironing involved in cocktail napkins; it is the inability of even one's best-brought-up friends to remember that these are not used handkerchiefs to be stuffed absently into pockets. I use paper napkins, often in some bright color, and allow about three per person; they get left on tables, get dirty and get wet. At an outdoor barbecue event, I provide bigger napkins.

Toothpicks there will probably have to be, and no intricate Japanese carving is going to make them truly elegant. Choose ones that are sufficiently sturdy that they won't break off under a load of food. Toothpicks along with the tails from boiled shrimp and the pits from olives will require discard spots. Otherwise, they end up in the flowers and potted plants. I use what used to be ashtrays and stick a pit or toothpick in each at the beginning of the party to give people the idea.

A *very elegant afternoon or late-evening alternative to a more complex assortment can be a decanter of a good Port and walnuts to crack ad lib. Small glasses with stems, please.*

Scatter these around the room along with real ashtrays and matches if needed and tolerated. People don't go to the pit stop; it has to come to them. Be sure to have garbage bags.

Plates are not a major concern, but if the food requires them, use all your bread-and-butter plates; it doesn't matter if they don't match. Bowls, platters and baskets for serving are needed. At a large party you need at least double the amount of serving dishes as food items. It is much better to bring in a fresh bowl of dip when the one that's out looks used and sorry than to leave an empty space next to the chips or try to refurbish the used container. Remove the offender to the kitchen and freshen it up or use it as a refill when the new bowl, in turn, gets sorry.

Flowers and candles are nice, but the greater the crush, the less they will be noticed. If it's cold or rainy, remember hangers along with a place for the drippy umbrellas. Stock the bathrooms. If it's a big outdoor event, think about a tent (not the kids' pup tent) and if it's likely to be chilly, heaters.

Storing the food can be a problem. If the weather's cold but not freezing and you have an outdoor space—I have an areaway between my back door and an external gate—use nature's refrigerator. If not, consider one of those big Styrofoam boxes or other camping-picnicking container. Get Blue Ice or other freezable chiller, freeze and line the bottom of your container and use that for food. If you give big parties often, consider buying extra baking sheets, loaf pans, bowls and large-capacity freezer and refrigerator containers. All parties, especially those with cook-

Although I'm not a big one for theme parties, it is sometimes fun to dig out all the artifacts brought from a trip or amassed over the years that have some relevance to the food served to make a festive presentation. In this case, the food is mainly Central American: **1** easy-to-make Nachos (page 57); **2** Guacamole (page 13); **3** Fried Empanadas (page 217); **4** Fresh Tomatillo Salsa (page 23); **5** Spicy Papaya Salsa (page 24); sliced chorizos and sour cream.

ing done ahead, will require plastic wrap, aluminum foil, paper towels, sponges and dishwashing stuff. Have a dustpan and whisk broom handy, along with a sponge or two for spills.

If you don't already have one, consider a wok and Chinese skimmers. Everything else is pretty standard. I always need more potato peelers and small knives than I have, but you may be more provident. I have a mandoline (page 233). It is hardly essential. Essential for me are a blender, a food processor, a food mill and a heavy-duty mixer.

A cautionary tale before planning: I will never forget going to a party in my first ever and long-coveted cocktail dress, a swishy affair of off-the-shoulder pale blue (I was very young) taffeta—in the days of chafing dishes, Swedish meatballs and toothpicks—only to have the sauce and the meatball slide ferociously down my décolletage, leaving a hideous indelible stain. If the food is messy and the dress fancy, provide bread and butter plates and forks.

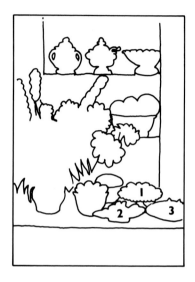

Any piece of furniture, here a rustic jelly cabinet, can look festive with graphic china, such as ironstone, and flowers, along with a small assortment of foods: **1** *miniature quiches (pages 98–102),* **2** *Chiles Relleños (page 246) and* **3** *rice paper–wrapped goodies (pages 208–212).*

off-the-shelf food

Don't start from scratch every time you want to have people over. Read the recipes. Many of the staples, as well as the seasonings, can be kept on hand. Read the Ready-Mades sections in the various chapters and see what emergency rations appeal to you. Be sure to have condiments such as mustard, cocktail sauce, horseradish and pickles on hand; they go with so many things.

Happy parties!

PARTY FOOD

chapter 1

dips, spreads and sauces

To me the most noticeable thing about party giving in the second half of the twentieth century is dips. Dips and their accompanying chips (pages 233 and 238–239), Crudités (pages 67–69) or other things eaten for their dippability are an almost inevitable part of any informal party. While many of the pleasantly gloppy mixtures owe their existence to cultures around the world, it is my belief that they strode front and center at cocktail parties in America where at one time they were so important there were special chip-and-dip platters for serving them. It is my guess that the virtual disappearance of household help after World War II and in the ensuing decades brought with it the virtual disappearance of the passed canapé and hors d'oeuvre at any but the most formal—probably catered, possibly at a hotel—event.

Dips require serving dishes but not individual plates, eaters but not waiters. We can stand and eat dips, at the same time managing a drink with our other hand. Most of them have the added advantage that they can be

A *small party can be gala with one familiar dip, Guacamole (page 13), one that is less familiar, Fresh Mint Salsa (page 25), and some tortilla chips. Pile them all into informal bowls.*

3

Green Olivada (page 22) is an
exotic-seeming dip or spread that
is easy to make, good on Heroes
(page 130) or with raw
vegetables. Pick brightly colored
ones.

made ahead and kept in the refrigerator for several days—a great help when planning a largish party.

The prototype of the dip may be the cocktail sauce. Perhaps it was some genius of a party giver who first stationed the cooked, tail-on shrimp next to a bowl of spicy tomato sauce so people could dunk their shrimp. Toothpicks then came into their own. In its 1946 edition, *The Joy of Cooking* called for hollowing out a red cabbage, filling it with mayonnaise and surrounding it with shrimp on toothpicks.

Many of today's dips started life elsewhere as a sauce. Others were part of the cold mixed hors d'oeuvre table. They range from the fish salads of Scandinavia, such as Herring in Sweet Mustard Sauce (page 184), through Romanian Eggplant Dip (page 12), to some of the meze of Greece, such as Taramasalata (page 31). However, far and away the most made dip in America had no life except as a dip, although its ancestors may include all the creamed dishes that began "Mix a can of cream of mushroom soup with . . . ." It is that combination of sour cream and dried soup mix—onion or vegetable—whose recipe has come to dwell on the box of the soup-mix maker.

The "California Dip" made with sour cream and onion-soup mix can be dated accurately. It started as a groundswell recipe. In 1954, Lipton's noticed that the sales of its soup mix were surging in California. When they investigated, they found the dip. Even in 1950, Heinz was promoting a "dunking sauce" made with spices and cream cheese. In 1951 Kraft, the owners of Philadelphia cream cheese and Breakstone's sour cream, promoted a clam appetizer dip. The first reference to the word "dip" I have found—but it probably was in spoken use earlier, as Helen

Evans Brown could assume that people knew what she meant when she wrote about guacamole in 1952—is in the *West Coast Cook Book:* "Here is our favorite dip." Incidentally, it still is a favorite—guacamole. Friends who would die of embarrassment before they admitted to liking—I still do—that fifties onion concoction will dig into salsa with blue corn tortilla chips or happily serve a tapenade or a bagna cauda.

As much as to ingredients, dips probably owe a large debt to the development of the blender, originally marketed in 1937 for making drinks, both ice cream and alcoholic. It wasn't until blenders came back on the market after World War II that they really got used for food. The introduction of the food processor varied the possibilities even more.

Long before dips came on the scene, English pubs were putting out on the bar crocks full of cheese spreads to be flattened with knives onto British biscuits. The spreads were made with the last of a Cheddar or Stilton that had been creamed with butter and Port, Sherry or Cognac. These spreads date from an even earlier custom of serving a large cheese such as a Stilton with a small rounded shovel called a cheese scoop. A hole would be cut in the top of the rind or wax outer cover of the cheese and the cheese would be scooped out until only the rind and a modicum of cheese remained. By this time, the cheese would be rather dry, and Port would be sloshed into the well to moisten the cheese and let the last bits be scooped out. Coming forward in time, manufacturers realized how popular the crocks of spread were becoming and started marketing cheese as a spread all ready in crocks.

Americans were spreading their equivalent of biscuits—crackers—with cream cheese, white and bland, mixed with any number of elements such as olives, nuts and smoked salmon and seasonings such as paprika, chives and dill to make spreads. In more recent years, the cheese is often cut with low-fat yogurt to make a less caloric and slightly more acid spread.

Both English and American cheese spreads had an earlier model as well, the softened butter spreads in tea sandwiches. The butters were used in a thin slick on bread or toast as the underpinning of canapés.

This chapter contains some of all these kinds of dips, spreads and sauces. If any of them are too thick for the way you want to serve them, thin with water or other liquid. Remember the dips will be thinner at room temperature than straight from the refrigerator. We begin with the true dips—most of them vegetarian, some of them cheese-, yogurt- or sour-cream-based (pages 17–19), all of them guaranteed to stick on the chip. We go on to the thinner, drippier dipping sauces from salsa to Anchovy Dip (anchïoade) and move briskly into mayonnaise-based sauces, which can be spread or dipped into. Then there are spreadable cheese mixtures, including our old friends the cream cheese spreads, and the very basic compound butters.

Look out for hints and photographs of ways to use these gooey glories. They do not all have to be used as dips. Consider them also as toppings for Crostini and Bruschette (page 131), Oven-Fried Potato Chips (page 233), Blini (page 220), Swiss Potato Pancakes (page 85) and Corn Pancakes (page 85), as well as fillings for Savory Pastry shells (pages 96–97) and Pâte à Choux (page 106).

Not everything that can be spread or even dipped into is in this chapter. Check the Index; check Chapter 4, Mousses and Pâtés; watch out for dividends in other chapters like the Chicken Liver Spread (page 132) that can be served on its own as well as a topping for crostini. Think of some of the fillings for vegetables (listed page 72), various leaves and pastries as dips. Quintessential Tuna Salad (page 183), Chicken Salad (page 263) and some of the salads in Chapter 2, Veggie Good, can be excellent dips. If you are uncomfortable serving bowls of dip, look in Chapter 3 for shells you can pop them into, or examine the ideas for Crudités (page 67–69) for other places to tuck them so that they can be picked up easily. The breads for dipping will be in Chapter 3, the vegetables for dunking in Chapter 2, the chips are in Chapter 7.

French Olive Spread (page 22)
can go on bread, but is a stunner
accompanied by slices of daikon
(Japanese radish), peeled, sliced
thin and crisped in cold water
until they curl.

The sun-dried tomato dip is a real breakthrough. At a recent cocktail party seven guests demanded the recipe.

Buying sun-dried tomatoes dry in bulk instead of packed in oil makes them less expensive. Reviving them in the microwave oven means that you can use a minimum of liquid for optimum intensity of flavor. Then they can be packed up in good-quality olive oil (much better than that which comes with them in jars) to use as needed or to turn into this dip, with its rich, mystifying flavor. The dip keeps for weeks in the refrigerator. You will want to have the ubiquitous sliced raw vegetables . . . fennel does well with the Sun-Dried Tomato Dip.

You don't have to use a microwave oven; you can still make this dip even if it is slightly less intense in flavor. The reward is the cooking water. Save it to use for boiling pasta.

Cooked either way this dip makes a delicious pasta sauce.

The box on page 10 gives timings for other amounts of sun-dried tomatoes so that you can multiply and divide the recipe as you want.

Makes 3 cups

½ pound sun-dried tomatoes, dry (not in oil)
2 cups water
10 medium cloves garlic, smashed and peeled
1½ teaspoons dried oregano
1½ teaspoons dried thyme
1¼ cups olive oil
¼ cup vegetable oil

Microwave-Oven Method.
Combine tomatoes, water, garlic, oregano and thyme in a 13 × 9 × 2-inch oval glass or ceramic dish. Cover tightly with microwave plastic wrap. Cook at

dips

The thing that makes a dip different from a dipping sauce is that it is thicker. It is not meant to be absorbed, as is a dipping sauce for bread, nor is it meant to coat lightly, as do dipping sauces for skewered meats and vegetables. On the other hand, it is not as stiff as a spread, which requires the guest to use a knife. Like Baby Bear's porridge, it is just right. It is smooth enough to be scooped up with a shrimp, a vegetable stick, a chip or a bit of bread, but not so liquid that it immediately drips off onto the floor.

I find that everybody goes for the red dips first, then the well-known guacamole and then they adventure. For a largish party, I would have at least three dips: one red and fully flavored, one mainly white, with a cream or cheese base, and one that is more original. If I have a white dip, like the very sexy Brandade of Sole (page 32), I wouldn't have another mainly white dip. The aim is to balance the colors and flavors and choose dippers that are a little different for each even if it is only the color of the pepper strip.

Almost every informal party requires at least one dip. Allow a quarter cup per guest. At bigger parties, I often supply two or three, spacing them around the room(s) with dippers at each location.

100% in a high-wattage oven for 8 minutes. Prick plastic to release steam.

Remove from oven and uncover. Stir well. Re-cover and cook for 8 minutes longer. Prick plastic to release steam.

Remove from oven and uncover. Stir well and allow to stand, stirring occasionally, until cool and most of the liquid has been absorbed.

Transfer to a 1½-quart soufflé dish. Pour ¾ cup of the olive oil and the vegetable oil over the tomato mixture. Cover tightly with microwave plastic wrap and cook for 5 minutes. Prick plastic to release steam.

Remove from oven and uncover. Stir and allow to stand until cool. Transfer to the work bowl of a food processor and purée until smooth.

Scrape into a large bowl and stir in remaining olive oil if serving immediately. Otherwise, pack in a refrigerator storage container with a tightly fitting lid. The dip will keep as long as a month, so think about making the whole quantity.

Stove-Top Method. Reconstitute as in box. Cook with oil, garlic, oregano and thyme over low heat, covered, for 20 minutes. Purée.

romesco sauce

This is a standard and very good Catalan recipe. For slightly different versions, see Colman Andrews' Catalan Cuisine. The sauce evidently derives from a combination of Spanish and Arabic foods, just as Creole cooking in America has roots in African, Spanish and Italian cooking along with American ingredients. The ground nuts that are used as the base show an Arabic influence. The peppers and tomatoes were all pounded with the nuts in a mortar with pestle.

Traditionally, Romesco is stirred into fish soups or sauces with grilled fish and meats. I would serve it as a simple dipping sauce with Boiled Shrimp (page 168); Marinated Grilled Shrimp (page 172); or skewers of either vegetables (page 79), chicken (page 269) or meat (page 273), or use it as a filling for Mini-Strudels (page 214), Miniature Biscuits (pages 108–109) or Pâte à Choux (page 106) or as a topping for Crostini (page 131).

You cannot take a short cut around the grilling; it is essential to the flavor. If you make this ahead, cover it with a little olive oil and then put some plastic wrap directly on top of the Romesco before covering the container. Wonderful as this sauce is, it discolors when exposed to the air for any length of time. Serve in a smallish bowl and refill with fresh sauce as needed.

Makes 2½ cups

3 ancho chilies
1 cup water
2 ripe tomatoes, about 4 ounces each
1 red bell pepper, about 7 ounces
¼ cup plus 1 teaspoon olive oil
1 ounce whole blanched almonds (about 40)
1 ounce whole hazelnuts (about 20)
2 slices crustless French or Italian bread (about 1 ounce each)
6 medium cloves garlic, smashed and peeled
1 jalapeño pepper, stemmed and seeded
2 tablespoons red wine vinegar
2½ teaspoons kosher salt
Freshly ground black pepper, to taste

Preheat grill or broiler with rack about 4 inches from heat.

Place anchos and water in a 1-quart soufflé dish, cover tightly with microwave plastic wrap and cook at 100% in a high-wattage microwave oven for 4 minutes or in a low-wattage oven for 6 minutes, or simmer covered on top of the stove until softened. If using microwave oven, prick plastic to release steam. Remove from oven and uncover. Allow to stand, covered with a plate, until cool enough to handle. Drain and remove seeds. Place in the work bowl of a food processor.

Meanwhile rub outside of tomatoes and bell pepper with 1 teaspoon oil. Either grill them or place them on a broiler pan about 4 inches from the heat. Cook for 10 to 15 minutes, turning frequently so that the skin is evenly charred all over. Remove from grill or broiler pan and place in a bowl. Cover with a plate and allow to steam for about 10 minutes. Peel, core, seed and add to food processor.

Allow heavy skillet to become hot over medium to high heat for about 2 minutes. Add almonds and cook, stirring continuously, for about 5 minutes, or until golden brown all over. Transfer to food processor. Add hazelnuts to pan and cook in the same manner. Transfer to a kitchen towel and rub off skins. Add to food processor.

Brush bread slices with about 3 tablespoons of oil and either broil about 3 inches from the heat for 2 minutes on each side or cook in skillet over moderate heat for about 5 minutes, or until golden brown, turning once. Break up into pieces and add to food processor with remaining ingredients. Process until coarsely chopped and season to taste with salt and pepper. For a less chunky sauce, process until very smooth.

Reconstituting Sun-Dried Tomatoes

Drained, reconstituted tomatoes can be halved and put out with toothpicks as a nice snack. A ½ pound dried makes 4 cups reconstituted—about 27 tomato pieces in each cooked cup, which will make 54 snacks (216 per ½ pound). Each cooked cup is enough for 12 to 15 guests. If you have packed them in oil for storage, the oil can be used for another batch.

Microwave-Oven Method.

For ¼ pound dried tomatoes: With 1 cup water in a 2½-quart soufflé dish, cook, covered, at 100% in a high-wattage oven 5 minutes; prick plastic to release steam; stir; cook, uncovered, 5 minutes. In a low-wattage oven, cook 9 minutes and 9 minutes.

For ½ pound dried tomatoes: With 2 cups water in a 13 × 9 × 2-inch oval glass or ceramic dish, cook in a high-wattage oven 8 minutes, then 8 minutes. In a low-wattage oven, cook 12 minutes and 14 minutes.

For 1 pound dried tomatoes: With 4 cups water in a 5-quart casserole, cook in a high-wattage oven 14 minutes, then 14 minutes. In a low-wattage oven: cook 20 minutes and 20 minutes.

Stove-Top Method. Cover sun-dried tomatoes with water in nonreactive saucepan. Bring to a boil over medium heat, about 8 minutes. Reduce heat to a simmer and cook, covered, for 22 minutes. Allow to cool. Drain.

eggplant moroccan

One day, I had peeled eggplant left after testing the Caponata (page 14) and I needed a dip for a party. I made this and everybody seemed to like it. The "Moroccan" in the title is purely honorary. This is a large batch that will easily serve thirty-six to forty people, but it's worth making the whole thing, since it keeps so well and for such a long time in the refrigerator. If you want to make a smaller amount, halve or quarter the recipe.

This would make an untraditional but good topping for Crostini (page 131). Top each with a couple of extra pine nuts.

Makes 9 cups

¾ to 1 cup olive oil
1 medium onion (4 ounces), finely chopped (⅔ cup)
6 ounces garlic cloves, smashed, peeled and finely chopped
1½ pounds peeled, finely chopped eggplant
2 28-ounce cans Italian plum tomatoes, drained and squeezed, 2 cups of the liquid reserved
2 bay leaves
½ teaspoon ground cinnamon
1 teaspoon ground cumin
1 teaspoon red pepper flakes
1½ cups golden raisins
1 3-ounce jar pine nuts
2 1-gram vials saffron threads
2 tablespoons kosher salt
½ cup fresh orange juice
⅓ cup fresh lemon juice

Heat ¼ cup of the olive oil in a 12- to 14-inch skillet or braising pan. Add onions and cook over low heat until translucent, about 20 minutes. Add ⅓ of the garlic and cook over low heat for 10 minutes.

Stir in eggplant and ¼ cup of the olive oil. Increase heat to medium. Cook until eggplant is translucent but not brown. Add tomatoes, bay leaves, cinnamon, cumin, red pepper and ½ of the remaining garlic. Cook over low heat for 1 hour, stirring occasionally.

While eggplant mixture is cooking, place raisins in a medium saucepan for stove-top cooking or a glass or ceramic soufflé dish for microwaving. Separate the raisins if they are sticking together. Stir in reserved tomato juice. Either cook, covered, in a small pan over very low heat until plumped or cover tightly with microwave plastic wrap in a 1-quart soufflé dish and cook at 100% in a high-wattage oven for 10 minutes, low-wattage 15 minutes. Prick plastic to release steam.

Add raisin mixture, ¼ cup of the olive oil, pine nuts, saffron, salt and orange juice to eggplant mixture. Cook for 10 minutes. Taste and add remaining garlic and remaining ¼ cup olive oil, if desired. Cook over medium-low heat, stirring occasionally, until mixture has a thick dip consistency, about 45 minutes. Remove bay leaf.

Remove from heat and stir in lemon juice. Store in refrigerator, tightly covered, up to 3 weeks.

Clockwise from top: Come late spring, seasonal vegetables like cherry tomatoes; baby carrots and rinsed, tightly furled fiddlehead ferns can star in a simple assortment with Bread Sticks (page 129), homemade or store-bought; Schiacciata (page 128) and a full-flavored dip like Eggplant Moroccan.

romanian eggplant dip

The simplest of the eggplant dips, **baba ghanouj,** *is very good and easily multiplied or divided using the timings in the box.*

Makes about 3 cups

1 medium eggplant (about 1 pound), baked as in box

Seasoning Mix
¼ cup olive oil
2 tablespoons fresh lemon juice
1 to 2 medium cloves garlic, or to taste, smashed, peeled and minced
2 teaspoons kosher salt
Freshly ground black pepper, to taste
¼ cup loosely packed chopped fresh Italian parsley leaves, optional

Shred eggplant, or purée in food processor. Beat in remaining ingredients. Store, covered, in refrigerator at least overnight to let flavors develop. Make up to 1 week ahead.

Baking Eggplant

Conventional-Oven Method

Place the oven rack in the center position. Heat oven to 400°F. Roast large eggplants on a heavy, ungreased baking sheet (do not use an air-cushioned cookie sheet) until they burst and the centers become very tender. This will take about 1½ hours. Smaller—not baby—eggplants will take less long. You can tell when they are done because the skin gets dark and the eggplant looks a bit like a deflated balloon.

Remove baking sheet from oven. Using two forks, immediately tear each eggplant open. Scrape out the pulp onto the hot baking sheet. Let it sizzle and brown. This will help some of the liquid to evaporate. Discard the dry skins.

Transfer the pulp to a bowl. Continue to pull it apart with the two forks until it is very finely shredded.

Microwave-Oven Method

Prick each eggplant several times with the tip of a knife. Put on double thickness of paper towels in bottom of oven. Cook, uncovered, at 100%, or until eggplant deflates.

½ pound:
High-wattage oven: 8 min.
Low-wattage oven: 11 min.

1 pound:
High-wattage oven: 12 min.
Low-wattage oven: 16 min.

1½ pounds:
High-wattage oven: 15 min.
Low-wattage oven: 20 min.

2 pounds:
High-wattage oven: 19 min.
Low-wattage oven: 28 min.

2½ pounds:
High-wattage oven: 22 min.
Low-wattage oven: 35 min.

3 pounds:
High-wattage oven: 45 min.
Low-wattage oven: 1 hour

---

russian eggplant dip

This mildly sweet and sour dip is very good and qualifies as a red one. Multiply or divide by using the timings in the box.

Makes about 4 cups

1 medium eggplant (about 1 pound), baked as in box

Seasoning Mix
¼ cup olive oil
2 tablespoons fresh lemon juice
3 to 5 medium cloves garlic, or to taste, smashed, peeled and minced
2 teaspoons kosher salt
Freshly ground black pepper, to taste
⅓ cup Plum Tomato Sauce (page 27) or canned tomato purée
3 tablespoons tomato paste
Pinch cayenne pepper
2 Roasted Peppers (page 58), red or green, chopped

Combine all ingredients except roasted pepper in food processor and purée. Stir in pepper. Store, covered, in refrigerator at least overnight and for up to 1 week. Refrigerate, covered.

---

east of the pacific eggplant dip

I've never had an eggplant dip in the Far East, but I have had many wonderful eggplant dishes there. I adopted some of their seasonings for this dip made with fat purple eggplants rather than their slim lavender ones or the short, curved purple ones. If you can find them, consider Asian, thin rice-flour crackers as the dippers.

If you want to make a greater quantity, simply multiply, using the eggplant cooking times in the box.

Makes 2 cups

1 medium eggplant (about 1 pound), baked as in box

Seasoning Mix
2 teaspoons rice wine vinegar
1 medium clove garlic, smashed, peeled and minced
2 scallions, white and green, chopped
¼ cup chopped fresh coriander (cilantro) leaves
1 tablespoon peeled and grated fresh ginger
2 teaspoons tamari soy sauce
2 teaspoons toasted sesame oil

When eggplant is cool enough to handle, cut in half lengthwise and scoop out flesh. Place flesh in a food processor with remaining ingredients. Process until mixture is coarsely chopped.

Transfer to a serving bowl. Serve at room temperature. The dip may be refrigerated, covered, for 2 to 3 days, but be sure to let it come to room temperature before serving.

creamy asian dip

I don't think tofu can go in everything, but it does very well in this creamy dip. Try to find tofu pillows, which are a little firmer and less watery than the squares. If you can only find the squares, put them in a baking pan, place another pan on top of them and weight it with a few heavy cans. Leave for an hour; drain and use.

Makes 2 cups

3 tofu pillows (3 ounces)
½ ounce peeled fresh ginger, cut into small pieces
1 cup loosely packed fresh coriander (cilantro) leaves

¾ teaspoon wasabi paste
3 tablespoons tamari soy sauce
2 to 3 tablespoons toasted sesame oil, to taste
2 tablespoons water
2 to 3 tablespoons rice wine vinegar
¼ cup chopped fresh coriander (cilantro) leaves

Place all ingredients except chopped coriander in a blender or food processor and process until very smooth. Refrigerate for at least an hour to let flavor develop. Just before serving, sprinkle with chopped coriander and serve with daikon radish or fennel (see pages 67–69). May be made up to 2 days ahead.

guacamole

So much green glop masquerades under this name that I hesitate to recommend it; but when you try it with really ripe dark-skinned Haas avocados that have been mashed, not puréed, I think you'll find it worth rescuing. This version is pleasant, mild and fresh. If you like things hotter or your guests do, add more peppers. If you cannot bear to

serve anything this unadorned, you can stir in a tablespoon of grated onion and two of chopped coriander.

Don't add tomato to the guacamole. Tomato makes it watery. Consider making one of the salsas (page 23–25) and serving it with the guacamole and tortilla chips. (Blue corn chips make a beautiful color contrast.)

If you cannot find fresh hot peppers, substitute a third of a green bell pepper and hot red pepper sauce to taste. Do not use dried peppers or pepper flakes. The guacamole will keep for the length of the party because of the amount of lime juice.

If multiplying the recipe several times, purée the flavoring mixture in a blender.

Makes 2¼ cups

Flavoring Mixture
1 tablespoon kosher salt
5 medium cloves garlic, smashed and peeled
3 small, fresh, hot peppers such as jalapeños, stemmed, halved, seeded and deribbed
5 tablespoons fresh lime juice

3 large ripe Haas avocados (1½ pounds)

Sprinkle salt over garlic cloves and mince very fine, pressing them into the salt with the flat of the knife from time to time until they form a paste. Add the peppers to the garlic paste and mince again, pressing on the pepper, salt and garlic mixture to make a fine paste that retains all the pepper juices. Scrape into a small bowl, stir in 2 tablespoons of the lime juice and set aside.

Just before serving, cut avocados in half lengthwise. Remove the pit and scoop the meat from the skin with a teaspoon. In a nonmetallic serving bowl, mash the avocados with fork. Stir in garlic mixture and remaining lime juice.

ready-mades

Making your own dips, spreads and sauces will really save you money, particularly important for a large party. The improvement in quality goes without saying. Not only can many of the store-boughts be duplicated at home; they can also be kept for fairly long times in the refrigerator or sterile-packed in jars (page 56). The one case where I would never substitute ready-made for homemade is guacamole. Making your own is so easy and store-bought is seldom good or fresh, and its off-taste has become a cliché.

Store-bought cocktail sauce, horseradish sauce, barbecue sauce, tartar sauce, relishes and mayonnaise can be kept on hand for emergencies. Mix and match using soy sauce, prepared mustard, store-bought pesto and vinegars as desired.

There are some jarred products, often imported, that can be used as dips. Taramasalata comes ready-prepared—not just the roe base, although that or vacuum-packed red caviar (salmon caviar) can be on-shelf staples to make your own quickly (page 31). Salsas can be bought although homemade (pages 23–25) are much better. A limited variety of chutneys is available. Greek eggplant meze, caponata and black olive olivada are all findable. All of these except the olivada will be dramatically improved by some freshly squeezed lemon juice—no, not out of a bottle—and a spoonful or so of really good olive oil. Consider some freshly ground black pepper.

A sprinkling of finely chopped fresh herbs from parsley to coriander to mint will certainly disguise the store-bought look and flavor.

You can buy sun-dried tomatoes packed in oil—better in olive oil—but once you have figured out how much cheaper it is to reconstitute the dried yourself (page 10), I think you will do that for snacks and dips that keep virtually forever in the refrigerator as long as they are fully covered by oil.

Deli fish salads are usable, but I would avoid tuna fish. Some delis or specialty stores can provide cheese spreads, a few of which come in crocks of great price in supermarkets.

caponata

This is a delicious sweet and sour southern Italian vegetable stew meant to be eaten at room temperature. Olives are traditional in caponata. Using them does mean some additional work in pitting them (see box, page 22). Also, it is very important that you use good-quality olives, not the canned California sort or the somewhat bitter dry, oil-cured ones.

This recipe can easily be doubled or tripled. Packed into sterile jars (see box, page 56), it will keep in the refrigerator up to two months.

Makes 4 cups

1/3 cup olive oil
2 medium onions (4 ounces each), peeled and diced fine (about 1 1/2 cups)
2 ribs celery (3 ounces each), halved lengthwise and cut crosswise into 1/2-inch-thick slices (about 1 1/2 cups)
1 medium eggplant (1 1/4 pounds), peeled and cut into 1/2-inch cubes (about 4 1/2 cups)
1/4 cup canned tomato purée
2 canned Italian plum tomatoes, squeezed of liquid and chopped (about 1/4 cup)
1 ounce pitted olives (see box, page 22), chopped
2 tablespoons raisins, soaked in warm water for 10 minutes and drained
1/4 cup red wine vinegar
2 tablespoons capers, drained and rinsed
2 tablespoons tomato paste
1 tablespoon sugar
1 tablespoon pine nuts
2 teaspoons kosher salt
Freshly ground black pepper

Heat the oil in a heavy 4-quart saucepan over medium heat until rippling. Add the onions and celery; sauté until wilted, about 4 minutes. Stir in the eggplant and sauté, stirring occasionally, until the eggplant is lightly browned, about 8 minutes. Stir in the remaining ingredients. Heat to simmering, reduce the heat to low and simmer, covered, until the eggplant is very tender and the flavors are blended, about 30 minutes. Cool completely to room temperature and let stand at least 3 hours before serving. The caponata can be stored in the refrigerator up to a week. Bring to room temperature and check the seasoning.

roasted red pepper spread

Very pretty, very good and a last-minute savior if you use jarred red peppers, which are quite satisfactory. This is easily multiplied and will keep for up to five days, covered, in the refrigerator; it is good with Crudités (page 67) or on Crostini (page 131).

Makes 2 cups

1 recipe Roasted Peppers, red (page 59), or 2 jars roasted red peppers, drained (7 ounces each)

2 tablespoons extra-virgin
   olive oil
2 tablespoons minced fresh
   Italian parsley leaves
1 tablespoon fresh lemon juice
2 teaspoons capers, drained
1 medium clove garlic,
   smashed, peeled and
   mashed to a paste with
1/4 teaspoon kosher salt

Arrange the drained peppers on a double layer of paper towels and let them dry while preparing the recipe.

Combine the remaining ingredients in the work bowl of a food processor. Process until the capers and parsley are very finely chopped, or work hard with a large knife. Add the drained peppers and process, using on/off pulses, or chop until the peppers are coarsely chopped. Stop several times to scrape down the sides of the work bowl to make sure the mixture is evenly chopped. Check the seasonings and adjust as necessary. Store the spread in a covered container in the refrigerator for up to 5 days. Remove to room temperature at least 30 minutes before serving.

Crostini (page 131) with Roasted Red Pepper Spread and flirtatious top leaves of basil.

Instead of cold, raw vegetables in winter, dunk Steamed New Potatoes (page 69) in quickly made Parsley and Scallion Dip. It will taste just fine if the potatoes cool. Other creamy dunks can be used, as well as the dry seasoning mixes.

chickpea dip

A wonderfully warm-tasting simple dip to serve with vegetables. It is common in the Middle East, where it is called **hummus.** *Easily multiplied, it will keep, covered, in the refrigerator for up to five days. If you don't like the somewhat dry texture and flavor of tahini, omit it.*

Makes 2 cups

- 1 19-ounce can chickpeas, drained and rinsed (a scant 3 1/3 cups)
- 1/3 cup toasted sesame oil
- 1/4 cup sesame tahini
- 1/4 cup fresh lemon juice
- 4 medium cloves garlic, smashed and peeled
- 1 teaspoon kosher salt
- 3 to 4 dashes hot red pepper sauce
- 1/4 cup water
- 4 teaspoons chopped fresh mint leaves, optional
- 4 teaspoons sesame seeds (use only 1 teaspoon if also using mint), optional

Place chickpeas in a food processor or blender and process until smooth, stopping two or three times to scrape down sides of bowl. Add all remaining ingredients except water and optional ingredients and process until smooth.

With motor running, pour water through feed tube in a steady stream. Scrape mixture into a bowl and stir in optional ingredients, if using.

walnut dip

I don't usually think of the Greeks as the great sauce makers of the world, but in this puréed walnut sauce, **skorthalia,** *they have a winner. We had actual disputes in the kitchen about who was going to get to take it home. In some parts of Greece, it is made with almonds instead of walnuts and in others it is really a bread-thickened mayonnaise without any nuts. This is my favorite version. If you have some left over, serve it over steamed vegetables or fish. I particularly like it with boiled potatoes. You don't have to serve it right after the party, as the sauce will keep in a covered glass jar in the refrigerator for at least two weeks. Which is good to know for make-ahead party planning.*

Makes 4 1/2 cups

- 1 pound shelled, unsalted walnuts
- 15 medium cloves garlic, smashed, peeled and green germ removed
- 2 1/2 ounces crustless Italian bread (about 6 inches x 2 inches), torn into pieces
- 2 1/2 tablespoons fresh lemon juice
- 2 1/2 cups olive oil
- 2 teaspoons kosher salt
- Freshly ground black pepper, to taste

Chop the nuts, garlic and bread in a blender or food processor until mealy—very finely chopped but not quite a purée. Add the lemon juice and process. With the machine still running, pour in the olive oil in a thin stream. When all the oil is incorporated, add salt and pepper to taste.

This can be used immediately or it can be refrigerated up to two weeks, covered.

Blender vs. Food Processor

I keep both a blender—at least twenty-five years old—and a food processor out on my counter because they give quite different results. I use the food processor for chopping, as I would a superefficient knife. I use the blender for silkier, smoother mixtures rather like working with a mortar and pestle, even like a mixture put through a fine sieve.

There are times when the two pieces of equipment are interchangeable. Then, I would probably use a food processor, which is less finicky: you don't have to stop as often to push the food down and more food fits in. There are times when a blender is preferable. It makes a thicker mayonnaise than a food processor with the same amount of oil, as in Taramasalata (page 31). If you want the sauce to accept more olive oil, use the food processor. When a sauce is thickened with bread or nuts, such as Walnut Dip (this page), a much smoother sauce results with a blender.

cheese, yogurt or sour cream dips

Anyone who has ever made an onion-soup dip will recognize how versatile a container of sour cream is. Yogurt, cottage cheese and various other white cheeses are just as usable and will often take down the calories as well. Such dips have the added merit of being inexpensive and easy to make. They are vegetarian as well, but not vegan.

●

crunchy vegetable dip

Pretty colors and crunchy vegetables to serve with more raw radishes and scallions (page 68) for dunking, as well as bought potato chips or homemade Vegetable Chips (page 238).

Makes 1½ cups

- 1 small bunch radishes, trimmed and cut into quarters (⅔ cup)
- 4 scallions, whites and about 2 inches of the green, cut into ½-inch lengths
- 2 tablespoons fresh dill sprigs
- 1 scant cup nonfat fromage blanc (8 ounces) or part-skim cottage cheese
- Kosher salt, to taste
- Freshly ground black pepper, to taste

Place radishes, scallions and dill in the work bowl of a food processor and process until they are finely chopped but not puréed. Scrape into a medium bowl and stir in remaining ingredients. Serve immediately or the dip will get watery as the vegetables start giving off liquid.

cucumber tzatziki

I make this dip when cucumbers in the garden grow to giants without my discovering them first. You can make it with normal cucumbers. It is a traditional Greek first course often served as part of meze, which are usually eaten on little plates when the diners are seated. Without a plate, it is best served with dunkers such as Herb Focaccia (page 128) or Crudités (page 67), as it has the texture of a chunky sour cream. It is virtually identical to the Indian raita.

You can divide this recipe if it makes too much.

Makes 6 cups

- 12 medium cucumbers (5¼ pounds), trimmed, peeled, quartered, seeded and cut into 2-inch lengths (about 10 cups)
- 2 tablespoons kosher salt
- 20 medium cloves garlic, smashed and peeled
- 1 cup packed fresh mint leaves
- 1 quart yogurt, sheep's milk is best, whole cow's milk or other
- Freshly ground black pepper, to taste

Working in batches, place cucumber in a food processor and process until medium fine. Scrape each batch as it is done into a large bowl. You will have about 6 cups. Stir in salt. Let stand 1½ hours.

Drain cucumber, pressing lightly, through a medium sieve. Discard the liquid. You will have a scant 4 cups of cucumber.

Place garlic and mint in food processor and process until finely chopped. Scrape into a large bowl. Stir in cucumber and remaining ingredients. Refrigerate, covered, for at least 1 hour. Will keep for up to four days.

parsley and scallion dip

Much like scallion cream cheese, but looser in texture. A good last-minute solution for a small party.

Makes 1 cup

- 4 ounces cream cheese (½ cup)
- ¼ cup plain yogurt
- ½ cup 1-inch pieces of green and white of scallions, loosely packed
- ½ cup loosely packed fresh Italian parsley leaves, chopped
- ¼ cup fresh lemon juice
- Kosher salt, to taste
- Freshly ground black pepper, to taste

In a food processor, combine the cream cheese, yogurt, scallion pieces and chopped parsley. Process until the mixture is smooth and turns light green. Taste and adjust the seasoning with lemon juice, kosher salt and black pepper. Pour the dip into a bowl and whisk to crush any lumps of cream cheese.

spicy goat cheese dip

Aside from an all-out event like fondue, most of the cheese dips are not warm. This microwave-cooked dish is. It can be made ahead and reheated briefly. On a buffet, it can be kept warm in an old fondue pot with a candle for heat; you don't want it to boil. Sliced raw vegetables are the nicest dippers.

Makes 2 cups

1-ounce package plain Boursin cheese
½ cup milk
2 teaspoons cornstarch dissolved in 4 teaspoons cold water
½ pound mild goat cheese, such as Bucheron
⅓ cup packed chopped fresh coriander (cilantro) leaves
⅓ cup sliced scallions, equal parts green and white
1 tablespoon chopped jalapeño pepper
2 teaspoons kosher salt

Combine Boursin, milk and dissolved cornstarch in a 4-cup glass measure. Cook, uncovered, at 100% for 3 minutes in a high-wattage oven, 5 minutes in a low-wattage oven. Whisk thoroughly and cook for 2 minutes more in a high-wattage oven, 3 minutes in a low-wattage oven. Whisk again.

Break goat cheese into chunks and whisk into hot cheese mixture until melted. Add remaining ingredients and stir to combine. Cook, uncovered, for 2 minutes to heat through. Serve warm.

To reheat from the refrigerator, cook, uncovered, for 3 minutes in a high-wattage oven, 4½ minutes in a low-wattage oven, stirring twice during cooking.

liptauer cheese

Liptauer cheese, a classic in Vienna and Hungary, is not usually of dip consistency. If you want to use it as a spread, as the natives do, omit the yogurt. This is a dip that tends to thin if it sits out. Don't make it too far ahead. Leftovers can be thinned with more yogurt to make a good salad dressing.

Makes 1½ cups

8 ounces cream cheese, at room temperature
2 teaspoons sweet paprika
¼ cup plain yogurt
3 tablespoons coarsely chopped sweet gherkins
3 tablespoons coarsely chopped Roasted Peppers, red (page 59), or fire-roasted from a jar, rinsed
¾ ounce onion, coarsely chopped (2½ tablespoons)
1½ teaspoons capers, drained
2 teaspoons caraway seeds
1 teaspoon fresh lemon juice
1 teaspoon kosher salt
2 dashes hot red pepper sauce

Place cream cheese and paprika in a food processor and process until smooth. Scrape mixture into a bowl and stir in remaining ingredients. Let stand, refrigerated, for 1 to 2 hours.

herb dip

I made up this recipe when I had a mountain of mint growing and I needed to provide a dip for the thirty pounds of shrimp I was bringing to a birthday party for a hundred people. It was a great success. If you want to multiply the recipe, be sure to work in batches, as it is too much of a load for the food processor at one

time. The processor makes this completely creamy, no hint of curds anywhere. Feel free to substitute other combinations of herbs. Two cups of parsley leaves and a cup and a half of dill work well.

Makes 2½ cups

8 ounces cottage cheese or part-skim ricotta
6 medium cloves garlic, smashed and peeled
¼ cup loosely packed fresh tarragon leaves
¼ cup plus 2 tablespoons loosely packed fresh apple mint leaves or ¼ cup peppermint or spearmint
2¼ cups loosely packed fresh Italian parsley leaves
1 cup sour cream (8 ounces)
½ cup plain yogurt (4 ounces)
1 tablespoon kosher salt
Lots of freshly ground black pepper

Place cottage cheese, garlic and herbs in a food processor. Process until herbs are finely chopped. Scrape mixture into a large bowl.

Stir in sour cream, yogurt, salt and pepper. Refrigerate for at least 3 hours and up to one day before serving.

macedonian cheese dip

Until I went to Thessaloniki, I never knew that Greeks used hot peppers. They have their own version of red pepper flakes—less dry than those sometimes used in Italian cooking—and mixed with cumin. You can use either kind, but if you find the Greek one, you might enjoy comparing.

This is not very spicy, so it will not overwhelm Greek foods like Stuffed Grape Leaves (page 203) and some olives.

Makes scant 3 cups

18 ounces feta cheese, removed from brine, rinsed and broken into pieces
1 cup plain yogurt, ewe's milk is best
2 tablespoons very good olive oil, optional (if you use sheep's milk yogurt, you won't need this)
1 tablespoon Greek or other red pepper flakes with ½ teaspoon ground cumin

Place feta pieces and yogurt in a blender or food processor and process until very smooth. If using olive oil, dribble it in, maintaining a thin stream while the machine is running. Scrape into a serving dish. Stir in the pepper flakes. Refrigerate covered at least overnight but not more than 2 days. Serve the next day at room temperature.

crimson menace

This is a spectacular color, and even those who think they don't like beets will like it. It can be used on bread or as a dip. I would choose raw or blanched cauliflower to serve with this.

Makes 1¾ cups, enough for about 80 open sandwiches

1½ cups Pickled Beets (page 89), or 1 16-ounce can sliced beets, drained
1 scant cup fromage blanc (8 ounces) or part-skim cottage cheese
Kosher salt, to taste
Freshly ground black pepper, to taste
Slices of pickled beets, for garnish
Sprigs of fresh dill, for garnish

Beet canapés are quickly, vividly made on store-bought pumpernickel with Crimson Menace and slices of Pickled Beets (page 89) and onions.

Combine beets and fromage blanc in a blender and process until completely smooth, stopping the machine and scraping down the sides occasionally. Season to taste with salt and pepper.

Spoon about 1 teaspoon of the mixture onto a small slice of pumpernickel or dark rye bread and garnish with a slice of beet and sprig of dill.

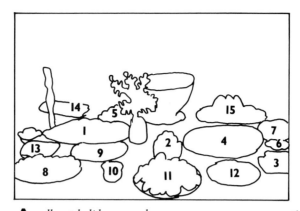

An all-out holiday spread centered on a gala bowl of Eggnog (page 305). Finger food replaces dinner. No one has to make all this; you can pick or choose to substitute other dishes that serve the same purpose. However, some of the combinations are nice to keep in mind. A **1** *Roast Loin of Pork (page 286) to slice thin and put on plates—a good idea if this is dinner—or tucked into Biscuits (pages 108–109). The pork can be enlivened by* **2** *Green Olivada (page 22) or* **3** *Bagna Cauda (page 29) painted on bread. Or dip* **4** *crudités—here color-related yellow pepper strips and orangey cherry tomatoes—into sauces. The* **5** *Plantain Chips (page 241) can be dipped into the olivada or the* **6** *Tomato Basil Dipping Sauce (page 27), which serves as a dunk for the squares of* **7** *Spinach and Mushroom Frittata (page 226) or a sauce for the* **8** *Spinach and Fish Pâté (page 147). The* **9** *Mahogany Quail with Peppercorns (page 264) should be served with their own* **10** *Seasoned Salt.* **11** *Empanadas (pages 218–220);* **12** *Vegetable Confetti Pancakes (page 84), here topped with sour cream and chervil flowers,* **13** *Mini–Moussaka Rolls (page 202), and* **14** *Tropical Fruit Brochettes (page 82) are easy to pop in the mouth and could be placed around the room. If there aren't plates, then the* **15** *Southwestern Seviche can go in individual shells, as on page 96.*

olive spreads

Where olives grow in France and Italy, they are made into spreads, often presented in little crocks, as if the spreads were butter, before the meal begins. A small snack for a few people before dinner at home or before going out could be made of any of these olive dishes, a good focaccia (pages 126–129), trimmed radishes, a crock of sweet butter and a few red pepper strips.

These olive preparations can also be used in risottos and in Olivada Focaccia (page 129), as well as in pasta sauces. They keep, covered and refrigerated, virtually indefinitely, so it is worth making more than you need and keeping the rest to have on hand.

To find out more about the various olives, see box, page 22.

To Pit Olives

Making olive dips and spreads means pitting olives. (Pitted olives that you can buy are generally not suitable.) It is not as bad as you think. There are olive pitters that look like cherry pitters, but I find them worthless. Soft olives—such as Kalamatas, Gaetas and Alfonsos—can be pitted by squeezing them hard between your thumb and first two fingers. The pit either will slip out or can be easily picked out. Alternatively, you can put these olives on a counter and push on them with your palm as you slide it forward. Hard olives should be put in a single layer on a counter, covered with a cloth and whacked several times with a heavy pot. This will break the flesh and make it easy to extract the pit. Oil-cured olives are best pried open with fingernails and the pit taken out.

french olive spread

This French **tapenade** *is perfect for parties, since it needs to be made ahead in any case. The flavor is mildly spicy and slightly salty. Serve with a crusty bread in chunks or as Crostini (page 131), or with slices of fennel or turnip or daikon radish. Multiply as long as your pitting fingers hold out.*

Makes 1 cup

1 cup oil-cured black olives
  (6 ounces), about 3/4 cup
  pitted (see box)
1/4 cup tightly packed fresh
  basil leaves
6 oil-packed anchovy fillets,
  drained
1 tablespoon fresh lemon juice
1 medium clove garlic,
  smashed, peeled and sliced
  thin
1/2 small dried red chili
  pepper, or 1/4 teaspoon red
  pepper flakes
1/4 cup olive oil

Combine all ingredients except the olive oil in the work bowl of a food processor fitted with the metal blade. Process, scraping down the sides once or twice with a rubber spatula, until coarsely chopped. Add the oil slowly with the motor running and process a few seconds until and process a few seconds until the mixture is a smooth purée. Check the seasonings and adjust if necessary. Store, covered, in the refrigerator for at least 24 hours and up to 4 weeks. Bring to room temperature before serving.

black olivada

This Italian version is the simplest of the olive spreads and delicious. It's the one I use in Focaccia (page 128).

Makes 2 cups

3 cups Gaeta olives, or other
  large, fleshy black olive like
  Alfonso or Kalamata (1
  pound), pitted (see box)
1/3 cup extra-virgin olive oil

Process the olives, stopping once or twice to scrape down the sides, until coarsely chopped. Add the oil in a steady stream with the motor running until the mixture is a smooth purée. Store in a container with a tightly fitting lid in the refrigerator for up to 6 weeks. Remove to room temperature at least 30 minutes before serving.

green olivada

This is not a traditional olive spread, but it is very good and has the great advantage of using already pitted olives.

Makes 3/4 cup

1 5-ounce jar pitted, green
  Spanish olives (1 cup)
2 tablespoons blanched
  almonds
1 teaspoon dried basil
1/2 teaspoon dried oregano
1/2 teaspoon dried thyme
1/4 cup olive oil

Drain and rinse the olives well. Drain again thoroughly.

Combine the olives, almonds, basil, oregano and thyme in a food processor fitted with the metal blade. Process until coarsely chopped, scraping down the sides of the bowl once or twice.

Add the oil in a thin stream with the motor running and continue processing until the mixture is a coarse purée. Store the olivada in a covered container in the refrigerator at least 3 days, or up to 2 weeks, before serving. Remove to room temperature at least 30 minutes before serving.

All set for a simple Tex-Mex drink time with the bright colors of Fresh Tomatillo Salsa and Spicy Papaya Salsa (page 24). Add chips and a Margarita (page 305); olé.

salsas

Salsas started out, as their name indicates, as sauces, but by now they have taken on a yet more important life as dips. We see them in a vast number of bars served with tortilla chips and Guacamole (page 13), or with Nachos (page 57). They are good with vegetables, with Calzones made with Southwestern Cheese Filling (page 220), on Vegetable Pancakes (page 84) or on Corn Pancakes (page 85). Salsas are also good in bread and cheese sandwiches: put a slice of good cheddar topped with salsa in a Cornmeal Jalapeño Biscuit (page 108), or put Cheddar-Sherry Spread (page 39) or Scallion Cream Cheese (page 42) on toasted Pepper Brioche (page 133) and top with salsa.

How much hot pepper you want in your salsa probably depends on how much of it you usually eat and in what part of the world. I give a range. Add the smaller amount; let the salsa sit for a half hour—the flavor will get stronger—then add more pepper if you want. Remember all guests may not have asbestos mouths.

You can add chopped green or red bell peppers to the salsas if you like more crunch, but they will be harder to dip up.

Salsas should not be made too far ahead, as they give off more and more water. They are OK the day after you make them, but not great, so don't make more than you need.

Some very good salsas are latter-day inventions that you might try.

fresh tomatillo salsa

In northern climes, tomatillos—the green tomatoes with the brown, papery husks—may be hard to find except for a brief season. They are nicely astringent. Serve tomatillo salsa at the same time you are serving a more conventional red tomato salsa. If you can't find the fresh, skip right to the next recipe.

Finely chopped green bell pepper will improve the color of this dish. Multiply as needed.

Makes 1½ cups

2 medium cloves garlic, smashed and peeled
1 small fresh jalapeño pepper, stemmed, seeded and deribbed
½ pound tomatillos, husks removed, cored and coarsely chopped
2 scallions, white and green parts cut into 2-inch lengths (⅛ cup)
⅓ cup water
2 tablespoons chopped fresh coriander (cilantro) leaves
1 tablespoon fresh lime juice
1 teaspoon kosher salt
Freshly ground black pepper, to taste

Place garlic and jalapeño in the work bowl of a food processor and chop very fine. Add tomatillos and scallions and process until finely chopped but not puréed.

Transfer mixture to a bowl and stir in remaining ingredients. Allow to stand for about 30 minutes and adjust seasoning.

canned tomatillo sauce

Yes, canned, and not bad, but probably not for purists, although one of my assistants who is from Texas took it home to eat. Multiply at will.

Makes 1 1/4 cups

2 medium cloves garlic, smashed and peeled
2 hot green peppers (such as jalapeños), stemmed and seeded (3/4 ounce)
3/4 cup loosely packed fresh Italian parsley leaves
3/4 cup loosely packed fresh coriander (cilantro) leaves
1 18-ounce can tomatillos, drained
1 small onion, chopped (1/3 cup)
1 teaspoon fresh lemon juice
Pinch sugar
1/2 teaspoon kosher salt

Place garlic, peppers, parsley and coriander in a food processor and process until finely chopped. Add tomatillos and process until smooth.

Scrape mixture into a small bowl. Stir in onions, lemon juice, sugar and salt.

fragrant mango salsa

This very pretty salsa with bits of red onion and apricot-gold mango has no heat, but lots of fresh flavor. I based it on a relish I had at Mise en Place in Tampa. Consider using it as a filling for Fried Bread Puffs (page 125), with or without a little goat cheese. This can be made up to a day before serving, refrigerated, stirred and then served cold.

Makes 3 3/4 cups

1 3/4-pound ripe mango, peeled, flesh cut from pit and diced in 1/4-inch pieces (a scant 3 cups)
4 ounces red onion, peeled and cut into very fine, 1/8-inch dice (1 cup)
1/2 cup loosely packed fresh coriander (cilantro) leaves, coarsely chopped
1/4 cup fresh lime juice
1 1/2 teaspoons kosher salt

Combine all ingredients in a glass or ceramic serving dish. Let rest at least 20 minutes before serving.

spicy papaya salsa

The golden yellow cubes of papaya bathe in a bright, jade green sauce that is hot to taste—not killing. If you can find jícama or daikon radish, peel it, cut it into one-quarter-inch dice and add it to the salsa for a little crunch. Make up to two hours before serving; stir and serve, but do not try to make a day ahead.

Makes 2 cups, 2 3/4 if jícama is added

2 jalapeño peppers, halved, seeded and cut in strips
6 medium cloves garlic, smashed and peeled
1 cup loosely packed fresh coriander (cilantro) leaves
3 tablespoons fresh lime juice
1 1/2 pounds ripe papaya, peeled, seeded and cut into 1/4-inch cubes (about 2 1/2 cups)

Combine all ingredients except papaya in a blender or mini-chop. Let machine run until a smooth green sauce forms. Scrape over papaya and stir. Stir in jícama if desired. Let stand at room temperature for 15 minutes before serving.

tomato-cranberry salsa

This is certainly not traditional, but it is a godsend in winter, when the tomatoes are faded.

Makes 3 1/2 cups

2 cups fresh cranberries (8 ounces)
1/2 cup peeled and coarsely chopped red onion
3/4 pound ripe tomatoes, cored, seeded and cut into 1/2-inch dice (about 1 3/4 cups) (if using canned tomatoes, use 3/4 cup, drained and coarsely chopped)
1 fresh jalapeño pepper, seeded and deribbed, or 1 canned jalapeño pepper, rinsed and drained
2 teaspoons kosher salt
2 tablespoons fresh lemon juice
1/2 teaspoon ground cumin

Place cranberries and onion in food processor. Pulse until coarsely chopped. Add tomato and jalapeño. Pulse 2 or 3 times in short bursts just to combine.

Scrape mixture into a ceramic or glass bowl. Stir in salt, lemon juice and cumin. Allow to ripen for 45 minutes at room temperature or overnight in the refrigerator.

*F*ried Bread Puffs *(page 125) can be split to form miniature pockets just like miniature pitas. Fill as desired with dips or salsas, here the coriander variation of Fresh Mint Salsa.*

fresh mint salsa

This is a salsa I made for a friend who loathes coriander. You can substitute coriander, but only use one cup, otherwise it will be too strong. The mint keeps its color in the lime juice better than the coriander. Multiply as desired.

Makes 2 cups

2 cups loosely packed fresh mint leaves, finely chopped (I cup)
12 ounces ripe tomatoes, cored and finely chopped (about I ¼ cups)
2 medium cloves garlic, smashed, peeled and minced
I to 2 small jalapeño peppers, stemmed, seeded, deribbed and finely chopped
2 tablespoons finely chopped yellow onion
2 tablespoons fresh lime juice
I teaspoon kosher salt
Freshly ground black pepper, to taste

Place all ingredients in a small bowl and mix until thoroughly combined. Allow to stand for about 30 minutes and adjust seasonings to taste.

Coriander Salsa
Omit mint. Use 1 cup loosely packed fresh coriander (cilantro), finely chopped.

Bruschetta Topping Salsa
Omit jalapeño. Substitute basil for mint.

25

dipping sauces

Some of these sauces, like the Peanut Dipping Sauce (page 28) or the Bagna Cauda (29), are traditional in the countries that they come from, although I may put them to untraditional uses. The others I invented mainly to enjoy one of my favorite pastimes, dipping bread in a savory sauce. The focaccias (pages 126–129) are wonderful cut into chunks and then dipped by your guests into these savory sauces. You may have to encourage them at first, but you won't have to do it a second time.

The tomato dipping sauces are a little thin to be conventional dips, but I have found friends dunking their vegetables and chips into them anyhow. Slightly reduced, they make good pasta sauces. These are good sauces with fried and grilled foods.

While Tomato Focaccia (page 129) cut in wedges to dunk in Tomato Basil Dipping Sauce can show up as part of a lavish Italian party (page 101), the pair does just fine on its own—although you could add a few olives.

pacific tomato dipping sauce

This sauce is unexpected but good with Tempura (page 246) or Corn Fritters (page 249).

Makes 1¼ cups

- 1 cup Plum Tomato Sauce (opposite page) or puréed canned plum tomatoes with their liquid
- ½ ounce peeled fresh ginger
- ½ cup loosely packed fresh coriander (cilantro) leaves
- 5 medium cloves garlic, smashed and peeled
- 2 tablespoons tamari soy sauce
- 2 teaspoons rice wine vinegar
- ¼ teaspoon hot red pepper sauce

Combine all ingredients in blender until smooth. Let stand at least 1 hour to let flavors develop.

plum tomato sauce

The base for the dipping sauces and as many pasta sauces as you wish to invent.

Makes 4 cups

2 pounds plum tomatoes, cored and cut into 1-inch pieces (about 6 cups)
5 medium cloves garlic, smashed and peeled
¼ cup fruity olive oil
Kosher salt, to taste
Freshly ground black pepper, to taste

Microwave-Oven Method. Combine all ingredients in a 2½-quart casserole dish with tightly fitting lid. Cover and cook in a high-wattage microwave oven at 100% for 15 minutes, low-wattage oven 23 minutes.

Remove from oven and uncover. Pass mixture through a food mill fitted with medium blade. Discard the pulp and return the purée to casserole. Cook, uncovered, at 100% for about 25 minutes in a high-wattage oven, 43 minutes in a low-wattage oven. The time will depend on the tomatoes used and the amount of water they contain.

Remove from oven and allow to cool.

Stove-Top Method. Proceed as in microwave-oven method, cooking over very low heat in a nonreactive pan, covered, for 35 minutes or until tomatoes get soft and break down. Put through food mill. Cook, uncovered, on top of the stove in a nonreactive pan over low heat, stirring frequently so the sauce does not scorch. It will take about 1½ hours.

spicy middle eastern tomato sauce

Use this as a dipping sauce for Koftah (page 278) or Fried Kibbeh (page 277) or as a sauce for Grilled Flank Steak (page 273), or add some hot red pepper sauce and use it with Caribbean Vegetable Fritters (page 249).

Makes 2½ cups sauce, or 3⅓ cups with added yogurt

2½ cups Plum Tomato Sauce (this page) or puréed canned plum tomatoes with their liquid
15 medium cloves garlic, smashed and peeled
2 teaspoons ground cumin
2 teaspoons ground coriander
2 teaspoons sweet paprika
1 teaspoon ground cardamon
1 teaspoon kosher salt
½ teaspoon cayenne pepper
Pinch ground cinnamon
Pinch ground clove
2 tablespoons fresh lime juice
1 cup plain yogurt, optional

Place all ingredients except lime juice and yogurt in blender and process until completely smooth. Allow sauce to stand for at least an hour for the flavors to blend.

If using warm as a steak sauce, heat gently on top of the stove. Stir in lime juice. If using as a cold dipping sauce, stir in yogurt.

tomato basil dipping sauce

I originally made this sauce to use up the canned plum tomatoes and their liquid left after making Tomato Focaccia (page 129). The sauce was so good that we all stood around dunking chunks of the still-warm bread into it.

If you would like to serve Spinach Terrine (page 143) or Smoked Fish Mousse (page 145), sliced, as a first course at a dinner, you could pour a few tablespoons of this sauce on the plates first, or use it as a dipping sauce with Calzones (page 220) or Italian Rice Dumplings (page 248).

Makes 1⅔ cups

1 cup Plum Tomato Sauce (this page) or puréed canned plum tomatoes with their liquid
⅔ cup medium-packed fresh basil leaves
10 medium cloves garlic, smashed and peeled
2 tablespoons tomato paste
1 tablespoon fresh lemon juice
6 tablespoons olive oil
2 teaspoons kosher salt
Freshly ground black pepper, to taste

Place all ingredients in a food processor and process until smooth.

peanut dipping sauce

There are two basic kinds of peanut dipping sauces used in the Malay Straits area and the rest of Southeast Asia. One is thin with flecks of peanuts and spices floating in it—next recipe. This is the other kind—smooth, creamy and mildly spicy, particularly good with grilled seafood, Yakitori and Saté (page 272). Since many items to be dipped are on skewers, put the sauce in a shallow dish so the skewers can be well coated.

Makes 1²/₃ cups

5 ounces roasted unsalted peanuts
2 slices (¹/₈ inch thick) peeled fresh ginger (¹/₄ ounce)
1 medium clove garlic, smashed and peeled
2 teaspoons sugar
¹/₂ teaspoon crushed red pepper
4 teaspoons tamari soy sauce
1 tablespoon rice wine vinegar
1 cup warm water
5 teaspoons fresh lime juice

Combine all ingredients except water and lime juice in a food processor. Process until smooth. With motor running, add water in a thin stream and process until incorporated. Stir in lime juice. Serve at room temperature.

southeast asian dipping sauce

This sauce can be made even prettier by stirring in a tablespoon of thinly shredded peeled carrot and a tablespoon of peeled, seeded, shredded cucumber.

Although usually used in Asia as a dipping sauce for Thai and Vietnamese eggrolls (page 258) or grilled meats, this is a good salad dressing. Or use with Steamed Napa Cabbage Rolls (page 207), Stuffed Cabbage with Pork Filling (pages 207 and 153) or Corn Fritters (page 249), or on Shrimp Balls (page 251) or Tempura (page 246).

You can make a large quantity to store, covered, in the refrigerator for months by omitting the scallion and fresh coriander and adding them proportionately about thirty minutes before serving, along with the carrot and cucumber, if you want.

Makes 1¹/₄ cups

¹/₂ cup Thai or other fish sauce (nuac nam)
¹/₃ cup fresh lime juice
¹/₄ cup tamari soy sauce
¹/₄ cup coarsely chopped toasted unsalted peanuts
1 scallion, trimmed, washed, and sliced on the bias very thin (about ¹/₄ cup)
2 tablespoons sugar
2 tablespoons chopped fresh coriander (cilantro) leaves
1 small fresh jalapeño pepper (with seeds), cored and diced very fine (about 1¹/₂ tablespoons)

Combine all ingredients in a pint jar with a tight-fitting lid. Shake vigorously until the sugar is dissolved. Let stand at room temperature up to 4 hours or in the refrigerator for up to 2 days. Bring to room temperature and shake vigorously before serving.

harissa sauce

This pungent red sauce can be made as spicy as you like or think your guests might enjoy by upping the quantities of sambal and harissa. Increase the other seasonings to taste so as to maintain the flavor balance. As with rouille (page 34), incremental amounts of the harissa are added to couscous as it is eaten and the palate numbs. It is a good sauce for any cold, steamed vegetable (page 69), or for Fried Kibbeh (page 277). For those with less spice-hardened palates, its spiciness can be diluted—nontraditionally—and the texture thickened with a good mayonnaise. The ingredient list looks long, but it is mainly composed of spices that require no work beyond purchase.

Makes 2 cups

1 cup tomato juice
³/₄ cup chopped tomatoes (canned, drained or fresh, cored and seeded) (about 7¹/₃ ounces)
1 teaspoon sambal olek
1 teaspoon harissa paste (the best is French, in tubes)
³/₄ teaspoon anise seed
Pinch allspice
Pinch nutmeg
¹/₄ teaspoon ground coriander seed
¹/₈ teaspoon ground cinnamon
¹/₄ teaspoon ground cardamom
2 teaspoons ground cumin
¹/₂ teaspoon ground ginger
2 tablespoons fresh lemon juice
2 tablespoons fresh lime juice
3 medium cloves garlic, smashed, peeled and finely chopped
1 cup Mayonnaise (pages 31–38)
1 tablespoon olive oil

Bring all the ingredients except the olive oil to a boil in a heavy nonaluminum pot. Reduce heat to simmer. Cook for 5 minutes. Turn off heat; stir in olive oil. Serve warm.

bagna cauda

Bagna cauda is literally a warm bath in Italian. Dig your old fondue pot out of the back of the closet and use it to keep this warm on the table. Put the pot in the middle of a large platter and surround with pieces or slices of vegetable and chunks of crusty bread. Make the slices long enough—leave some stem on the broccoli—so that friends don't get their fingers in the oil. It can be made ahead and reheated, but not in the microwave in plastic—it gets too hot. Also use it to brush on Hero Sandwiches (page 130) before adding your choice of filling.

When I have this on hand—the recipe can easily be multiplied—I use it as a pasta sauce.

Makes 1 cup

1 3-ounce jar or can anchovy fillets (about 18 anchovy fillets), drained
½ cup milk
35 medium cloves garlic, smashed and peeled
½ cup unsalted butter
½ cup olive oil

Place anchovies in a small bowl. Cover with milk and let stand for 1 hour.

Microwave-Oven Method. Place garlic, butter and oil in a 2½-quart soufflé dish. Remove anchovies from milk and dry on paper towels. Add to soufflé dish. Cover tightly with microwave plastic wrap. Cook at 100% in a high-wattage oven for 8 minutes, low-wattage 12 minutes. Prick plastic to release steam.

Remove from oven. Uncover carefully. Transfer mixture to a blender and blend until smooth (the mixture will look separated). Return to soufflé dish or ceramic serving bowl. Reheat, uncovered, for 30 seconds in a high-wattage oven,

1 minute in a low-wattage oven, or until hot.

Stove-Top Method. Melt butter in a medium pan over low heat. Drain and dry anchovies. Thinly slice garlic cloves and stir into butter with anchovies and oil. Gently simmer over very low heat, stirring occasionally, for about 15 minutes, or until the garlic is very soft.

Blend as above and return to the pan to reheat.

anchovy dip

Anchöiade, *the Provençale delight, is not a sauce to give friends who hate anchovies, but I love it and I pick the anchovies out of the Caesar salad. It is particularly good with fennel, Belgian endive and radishes. It's also good on bread, either dipped up with or spread on Crostini (page 131) and makes a terrific salad dressing; use a quarter cup for three cups torn-up romaine.*

Makes 2 cups

4 cans anchovy fillets (2 ounces each), packed in olive oil
25 medium cloves garlic, smashed and peeled
1 cup olive oil
1 cup packed fresh basil leaves, washed and dried (2¼ ounces)
4 teaspoons red wine vinegar
Freshly ground black pepper, to taste

Combine anchovies (with their own oil) and garlic in a blender and process until smooth. With the motor running, add olive oil in a steady, thin stream. Add remaining ingredients and process until thoroughly combined and smooth.

Transfer to a container and store, covered, in the refrigerator for up to 5 days. Let come to room temperature.

sweet mustard sauce

If this were only a sauce for Gravlax (page 177), it would live on the same page, but I like this cinnamon heightened variation so much that I use it in a number of other preparations, like the Herring in Sweet Mustard Sauce (page 184) and the Sweet Mustard Shrimp Salad (page 169). Once you have it, I think you will find lots of ways to use it. Spread it on bread before topping with smoked salmon. Serve it with boiled potatoes— incidentally, it makes a great potato salad if you let the potatoes cool before tossing them in the sauce with some thinly sliced red onion.

As it keeps so well, you may want to multiply the recipe.

Makes 1½ cups

½ cup spicy German mustard
2 teaspoons dry mustard
6 tablespoons sugar
¼ cup white wine vinegar
1 teaspoon ground cinnamon
⅔ cup vegetable oil
6 tablespoons finely chopped fresh dill sprigs

In a medium bowl combine mustards, sugar, vinegar and cinnamon. Slowly whisk in oil. Stir in dill. The sauce will keep in a closed jar in the refrigerator up to 1 month. Before serving, allow to come to room temperature and stir briskly.

mayonnaise and mayo-based sauces

After ketchup, mayonnaise may be our most ubiquitous sauce, on its own or as the base for Tartar Sauce (page 36), Rémoulade (page 36) and on. Mayonnaise is a cold sauce most often made with egg yolks that are beaten up with oil to form a stable emulsion. Bread, the roe of fish (see Taramasalata, this page), cooked potatoes (see Brandade of Sole, page 32) and even almonds ground to a smooth paste are sometimes used as thickeners. The mayonnaise-type sauces are rich and almost infinitely variable.

The egg yolks provide some problems in today's far-from-pure world, and I have offered two variations that avoid raw egg yolks. I still take the risk, but the decision is up to you. If you want to avoid the cholesterol in egg yolks—this will not avoid salmonella—substitute an equal amount of egg whites for the yolks.

I also use bottled mayonnaise from time to time particularly on sandwiches, in tuna salad, egg salad and potato salad. Those are the tastes of my childhood; but it is not suitable for everything.

All the mayonnaises keep well, covered, in a glass jar in the refrigerator—up to a month—so you may want to multiply the recipes.

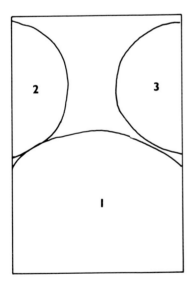

A *simple Greek assortment of* **1** *Walnut Dip (page 16),* **2** *Taramasalata and* **3** *Macedonian Cheese Dip (page 18) to go nicely with ouzo (page 203) and slices of fennel or wedges of toasted pita (page 93).*

taramasalata

Just for fun, we will start with a Greek, fish-roe mayonnaise that also uses bread as a thickener. Traditionally, taramasalata is made with cod roe that have been preserved with salt. The tarama can be bought in jars, as can a prepared taramasalata. Since jarred tarama is often terribly salty, I prefer to start with salmon roe (caviar), which can be fresh or jarred. It is generally less salty. If it is the right season of the year and you have a very good fish person, you may be able to get really fresh—unsalted—fish roe, which will make an even better dish.

This recipe makes a very thick sauce. If you want a thinner one, make it in a food processor and add about a quarter cup more oil; or make the sauce as below and just before serving whisk in some heavy (whipping) cream.

Don't use your greenest, heaviest tasting olive oil for this or nobody will be able to taste the fish roe. Serve with toasted sections of pita bread.

Makes 2 cups

7 medium cloves garlic, smashed and peeled
1¼ cups salmon roe (caviar)
1 ounce crustless Italian bread, broken into chunks
¼ cup fresh lemon juice
1 cup olive oil

In a blender, purée the garlic. Add the roe, bread chunks and lemon juice, and start processing. Dribble in the olive oil in a very thin stream; by the time the oil is completely incorporated, the mixture will be smooth and very thick. You will need to stop the blender from time to time in order to scrape down the sides and to break any air bubble that occurs over the blades. You can tell if that is happening because the noise the blender makes will change to an empty whirring.

If not using immediately, refrigerate, covered. It will last at least one week. Bring to room temperature before serving.

31

brandade
of sole

One of the few nonvegetarian
dips, this potato-fish mayonnaise
is a variation by London chef
Brian Turner of a classic
brandade of salt cod. Since sole
doesn't need desalting, the dip is
quicker to make and is less salty.
For a salt cod brandade, make
the mixture for the Salt Cod Pâté
(page 146) and eliminate the
eggs; do not bake.

Brandade of Sole is silky and
elegant, worth considering as a
starter for an elegant dinner. At a
stand-up party, serve it with New
Potatoes (page 69) or with slices
of carrot or stalks of celery.

After the Brandade is cooked
and chilled, taste it and adjust the
cream and the olive oil. How
much you need will depend on
how much liquid was in the fish
and how much evaporated during
cooking. Whether to thin with
olive oil or cream depends on the
flavor of your olive oil. Its taste
should not overwhelm the fish.

It may seem silly to dirty
both a food processor and a
blender, and you can make do
just using the food processor; but
the double whammy will give you
a much silkier texture.

Makes 4 cups

9 ounces sole fillets
½ cup heavy cream
**9 ounces Maine or Long Island
  boiling potatoes, peeled and
  cubed (about 1½ cups)**
¼ cup olive oil
**4 medium cloves garlic,
  smashed and peeled**
2 teaspoons kosher salt

Finishing
**Additional heavy cream and/or
  olive oil**

Microwave-Oven Method. Fold
fillets in half and place in a
1½-quart dish. Pour cream over
the fish. Cover tightly with
microwave plastic wrap. Cook at
100% in a high-wattage oven for
3 minutes 30 seconds, 4 minutes
30 seconds in a low-wattage
oven. Prick plastic to release
steam. Immediately scrape fish

and cream into a food processor.
Process until smooth.

Place potatoes in a 4-cup
measure with 1 cup water. Cook,
covered, for 8 minutes in a
high-wattage oven, 12 minutes in
a low-wattage oven. Prick plastic
to release steam. Remove from
oven.

Drain potatoes and place in
food processor with fish mixture.
Process until smooth. Add olive
oil, garlic and salt and process
until smooth.

Working in batches, scrape
mixture into a blender and blend
until silky smooth. Refrigerate
until cold. Adjust the brandade
with cream, olive oil or salt to
taste.

Stove-Top Method. Bring 3 cups
of water to boil in a medium
saucepan. Add potatoes, let
water return to the boil and
cook for 10 minutes. Remove
from heat and drain.

While potatoes are cooking,
cut fish into 1½-inch pieces.
Place in a very small sauce pan
with 2 tablespoons of water.
Pour cream over fish. Bring to a
simmer over low heat and cook
until fish is just opaque, about 5
minutes.

Immediately scrape fish and
cream into a food processor.
Process until smooth.

Add potatoes and finish
recipe as above.

classic
mayonnaise

This is classic mayonnaise; the
dried mustard can be omitted,
vinegar used instead of lemon
juice and all olive oil used instead
of part vegetable oil. I use a
strong-tasting olive and cut it with
vegetable oil—usually canola
(rapeseed) oil—to save money
and to not have an overwhelm-
ingly olivey sauce. Adjust

according to the oils you have on hand. Mayonnaise made in a food processor will be a little more stable—less likely to separate— than that made by hand. Classic mayonnaise is less satisfactory when made in a blender, as it quickly gets too stiff to accept all the oil needed.

Makes 2 cups

3 egg yolks
I tablespoon plus I teaspoon fresh lemon juice
I ¹/₂ teaspoons kosher salt
Freshly ground white pepper
I teaspoon dried mustard
I cup vegetable oil
¹/₂ cup olive oil

Place egg yolks in food processor fitted with the steel blade. Process 1 minute. Add lemon juice, salt, white pepper and mustard. With the machine running, gradually add oil through the feed tube, beginning with droplets and working up to a thin stream as the mayonnaise begins to set up.

Or in a large nonreactive bowl, work with a large whisk in the same manner.

cooked-yolk mayonnaise

This technique was developed by Harold McGee, author of The Curious Cook. *To learn more about it, read his book. The yolks cook in this way sufficiently so that they are no longer possibly contaminated. The mayonnaise has a slight taste of cooked yolks, but is eminently satisfactory.*

Makes I ³/₄ cups

Separate 2 large eggs, saving the whites for another purpose. Put the yolks in a 2-cup glass measure and whisk thoroughly with 2 tablespoons plus 1 teaspoon each of water and fresh

lemon juice. Wash the whisk with very hot, soapy water. Cover the measure tightly with microwavable plastic wrap. Cook at 100% in a high-wattage oven 45 seconds to 1 minute or until it just begins to boil (when first bubbles appear). Prick plastic to release steam. Remove from oven. Uncover. Whisk with cleaned whisk. Return to oven uncovered and cook for 20 seconds. Remove from oven. Whisk with a *clean* whisk—yes, another one—until cool. Now, continue by whisking in oil as if making any other mayonnaise. Use 1½ cups of the oil of your choice, seasoning with salt, pepper and mustard if desired.

sweet garlic "mayonnaise"

This mayonnaise has no eggs whatsoever. It is thickened by the sticky texture of long-cooked garlic. The long cooking— particularly easily accomplished in the microwave oven—also gentles the taste of the garlic. It still is not a sauce for those who loathe garlic, but it is very good in fish soups and with cold fish preparations such as Cold Cooked Salmon (page 179).

Makes I ¹/₂ cups

¹/₂ cup Sweet Garlic Purée
I cup olive oil or a combination of olive and vegetable oils
Kosher salt to taste
Freshly ground black pepper, to taste
Fresh lemon juice, optional
Prepared mustard, optional

Place Sweet Garlic Purée in blender jar. With the motor running, gradually add the oil in a thin, steady stream. When fully combined, add optional flavorings, if desired.

sweet garlic purée

The Sweet Garlic Purée can be used in sauce bases and as a flavoring agent and can easily be made in the microwave oven or on top of the stove. It will be a little less sharp, a little rounder, in the microwave.

Sweet Garlic Purée becomes the base for a surprisingly stable mayonnaise that can be seasoned or used as the foundation for other sauces.

Makes 2 cups

3 medium heads garlic, cloves separated, smashed and peeled
I ¹/₂ cups chicken broth, preferably homemade

Microwave-Oven Method. Combine garlic and chicken broth in a 4-cup glass measure. Cover tightly with microwave plastic wrap and cook at 100% in a high-wattage oven for 15 minutes or in a low-wattage oven for 25 minutes. Prick plastic to release steam. Remove from oven and uncover.

Transfer softened garlic and broth to work bowl of a food processor or blender and process until completely smooth.

Scrape into a container and store, tightly covered in the refrigerator or freezer.

Stove-Top Method. Combine garlic and chicken broth in a medium saucepan, cover with lid and bring to a boil over medium heat. Reduce heat to low and simmer, covered, for 25 minutes. Remove from heat. Finish recipe as above.

33

aïoli

Aïoli is a sauce that turns up all along the Mediterannean with its name spelled variously. It is made in three different ways: The hardest and yet the simplest is to pound the garlic with the salt in a mortar until it becomes a smooth purée. Then the oil is dripped in very slowly, working the pestle constantly—good luck. The most common today is to add garlic to a classic mayonnaise. If you are making the mayonnaise in a food processor, just throw in the garlic cloves about halfway through adding the oil and continue processing. You will need about eight medium cloves of garlic, or to taste. Remember, the garlic flavor will become more intense as the aïoli sits. The third way is to use a cooked potato as a base (this page) or bread (this page).

Aïoli is known as the butter of Provence and is spread on bread or served with steamed fish. When an assortment of steamed fish (notably salt cod), steamed chicken and meat and many steamed vegetables are served, this is a great feast called the Grand Aïoli. The sauce is also stirred into soup-stews like the French bourride and the Italian bourrida as a thickening and flavoring agent. Oddly, it doesn't separate in the heat.

Bouillabaisse is heightened by a version of aïoli called **rouille,** which describes its color, a rusty red. The color is achieved by adding some of the soup from the bouillabaisse and sometimes some roasted peppers, sweet and hot (red). To make rouille when you are not making bouillabaisse, add Roasted Peppers, red (page 58), and some hot, fresh red peppers to taste by puréeing along with the aïoli in the food processor or by reducing to a purée in a mortar. Also add some stem saffron that has been allowed to dissolve in a little, acid white wine. Rouille is

good with Boiled Shrimp (page 168) or Crudités (page 67).

●

aïoli (with potato)

Makes 1 cup

10 ounces boiling potatoes, peeled and cut into 1-inch cubes (1¾ cups)
¼ cup water
6 medium cloves garlic, smashed and peeled
½ cup olive oil
4 teaspoons fresh lemon juice
1 teaspoon kosher salt
Freshly ground black pepper, to taste

Microwave-Oven Method. Put potatoes and water in a 1½-quart soufflé dish. Cover tightly with microwave plastic wrap and cook at 100% in a high-wattage oven 10 minutes or in a low-wattage oven 17 minutes. Prick plastic to release steam.

Remove from oven and uncover. Strain off any remaining liquid and pass potatoes through a food mill fitted with a very fine disc. Reserve.

Stove-Top Method. Place potatoes in a steamer basket over boiling water; cover. Steam until easily pierced with the tip of a knife. Put through a food mill.

Place garlic and ¼ cup of the oil in a food processor and process until smooth.

Stir garlic mixture into reserved potato until thoroughly incorporated. Gradually add remaining ¼ cup oil, stirring well after each addition. Stir in lemon juice and add salt and pepper to taste.

aïoli (with bread)

Makes about 1 cup

6 medium cloves garlic, smashed and peeled
½ cup olive oil
1 cup finely ground fresh bread crumbs (2½ ounces), whirring in a food processor is fine
4 teaspoons fresh lemon juice
1 teaspoon kosher salt
Freshly ground black pepper, to taste

Place garlic in a blender jar and process until finely chopped, stopping the machine and scraping down the sides occasionally. Add about half the oil and process until very smooth. Add bread crumbs in three batches and process until combined after each addition.

With the motor running, gradually add the remaining oil in a steady, thin stream. Add remaining ingredients and process until mixture becomes completely smooth, stopping the machine occasionally and scraping down the sides.

Transfer to small bowl and store, refrigerated and covered.

sweet potato aïoli

I know of no traditional recipe like this, although I have had sweet potatoes in a Grand Aïoli. It makes a sensational, brightly pumpkin-colored sauce that goes well with almost any vegetable, looks different from standard dips and can vary your main courses as well.

Makes 4½ cups

2½ pounds sweet potatoes

16 medium cloves garlic, smashed and peeled

1 ½ cups olive oil

2 tablespoons fresh lemon juice

4 teaspoons water

Scant 1 teaspoon hot red pepper sauce

2 teaspoons kosher salt

Freshly ground black pepper to taste

Microwave-Oven Method. Prick potatoes several times with a fork. Cook at 100% in a high-wattage oven for 20 minutes. Remove from oven. When cool enough to handle, peel potatoes. Set aside to cool.

This quantity cannot be done at once in a low-wattage oven.

Stove-Top Method. Steam sweet potatoes over a small amount of water until easily pierced with a fork. Do not boil potatoes; they get too watery.

Chop the garlic in a food processor. Add peeled sweet potatoes and process until mixture is very smooth. A little at a time, add olive oil, lemon juice and water, stopping occasionally to scrape down the sides of the work bowl. Add hot pepper sauce, salt and pepper and process until incorporated.

A *simple dip, Sweet Potato Aïoli, and an appropriate Crudité (page 67) of red pepper strips can gain entertainment value by having their colors flattered by the choice of containers and even nibbles—here pistachios in their traditional red shells.*

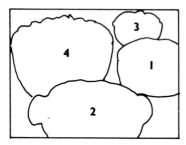

An international mix of dips,
1 Spicy Rémoulade and **2** Tartar
Sauce; spreads like **3** Cheddar-
Sherry Spread (page 39) and a
simple vegetable preparation like
4 Caponata (page 14) can go
with Biscuits (page 108) and one
sliced or grilled meat or
Fishburgers (page 187) for a
mix-and-match party.

tartar sauce

This is the great American
standard for fried fish and
seafood, as well as Fishburgers
(page 187) and Crab Cakes (page
187). The recipe can be easily
multiplied and will keep for at
least one week.

Makes 2 cups

**2 cups commercial
     mayonnaise
2 tablespoons white wine
     vinegar
3 sweet gherkins, minced
3 scallions, minced
¼ cup plus 2 tablespoons
     capers, drained**

Combine all ingredients in a
small bowl. Refrigerate, covered,
until cold.

rémoulade sauce

While extremely similar to
American tartar sauce and good
on similar foods, this sauce has an
extremely French air. It really
needs homemade mayonnaise,
which I would make with
tarragon vinegar. The recipe is
easily multiplied and will keep,
covered, in the refrigerator for at
least a week.

Makes about 2 cups

**1 ½ cups Classic Mayonnaise
     (page 32), or Cooked Egg
     Yolk Mayonnaise (page 33)
3 tablespoons minced
     Cornichons (page 152) or
     commercial, drained**

3 tablespoons rinsed, drained, and minced capers
4 tablespoons minced fresh herbs (Italian parsley, chervil, chives, tarragon)
½ teaspoon anchovy paste

Beat the flavorings into the mayonnaise.

spicy rémoulade

In the South, there are many sauces called rémoulade that the French would never recognize. They are spicy and go well with boiled seafoods and on Crab Cakes and Spicy Crab Cakes (page 187) and fried fish and seafood.

I would make this with homemade mayonnaise, but the seasonings are sufficiently sharp that you may be able to get away with commercial mayonnaise; just make sure it's not sweet.

Makes about 1½ cups

1 cup Classic Mayonnaise (page 32), Cooked Egg Yolk Mayonnaise (page 33) or commercial mayonnaise
2 tablespoons Dijon mustard
2 tablespoons prepared horseradish, drained
1 tablespoon fresh lemon juice
¼ cup chopped celery (about 2 ounces)
¼ cup chopped scallions (1½ ounces)
½ teaspoon cayenne pepper
1 tablespoon sweet paprika
1 medium clove garlic, smashed and peeled

Mix everything together, blending well. Refrigerate for several hours before using.

new orleans spicy rémoulade sauce

Now, this is clearly not authentic, as it uses Sweet Garlic Mayonnaise. I think it is very good. If you want to be more authentic, substitute Classic Mayonnaise (page 32) made with tarragon vinegar and add at least four cloves of garlic to the recipe. The spicy rémoulade may not seem very hot when you first make it, but its true flavor will show as it sits in the refrigerator for a few hours. It's famous with fried foods, which would negate all the health benefits of non-egg mayonnaise, but grilled foods can be successfully substituted.

Makes 1½ cups

1 cup loosely packed fresh Italian parsley leaves
2 scallions, white and green parts cut into 1-inch pieces (½ cup)
2 slices fresh horseradish, peeled and cut into small pieces (about ½ ounce)
1 rib celery, peeled and cut into 1-inch pieces (½ cup)
2 tablespoons tarragon vinegar
1 tablespoon sweet paprika
2 teaspoons tamari soy sauce
2 teaspoons dry mustard
¼ teaspoon hot red pepper sauce
¾ cup unseasoned Sweet Garlic "Mayonnaise" (page 33)
Kosher salt, to taste

Combine all ingredients except "Mayonnaise" and salt in the work bowl of a food processor and process until finely chopped. Add remaining ingredients and process to combine. Scrape into a container and store, tightly covered, in the refrigerator.

green goddess dressing

Anybody who has read James Beard or Helen Evans Brown will be familiar with this San Francisco dressing traditionally used with cold crab meat. I have used it in chicken and shrimp salads as well.

The day I was shooting the photograph of the Spinach and Fish Pâté (page 147), the owners of the house, Leo Lerman and Gray Foy, ate up the pâté, slathering it with the dressing. I hadn't thought of the combination, but it was excellent, which leads me to believe that it could accompany many of the simple fried foods in Chapter 7 and the fish pâtés and mousses in Chapter 4, as well as other things to which your thoughts may lead you.

Makes 2¼ cups

1 cup of the homemade mayonnaises (pages 32–33) or commercial mayonnaise
1 cup sour cream
1 2-ounce can anchovies, chopped
1 tablespoon fresh lemon juice
3 tablespoons tarragon vinegar
2 teaspoons chopped fresh tarragon leaves
3 tablespoons chopped fresh chives
½ cup chopped fresh Italian parsley leaves
½ teaspoon kosher salt
Freshly ground black pepper, to taste

Combine all ingredients in a food processor and process until smooth. Chill.

cocktail sauce

As I noted in the introduction to this chapter, cocktail sauce may have been the start of dipping. I would rather dip my boiled shrimp, raw oysters or clams or boiled lobster chunks, into one of the many other dips and sauces in this chapter, such as Romesco Sauce (page 9), Herb Dip (page 18), a salsa (pages 23–25) and the Rémoulade Cocktail Sauce that follows. This is the traditional sauce and cannot be ignored.

Makes 1 ½ cups

1 ½ cups ketchup
2 tablespoons finely grated peeled fresh horseradish, or 2 tablespoons drained prepared horseradish
1 tablespoon Worcestershire sauce
2 ¼ teaspoons fresh lemon juice
6 dashes hot red pepper sauce

Combine all ingredients in a small bowl. Let stand at least 2 hours to let flavors develop.

rémoulade cocktail sauce

This wasn't the sauce at the birthday, but it's terrific. Try it for a change.

Makes 2 cups

1 ½ cups ketchup
¾ cup New Orleans Spicy Rémoulade Sauce (page 37)

Combine both ingredients in a small bowl.

cheese and butter spreads

Different cheeses and butter are often creamed and seasoned to be placed in crocks for guests to spread on crackers or bread or to be used by the cook as the base of a bread- or pastry-based mouthful. A good serving temperature is about 70°F, spreadable but with no fat separating out. As your kitchen may be a good deal hotter when you are cooking for a big party, remember to remove the spreads to a cooler location once they are ready. Do not try to spread them refrigerator-cold; they will tear the bread and break the cracker.

Go for simplicity: crisp radishes with Liptauer Cheese (page 18). A crusty bread would be a good addition.

cheddar-sherry spread

This is much like the cheese spread that you find in crocks, but with a little more oomph. It would be particularly good at a sherry party. Serve in an herb-crusted roll or a crock surrounded by bread, or spread on toasted rye bread. Spread on bread, it can be topped with minced herbs or with a thin slice of canned jalapeño or Roasted Pepper (page 58), a slice of olive or an almond sliver.

Makes 1½ cups

8 ounces mild Cheddar cheese, preferably yellow but white will do, cut into ½-inch cubes, at room temperature
6 tablespoons unsalted butter, at room temperature
2 tablespoons dry sherry
2 teaspoons Dijon mustard
¼ teaspoon freshly ground white pepper
Large pinch cayenne pepper
2 tablespoons chopped fresh Italian parsley leaves, optional
2 tablespoons very finely sliced fresh chives, optional

Combine cheese, butter, sherry, mustard, white pepper and cayenne in the work bowl of a food processor. Process, stopping to scrape down the sides of the bowl as needed, until the mixture is smooth.

At this point the cheese spread can be wrapped tightly and stored in the refrigerator for up to 3 weeks. Bring the cheese to room temperature before serving. If desired, roll the cheese mixture into a log shape before chilling and coat with an even layer of the chopped parsley and chives when you remove it from the refrigerator just before serving.

blue cheese and port spread

Serve this with Port. Instead of spreading it on bread, place a heaping spoonful in a pastry tartlet (pages 96–97) and top with a piece of walnut.

Makes 1½ cups

8 ounces rindless mild blue cheese, like Saga, at room temperature
6 tablespoons unsalted butter, at room temperature
¼ cup port
¼ teaspoon freshly ground white pepper
Large pinch cayenne pepper
¾ cup coarsely chopped walnuts

Combine all ingredients except walnuts in the work bowl of a food processor. Process, stopping occasionally to scrape down the sides, until the mixture is smooth and well blended. Refrigerate, covered, up to 2 weeks. Remove from the refrigerator about 1 hour before serving and stir in the walnuts when softened. (You may add the nuts right away if you're serving the spread within a few hours.)

horseradish cream cheese

This is simple and surprisingly good. In addition to using it to fill Salami Roll-Ups (page 202), spread Buttermilk Biscuits (page 108) with this and add a slice of ham. Or stir in some chopped herbs and pipe into Pâte à Choux (page 106). This can be made up to a week ahead of time and kept covered and refrigerated.

Makes 1 cup

8 ounces cream cheese, at room temperature (1 cup)
½ cup prepared horseradish, drained and liquid squeezed out (4½ ounces)
Kosher salt, to taste
Freshly ground black pepper, to taste

Combine all ingredients in the work bowl of a food processor and process until completely combined.

smoked salmon cream cheese

This is best made two or three days before needed. Serve in a crock, spread on thinly sliced toast or pipe into a Sour Cream Pastry (page 96) or Cream Cheese Pastry (page 96) tartlet.

Makes 1¼ cups

8 ounces cream cheese, at room temperature (1 cup)
3 ounces smoked salmon or lox
2 teaspoons fresh lemon juice
¼ teaspoon coarsely ground black pepper
¼ teaspoon kosher salt
1½ tablespoons thinly sliced fresh chives
1 tablespoon finely chopped fresh dill sprigs

Process the cream cheese in the work bowl of a food processor until creamy. Add the remaining ingredients and pulse until the cream cheese is a pale pink and the smoked salmon is finely chopped. Store in a tightly covered container in the refrigerator for up to 5 days.

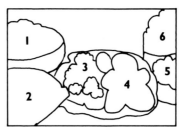

A gala Franco-Russian zakouski assortment of **1** Creamed Herring (page 185), **2** Marinated Anchovies with Fennel (page 182), **3** Fried Bread Boxes (page 121) filled with sour cream and fresh whitefish roe, **4** Puff Pastry (page 103) and Russian Turnovers (pages 217–218), **5** Scallion Cream Cheese (page 42) waiting for smoked fish and toast, and **6** Chicken Liver Crock with Apples and Onions (page 149) to spread on the toast as well. Vodka is obvious.

scallion cream cheese

Again, make a day or so ahead of serving. Use on canapés under smoked salmon instead of butter, if desired.

Makes 1¼ cups

3 scallions (green onions), trimmed and cut into 2-inch lengths
8 ounces cream cheese, at room temperature (1 cup)
2 teaspoons fresh lemon juice
¼ teaspoon coarsely ground black pepper
¼ teaspoon kosher salt

Process the cream cheese in the work bowl of a food processor until creamy. Add the remaining ingredients and pulse until the cream cheese is a pale green and the scallions are finely chopped. Store in a tightly covered container in the refrigerator for up to 5 days.

olive cream cheese

This is an old lunch box favorite that is still good today. Spread on Whole-Wheat Soda Bread (page 114) and top with a slice of olive.

Makes 2½ cups

16 ounces cream cheese, at room temperature
1 cup drained pimento-stuffed green olives
¼ cup sour cream
1 tablespoon fresh lemon juice
Freshly ground black pepper
½ cup pecan pieces, chopped, optional

Place the cream cheese in the work bowl of a food processor. Process until smooth

and creamy. Add the remaining ingredients and pulse until the olives are coarsely chopped and the ingredients are mixed.

Bring to room temperature and, if desired, stir in the pecans before serving.

sage butter

This is good with thinly sliced cooked meat.

1 cup unsalted butter
2 tablespoons chopped fresh sage leaves
4 teaspoons fresh lemon juice
1 teaspoon kosher salt
Pinch cayenne pepper

Make as in box.

dill butter

Particularly good with smoked salmon and Rye Soda Bread (page 114). Top with a dill sprig. The spread bread could also be topped with a little pile of peeled bay shrimp or other tiny shrimp and a twist of lemon.

1 cup unsalted butter
½ cup loosely packed fresh dill sprigs
3 teaspoons fresh lemon juice
1 small clove garlic, smashed and peeled
¼ teaspoon kosher salt

Make as in box.

Basic Formula for Butters

• Allow butter to reach 72°F. Place herbs, garlic and any other ingredients to be chopped in a food processor. Process until coarsely chopped. Add butter, cut into chunks, and spices; process until smooth. With machine running, slowly pour lemon juice and any other liquids through the feed tube. Process until completely incorporated, stopping to scrape sides of bowl as necessary.

• Wrap and refrigerate if not being used immediately. A convenient way to wrap it is to spoon it onto a sheet of waxed paper and roll it in the waxed paper so that you have a stick about an inch in diameter. Wrap tightly in waxed paper and then in aluminum foil. The butter can be refrigerated or frozen virtually indefinitely.

• If using as a topping for hot vegetables, fish, chicken or meat, slice off a thin round and place on hot food where it will soften.

• If using as a spread, allow to come to room temperature. Cream with a wooden spoon or in a food processor and spread with a sandwich spatula or a broad-tipped table knife.

• Many of these butters are good in tea sandwiches and on canapés. See pages 118 and 116 for a list of combinations.

maître d'hôtel butter

This is a basic tea-sandwich fixing. Sometimes the parsley is omitted.

Makes 1 cup

1 cup unsalted butter
1 cup loosely packed fresh Italian parsley leaves
1/4 cup fresh lemon juice
1/4 teaspoon kosher salt
Freshly ground black pepper

Optional (choose one group)

4 large cloves garlic, smashed and peeled and 1/8 teaspoon hot red pepper sauce
or

2 1/2 tablespoons Dijon mustard, 2 1/2 tablespoons Worcestershire sauce and 1/4 teaspoon freshly ground black pepper
or

2 tablespoons anchovy paste

Make as in box opposite.

minted butter

This is particularly good with thinly sliced rare lamb. Top with a mint leaf.

1 cup unsalted butter
1 cup loosely packed fresh mint leaves
5 shallots
1 medium clove garlic, smashed and peeled
5 strips lemon zest, chopped
8 teaspoons fresh lemon juice
1 1/3 teaspoons Worcestershire sauce
1/4 teaspoon kosher salt
Freshly ground black pepper
Pinch cayenne pepper

Make as in box opposite.

green peppercorn butter

A terrific accompaniment to almost all meats and sliced cheeses.

1 cup unsalted butter
2 tablespoons green peppercorns
1 medium clove garlic
1 slice peeled fresh ginger
1 tablespoon fresh lemon juice
1/4 teaspoon kosher salt
Freshly ground black pepper

Make as in box opposite.

mustard-anchovy butter

This is fabulous with cold sliced steak or sliced hard-boiled egg.

1 cup unsalted butter
2 tablespoons anchovy paste
1 tablespoon dry mustard

Make as in box opposite.

watercress butter

This brilliantly green butter is not only beautiful but virtually all-purpose as well.

1 cup unsalted butter
8 cups loosely packed watercress leaves (about 9 ounces)
2 tablespoons plus 3/4 teaspoon fresh lemon juice
1/2 teaspoon kosher salt

Make as in box opposite.

coriander butter

Try this with thinly sliced chicken, or a bit of cold fish.

1 cup unsalted butter
8 teaspoons finely chopped fresh Italian parsley leaves
1 teaspoon ground coriander
4 teaspoons fresh lemon juice
1/4 teaspoon kosher salt
Freshly ground white pepper to taste

Make as in box opposite at least 1 hour before using.

curry butter

This is a pleasant surprise with smoked fish or chicken. Add a thin slice of a cherry tomato for contrast.

1 cup unsalted butter
8 teaspoons finely chopped fresh Italian parsley leaves
4 teaspoons curry powder
1/4 cup fresh lemon juice
1/4 teaspoon kosher salt
Freshly ground white pepper, to taste

Make as in box opposite at least 1 hour before using.

horseradish butter

This is good with smoked fish or thinly sliced leftover cold meat.

1 cup unsalted butter
8 teaspoons drained, prepared horseradish
8 teaspoons finely chopped fresh Italian parsley leaves
1/4 cup fresh lemon juice
Kosher salt, to taste
Freshly ground white pepper, to taste

Make as in box (page 42).

red pepper butter

Another good base for hard-boiled eggs (see box, page 88), topped with a slice of roasted pepper; it's also nice under very thinly sliced carrots.

1 cup unsalted butter
6 ounces Roasted Peppers, red (page 59), or canned roasted red peppers, drained
Kosher salt, to taste
Freshly ground black pepper, to taste

Make as in box (page 42).

A *substantial smørrebrød that isn't at all Scandinavian. A thin slice of packaged German rye bread is amply spread with Watercress Butter (page 43) and then mounded with Chicken Salad (page 263) sprinkled with extra caraway.*

prosciutto spread

If you want, you can top this with a slice of prosciutto, but it's good alone on bread or in a Cheddar Cheese Pastry (page 97) tartlet.

Makes 2 cups

1/2 pound prosciutto, cut into thin strips
1 cup unsalted butter, cut into 1/2-inch pieces, cold
4 teaspoons fresh lemon juice
Freshly ground black pepper, to taste

Place all ingredients in a food processor and pulse until prosciutto is finely chopped. Process until smooth. Serve at room temperature.

ham spread

This is delicious in a Cornmeal Biscuit (page 108) with a slice of cheese or piped into a Pâte à Choux (page 106).

Makes 2 cups

2 tablespoons Cognac
3/4 pound boiled ham, cut into 1-inch cubes
1 tablespoon Worcestershire sauce
2 1/2 teaspoons dry mustard
1/8 teaspoon cayenne pepper
Freshly ground black pepper, to taste
1/2 cup unsalted butter, at room temperature

Place Cognac in a small saucepan and warm slightly over low heat. Ignite with a match, turn off the heat and let stand until flames subside.

Place Cognac and remaining ingredients except butter in a food processor. Process until ham is finely chopped. Transfer mixture to a bowl.

Place butter and 1/2 cup of the ham mixture in the food processor and process until smooth. Scrape butter mixture into ham mixture and stir to combine. Let stand at least 2 hours to let flavors develop. Serve at room temperature.

sardine paste

This is a classic filling for tea sandwiches or as a spread for a cracker.

Makes 1 1/4 cups

2 4 3/8-ounce cans boneless sardines in oil
4 tablespoons unsalted butter
2 teaspoons fresh lemon juice
2 teaspoons Dijon mustard
1/2 teaspoon kosher salt
1/4 teaspoon freshly ground black pepper
1/4 teaspoon hot red pepper sauce

Drain the sardines well and place them in the work bowl of a food processor fitted with the metal blade. Add the remaining ingredients and process until the mixture is a smooth paste. Stop once or twice during processing to scrape down the sides of the bowl.

Store the sardine paste in a covered container in the refrigerator up to a week. Bring to room temperature at least 30 minutes before serving.

chapter 2

veggie good

At least since the 1960s, vegetables have been a part of any cocktail party. The quantity of them is increasing as the dieters and health-conscious among our friends go to them as if to a magnet. They are most visible as crudités—strips or pieces of vegetables arranged with more or less artifice in baskets, bowls and platters to use with dips (pages 8–13). Individual leaves or whole small vegetables, raw or blanched (page 72), are stuffed with mousses, salads and cooked stuffings. (Look in the Index for lists of possibilities.) Of these vegetables, more below. Of course, the dips themselves are often made from vegetables, as you can see in the previous chapter. There are also vegetable molds and mousses (pages 140–143), blanched vegetable leaves used as wrappers for things like stuffed cabbage (pages 204–207), vegetable frittatas to cut in strips or dip in spicy sauces (pages 26–38) and batter-dipped vegetables that are crisply fried (page 245) and Vegetable Chips (page 238) to gobble or dip.

Two of my favorite vegetable nibbles are reconstituted sun-dried tomatoes (see box, page 10) and Sage Potatoes (page 238). The first probably needs a toothpick; the second doesn't.

This chapter ranges from nibbles like seasoned olives and nuts, through cooked spiced vegetables for nabbing on a toothpick or to use as a salad, to marinated peppers, to crudités and steamed vegetables, before plunging on to grilled vegetables, stuffed vegetables, vegetable pancakes, such as potato rösti and corn pancakes, to a few good egg dishes that seem to fit in this chapter better than any place else.

The recipe for Spiced Green Olives (page 54) can be made with an assortment of olives in different colors and flavors from different countries.

Beet Pickled Eggs (page 89) look like the endpapers of a very rare book. Serve with a saucer or shaker full of Seasoned Salt.

nibbles

The supermarket, the gourmet shop and the deli are all filled with things to nibble on while drinking or waiting for dinner. They come loose, in paper packages, in cans and bottles. If you look at Ready-Mades (opposite page), you'll find some of the better choices and how to select them or vary them. I have in my life served nuts right from the can and olives right from the jar. I certainly have used taco chips and potato chips. I don't think I have ever gone as far as beer nuts, but I have served—at football games—large pretzels with a jar of mustard.

It is nice to have a few homemade alternatives to dry cereal and Japanese assorted snacks, especially if they are not too hard to make. These are pretty easy. Look in Fear of Frying (pages 231–259) for all the fried chips made at home.

I find that nibbles should be fairly spicy. If you want people to drink less, cut down on the salt. Most nibbles are very fattening, if that is a concern; the most fattening and one of the tastiest is cracklings left over from Rendering Fat (box, page 150).

nuts

There is no easier route to cocktail party snacks than keeping an assortment of nuts in cupboard and freezer. Sealed jars of unsalted peanuts and macadamia nuts go on the shelf along with cans of whole blanched almonds, walnuts and pecans. Opened or loose nuts, such as bulk-bought hazelnuts, go in plastic bags in the freezer. Pistachios keep in the shell for quite a long time.

On the most hurried days, just open the container and pour the nuts into a bowl, or serve with Seasoned Salt (opposite page). A very little more time will let you make the seasoned nuts below, or they can be made and refrigerated, tightly covered, for as long as a week. Nuts that are best at room temperature will need about an hour out of the refrigerator. Those that are meant to be eaten warm can be reheated on a baking or cookie sheet in the oven (350°F) for four minutes.

For large parties, you may want greater quantities of any kind of nut. It is a better idea to make batches than to try to cram more into a pan. They won't heat and flavor properly in larger batches.

If you are only serving nuts and olives—very Spanish—with drinks, two cups will be right for around six people. If it is a party with lots of different kinds of food, I wouldn't even put the nuts with the main group of foods. I would put them in little bowls around the room. In that case, two cups of nuts will spread to ten to twelve people.

48

ready-mades

This is a category where from the jar or from the can or even the bag can be a big help. Salted nuts of many kinds are good. Buy single kinds of nuts for better value. In mixed nuts, you are likely to get a plethora of peanuts and few cashews. Pistachios keep very well. Chilied or otherwise flavored nuts are acceptable, if not as good as homemade. Pickled walnuts are a luxury to add to sliced meats. Health food or Indian stores may sell spiced and toasted seeds. A myriad of olives come packed in jars, from the tiny Niçoise to the big Gaetas and the marvelous purple Kalamatas, and some better stores sell their own spiced olives. For the right people, an olive assortment with a few nuts can be a whole party.

While we're on the nibble-y things, I must concede that there are things like miniature pretzels and Japanese pre-made party snacks. I cannot say I like any of them. If you're looking for a list of fried ready-mades, see page 234.

I love peperoncini, the small hot Italian brine-packed peppers; I eat them as a low-calorie, hunger-reducing snack. Fire-roasted red peppers are also available in jars—rinse well and marinate as on page 60. Although I find them very expensive, marinated artichoke hearts or pickled mushrooms can be bought in jars. In some places, you can find tiny eggplants, about an inch and a half long, stuffed and put up in oil.

You are better off with firm, nonrunny cheeses at cocktail parties. Allow about two ounces per person. Blocks of cheese can be put out whole, or the cheese can be cut into three-quarter-inch cubes to snare with toothpicks. You can put out a bowl of seeds that makes an appropriate dunk for the cheese, or pre-dunk and skewer them. Feta cubes are good dipped in anise seeds; Appenzeller, Muenster or Gruyère in caraway; Cheddar in Sheila's Dry Dunk (page 70); firm mozzarella in mixed Italian herbs; a firm goat cheese in finely chopped fresh herbs and Port Salut in sesame seeds. Slab cheeses need bread and/or crackers. Creamier and more distinctively flavored cheeses are best served for spreading, accompanied, perhaps, by walnuts or pecans.

Finally, for last-minute parties, consider a dash to a nearby salad bar for already sliced vegetables.

seasoned salt

Sprinkle this on nuts, crudités or boiled eggs, or put it out in a little dish so that people can dunk in it, particularly if you have some salt-shy friends. I like to put it in an old sugar canister, but that may be because my daughter gave me such a handsome ruby glass one. You can use Sheila's Dry Dunk (page 70) the same way. This quantity will season about two and a half to three pounds of nuts. It stores well in a tightly closed glass jar if kept in a cool, dark place so make the whole quantity and use it as needed. Use one and a half teaspoons for each cup of nuts.

Makes ⅔ cup

- 1 tablespoon coriander seeds, picked over to eliminate stems
- 1 tablespoon whole, dried green peppercorns
- 1 tablespoon pink peppercorns
- 1 teaspoon white peppercorns
- 1 tablespoon five-spice powder
- ½ cup kosher salt

Combine all ingredients other than salt in a small nonstick skillet. Over medium heat, cook, stirring frequently with a wooden spoon and being sure to scrape the pan as you go so as not to burn the five-spice powder, for about 3 minutes, or until the first peppercorn pops and/or the five-spice powder is a darkish brown. Scrape contents of pan into a spice mill. Grind until the mixture is powdery. In a separate glass bowl or container, combine ground spices with the salt.

marinated artichokes

While marinated artichokes can be bought ready-made in jars and are fairly satisfactory, they are better made at home and pretty easy if you can find frozen or canned artichoke hearts. There are about as many hearts in a tin as there are in a box. Be sure to rinse these well before marinating.

Makes 1½ cups

1 9-ounce box frozen artichoke hearts, defrosted in a sieve under warm running water
½ cup olive oil
½ teaspoon dried thyme
½ teaspoon dried oregano
1 grind fresh black pepper
2 teaspoons kosher salt
1 tablespoon fresh lemon juice

Combine artichokes, oil and herbs in a small saucepan. Place over very low heat and cook, covered, for 10 minutes. Remove from heat and stir in salt. Let mixture cool completely. Stir in lemon juice. Keep refrigerated. Bring to room temperature before serving.

sesame curried almonds

This combination of two nutty flavors—sesame and almond—may seem odd; but it is very good. The nuts will end up being lightly browned rather than ivory. This recipe can be multiplied.

Makes 1 cup

1 teaspoon toasted sesame oil
5 ounces whole unblanched, unsalted almonds (scant 1 cup)
1 teaspoon sesame seeds

1½ teaspoons curry powder
1 teaspoon kosher salt
1 teaspoon sugar
2 teaspoons fresh lemon juice
1 tablespoon water
½ teaspoon hot red pepper sauce

Heat the sesame oil in a heavy medium skillet over medium-low heat. Add the almonds and sesame seeds and stir until coated with oil and the almonds begin to sizzle, about 4 minutes. Sprinkle the curry powder, salt and sugar over the almonds and toss to coat. Cook until the curry powder begins to brown, about 2 minutes. Remove the pan from the heat. Stir the lemon juice, water and hot red pepper sauce in a small bowl and sprinkle this mixture over the almonds. Toss until the liquid is evaporated and the spice mixture clings to the nuts. Turn onto paper towels and cool to room temperature.

chili pecans, almonds or macadamias

Whatever nuts you choose to do this with, they will be addictive. The slight bitterness of pecans adds some punch to the taste, but the shape and light color of the macadamias are particularly attractive.

Makes about 1½ cups

2 teaspoons peanut or vegetable oil
6 ounces shelled pecan halves (1½ cups), or
7½ ounces macadamia nuts (1½ cups), or
9 ounces blanched, unsalted, whole almonds (1½ cups)
1½ teaspoons chili powder
¾ teaspoon cayenne pepper
1½ teaspoons kosher salt

½ teaspoon sugar
1 teaspoon fresh lemon juice

Heat oil in a heavy skillet over medium-low heat. Add nuts. Stir until nuts are dry and begin to sizzle, about 8 minutes.

Sprinkle chili powder, cayenne pepper, salt and sugar over them and stir until evenly coated. Sprinkle lemon juice into the skillet and cook until it has completely evaporated.

Turn nuts out onto several thicknesses of paper towels to drain. Let cool slightly. The nuts are best when served warm. Place them in a moderate oven (350°F) for 4 minutes to reheat if need be.

soy-anise macadamia nuts

These are absolutely delicious, but not quite like any other spiced nuts I know. They are virtually candied even though spicy. The reason they are served on a plate is so they won't clump together and be impossible to eat. People will need napkins, but they will come back for more of these glistening, darkly brown nuts. This recipe can be halved.

Makes 3 cups

1⅓ cups cold water
¼ cup sugar
¼ cup tamari soy
4 whole star anise
14 ounces macadamia nuts (about 2⅔ cups)
½ teaspoon kosher salt, optional

Combine water, sugar, soy and anise in a medium saucepan. Heat over medium heat to simmering. Cover and simmer 10 minutes. Add the nuts and toss

Soy-Anise Macadamia Nuts.

to coat. Increase the heat to medium-high and boil until the liquid is almost entirely evaporated. Reduce the heat to low. Stir continuously until the nuts are coated with a thick syrup. Spread on a cookie sheet or flat platter and sprinkle with the salt if you like. Cool to room temperature, stirring once or twice to keep the nuts from sticking together.

Serve the nuts in a single layer on a plate (not in a bowl) at room temperature.

toasted pumpkin seeds

These salty snacks are a dividend when you use a pumpkin or *acorn squash. They can be left at room temperature for a day or so or stored in a covered jar in the refrigerator for months. If refrigerated, toast in microwave oven or 300°F conventional oven just until warm.*

Makes 1 ½ cups

1 ½ cups (10 ½ ounces) pumpkin seeds (from 3 2 ½-pound pumpkins, seeds separated from fibers and rinsed)
1 tablespoon vegetable oil
1 ½ teaspoons kosher salt, or Seasoned Salt (page 49)

Preheat oven to 350°F. Toss seeds in oil. Place on a baking sheet. Bake in the lower third of oven for 15 minutes, stirring twice. Remove from oven and sprinkle with salt.

Quick and yet stylish: feta cheese rinsed and cut in one-inch cubes, put out with toothpicks for picking up the cheese, and a bowl of anise into which to dunk them, served with shiny purple-black, briny Gaeta olives. Black and white bowls give the simple feed an intentional look.

spicy glazed walnuts

Frankly, many years ago I learned and stole a version of this from Barbara Tropp, the great Chinese cook and better friend. I like to do this in the microwave oven. I find that the blanching goes particularly well and I can use a minimum of fat in the glazing. If you want to do it on top of the stove, bring a large pot of water to a boil and blanch the nuts for twelve minutes. Glaze the nuts in a large skillet, increasing the oil to a quarter of a cup. Cook until nuts are shiny and liquid is pretty well absorbed.

Makes 5 1/3 cups

1 1/4 pounds shelled, unsalted walnuts (5 cups)
3 cups cold water

2 teaspoons vegetable oil
1 1/2 teaspoons kosher salt
1/3 cup sugar
1 1/2 teaspoons cayenne pepper

To Blanch. Place walnuts and water in a 14 × 11 × 2-inch oval dish. Cook, uncovered, in a high-wattage oven, at 100% for 10 minutes.

Remove from oven. Drain nuts in a colander. Rinse with cold water and dry on paper towels. Rinse out dish and dry and return walnuts to it.

To Glaze. Combine remaining ingredients in a small bowl. Add to walnuts and stir to coat. Cook, uncovered, at 100% for 8 minutes, stirring several times.

Remove from oven. Spread hot nuts on wax paper to dry. Stir from time to time to prevent sticking. Store, tightly covered, at room temperature or in the refrigerator for up to 2 weeks.

For Low-Wattage Ovens. Halve all ingredients. Place walnuts in a 10-inch quiche dish. Cover with 2 cups water and cook, uncovered, at 100% for 15 minutes. Drain nuts, rinse with cold water and pat dry. Return to dish. Stir together remaining ingredients and add to nuts. Cook, uncovered, at 100% for 8 minutes. Finish as above.

cumin toasted peanuts

This is quick, easy and delicious. It can be multiplied and the stove-top cooking done in one batch. Do not try to put more than one batch in an oven pan. Instead, divide multiple batches into multiple pans. More than one pan of nuts can be cooked at a time.

Makes 1 ¾ cups

1 tablespoon olive oil
2 ½ teaspoons ground cumin
2 ½ teaspoons ground coriander
1 ½ teaspoons kosher salt
1 ½ teaspoons sugar
½ teaspoon hot red pepper sauce
½ teaspoon freshly ground black pepper
8 ounces roasted unsalted peanuts (about 1 ½ cups)

Heat the oven to 300°F with rack in center of oven. Combine all ingredients except the peanuts in a medium skillet over medium heat. Stir until the spices begin to sizzle. Add the peanuts and stir until coated.

Transfer the peanuts to a baking pan with sides, such as a jelly roll pan, lined with a double thickness of paper towels. Bake 10 minutes. Remove pan from oven and cool completely before removing peanuts from the paper towels.

olives

Ripe olives are not a mystery to me. I can understand how people decided to eat them—but green olives! Nevertheless, almost all olives except the galvanized rubber ones from California make good nibbles. While I have specified a special kind of olive for Moroccan Spiced Olives, Spiced Niçoise Olives, Spiced Green Olives and Lemon Spiced Olives, a variety of olives can be mixed together for an attractive result (see picture, page 46). The "Martini" Olives should be left as is.

Since these olives require making ahead to develop full flavor, they are perfect do-aheads for large parties. Even without a large party, make up a large batch of olives. In the refrigerator, they keep for about four weeks, tightly covered. Let them come to room temperature before serving in an attractive crock.

Olives are good on their own and with pâtés (see page 135) and sliced meats. Most of these olives are prepared with their pits in. Leave little empty dishes—what used to be ashtrays—around for the pits.

moroccan spiced olives

The vanilla in these may seem surprising, but it adds a nice background flavor and aroma that blends everything together. See these olives with the pâté on page 152. There, I have added a quarter cup of diced Roasted Red Peppers (page 59), or you could use canned fire-roasted peppers that have been well rinsed. The olives won't keep as well with the
peppers mixed in, so add them at the last minute.

Makes 2 cups

2 cups oil-cured olives (10 ounces)
¼ cup olive oil
2 teaspoons whole cumin seed
2 teaspoons whole coriander seed
2 teaspoons fennel seed
½ teaspoon ground cardamom
Pinch each: ground cinnamon, ground nutmeg, crushed red pepper flakes
2 tablespoons fresh orange juice
2 tablespoons fresh lemon juice
2 teaspoons vanilla extract
6 cloves garlic, smashed, peeled and cut into thin strips

If olives have been refrigerated, remove to room temperature about 30 minutes before preparing seasoning mix.

Warm the oil in a small skillet over medium heat. Add the cumin, coriander, fennel, cardamom, cinnamon, nutmeg and red pepper flakes. Cook until fragrant, about 2 minutes.

Remove the skillet from the heat, add the olives and toss to coat. Add the orange and lemon juices, the vanilla and the garlic and toss.

Transfer the olives to a 1-pint container with lid. Store in the refrigerator for at least 4 days (or up to 4 months), shaking the container occasionally. Bring the olives to room temperature and toss once or twice before serving.

spiced niçoise olives

These are the kind of olives you are likely to get on a cool, stone terrace at sunset overlooking the bay of Nice to go with Campari and soda or pastis. They are good on a winter's evening at home.

Makes 2 cups

2 cups Niçoise olives in brine (10 ounces)
¼ cup dry red wine
¼ cup olive oil
1 teaspoon dried basil
½ teaspoon dried oregano
½ teaspoon dried thyme
¼ teaspoon rosemary
4 medium cloves garlic, smashed, peeled and sliced thin
¼ teaspoon freshly ground black pepper

Drain olives and reserve the brine. Rinse the olives briefly under cold running water.

Combine remaining ingredients in a medium saucepan over low heat. Heat to simmering; reduce the heat to low and simmer 1 minute. Remove from heat, add the olives and toss to coat them with the spice mixture.

Transfer the olives to a 1-pint container with lid. Add brine as needed to cover olives. Store in the refrigerator for at least 4 days (or up to 4 months), shaking the container occasionally. Bring the olives to room temperature and toss once or twice before serving.

spiced green olives

Over the years, I have spiced most varieties of olives in this way. It's my standby.

Makes 2 cups

2 cups good, brine-packed, large Spanish olives, with pits (7½ ounces)
10 medium cloves garlic, smashed and peeled
1 tablespoon olive oil
4 strips (2 x ¼-inch) orange zest
4 strips (2 x ¼-inch) lemon zest
½ teaspoon cumin seeds
½ teaspoon coriander seeds
½ teaspoon fresh lemon juice

Drain and rinse the olives briefly and poke each once or twice with the tip of a paring knife. Mix remaining ingredients in a small bowl and pour over the olives. Toss to coat evenly.

Transfer the olives to a 1-pint container with lid. Store in the refrigerator for at least 3 days (or up to 4 months), shaking the container occasionally. Bring the olives to room temperature and toss once or twice before serving.

"martini" olives

I am not a martini drinker; but I find that I am constantly begging my friends for their olives. This way you can have the flavor without the martini. Incidentally, small pickled onions can be drained and rinsed and covered with the same mixture.

Makes 2 cups

One jar small green Spanish olives with pits (10 ounces)

4 strips (2 x ½-inch) lemon zest
1 cup dry white vermouth
20 juniper berries

Drain the liquid from the olives; rinse the jar and olives. Drain the olives well. Place them on a flat surface and cover with cloth or paper towels. Lightly whack the olives with a pot just enough to crack each olive, not crush it. Return the olives to the jar, discarding any that are overly cracked or bruised. Slip a strip of the lemon zest into the jar after each addition of olives.

Heat the vermouth and juniper berries in a small pan over medium heat. Carefully tilt the pan away from you toward the flame to ignite. Simmer until the flames die down. You should have about ⅔ cup liquid. Pour the vermouth mixture over the olives. If necessary, add enough vermouth from the bottle to cover the olives. Shake the jar well.

Store the olives in a cool place (or the refrigerator) at least 3 days before serving. Bring the olives to room temperature and shake the jar once or twice before serving.

lemon pickles and green pickled lemons

Makes 2 cups

3 large lemons

Lemon Pickle Seasonings
¼ cup kosher salt
3 small whole dried chili peppers
½ teaspoon ground cumin
½ teaspoon ground cardamom
1 cup water

Green Pickled Lemon Seasonings

- ½ **cup packed fresh coriander (cilantro) leaves, washed and picked over**
- ½ **cup packed fresh Italian parsley leaves, washed and picked over**
- ½ **cup packed fresh mint leaves, washed and picked over**
- 2 **medium cloves garlic, smashed and peeled**
- 1 **2-inch piece peeled fresh ginger, grated**
- ½ **cup vegetable oil**
- 1 **tablespoon rice or white wine vinegar**
- ½ **teaspoon hot red pepper sauce**
- 1 **teaspoon ground cumin**
- 2 **teaspoons kosher salt**
- ½ **teaspoon freshly ground black pepper**
- 2 **tablespoons harissa (optional)**
- 3 **canned plum tomatoes, thoroughly drained**

To Prepare Lemons. Bring a pot of water to a rapid boil. Wash the lemons and add them to the water. Cover the lemons with a plate or a lid from a smaller pot to keep them submerged. As soon as the water returns to a boil, remove the lemons to a colander and cool them under cold running water.

Cut off the ends of the lemons. Cut the lemons in quarters lengthwise, then cut away the membrane from the edge of the lemon wedges. Pick out the seeds. Cut each lemon wedge in half lengthwise, then crosswise into ½-inch pieces.

lemon pickles

Combine Lemon Pickle Seasonings and the 1 cup water in a 1-quart saucepan. Heat to simmering, stirring to dissolve the salt, and add the lemons. Simmer over very low heat until the lemons are tender, about 20 minutes. Process as in To Store Pickles and Chutneys (page 56).

green pickled lemons

In a food processor, purée Green Pickled Lemon Seasonings until you have a thick green sauce. Stop the machine; taste and adjust the seasoning if necessary.

Pour a little of the sauce into the sterilized jar(s). Alternately add lemon pieces and remaining sauce. Process as in To Store Pickles and Chutneys.

lemon spiced olives

This recipe requires some forethought both to make the Lemon Pickles and to allow time for the olives to marinate, but at the end you will have a very refreshing brew. Be sure to have some chunks of bread available, such as the Whole-Wheat Focaccia (page 128), because people will want to dunk in the sauce.

Makes 2 cups

- 1 **cup Lemon Pickles**
- 1 **jar (7 ounces) Niçoise olives, to yield 1½ cups olives and ½ cup brine**
- 1 **teaspoon dried oregano**
- ½ **teaspoon dried thyme**

Combine all ingredients in a small saucepan. Heat to simmering over low heat. Simmer 5 minutes. Transfer to a jar and cool to room temperature. Cover the jar and store at room temperature at least 3 days before serving. The spiced olives can be kept refrigerated up to 2 weeks.

pickled lemons

Ever since I read Paula Wolfert's *Couscous and Other Good Food from Morocco,* I have been intrigued by pickled lemons on their own and as an ingredient. Tasting other kinds of pickled lemons both from India and the Middle East that are packed in jars, I became yet more intrigued. Unfortunately, I am a far-from-patient person, and the time-consuming procedure in traditional recipes was not for me, especially after I had a whole batch go moldy on me. Instead, I have created this short-cut method, which I find very satisfactory.

With it, I make two different kinds of pickled lemons. The first, Lemon Pickles, is a very good ingredient for Lemon Spiced Olives and for tagines. The second, Green Pickled Lemons, is a delightful relish on its own to serve with cooked meats, fish and pâtés. If you like a spicier pickle, add the harissa and the tomato. This will turn the pickle a brownish red.

Put up the pickled lemons and all other pickles and chutneys according to the instructions To Store Pickles and Chutneys (see box, page 56). Lemon pickles are particularly safe because of their high acidity.

Both of these recipes can be multiplied as often as you want as long as you multiply the number of jars and make sure that whenever there is the instruction "return to a boil," a full rolling boil is achieved.

pumped-up popcorn

Consider this at large informal parties such as those that attend a football game. See photograph.

It is terribly simple to do with popcorn you have just popped or with store-bought popped popcorn. Try to buy air-popped, unsalted popcorn and then salt the final product to taste.

Makes 14 cups

3/4 cup vegetable oil
8 medium cloves garlic, smashed, peeled and minced
2 1/4 teaspoons chili powder
Scant 1/4 teaspoon cayenne pepper
1 4-ounce bag plain popcorn
Kosher salt

Place oil, garlic, chili powder and cayenne in a small saucepan over very low heat. Cook, stirring occasionally, for 5 minutes.

Place popcorn in a large bowl. Pour the spice mixture over and toss to coat; hands are best. Season with salt to taste.

Put out Pumped-Up Popcorn in lots of medium-sized bowls at a large party or in large bowls at a television-sports party.

To Store Pickles and Chutneys

Wash canning jar(s), lid(s) and ring band(s) with soap and hot water. Bring to a boil a pot of water large enough to submerge the jars. Add jars, lids and rings; return to a boil and boil for 5 minutes. Remove and drain on a clean towel.

Fill jars and rap against a counter so fruit or vegetable pieces are tightly packed and no air pockets remain.

To Keep for Up to 2 Weeks. Pack into hot jars. Close with lids. Allow to cool. Label and store in refrigerator.

To Keep for Up to 6 Months. Leave about 1/2-inch space between the top of the mixture and the top of the jar. Cover with the ring band seal and the lid. Bring a large pot of water to a boil. Submerge the jars in the pot, cover and boil slowly for 10 minutes. Carefully remove the jar; tighten lid; cool completely before labeling. Does not need refrigeration.

nachos

The simplest and one of the most popular cheese snacks is the nacho. This recipe can be multiplied as needed. Set up the nachos on baking sheets and broil as wanted. Serve one or more of the salsas (pages 23–25).

Makes 24

6 jalapeño peppers
24 tortilla chips
6 ounces yellow Cheddar cheese, grated (2 cups)

Preheat broiler.

For very hot nachos, cut peppers across into thin slices with seeds left intact. For milder nachos, cut off stem end of peppers. Use a potato peeler or a small knife to remove seeds and core. Cut into thin slices.

Place chips on a baking sheet. Place about 2 teaspoons of cheese on each one. Top with one pepper slice.

Broil until cheese melts.

A *quick Tex-Mex party can be as simple as Nachos with Guacamole (page 13) and sour cream for toppings and some sliced chorizo. Serve a Mexican beer or Margaritas (page 305).*

Tomatillos, in their husks, husked, and sliced (looking like green tomatoes), are tart and good in Southwestern food.

lacy cheese cookies

These are irresistible cool or cold. The recipe is the result of a cooking mistake. I was making Phyllo with Tyropitta (Cheese) Filling (page 216) and the filling kept seeping out onto the hot baking sheet. As I was standing around deciding what to do to correct the recipe, I idly picked at the now crisp, cooked, thin disk of cheese mixture on the baking sheet. It was delicious, so I decided to make a recipe from my mistake.

These go quickly, and this amount will feed only two to three people unless there is a lot of other food. Fortunately, the recipe can be multiplied as often as you want. Unfortunately, if the weather is very humid, these will not stay crisp for a long time. I make these early in the afternoon of an afternoon or evening party, first thing in the morning for a lunch party.

Makes about 16 crisps

8 ounces feta cheese, broken into small pieces and rinsed under cold water

¼ cup grated Parmesan cheese
½ teaspoon ground nutmeg
¼ teaspoon dried oregano
¼ teaspoon dried thyme
Freshly ground black pepper, to taste
Olive oil, for greasing baking sheet

Preheat oven to 400°F.

Place feta, Parmesan, nutmeg, oregano and thyme in work bowl of food processor. Process until very finely crumbled. Transfer to a medium bowl and season to taste with pepper.

Lightly grease baking sheet—not an air-cushioned one—with olive oil and form one rounded teaspoon of the feta mixture into a ball. Place on baking sheet and repeat with remaining mixture, placing the balls about 3 inches apart. Bake in the center of the oven for 10 minutes, or until cookies are golden brown.

Remove from oven and immediately loosen cookies from baking sheet with a metal spatula. Carefully transfer them to a wire rack to cool.

roasted peppers

Today, bell peppers come in a bewildering variety of beautiful colors, all of which can be cooked in a variety of ways—in the microwave oven, over a flame or under a broiler—and used in many more. Strips of roasted peppers make attractive garnishes for canapés. Diced peppers can be tossed with olives or salads to add color and flavor. They can be chopped and seasoned to make dips. They can be used in Kalamata Antipasto (page 64), Roasted Red Pepper and Mushroom Salad (page 64) or Roasted Red Pepper Spread (page 14), or they can be marinated as in the variations below and served on their own. Provide forks and plates or serve them with miniature biscuits like the ones on pages 108–109 to make attractive sandwiches.

If you don't have time to roast your own, you can buy fire-roasted peppers in jars and rinse them off before proceeding with the marinating or other recipes. Peppers will keep, marinated, in the refrigerator for a week.

Note Fire-roasted peppers are packed about 15 pieces to the jar. They vary in size from 1½ to 3 inches in length. Smaller ones are better for cocktails.

roasting bell peppers

If possible, choose squarish peppers; they will be easier to roast and peel.

Makes 3 cups diced peppers or 4 cups pepper strips of the size used in Marinated Peppers (page 60)

6 medium-size firm red, yellow, orange or green bell peppers (purple peppers will lose their color when the skins come off)

Microwave-Oven Method. Cut the peppers into quarters and cut out the cores, ribs and seeds. Remove the peel with a vegetable peeler, being careful not to remove too much of the flesh. Arrange the peeled pepper pieces overlapping in an 11 × 7-inch baking dish. Cover tightly with microwave plastic wrap. Cook at 100% in a high-wattage oven 12 minutes or in a low-wattage oven for 18 minutes. Pierce the plastic to release steam. The peppers should be tender but still firm, with a small amount of liquid in the bottom of the dish. Cool to room temperature, tossing occasionally in the liquid.

Fire-Roasted Method. Leave the peppers whole; rinse them under cold running water and drain well. Roast the peppers directly over the gas burners on medium-high, rotating them until all sides are blackened and peeling. Some parts may roast more quickly than others. Check continually and turn the peppers with a pair of long tongs as necessary. As the peppers are blackened, transfer them to a large mixing bowl. Cover with plastic wrap and let stand until cool enough to handle.

Pull out the cores from the pepper and drain the liquid carefully. (The liquid may remain hot for a while after the peppers have cooled.) Gently tear each pepper into sections along the creases. Scrape the seeds and blackened skin from the peppers. (Avoid rinsing the peppers if possible—a few remaining specks of black won't matter.) Drain the peppers on paper towels.

Broiler Method. Heat the broiler with the oven rack at its highest setting. Broil the peppers until blackened on all sides, turning as necessary with tongs, about 8 minutes. Remove to a large bowl, cover with plastic wrap and proceed as for fire-roasted method, above.

microwave roasted peppers and red pepper purée

Using a microwave oven saves a lot of work, particularly when you want a purée to use as an ingredient in Red Pepper Butter (page 45). It is also useful if you don't object to serving peppers with the skin on.

Stem, seed and derib peppers. Place in the dish indicated below and cover tightly with microwave plastic wrap. After cooking, prick wrap with the tip of a sharp knife to release steam. Remove dish from oven and uncover. If making purée, pass peppers through a food mill fitted with a medium disk. Store, covered, in the refrigerator.

1 pound
in a 2½-quart soufflé dish
High-wattage oven: 10 minutes
Low-wattage oven: 15 minutes
Makes 1 cup purée

2½ pounds
in a 2½-quart soufflé dish
High-wattage oven: 15 minutes
Low-wattage oven: 25 minutes
Makes 2½ cups purée

5¼ pounds
in a 5-quart casserole:
High-wattage oven: 22 minutes
Low-wattage oven: not recommended
Makes 5¼ cups purée

Raw vegetables (Crudités, page 67) can be as simple as a few kinds of small cherry tomatoes.

marinated peppers

Cut the roasted peppers from top to bottom into 1- to 1½-inch-wide strips. Marinate as below. Each recipe is enough for 6 roasted peppers (page 59).

in oil (sott'olio)

Whisk ⅓ cup extra-virgin olive oil, 2 teaspoons kosher salt, 1 teaspoon minced fresh sage and ¼ teaspoon freshly ground black pepper in a mixing bowl until the salt is dissolved. Add the peppers and their liquid and toss to coat. Let marinate, tossing occasionally, for 2 hours at room temperature or up to 2 days in the refrigerator. Bring to room temperature and check the seasonings before serving.

in vinegar (sott'aceto)

Stir ¼ cup balsamic vinegar, 1½ teaspoons kosher salt and ¼ teaspoon freshly ground black pepper in a mixing bowl until the salt is dissolved. Add the peppers and their liquid and toss to coat. Let marinate at room temperature 2 to 4 hours or store in the refrigerator up to 4 days. Bring to room temperature and check the seasonings before serving.

roasted peppers with fresh thyme

Whisk ¼ cup extra-virgin olive oil, 2 tablespoons red wine vinegar (or fresh lemon juice), 1½ teaspoons kosher salt and ¼ teaspoon freshly ground pepper in a mixing bowl until blended. Add the peppers and their liquid and toss to mix.

roasted peppers with anchovies and chives

Use a recipe's worth of any of the marinated peppers above. Feel free to mix the colors. Lay the strips out flat or overlapping on a large platter (see photograph). Rinse the anchovies from three cans in warm water and use them to top the peppers in any attractive pattern. Dribble the marinade over both anchovies and peppers. Sprinkle with the petals from 6 or 7 chive flowers. Separate the petals from the flower by holding the petals in one hand and the green base in the other. Twist and pull.

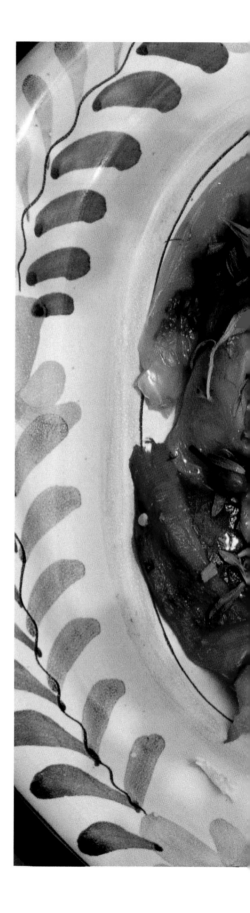

By varying the colors of your Roasted Peppers (page 58), you can make a stunning platter to top with anchovies and an herb flower, such as chive, or nasturtium buds.

vegetable
salads

Vegetable salads are a nice addition to big buffets, as they don't get soggy the way lettuce salads do when they are not made at the last minute. In the world of finger foods, they can be piled onto Crostini or into any of the savory pastries (pages 96–97), stuffed into Mini-Biscuits (pages 108–109) or Fried Bread Puffs (page 125) or piled onto a small, crisp leaf of endive or lettuce.

If you are caught unprepared by company, look in the refrigerator and see if there are any leftover cooked vegetables. Snare celery stalks and onions out from their hiding places in the back of vegetable drawers. Add an apple if you are short of vegetables. A can of nuts can be helpful. Mozzarella or Swiss cheese can be used. Cut everything you have found into small dice. Mix your ingredients with a little mayonnaise—about two tablespoons to a cup of ingredients—add a little lemon juice, black pepper or cayenne and serve.

Lemon Dill Antipasto (page 66).

roasted red pepper and mushroom salad

This simple dish can be turned to many uses. It can be spooned onto Crostini (page 131) or into endive leaves. At another meal, it makes a good accompaniment to grilled fish or chicken, and a quarter cup is an attractive topping for a portion of pasta. A tablespoon makes a taste, three a serving. The whole will make forty tastes, about enough for a dozen people.

Makes 2 1/2 cups

3 medium red peppers, roasted as on page 59 and cut into 1/8-inch-wide strips
1/4 pound mushrooms, trimmed and sliced thin (1 cup)
1 1/2 tablespoons fresh lemon juice
1 1/2 tablespoons anchovy paste
1 tablespoon chopped fresh Italian parsley leaves
6 tablespoons olive oil
1 tablespoon brine-packed capers, well rinsed, optional
Kosher salt, to taste
Freshly ground black pepper, to taste

Combine pepper strips and mushrooms. In a small bowl, combine the remaining ingredients. Mix well and toss with the peppers and mushrooms.

Let marinate at least 1 hour before serving. Serve at room temperature.

mushrooms with yogurt and dill

The mushrooms virtually cook in the dressing. They are particularly good in the Cheddar Cheese Pastry (page 97). You can multiply this recipe as many times as you want. Since it takes about a tablespoon to fill each small tart shell, the basic recipe will make thirty-two hors d'oeuvre, enough for ten guests.

Makes 2 cups

1/2 pound mushrooms, wiped clean, quartered and cut into 1/4-inch slices (2 1/3 cups)
2 tablespoons fresh lemon juice
3 tablespoons plain yogurt
1 1/2 tablespoons Dijon mustard
2 tablespoons chopped fresh dill sprigs
1/2 teaspoon kosher salt
2 to 4 drops hot red pepper sauce
Freshly ground black pepper, to taste

Toss mushrooms with lemon juice in a medium bowl. Set aside. In a small bowl, whisk together remaining ingredients. Pour over mushrooms and toss to combine. Let stand at least 1 hour to let flavors develop. Packed in a crock and refrigerated, these will keep for several days.

kalamata antipasto

Various Mediterranean countries make up lightly pickled antipasto mixtures of vegetables to use as needed. Toothpicks or small forks

are all the equipment needed. This faintly Greek version would go well with Greek Stuffed Grape Leaves (page 203), Taramasalata (page 31) and lamb brochettes in Greek Marinade (page 269). Add some chunks of feta that have been rinsed in water. Pass an attractive bottle or cruet of good Kalamata olive oil for guests to dribble on top if they want.

On a hot summer evening, just serve a half cup of this to each of six guests with the cheese and the olive oil. The recipe is easily multiplied. At a cocktail party, allow a quarter cup of this per person.

Makes 3 cups

10 ounces Kalamata olives in brine
1 cup fresh fennel cut into strips (2 x 1/4-inch), about 1/2 head (7 ounces)
1/2 cup Roasted Peppers (page 59) or bottled roasted red peppers (about half a 7-ounce jar), cut into 2 1/2 x 1/4-inch strips
2 tablespoons minced fennel fronds
1/4 cup red wine vinegar
1/4 cup water
1/4 teaspoon freshly ground black pepper

Combine all ingredients, including olive brine, in a large bowl. Toss to mix. Transfer to a jar with tight-fitting lid. There should be enough liquid to cover all ingredients. Cover and store in refrigerator, shaking occasionally, at least 3 days and up to one week.

Bring to room temperature and drain the brine before serving. Reserve the brine. If there is any of the antipasto left at the end of the party, put it back in the brine and store in the refrigerator.

Easy and informal along with a good beer: Crudités (page 67) of celery, carrots and cucumbers, with tortilla chips and Fresh Tomatillo Salsa (page 23).

pickled vegetable antipasto

An Italian-inspired, red-wine-brined vegetable antipasto, a cousin of the Kalamata Antipasto (page 64), is good with pâtés or simply with focaccia (pages 135 and 128) and slices of mozzarella. Try substituting some drained for the tomatoes in Insalata Caprese Hero (page 131), after brushing the bread with olive oil. Since this keeps very well, I make a large

quantity, but you can easily halve the recipe.

Makes 6 cups

- **1 bunch thin carrots (about 1¼ pounds), peeled, trimmed and cut into 2 x ¼-inch strips (about 3 cups)**
- **1 small head cauliflower, florets only, cut into pieces no larger than ½ inch (about 3 cups)**
- **1 bulb fresh fennel (14 ounces), trimmed and cut into 2 x ¼-inch strips (about 2 cups)**
- **6 small or 4 large bottled peperoncini**
- **3 cups dry red wine**
- **1½ cups red wine vinegar**
- **¼ cup kosher salt**

Heat a large pot of salted water to boiling over high heat. Add the carrots and blanch just until softened but still quite firm, about 2 minutes. Remove to a colander with a wire skimmer and run under cold water until cool. Repeat the blanching procedure with the cauliflower, blanching about 3 minutes. Drain the vegetables very well and combine with the fennel and peperoncini in a large bowl. Toss to mix the vegetables and transfer them to three 1-pint canning jars, dividing the vegetables and peperoncini evenly among the jars. (If you have a tall, thin 6-cup container, you can use that instead of three 1-pint jars.)

Heat the wine, vinegar and salt to boiling in a small saucepan over high heat. Boil 1 minute. Pour the wine mixture over the vegetables in the jar. Cool to room temperature. Cover and store in the refrigerator at least one day or up to two weeks before serving.

65

lemon dill antipasto

This is a light, fresh antipasto with no oil. While I have given indications for cutting up the vegetables, it is most efficient and attractive to cut them to just the height of your jars. If you have wide-mouthed canning jars, it will be easier to get the vegetable sticks out.

Makes 4 1-pint jars

Dressing
1 ½ cups fresh lemon juice
1 ½ cups water
1 cup lightly packed fresh dill
  sprigs
2 tablespoons kosher salt
4 teaspoons Dijon mustard
1 teaspoon freshly ground
  black pepper

2 medium zucchini (12
  ounces), trimmed, halved
  crosswise, then cut
  lengthwise into eight
  wedges (about 2⅔ cups)
1 each medium red and yellow
  bell pepper (5 ounces),
  cored, seeded and cut into
  ½-inch-wide strips (about 2
  cups)
1 small celery root (8 ounces),
  peeled and cut into
  2 x ¼-inch sticks (about
  2 cups)
16 thick spears asparagus
  (about 1 pound), peeled and
  cut into 4-inch lengths
  (about 3 cups)

Combine dressing ingredients in a blender until dill is finely chopped.

Arrange vegetable strips standing up in wide-mouth or other 1-pint canning jar. Add the marinade. Cover the jar and refrigerate, shaking occasionally, 2 to 3 days before serving. The vegetables can be kept refrigerated up to 7 days before serving. Bring to room temperature and drain thoroughly.

*D*elicious hot, warm or cold: Cumin Vegetables (page 70).

dhal

This makes a gently and roundly spicy mixture that is halfway between a dip and a salad. In India, it would traditionally be served as a side dish with curry, raita—see Cucumber Tzatziki, page 17—chutneys and other condiments. I like to serve a dollop of it on a small Bibb or cos lettuce or endive leaf. Some finely minced fresh coriander (cilantro) can be sprinkled on top. Where little plates are used, let guests assemble their own.

Makes about 2 cups

1 cup dhal (red lentils)
¼ teaspoon ground turmeric
2 ½ teaspoons ghee (clarified
  butter)
2 medium onions, sliced
1 medium clove garlic,
  smashed and peeled
3 small green chilies such as
  jalapeños, slit slightly at the
  stem end
6 ripe medium tomatoes,
  cored, cut into ¾-inch
  cubes
1 ½ teaspoons kosher salt
2 teaspoons tamarind liquid
¼ teaspoon black mustard
  seed
2 small dried red peppers,
  halved
5 dried curry leaves

Bring 6 cups water to a boil in a saucepan. Add the dhal, the turmeric, ½ teaspoon ghee, the onions, the garlic and the green chilies. Cover the pan and allow to boil gently until the dhal is soft, 15 to 30 minutes.

Add the tomatoes, salt and tamarind juice. Let the sauce continue cooking for 20 minutes. Remove from heat and purée the mixture in a food processor until smooth.

Heat a small frying pan over high heat. Add the remaining 2 teaspoons ghee. When very hot, add the mustard seeds. When they stop splattering, add the dried red peppers and the curry leaves. Fry for 30 seconds, then pour in ½ cup puréed dhal mixture, stirring all together. Stir this mixture into the remaining puréed dhal. Cover and let sit over low heat for 5 to 10 minutes to let the flavors mellow.

Serve at room temperature. The mixture will thicken as it cools.

66

crudités

I have been to catered events where whole vegetables and vegetables in pieces are arranged into magnificent gardens. There are three problems with this picture. First, I find that the party often ends with the garden virtually untouched. Guests seem to find it intimidating to disarrange perfection and seem somehow to treat the beautiful array much as if it were a centerpiece. Second, if guests do bravely disarrange the garden, it quickly looks like a disorderly wilderness, a hostess's despair. Third and perhaps most important is the unconscionable amount of time making such a display takes, time I would rather spend on the dips and pâtés, or the fried or grilled foods.

Since into each cocktail party some raw vegetables will fall, let's look at ways of limiting the labor and choosing among the vast variety of raw vegetables available. Choose the vegetables to be all in one or two colors, such as a green and white assortment composed ad lib of cauliflower and broccoli florets, strips of green pepper, slices of peeled turnip or daikon or white radishes, scallions, endive leaves, the edible parts of asparagus—peeled are better—and the whitish inner stalks of celery. A dramatic assortment could be made with whole, peeled, small carrots or carrot strips, red and yellow and orange pepper strips or squares, cherry tomatoes in reds and yellows and even small leaves of radicchio. The vegetables can be all white or all green. You might think of adding sugar snap or snow peas to the green assortment above if the stringing doesn't bother you or small green beans if it does. The advantage of this color limitation is that your arrangement looks attractive even if it is totally random—the eager hands of friends won't upset the vegetable cart.

Try to pick vegetables of a color that will go well with the dips or salads that you are providing. In a garden, flowers of every color may go well together, but it is another thing entirely when you set dishes of food out on a table.

I find I have to allow about three quarters of a cup of crudités per person no matter how much other food I am serving. Of course, if the whole three quarters of a cup is made up of cauliflower or broccoli, which is bulky, I will have to provide somewhat more, and if all the vegetables are cut in thin strips—mildly uninteresting—I can supply somewhat less.

Cherry tomatoes are the easiest vegetables to provide but the messiest to eat. Other vegetables require a little more work, but if you don't get carried away with Thai-inspired vegetable carving, it shouldn't take too long.

The work is in the cutting up. If you frequently entertain a large number of people at any kind of party, it is worth thinking about investing in a mandoline—a slightly tricky bit of French kitchen engineering, not the musical instrument. It makes the work go much more quickly. See page 233 for a description. Most of the vegetables can be cut a day or so ahead of time and kept in the refrigerator, covered with very cold water, until needed. If you are running out of refrigerator space, drain the chilled strips and store them in closed plastic bags. Before the party, drain the vegetables if need be; arrange them and throw a little crushed ice over them and drape a damp kitchen towel over the whole thing. The ice will melt and, along with the towel, keep the vegetables from looking dried out.

Crudités go well with almost all of the dips and salsas on pages 8–25 and are more decorative and less fattening than chips. They are essential for dipping into Bagna Cauda (page 29), but you may want to cut them into somewhat larger pieces than normal so that people don't burn their fingers. They also do well on their own or served with a shaker of Seasoned Salt (page 49) or Sheila's Dry Dunk (page 70).

crudités yields

artichokes
In Italy and the South of France, very young artichokes with pointed tips—sometimes called violets—have their points trimmed and any nasty outside leaves stripped off and are then quartered or thinly sliced lengthwise. There is usually no or almost no choke. If there is, it is scraped off with a paring knife. The slice is rubbed with or tossed in lemon juice and served raw. Larger artichokes can offer only their bottoms. Cut off leaves; trim bottoms and scrape out choke with a thin-edged spoon. Slice thinly and douse with lemon.

It is very hard to give a yield because of variations in size. I generally allow a small artichoke for each two people and a large bottom for four.

asparagus
Cut asparagus 3 inches from tip. Reserve stalks for another use. Peel each length below the tip. Eight ounces asparagus (medium thickness) = 15 tip pieces = scant ½ cup.

beans—fava, broad or lima

When very young, in the spring, these can be shelled and served raw. A pound and a half in the shell will give you about ½ pound shelled (depending on the size of the bean) = ⅔ cup. One-quarter cup per person will be plenty. For String Beans, green beans, wax beans, etc., see String Beans, below.

broccoli

Remove stems and cut into medium-sized florets. One medium head broccoli (1½ pounds) = 4⅓ cups.

carrots

Peel and trim carrots. Cut into 3 × ¼-inch sticks. One medium carrot (3 ounces) = 22 carrot sticks = ½ cup.

cauliflower

Cut off outside leaves. Core deeply with a small knife. Cut into small florets. One medium head cauliflower (2¼ pounds) = 4¾ cups.

celery

Wash, trim and peel celery stalks. Cut into 3 × ¼-inch sticks. One medium celery stalk (2½ ounces) = 15 celery sticks = ⅓ cup.

celery root

Trim and peel celery root. Either quarter lengthwise and cut across into ⅛-inch-thick slices or cut into 3 × ¼ × ¼-inch sticks. One medium celery root (1¼ pounds) = 14 ounces trimmed and peeled = 3½ cups slices = 4 cups sticks.

cherry tomatoes

One pint = 13 ounces = 20 tomatoes.

cucumbers

Trim cucumbers. Peel if the skins are waxed or heavy. Cut in half lengthwise. Scrape out seeds. Cut into 3 × ¼-inch sticks. One medium cucumber (8 ounces) = 30 cucumber sticks = ⅔ cup.

endive

Trim bottom. If using large endive, remove and discard the outer leaves. Carefully separate each leaf. Large endive (3½ ounces) = 10 leaves = 2 ounces; small endive (1¼ ounces) = 4 leaves = ½ ounce.

fennel

Trim and remove tops and tough outer leaves. Cut in ¼-inch-thick wedges around the core so that slices hold together. One fennel bulb (1½ pounds) = 5 ounces slices = 30 pieces = 1⅓ cups.

peppers

(red, purple, orange, yellow or green)
Trim, core, seed and derib peppers. Cut into 3 × ¼-inch sticks. One 6-ounce pepper = 3½ ounces sticks = 26 sticks = 1 scant cup.

radicchio

Trim bottom. Carefully separate each leaf. Large radicchio (7 ounces) = 13 big leaves = 4½ ounces; small radicchio (4 ounces) = 28 small leaves = 3½ ounces.

radishes

(red, daikon, white or black)
Scrub well. Trim root end. Very small radishes may be served whole with a small amount of stem attached. Medium radishes (usually white or red, about 11 in a bunch) can be either quartered lengthwise or cut across into ¼-inch-thick slices. One bunch radishes (½ pound with stems) = 4½ ounces trimmed = ¾ cup quartered pieces or ⅔ cup slices.

Large radishes such as daikon or black may be peeled or not. I usually peel daikon and do not peel the black. The daikon can be cut either into thin crosswise slices or into sticks, 3 × ¼-inch. The black radishes are nice cut across into thin slices, leaving a tiny rim of black around the white center. Of either kind, 5 ounces will give about ⅔ cup slices = 22 sticks = ¾ cup. These radish slices will curl up attractively if left to soak in ice cold water.

scallions

Trim root end and cut into a 3-inch length from the root end of each scallion. Reserve the remaining dark green leaf part for another use. One bunch scallions (4½ ounces) = 1½ ounces = 7 sticks.

snow peas

Tip, tail and string. Three ounces = 1 cup.

sugar snap peas

Tip, tail and string. Two and a half ounces = ½ cup.

string beans

Of course, most of the beans in this category—string beans, haricots verts, etc.—no longer have strings. Yield will vary with size. You will get more haricots verts, which only need to be tipped and tailed, in a pound or a cup than largish string beans. To give you a starting place for estimating how much to buy: Large Beans, tipped, tailed and cut in half crosswise: 2 ounces large string beans = 20 pieces = ½ cup.

turnips

The younger the better, and don't use rutabagas . . . too strong. Trim and peel. Depending on the size of the turnip, either cut in half lengthwise and slice across into ⅛-inch-thick slices, slice across into rounds, cut into tiny wedges or cut into 2½ × ¼ × ¼-inch-thick sticks. One medium turnip (4½ ounces) = ⅔ cup slices = 22 sticks = ¾ cup.

new potatoes

In a crudités bowl, allow two per person. Alone with a dipping sauce, allow three to four. Use a fairly thick dip so it doesn't slide off the round shape. Herb Dip (page 18) or Brandade of Sole (page 32) would be good.

New potatoes are micro-waved with minimal liquid. Without liquid, they tend to wrinkle. Buy potatoes that are all the same size—and as small as possible. If they are larger than you like, cut them in half after cooking.

Place in the dish indicated below and cover tightly with a lid or microwave plastic wrap. Prick wrap, if using, with the tip of a sharp knife to release steam. Remove dish from oven.

Small new potatoes will yield 14 potatoes to the pound.

¼ pound
with 1 tablespoon water in a 9-inch pie plate
High-wattage oven: 3 min.
Low-wattage oven: 4 min.

½ pound
with 2 tablespoons water in a 1½-quart soufflé dish
High-wattage oven: 4 min.
Low-wattage oven: 7 min.

1 pound
with ¼ cup water in a 1½-quart soufflé dish
High-wattage oven: 7 min.
Low-wattage oven: 14 min.

2 pounds
with ½ cup water in a 1½-quart soufflé dish
High-wattage oven: 14 min.
Low-wattage oven: 20 min.

3 pounds
with ¾ cup water in a 2½-quart soufflé dish
High-wattage oven: 17 min.
Low-wattage oven: not recommended

A basic Crudités (page 67) mix kept in attractive order by limiting the colors used.

steamed vegetables

If you have a little more time, some vegetables are more attractive and pleasanter when lightly steamed—like broccoli florets. Others must be cooked before including in an assortment—potatoes, for example. I have gotten used to steaming vegetables in the microwave oven, which is cool and quick and leaves my stove free for other things. You can steam the vegetables on top of the stove in a minimum of water. Unless you are serving the vegetables the minute they come out of the oven or steamer, uncover them and run cold water over them as soon as they are cooked. Then store them until serving time in bowls of cold water. Add ice if there isn't enough room in the refrigerator.

asparagus

Asparagus in the microwave oven stay bright green, retain all their vitamins and don't have to be bunched since they're not floating around. Arrange stalks in a flat layer in a microwavable dish, no more than 1½ inches thick. Cover tightly with microwavable plastic wrap. After cooking, prick plastic to release steam. Remove from oven and uncover.

To serve as part of a selection of crudités, keep the asparagus about 4 inches long. It's hard to know how many asparagus will get eaten. It also depends on their size. I usually allow about six spears per person. However, if it is asparagus season and I serve a large dish of them with a mayonnaise (pages 31–38), Parsley and Scallion Dip (page 17) or Green Goddess Dressing (page 37), I allow as many as ten spears per person. Medium asparagus will yield 30 spears to the pound.

¼ pound
High-wattage oven: 2 min.
Low-wattage oven: 4 min.

½ pound
High-wattage oven: 2 min. 30 sec.
Low-wattage oven: 5 min.

1 pound
High-wattage oven: 4 min. 15 sec.
Low-wattage oven: not recommended

2 pounds
High-wattage oven: 7 min.
Low-wattage oven: not recommended

2½ pounds
High-wattage oven: 11 min.
Low wattage oven: not recommended

broccoli florets

Broccoli rewards cooking, as it turns a bright green and has a milder, pleasanter flavor than the raw. Cooked in the microwave oven, it doesn't get waterlogged. Dripping vegetables are a threat to your guests' hands and clothing. Cut the florets fairly small so they go in the mouth in one bite.

Place florets in cooking dish specified below. Cover tightly with microwave plastic wrap or a lid. If using a lid, add a tablespoon of water for each 4 ounces of broccoli. Four ounces raw broccoli yields a scant 1 cup cooked.

4 ounces in a 1½-quart soufflé dish
High-wattage oven: 1 min. 30 sec.
Low-wattage oven: 3 min.

8 ounces in a 1½-quart soufflé dish
High-wattage oven: 3 min.
Low-wattage oven: 6 min.

1 pound in a 2½-quart soufflé dish
High-wattage oven: 6 min.
Low-wattage oven: 10 min.

1½ pounds in a 2½-quart soufflé dish
High-wattage oven: 8 min.
Low-wattage oven: 15 min.
Stir once.

2 pounds in a 5-quart casserole
High-wattage oven: 13 min.
Low-wattage oven: 23 min.
Stir once.

2½ pounds in a 5-quart casserole
High-wattage oven: 15 min.
Low-wattage oven: 27 minutes.
Stir once.

3 pounds in a 5-quart casserole
High-wattage oven: 17 min.
Low-wattage oven: 30 min.
Stir once.

sheila's dry dunk

A lovely Indian woman and good cook named Sheila provided this mildly spicy and slightly sweetish seasoning mixture at a party last summer. We all dunked raw vegetables into the little saucer filled with a brown powder. The more we ate, the deeper we dunked. The mixture was addictive, is easy to make and keeps for a long time in a jar. Cut-up raw vegetables have just enough moisture to stick the powder to them.

Makes ¾ cup

⅓ cup sugar
1 tablespoon dried oregano
1 teaspoon dried sage
½ cup good curry powder
1 teaspoon ground cumin
¼ teaspoon cayenne pepper
Kosher salt, to taste

Combine sugar, oregano and dried sage in a spice mill. Whir until the dried herbs seem to disappear and you have a fine powder.

Pour sugar mixture into a small nonstick skillet. Stir constantly over lowish heat for about 10 minutes. Be sure to scrape the bottom of the pan as you go. You want the mixture to turn a medium brown without having the bottom of the mixture scorch. Combine with remaining ingredients.

cumin vegetables

Cooked, savory and delicious if skewered on a toothpick and popped into the mouth between sips. If the mushrooms aren't small, halve or quarter them before cooking. If you make the carrots, the carrots and mushrooms can be tossed together.

Makes about 3 cups

1 pound, firm, small white mushrooms, wiped clean
or
6 cups whole tiny carrots, peeled and trimmed
or
8 medium carrots, trimmed, peeled and cut across into 1/4-inch-thick slices
or
12 medium carrots, trimmed, peeled and cut into 3 × 1/4-inch strips
1/4 cup vegetable oil
1 to 1 1/4 teaspoons ground cumin
1/8 teaspoon kosher salt, or to taste
Freshly ground black pepper

If using mushrooms, wipe them clean with the palm of your hand or a moistened paper towel. Cut off the stems and reserve them for another use.

In a skillet large enough to hold all the mushrooms or carrots in a single layer, heat the oil over medium heat. If your skillet is too small, use two skillets and divide the ingredients equally between them. Set the mushrooms in the pan, cut side down or add the carrots. Sprinkle with 3/4 teaspoon cumin, salt and several grinds of pepper. Reduce the heat to low. Cook, uncovered, turning occasionally, about 25 to 30 minutes, until mushrooms are very dark brown or carrots are golden and shriveled-looking.

Five minutes before removing from the heat, stir in 1/4 teaspoon cumin. Taste and adjust the seasonings. Transfer the mushrooms or carrots to a bowl. Cool to room temperature, tossing occasionally. Serve at room temperature.

stuffed vegetables

Vegetables can be stuffed raw, they can be cooked and then stuffed or they can be stuffed and then cooked. Different vegetables and different fillings determine the method of choice. Cherry tomatoes are best used as a raw container for a cooked stuffing. Miniature zucchini and pattypan squash are best cooked before stuffing and then either stuffed with a mixture meant to be eaten cold or reheated after stuffing. Somewhat larger zucchini are best stuffed when raw, cooked and then served sliced, hot or cold.

Mushroom caps can be used raw as containers for cooked fillings, but unless they are very small they tend to break when bitten, scattering filling around the room. Slightly cooked caps are easier to eat.

Summer squash with Thai Shrimp Stuffing (page 210) is elegant, not too hard, and good hot or cold.

71

stuffed miniature vegetables

These pretty miniatures combine vegetables and flavorful stuffings into one tasty mouthful. Obviously, the amount you make will depend on how many vegetables you prepare, how many stuffings you make and how much of each. Fortunately, the vegetable shells can be prepared up to two days ahead. The fillings can even be made three days ahead. The vegetables can be filled a day ahead of time. Just take the ones with unbaked fillings out and serve them. Bake the ones that have fillings that need to baked and serve them hot or cool.

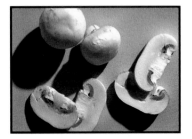

Several of the fillings, such as the Roasted Red Pepper Spread (page 14) the Orzo Filling (opposite page) and the Mushroom Purée (opposite page), are good for vegetarians. You might also want to consider filling the vegetables with Chicken Salad (page 263), Quintessential Tuna Salad (page 183), Smoked Trout Velvet (page 182), Brandade of Sole (page 32) or one of the cheese spreads (pages 38–42). Don't use a liquid filling such as Pacific Overture or a salsa—it will be too messy to eat.

Makes about 24 stuffed vegetables

**I pint ripe cherry tomatoes
  or**
**12 ounces miniature pattypan
  squash or**
**I pound miniature zucchini
  or**
**I pound small (2-inch)
  mushrooms**

suggested fillings

**Unbaked Fillings
(to serve at room
temperature):**
**Roasted Red Pepper Spread
  (with or without French
  Olive Spread, page 14)**
Orzo Filling, opposite page

**Baked Fillings
(to serve hot):**
**Mushroom Purée, opposite
  page**
Curry Lamb Stuffing, page 286
**Lamb-Tomato Stuffing,
  page 76**
Minted Rice Stuffing, page 76
Turkey Pâté, page 151
**Chinese Pork Terrine,
  page 153**
Thai Shrimp Stuffing, page 210

To Prepare the Vegetables
Cherry Tomatoes. Stem and wash. Drain well. Slice off about ¼ inch of the stem end of each tomato; reserve stem end as lid. If necessary, slice a thin sliver from the opposite end so the tomatoes can stand upright. Hollow out and discard the seeds and liquid. Reserve the lids.

Miniature Pattypan Squash and Zucchini. Wash and drain. Blanch in a large pot of boiling salted water 3 minutes. Drain in a colander and rinse under cold running water until cool. Drain thoroughly. Cut a thin slice from the end opposite the stem of the pattypan squash or from one side of the zucchini so they can stand upright. Cut off about ¼ inch of the top of each and hollow out the vegetable with a small paring knife, keeping the shells intact. Reserve the tops if desired.

Mushrooms. Remove the stems from the mushrooms and reserve for another use (see Mushroom Purée, opposite page). Toss the caps in a large bowl with 2 tablespoons of olive oil and 2 teaspoons kosher salt. Preheat oven to 350°F. Bake in a covered 8 × 8-inch dish 15 minutes. Cool before using.

For Unbaked Fillings
Spoon about 2 teaspoons of the filling into each vegetable shell. (About 1 teaspoon for pattypan squash.) Place the reserved tops of the cherry tomatoes, pattypan squash and zucchini over the filling, if desired. Refrigerate until ready to serve, covered with a slightly damp towel.

For Baked Fillings
Heat oven to 350°F, with rack in center of oven. Spoon about 2 teaspoons of filling into each vegetable shell (about 1 teaspoon for pattypan squash). Place in an ovenproof 11 × 7-inch baking dish. Pour in enough water to make an ⅛-inch layer in bottom of dish. Cover tightly with aluminum foil (may be done a couple hours ahead to this point) and bake 10 minutes. Remove the cover and continue baking until the filling is heated through, about 5 minutes. Serve warm.

sliced stuffed squash

These are very pretty with the green or yellow circle of vegetable rimming the variously colored stuffings. Allow at least three slices per person. You can mix the colors of the squashes and vary the fillings. Multiply this as many times as you want. If steaming, be sure the water comes back to a boil before timing, as more cold food will slow the cooking down. Use a very sharp knife or a tomato knife to slice the stuffed squash so the filling isn't pushed out. Serve hot or cold.

Makes about 40 slices

4 medium zucchini or summer squash, about 4 to 5 ounces each

**Suggested Fillings
(to steam and serve warm):
Salt Cod Pâté, uncooked,
    page 146
Turkey Pâté, page 151
Chinese Pork Terrine,
    page 153
Thai Shrimp Stuffing, page 210**

**Suggested Fillings
(to serve cold in steamed squash):
French Olive Spread, page 22
Chicken Salad, page 263
Quintessential Tuna Salad,
    page 183
Shrimp Salad, page 169**

To Prepare Squash. Trim both ends of the squash. Using a swivel-bladed vegetable peeler, hollow out the squash, making sure to remove all the seeds and leaving about ⅛ inch of white pulp attached to the skin.

To Cook Squash with a Filling. Prepare one of the fillings above. Use about 4 tablespoons of the filling to stuff each squash, firmly but not tightly packed. Steam the squash, covered, over boiling water until the filling in the center is cooked through, about 10 minutes. Remove and slice warm or allow to cool to room temperature before slicing.

To Cook Squash for Use with a Cold Filling. Steam the prepared squash, covered, over boiling water until tender but still firm, about 6 minutes. Remove, drain thoroughly and cool in cold running water before filling and slicing.

orzo filling

A nice vegetarian appetizer. The cheese holds everything together, so it is not for vegans. If you put the cheese in the freezer for five minutes or chill it thoroughly, it will be easier to cut it up.

Makes 1½ cups; enough for about 36 Stuffed Miniature Vegetables (opposite page)

**4 large shallots (about 3 ounces), peeled and sliced
4 mushrooms (about 3 ounces), cleaned and sliced
2 tablespoons unsalted butter
2 tablespoons olive oil
1 teaspoon kosher salt
Freshly ground black pepper
⅓ cup orzo pasta
2 canned Italian plum tomatoes, drained and diced (about ¼ cup)
2 teaspoons minced fresh thyme leaves, or 1 scant teaspoon dried thyme
½ cup chicken broth, or water
2 tablespoons minced, fresh Italian parsley leaves
½ cup shredded mozzarella cheese (about 2 ounces)**

Combine the shallots and mushrooms in a food processor. Chop fine using on/off pulses or chop with a stainless steel knife.

Heat the butter and oil in a medium skillet over medium heat until the butter is foaming. Add the mushroom mixture and sprinkle with 1 teaspoon of the salt and pepper to taste. Sauté, stirring occasionally, until the shallot is tender, about 5 minutes. Add the orzo and toss to coat. Add the remaining ingredients, except the cheese, and heat to boiling. Reduce to a simmer, cover and cook until the orzo is tender, about 6 minutes. Uncover and let cool to room temperature. Stir in the cheese and check the seasoning.

mushroom purée

This is a conventional—that is, stove-top—version of a recipe that appeared in Microwave Gourmet. *While I still use the microwave, this is too good a basic preparation for me to stop people who don't have a microwave.*

Makes 1¼ cups

**1 pound mushrooms and/or mushroom stems, wiped clean and sliced (almost any mushrooms can be used)
¼ pound shallots, peeled and sliced (about ⅓ cup)
6 tablespoons unsalted butter
1½ teaspoons kosher salt
½ teaspoon freshly ground black pepper
¼ cup finely chopped fresh Italian parsley leaves**

Finely chop the mushrooms and shallots separately in a food processor.

Melt the butter in a large heavy skillet over medium heat. When it's foaming, stir in the shallots and sauté until softened, about 5 minutes. Stir in the mushrooms and sprinkle with salt and pepper. Sauté, stirring occasionally, until the mushrooms have rendered their liquid, about 6 minutes. Boil off the liquid. This will take from 5 to 10 minutes, depending on the mushrooms and the size of the pan. There should be only butter—no liquid—remaining in the skillet. Reduce the heat to low, stir in the parsley and cook until the mushrooms are just beginning to brown, and no trace of liquid remains in the pan, about 5 minutes. Turn the mushroom purée out of the pan and cool.

Come games, particularly playoffs and final matches, people like to eat well and heartily without moving from the television screen or fussing with forks and knives. Bring one hot food in at a time. You don't need to make all these things unless you are feeling ambitious, but it gives you enough substantial food items from which to make a selection. Beer, without glasses, seems to be the chosen drink. The spreads, salsa and sauces can go on biscuits, tortilla chips, crudités, meats and mussels as desired. The same kind of spread is good at any cold-weather party. Cold: **1** Mussels (page 194); **2** Pumped-Up Popcorn (page 56); **3** Caponata (page 14); **4** Cheddar-Sherry Spread (page 39); **5** pistachios; **6** tortilla chips; **7** Crudités (page 67); **8** Fresh Tomatillo Salsa (page 23); **9** Spicy Rémoulade (page 37). Hot: **10** Crab Cakes (page 187) on **11** Cornmeal Biscuits (page 108) with **12** Tartar Sauce (page 36); **13** Marinated Lamb Riblets (page 283); **14** Spicy Popcorn Shrimp (page 242); **15** Salami Roll-Ups (page 202); **16** Miniature Tuna Melts (page 182); **17** Miniature Hamburgers (page 279); **18** Grilled Reuben Sandwiches (page 122).

minted rice stuffing

Simple, savory and thrifty with a mildly Greek taste—I like it.

Makes 1½ cups

2 tablespoons olive oil
1 small onion, finely diced (⅔ cup)
¾ cup long-grain rice
½ teaspoon dried mint
1½ cups chicken broth, or water
1 teaspoon kosher salt
2 teaspoons fresh lemon juice

Heat olive oil in a 2-quart saucepan over low heat. Add the onion and cook, stirring, until wilted, about 5 minutes. Stir in the rice and mint until coated with oil. Add the broth and salt, increase the heat to medium and heat to boiling. Reduce the heat to a bare simmer, cover the pot and cook until the rice is tender and the liquid is absorbed, about 16 minutes. Remove from the heat and stir in the lemon juice.

lamb-tomato stuffing

I think this is absolutely delicious. I got the idea for the recipe from a woman, Elsa, who works with me. She, a Chilean, uses it to stuff grape leaves, so in addition to using it in vegetables, I use it in grape leaves. I also doctor it and use it for the Mini–Moussaka Rolls (page 202).

Makes about 1¾ cups

Basic Filling

Makes about 40 Stuffed Miniature Vegetables (page 72) or 75 Chilean Stuffed Grape Leaves (page 206)

½ pound ground lamb
1 small onion, finely diced (about ½ cup)
2 medium cloves garlic, smashed, peeled and minced
⅛ teaspoon cayenne pepper
2 tablespoons long-grain rice
½ cup diced canned plum tomatoes with liquid
½ cup chicken broth, or water
2 tablespoons loosely packed chopped fresh coriander (cilantro) leaves
1½ teaspoons red wine vinegar
⅛ teaspoon ground cinnamon
1 teaspoon kosher salt
⅛ teaspoon freshly ground black pepper

Moussaka Filling

Makes about 2 cups filling; enough for 2 Spinach Roulades (80 slices) (page 225) or 75 Mini–Moussaka Rolls (page 202)

1 recipe Basic Filling
½ cup loosely packed grated Parmesan cheese
¼ cup ricotta cheese
2 large eggs

Crumble the lamb into a large saucepan. Place over medium heat and sauté, stirring, until no trace of pink remains. Stir in the onion, garlic and cayenne pepper. Sauté until the lamb is browned and the onion is tender, about 8 minutes. Stir in the rice and add the tomatoes, broth, coriander, vinegar, cinnamon, salt and pepper. Heat to simmering, cover the pan and cook until the rice is tender and the liquid is absorbed, about 15 minutes. Check occasionally and adjust the heat if necessary. If the liquid is evaporated before the rice is tender, add a little water or broth.

To Make Moussaka Filling. Cool the Filling slightly. Whisk the Parmesan, ricotta and egg in a mixing bowl until blended. Fold into Filling.

grilled vegetables

Where I live, grilled vegetables are strictly a mid-spring—early spring is beautiful but chilly—into late-fall event. I envy those people who can grill all year because the vegetables are spiffy. The best time to have them is when your party is out of doors and everybody can gather around the grill as you remove the done bits to platters. Add a Grilled Flank Steak (page 273) or Saté or Yakitori (page 272) to the grill or some butterflied shrimp and all you will need to complete the pleasure will be a cold dip and some good bread.

Sliced or halved whole vegetables (page 82) are somewhat messy food. My friends and I are happy to eat these foods with our fingers in informal clothes. If your friends will be in dressier clothes or have dressier manners, or if you are indoors, you will need to provide plates or provide the skewered vegetables and brochettes.

The fire should be white-hot. It will take a good half hour to get it there. Provide yourself with a long-handled brush for dabbing on marinade or sauce as the food cooks.

While the vegetables need to be good, much of the flavor is provided by olive oil and garlic, marinades or barbecue sauces. The inspiration for these sauces can come from many countries, since grilling is one of the most basic ways of cooking. Several of these sauces and marinades are called for in other parts of the book. They can be equally good with fish, seafood, chicken and meat. The marinades and sauces keep very well, covered, in the refrigerator for up to two months, so you may want to make larger quantities and store them for another time. It is easier to multiply nonmicrowave recipes than microwave recipes.

Leftover marinades can be used as sauces only after being brought to a full boil; watch out for bugs.

asian barbecue sauce

This thickened sauce is good with Vegetable Skewers (page 79), seafood, meats, chicken and pork. It is better than the Asian Marinade (page 78) when you want the skewers to be coated and glazed as well as seasoned.

Makes 1 1/3 cups

2/3 cup tamari soy sauce
1/2 cup rice wine vinegar
1/4 cup light brown sugar
2 tablespoons vegetable oil
20 medium cloves garlic, smashed and peeled
1 2-inch piece fresh ginger, peeled and cut into 1/2-inch dice
1 strip orange zest, 3 inches long and 1/4 inch wide
10 drops hot red pepper sauce
1 tablespoon cornstarch dissolved in 2 tablespoons water

Microwave-Oven Method. Combine all ingredients except the cornstarch mixture in a 4-cup glass measure or bowl. Cover tightly with microwave plastic wrap and cook at 100% for 5 minutes in a high-wattage oven, 8 minutes in a low-wattage oven. After cooking, prick plastic with the tip of a small knife to release steam. Purée thoroughly in a blender. Return to measure or bowl. Stir the cornstarch mixture into the sauce. Cover with microwave plastic wrap and cook for 3 minutes in a high-wattage oven, 5 minutes in a low-wattage oven, until thickened. Prick plastic wrap with tip of a sharp knife. Cool to room temperature before using.

Stove-Top Method. Combine all ingredients except cornstarch in a medium saucepan. Heat over medium heat to simmering. Gradually stir in the cornstarch mixture. Return to a simmer and cook, stirring constantly, 2 minutes. Cool to room temperature before using.

asian marinade

Asian Marinade is thinner in texture—not flavor—than the barbecue sauce above. Use it when you want the vegetables to really soak up the marinade, or when you need to tenderize meat.

Makes 1½ cups

6 medium cloves garlic, smashed, peeled and sliced
1 ounce fresh ginger, peeled and cut into small pieces
¾ cup water, if cooking on stove top
1 cup tamari soy sauce
¼ cup sugar
¼ cup rice wine vinegar
2 tablespoons Thai or other fish sauce (nuac nam), optional
Zest of 2 lemons, grated
½ teaspoon ground coriander
½ teaspoon ground cardamom
½ teaspoon Chinese chili paste with garlic (if unavailable substitute Chinese hot pepper oil or hot red pepper sauce)
1 teaspoon fresh lemon juice

Microwave-Oven Method. Combine all ingredients except lemon juice in a 4-cup glass bowl. Cover tightly with microwave plastic wrap and cook at 100% in a high-wattage oven for 6 minutes or in a low-wattage oven for 10 minutes. Prick plastic to release steam.

Remove from oven and uncover. Strain through a fine sieve and stir in lemon juice. Use or store, tightly covered, in the refrigerator.

Stove-Top Method. Combine garlic, ginger and water in a

medium pan and bring to a boil over medium heat. Reduce heat to very low and simmer, uncovered, for about 15 minutes, until almost all the liquid has evaporated and both garlic and ginger are soft.

Add remaining ingredients except lemon juice, allow mixture to come to a simmer and cook for 5 minutes.

Remove from heat and strain through a fine sieve, stir in lemon juice and proceed as above.

greek marinade

This is a light, clean-tasting marinade that is particularly good with Seafood Skewers (page 193), Lamb Kabobs (page 269) and vegetables.

Makes ½ cup

For 1⅔ cups, triple all ingredients

6 medium cloves garlic, smashed, peeled and sliced
1 cup water, if cooking on stove top, or ¼ cup if cooking in microwave
1 teaspoon dried mint, or ½ teaspoon dried oregano plus ½ teaspoon dried thyme
1 teaspoon kosher salt
¼ cup olive oil
3 tablespoons fresh lemon juice

Microwave-Oven Method. Place garlic, water and herbs in a 4-cup glass measure. Cover tightly with microwave plastic wrap and cook at 100% in a high-wattage oven for 6 minutes or in a low-wattage oven for 9 minutes. Prick plastic to release steam.

Remove from oven and uncover. Scrape into a blender, add salt and blend until smooth.

With the motor running, add oil in a thin stream. Add lemon juice and blend until well combined. Use or store, covered, in the refrigerator.

For Larger Quantity. Use a 2½-quart soufflé dish. Cook as above in a high-wattage oven for 9 minutes 30 seconds or in a low-wattage oven for 15 minutes. Finish recipe as above.

Stove-Top Method. Place garlic and water in a small pan and bring to a boil over medium heat. Reduce heat to very low and simmer for about 15 minutes, until garlic is soft and only about ⅓ cup water remains. Add herbs for last 5 minutes of cooking time.

Scrape into a blender and continue as above.

vegetable brochettes

These are very good and rather ample. If there is lots of food, one per person is probably adequate. Otherwise allow two each. The recipe can be multiplied as often as need be and the brochettes can be prepared, but not cooked, a day ahead. While better hot— cook in batches—these are also very tasty cold.

Makes 8 brochettes

1 cup Greek Marinade (this page)
16 small white onions (¾ pound), peeled with the stem end left on (if onions are large, halve through stem end)
16 medium mushrooms, trimmed and wiped clean (1 pound)
1 medium bulb fennel (14 ounces), stalks separated and cut into ½- to 1-inch squares (about 5 cups)

78

1 red bell pepper, stemmed, seeded, deribbed and cut into ½- to 1-inch squares (about 1½ cups)
16 cherry tomatoes

Pour marinade into a long dish that will fit the brochettes and reserve.

Bring a small pan of water to a boil over medium heat. Add white onions and cook for about 2 minutes, or until just soft. Drain and refresh onions under cold running water.

On eight 12-inch metal skewers thread onions with remaining vegetables in any order, ending with a piece of pepper or fennel at the tip end (these remain firmest during cooking so are least likely to fall off). Brush brochettes with marinade and allow to sit in the remaining marinade for about 30 minutes at room temperature or in the refrigerator overnight. If refrigerated, bring to room temperature and brush again with marinade.

Heat grill until coals are white hot. Cook brochettes on the grill for about 10 minutes, turning them occasionally to cook all sides and brushing with reserved marinade.

These can also be done in a pan under the broiler.

vegetable skewers

These are so good that I serve long skewers with double the amount of vegetables and brown rice or bulgur to vegetarian friends.

Makes about 20 skewers

1 recipe Asian Barbecue Sauce (page 77)

2 small red or yellow bell peppers (about 5 ounces), cored, seeded and cut into 1¼ × 1¼-inch squares
1 small zucchini or yellow squash (4 ounces), washed and trimmed, cut into ½-inch cubes
4 ounces small (2-inch) mushrooms, cut into quarters
5 small red onions (4 ounces each), peeled and quartered, leaving stem end on

Let 24 six-inch bamboo skewers soak in enough cold water to cover for at least 24 hours before skewering the vegetables.

Make the Asian Barbecue Sauce. Toss the vegetables in half the sauce until coated and let marinate, covered, in the refrigerator for one day or at room temperature 4 hours.

Up to four hours before cooking, you can arrange one piece of each vegetable on each skewer. Place the skewers in an 8 × 8-inch baking dish. Pour any extra marinade over the skewers, cover and refrigerate up to 4 hours.

Mildly spicy Tropical Fruit Brochettes (page 82). Sweet versions can be made by brushing fruit with a mixture of orange juice and sugar or honey.

To cook, heat the broiler and place the rack 4 inches from the heat. Heat the broiler pan 3 to 4 minutes. Carefully arrange the skewers in a single layer on the broiler pan. Broil, rotating the broiler pan once, until the vegetables are lightly browned and crisp-tender, about 3 minutes.

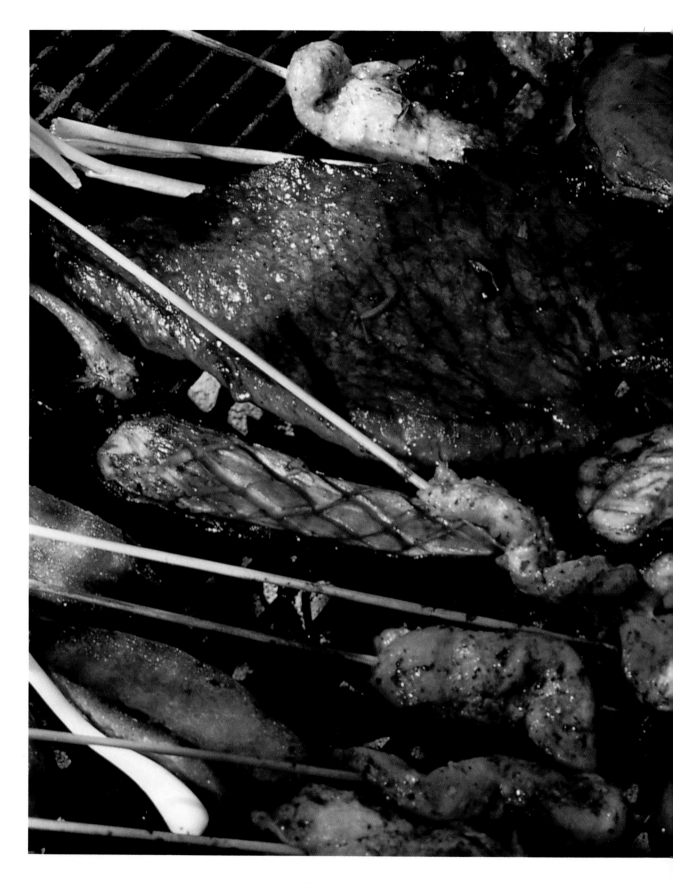

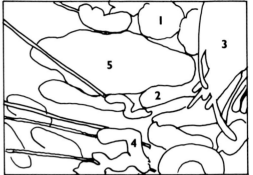

A *host or hostess can serve right from the grill to individual plates or to platters. The* **1** *portobello mushrooms (page 82) and* **2** *the eggplant (page 82) can be cut in wedges. As the vegetables, including the* **3** *Grilled Ramps (page 83), cool, many will be happy to eat them with their fingers, but you can have toothpicks for the elegant. The* **4** *Chicken Saté (page 272) can be eaten as is or with Peanut Dipping Sauce (page 28) on the side.* **5** *Sliced Grilled Flank Steak (page 273) gets mustard and a good bread, such as Herb Focaccia (page 128).*

tropical fruit brochettes

No, these aren't vegetables, but they seem to fit here better than anywhere else. Consider serving them with a ham (page 288) or with a spicy assortment of foods. The fruit is refreshing. Prepare these a day ahead and quickly cook at the last minute. If they get cold, it's no problem.

Makes 20 brochettes

Marinade
1 cup fresh orange juice
6 tablespoons guava paste
1/4 cup Dijon mustard
1 1/2 teaspoons curry powder
2 teaspoons fresh lime juice

Fruit
80 1/2 x 1/2-inch pieces from underripe papaya, mango, star fruit and loquat

Place 20 plain wooden toothpicks in a shallow dish. Cover with hot water and reserve.

Combine first four ingredients in a blender until smooth.

Scrape mixture into a small saucepan and bring to a boil over medium heat. Reduce heat to low and simmer for 20 minutes.

Remove from heat. Stir in lime juice.

Thread 4 pieces of fruit on each toothpick. Place brochettes in a medium bowl and pour marinade over. Refrigerate overnight.

Preheat broiler. Line a cookie sheet with aluminum foil. Roll brochettes in marinade; remove and place on the pan 2 inches apart (reserve marinade). Broil for 1 1/2 minutes per side.

Remove from oven and serve warm, using reserved marinade as a dipping sauce.

grilled vegetables

Vegetables don't need to be skewered into neat packages to be grilled. Many kinds can be cut and marinated and served to fingers—after cooling slightly—or plates. The amount of marinade you use and the amount of vegetables will depend on how many you are serving. I generally allow at least eight pieces of vegetable per person, although only two or three pieces of halved baby vegetables. You will be surprised at how popular these are. Serve them with slices of Grilled Flank Steak (page 273) for a robust outdoor meal, or combine with any of the seafood brochettes in Chapter 5, the chicken or meat ones in Chapter 8.

You can also put the sliced grilled vegetables (assorted) on a halved Italian Bread and slice across for small sandwiches. Sprinkle the filling with some chopped herbs and any leftover marinade.

Greek Marinade (page 78)
   or
Asian Marinade (page 78)
Sweet or baking potatoes, scrubbed and cut across into 1/2-inch slices
Red onions, peeled and cut across into 1/2-inch slices
Eggplant, washed and cut across into 1/3-inch slices, or baby eggplants (1 to 2 ounces each), cut in half lengthwise and scored in diamonds
Red and yellow bell peppers, stemmed, seeded, deribbed and cut into sixths
Zucchini and yellow squash, washed and cut on the diagonal into 1/4-inch slices, or baby squashes cut in half lengthwise

Heat grill until coals are very—white—hot, or cook under broiler on a baking sheet (not air-cushioned). Turn once with a spatula.

Brush all sliced vegetables with marinade or place halved baby vegetables, cut side down, in the marinade and allow to sit 15 minutes at room temperature.

You will need about a third cup of either Greek Marinade or Asian Marinade for each guest. Continue to brush vegetables occasionally with marinade as they are cooking. Cook potato slices toward the edge of the grill for about 15 minutes on each side, taking care that they do not become charred before they are cooked through. Cook red onions farther toward the center of the grill for about 5 minutes on each side. Cook eggplant slices for 4 minutes on each side. Cook pepper strips for 5 minutes on each side. Cook squash slices for 3 minutes on each side. Cook halved baby vegetables on grill for about 3 minutes on each side, brushing occasionally with reserved marinade. The amount of time will vary, depending on the size of the vegetables and the heat of the grill.

grilled mushrooms

There is no point in making these with small mushrooms, but if you can buy or pick mushrooms that are at least four inches across, these are a real treat.

About 1/2 cup olive oil to every pound of mushrooms
Kosher salt
Freshly ground black pepper, to taste

Large fleshy mushrooms such as cêpes, portobellos or field mushrooms (e.g., agaricus campesteris), stemmed and wiped clean of dirt with a damp paper towel

Preheat grill until quite hot. Combine oil with salt and pepper. Turn mushrooms in oil until well coated. Place around the edges of the grill, top side down. Longer-cooking vegetables, meat or fish can be cooked over the central, hottest part of the grill.

The length of time needed to cook the mushrooms will depend on the heat of the fire and the size of the mushrooms. When mushrooms are about half cooked, brush the underside with oil and turn over. Brush any remaining oil over the skins as required and continue grilling until cooked through.

Remove from grill and season to taste with salt and pepper.

If no plates and forks are being used, cut the mushrooms into wedges and serve with toothpicks. If cut, allow about 4 wedges per person.

grilled ramps

You can't make these very often—only in spring—but if you know how to pick ramps (they grow wild) or know someone who does, these are bound to be a favorite with friends who are not afraid to get their fingers greasy. Some very fancy stores may sell them. (Scallions can be substituted.) They are good cold, and I find that people devour them, so prepare more than you think you will need.

Serves 4 to 8

1½ pounds ramps (wild leeks)
1 cup olive oil
Kosher salt
Freshly ground black pepper

Wash ramps well and pull off the thin, outermost layer.

Preheat grill until coals are white hot. Brush ramps with oil and place in a single layer crosswise on grill so that they cannot fall through the rack and so that the green part is not actually over the heat but hanging off the side. Continue to brush with remaining oil as necessary.

When the white parts of the ramps start to turn brown, turn them over with a pancake turner and move them toward the center of the grill so that the greens are over the heat.

When fully cooked and quite soft, remove from grill with pancake turner. Season to taste with salt and pepper.

glazed garlic on brochette

These are not for everybody, but those who love garlic as I do will gobble them up. Be careful when cooking; check often: they burn easily.

Makes 30 brochettes

30 cloves garlic (1 large head), smashed gently and peeled
2 tablespoons balsamic vinegar
2 tablespoons honey
Kosher salt
Freshly ground black pepper, to taste

Place 30 plain wooden toothpicks in a shallow dish. Cover with hot water and reserve.

Combine garlic cloves and vinegar in a 1-quart soufflé dish.

Cover tightly with microwave plastic wrap and cook at 100% in a high-wattage oven for 4 minutes, 6 minutes in a low-wattage oven. Prick plastic to release steam.

Remove from oven and uncover. Pour most of the cooking liquid into a small bowl. Stir in honey, salt and pepper. Add mixture to cooked garlic and stir gently to coat well, being careful not to break up cloves. Allow to stand for about 15 minutes or until needed, stirring occasionally.

Preheat broiler until very hot. Thread 1 garlic clove on each toothpick.

Broil garlic, brushing occasionally with remaining marinade, until brown, about 1 minute on each side.

83

Vegetable Confetti Pancakes—as good at room temperature as hot—are topped with a dollop of sour cream and chervil flowers. Other herb flowers would be just as pretty and taste as good. The red flowers of pineapple sage are particularly striking. If this is not a spring or summer treat, the sour cream could be topped with a twisted strip of smoked salmon or some snipped chives.

vegetable pancakes

The world is full of delectable pancakes that can be made in miniature, from Crêpes (page 221) to Blini (page 220), and so serve as a base for a savory filling or as something to roll one up with. Miniature Vegetable pancakes, barely larger than a silver dollar, are crisper and more interesting.

vegetable confetti pancakes

Although these pancakes are brown and crisp, the pretty pattern of the variously colored vegetables shows through. They can be simply topped with plain yogurt and herb blossoms. A salsa

(pages 23–25) can be served on the side, but don't pretop the pancakes with it or they will get soggy. If you bought the mandoline (page 233), you can save your knuckles by using it for this. If not, back to an old-fashioned four-sided grater. Use the big-holed side. If you are making a lot of these for a large party, you may want to try the oven method. It also avoids a lot of fat.

Since the pancakes can be cooked, frozen and reheated as needed, you may want to make a multiple batch to stash in the freezer for unexpected guests or in preparation for a large party.

Makes 16 pancakes

- **1½ cups grated peeled potatoes from about one large potato (10 ounces)**
- **¾ cup grated peeled carrot (about one large, 5 ounces)**
- **¾ cup grated trimmed zucchini with skin (about one 4-ounce)**
- **2 tablespoons minced onion**
- **1 tablespoon chopped fresh Italian parsley leaves**
- **1 teaspoon kosher salt**
- **Freshly ground black pepper**

¼ cup all-purpose flour
Vegetable oil for frying or greasing baking sheet

Blanch the potatoes in a large pot of boiling water for 1 minute. Drain in a coarse strainer. Don't rinse; shake out excess water.

Combine the potatoes, carrot, zucchini, onion, parsley, salt and pepper in a mixing bowl. Stir until blended. Sprinkle the flour over the vegetable mixture and stir just until evenly distributed. Let the batter stand 10 to 15 minutes before frying.

Stove-Top Method. Pour oil into a large heavy skillet to a depth of about ⅛ inch. Heat over medium heat until wavy. For each pancake, spoon 2 tablespoons of the mixture into the pan and flatten with a spatula into a 2-inch circle. Fry only as many pancakes in each batch as will fit in the skillet in a single layer. Fry, turning once, until deep golden brown and crisp on both sides, about 6 to 8 minutes.

Remove the pancakes from the oil, drain on paper towels. Repeat with the remaining pancakes. Keep the fried pancakes warm on a baking sheet in a 250°F oven while cooking the rest.

Conventional-Oven Method. Preheat oven to 375°F. with rack in bottom third. Thoroughly grease a baking sheet (not air-cushioned). Slide the rack partway out of the oven and form the pancakes, or preform on a plate and carefully move with a spatula. Bake the pancakes, turning once, until well browned and crisped on both sides, about 30 minutes per side. Remove and drain on paper towels.

Note: The pancakes can be made up to 4 weeks in advance and frozen. Separate the layers of cooked pancakes with wax paper and cover the container tightly with aluminum foil. To serve: Heat the frozen pancakes in a single layer on a baking sheet in a preheated 375°F oven until heated through and crisp, about 6 minutes. Flip once during heating.

swiss potato pancakes

Swiss potato pancakes, or rösti, are usually made large and thick in big quantities for hearty, cold-weather appetites. I like them small and crisp as a base for sour cream and chives, or smoked salmon, caviar or smoked trout (pages 165–166) or Brandade of Sole (page 32). The variation will make a crisper cake that is easier for guests to pick up. These can also be made ahead, frozen and reheated.

Makes 36 2-inch rösti

1 ½ pounds boiling potatoes, peeled

2 teaspoons kosher salt
¼ teaspoon freshly ground black pepper
Vegetable oil for frying

Grate the potatoes lengthwise on a coarse grater into a mixing bowl, or use a mandoline. You should have about 4 cups. By pressing the potatoes firmly against the grater, you will get thicker strips and will make rösti that hold together more firmly. Add the salt and pepper; toss to mix.

Pour oil into a large nonstick pan to make a film about an ⅛ inch deep. Heat over medium-high heat till wavy. Form 2-inch pancakes using one tablespoon of the potato mixture. Don't crowd the pan; leave enough room to turn the rösti easily. Cook, turning once, until golden brown on both sides, about 6 minutes. Drain the rösti on a double thickness of paper towels. Keep them warm in a 200°F while cooking the remaining rösti or until needed. Serve hot.

Note: The pancakes can be made up to 4 weeks in advance and frozen. Separate the layers of pancakes with wax paper and cover the container tightly with aluminum foil; freeze. To serve: Heat the pancakes in a single layer on a baking sheet in a 375°F oven until heated through and crisp, about 6 minutes. Flip once during heating.

Variation
Add 1 medium yellow onion (4 ounces), peeled and grated, and ¼ cup rice flour to the potato mixture.

corn pancakes

These are more like traditional pancakes than the ones

above—tender and elegant. Try topping them with sour cream and a salsa (pages 23–25), or for a milder flavor, top with a spoon of Pacific Tomato Dipping Sauce (page 26) and a fresh coriander (cilantro) leaf. Sadly, these do not reheat well.

Makes 36

4 medium ears corn, shucked and silk removed
6 tablespoons heavy cream
6 tablespoons milk
3 large eggs, slightly beaten
6 tablespoons all-purpose flour
¼ teaspoon sugar
1 teaspoon kosher salt
3 tablespoons unsalted butter, melted

Preheat oven to 400°F with rack in bottom third of oven.

Using the point of a small knife, cut down the center of each row of corn, splitting the kernels in half. Use the blunt edge of the knife to scrape the corn pulp into a bowl, leaving the skins on the cob. You should have 1 cup of pulp.

Add all remaining ingredients except 1 tablespoon of the butter to the corn. Stir to combine.

Place a baking sheet (not air-cushioned) in the oven. Heat for 10 minutes. Remove baking sheet from oven and brush with the remaining tablespoon of butter. Working as quickly as possible, drop batter by scant tablespoons onto the baking sheet, about 2 inches apart (you will use about half of the batter).

Bake until pancakes are golden brown on the bottom, about 5 minutes. Turn pancakes over and bake until brown on the other side, about 2 minutes. Transfer to a baking sheet lined with paper towels. Wrap the pancakes in the towels to keep them warm.

Repeat with remaining batter.

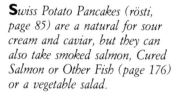 **S**wiss Potato Pancakes (*rösti, page 85*) are a natural for sour cream and caviar, but they can also take smoked salmon, Cured Salmon or Other Fish (*page 176*) or a vegetable salad.

To Prepare Hard-Boiled Eggs

Hard-boiled eggs and Deviled Eggs may sound old-fashioned, but I love them and they always get eaten. Hard-boiled eggs can be served, shelled, just with a bowl of Seasoned Salt (page 49) or Sheila's Dry Dunk (page 70), or be turned into any of the recipes that follow.

All recipes in this book call for USDA large eggs. Choose fresh eggs with no cracks in the shell. (If you're fortunate enough to have access to farm-fresh eggs, you should refrigerate them two to three days before cooking; they will be easier to peel.) Free-range eggs may be healthful. They certainly have flavor and brilliantly colored yolks.

Place six to twelve eggs in a 2-quart saucepan—not aluminum or copper. Add enough cold water to cover. Heat over very high heat to boiling. Immediately adjust the heat to maintain a bare simmer (one or two bubbles rising to the surface at a time). Cook exactly 10 minutes. Drain the eggs and, unless using hot, run under cold water until cool. Roll the eggs gently against a hard surface—I cover it with paper towels so it's easy to throw out the shell pieces—to lightly crack the shell without damaging the egg. Return the eggs to a bowl of cool water for 10 to 15 minutes. The eggs should peel very easily.

egg salad

I used to eat egg salad at lunch counters. It has virtually disappeared. I still love it plain or with the variations below. Make it into sandwiches using Pain de Mie (page 119) or any of the miniature biscuits (pages 108–109). Pile it into tart shells and top with chopped parsley, thinly sliced scallion greens or chives, a tiny bit of anchovy. Put a spoonful in the base of an endive leaf or plonk some in a Crisp New Potato Shell (page 241) or Pâte à Choux (page 106). Top red pepper variations with a lozenge of Roasted Red Pepper. Put a dill sprig on dill-flavored egg salad.

Puréed a little more finely, this is a good dip or spread.

Makes 1½ cups

6 large eggs, hard-boiled and peeled (see box)
⅓ cup commercial mayonnaise
¼ teaspoon kosher salt
⅛ teaspoon freshly ground black pepper
⅓ cup minced trimmed celery, optional
⅓ cup minced yellow onion, optional

Cut the eggs into quarters and place them in a mixing bowl with the mayonnaise, salt and pepper. Mash with a fork until the whites are finely chopped and the yolks are blended with the mayonnaise. The egg salad can be stored in the refrigerator up to a day before serving.

Variations
You may add any of the following to the above egg salad:
• 2 tablespoons finely chopped Roasted Red Pepper (page 59) or one from a jar and ¾ tablespoon minced fresh or canned jalapeño pepper

• 1½ teaspoons curry powder dissolved in 1½ teaspoons fresh lemon juice
• 1½ teaspoons chopped fresh dill sprigs and 3 teaspoons thinly sliced fresh chive

deviled eggs

A must for a real American feed with a Ham (page 288), Spicy Cheddar Biscuits (page 109), one of the hamburgers (pages 279–280) and any dip from Chapter 1 that takes your fancy. Allow two to three halves per person.

I always use mayonnaise out of a jar for this. It's the taste I remember from childhood, but if you are a purist, make your own.

Makes 24 halves

12 large eggs, hard-cooked and peeled (see box)
¾ cup commercial mayonnaise, or homemade
4 teaspoons Dijon mustard
1 tablespoon fresh lemon juice (omit if making mayonnaise)
Large pinch cayenne pepper
Sweet paprika, for garnish

Prepare and peel the eggs (see box). Slice each in half lengthwise through the yolk. Combine the yolks and the remaining ingredients except paprika in a small mixing bowl. Whisk until smooth.

Pipe the filling through a pastry bag fitted with a number 4 star tip, which is ¼ inch across, into the egg white, mounding it slightly. Sprinkle with paprika and serve at room temperature. The eggs can be cooked and the filling made a day in advance, both refrigerated. Pipe the filling into the eggs up to an hour in advance. Refrigerate.

Variations

• Add 3 tablespoons French Olive Spread (page 22) or Olivada (page 22) to the egg yolk mixture.

• Add ⅓ cup each finely minced yellow onion and celery to the egg yolk mixture. Use a plain round tip for piping the filling into the egg.

• Substitute ⅔ cup Spicy Rémoulade (page 37) for the mayonnaise. Add ½ teaspoon salt and decrease the mustard to 2 teaspoons and the lemon juice to 2 teaspoons.

Toppings

Each deviled egg half can be topped for decoration and for taste. The basic filling can be topped with a few capers, ⅛ teaspoon of a medium good caviar, say salmon roe, or a sliver of smoked salmon, a leaf or two of fresh chervil, tarragon or minced Italian parsley, or an herb flower. A French Olive Spread or olivida-enriched stuffing can be topped with an olive sliver, a bit of anchovy or a curled roasted-red-pepper strip.

pickled beets

I like these beets. Serve them with Cold Cooked Salmon (page 179) or Roast Loin of Pork (page 286) or turn them into Crimson Menace (page 19). You will use the leftover liquid for the gorgeous Beet Pickled Eggs (below).

Makes 8 cups

**4 pounds beets, scrubbed, cooked (page 184), peeled and sliced, or 3 cans (15 ounces each) sliced beets
20 whole black peppercorns
12 whole allspice berries
12 whole cloves
1½ cups dry red wine
1 cup water
¾ cup red wine vinegar
½ cup sugar
3 tablespoons kosher salt**

Drain beets and, if desired, reserve liquid. Transfer the beets to a deep 8-cup container (a soufflé dish works well).

In a 2 x 2-inch square of cheesecloth, tie up securely the peppercorns, allspice and cloves. Combine the red wine, water, vinegar, sugar and salt in a 4-quart nonaluminum saucepan over medium heat. Add the spice bag and heat to boiling. Boil 2 minutes. Pour the spice mixture over beets and cool to room temperature. Cover securely and store in the refrigerator at least two days or up to one week before serving.

beet pickled eggs

These are beautiful, like endpapers in an Italian book or oil slicks in a wet road that I stared at as a child. Peel them before serving, as in box. Serve with a shaker of Seasoned Salt

(page 49) or a bowl of Mayonnaise (page 32) or Tartar Sauce (page 36). Allow one egg per person.

Makes 12 eggs

**Juice retained from canned beets in Pickled Beets, or from 3 cans sliced beets
12 large eggs
¾ cup water
½ cup red wine vinegar
¼ cup pickling spices
¼ cup sugar
2 tablespoons kosher salt
1 tablespoon whole black peppercorns**

Drain the beets, reserving the liquid (save the beets for another use—see Pickled Beets above).

Place the eggs in a 3-quart saucepan. Add the reserved beet juice and water. Heat to boiling over high heat. Immediately reduce the heat to simmering. Simmer the eggs exactly 10 minutes.

Pour the beet liquid into a medium saucepan and set eggs aside to cool. Add remaining ingredients to the saucepan. Heat to simmering, simmer 2 minutes and remove from the heat.

When the eggs are cool enough to handle, spank them gingerly one by one with a wooden spoon until they are covered with fine cracks but the shells are still intact. Place the eggs in a tall, thin 2-quart jar (or two 1-quart jars) into which they fit comfortably with about 1 inch of headspace. Pour the warm pickling liquid over the eggs. There should be enough to cover. If not, add warm water as necessary.

Cool the eggs to room temperature, cover the container and refrigerate at least 2 days and up to 3 days before serving. Peel eggs. Bring to room temperature at least 30 minutes before serving.

chapter 3

crusts and shells

Many of the foods in this book come in neat packages to be picked up by fingers, toothpicks or a small fork. Still others are dippers or are dipped into and require no package. Then there are those that require a home before they are easily usable or edible by the guests who stand and the informal hosts. That is where the recipes in this chapter come into their own—the pastries, baked crusts and breads that serve as savory holders for salads, spreads, pâtés, cold meats, sausages and smoked fish. To liven things up, a few of the filling and topping recipes are given here

as well, but you will find many more in Chapters 1, 2, 4 and 6 or by looking in the Index.

There are other bases. See the suggestions for cooked and raw vegetables for stuffing (pages 72–73); the vegetable pancakes (page 84); the blini and crêpes (pages 220–221); the Phyllo Shells (page 213); Crisp New Potato Shells (page 241) and the Oven-Fried Potato Chips (page 233). When you are thinking of holders for somewhat messy foods like Pacific Overture (page 174) and Beet and Herring Salad (page 184), you may want to small seafood shells that have been emptied

People who no longer feel happy eating a large amount of quiche seem very happy to eat these mini ones filled with well-seasoned quiche fillings, such as Tomato-Basil (page 99), or a variation you invent, such as defrosted frozen peas and blanched asparagus tips in the Scallion-Pea Quiche Filling (page 99).

and cleaned (see box, page 174) as holders. Other good possibilities are tiny ceramic ramekins and even soup spoons holding, say, an individual oyster, hot or cold.

In this chapter, the doughs that are used for barquettes, tartlets and blind baked shells come first. These are the homes for the gooier mixtures and more than bread-slicking amounts of spreads. They also house miniature quiches—the recipes are here—or can be formed into crisp straws on their own.

There are a few recipes using bought puff pastry (pages 103–105). I don't attempt teaching the dough in this book.

Cream puff dough, Pâte à Choux (page 106), can be used on its own or be baked and filled. Then there are miniature biscuits (pages 108–109) to split and use for sandwiches of anything from ham and cheese to Crab Cakes (page 187).

Finally, on page 110, you will arrive at the breads, from loaf breads for slicing to focaccias to brioche, along with a myriad of ways to use them from Fried Bread Boxes (box, page 121) to Tea Sandwiches (page 118) to heros for slicing, as well as suggestions for toppings and fillings and recipes for them.

ready-mades

Some doughs are available from freezer or refrigerator sections of stores. I heartily recommend taking advantage of them. Buy puff pastry and phyllo or strudel leaves to keep in the freezer. Some uncooked bread doughs are available refrigerated. They won't keep forever; check the expiration date on the package. They are useful in emergencies for Pigs in Blankets (page 200) and Pizzas (opposite page).

Some stores sell dough-wrapped hors d'oeuvre, but I find them relatively unacceptable and I have never met a pre-made pastry shell I liked.

Availability of store-bought breads, doughs and crackers varies enormously with where you live. If you find breads that seem sensational for parties, consider buying a few, wrapping them tightly and individually and freezing them to keep on hand. See page 111 for reheating frozen breads like focaccia. Some packaged breads, like party rye, keep for a long time if their package isn't opened. Dried or toasted breads are useful for any party giver: Melba toast, bagel chips or pita chips along with bread sticks. Store-bought pita and mini-pitas will keep for about a week in the package.

Indian stores sell packages of thin breads for cooking; some are quite good and keep well. Lavash in packages will keep about two weeks. Various kinds of dry Scandinavian flat breads keep virtually indefinitely, as do crackers and English biscuits such as Bath Olivers and wholemeal biscuits. French pastry shops often sell cheese straws that they make with the trimmings from their pastry. These are so easy and inexpensive to make (pages 103–104) that I seldom buy them, but it's good to think about in an emergency.

mini-pizzas

Pizza is a perennial favorite with adults and children alike. My favorite is the closest to the kind I have eaten on the Costa Amalfitana—no sauce. You can vary these with other ingredients, such as Roasted Peppers (page 58) or grilled eggplant (page 82). The bought dough works perfectly well, but if you are inspired, make the focaccia dough of your choice (pages 128–129) and adapt your pizza to suit. For instance, top Olivada Focaccia dough with a little extra olivada before adding other ingredients.

Makes 24 pizzas

7 cherry tomatoes
10 ounces store-bought refrigerated bread dough, or Focaccia (page 128)
¼ cup olive oil
⅔ cup loosely packed fresh basil leaves, cut crosswise into a thin chiffonade
Kosher salt

Pepper
1¼ cups grated mozzarella cheese (5 ounces)

Preheat oven to 400°F.

Cut tomatoes across into very thin slices and lay out on a double sheet of paper towels to drain for about 10 minutes.

Meanwhile roll dough into a sausage shape (about 18 inches). With a sharp knife cut across into 24 equal pieces. With the tips of your fingers knead each piece into a small ball on a lightly floured surface and then roll out each ball to a 3-inch disk. Place ½ inch apart on a baking sheet lined with parchment paper.

Place three slices of tomato on each piece of dough, slightly overlapping. Brush tops with oil so that the edge of the dough is also coated with oil. Scatter a little basil over tomatoes and lightly sprinkle with salt and pepper. Top with grated mozzarella.

Bake in the center of the oven for 12 minutes. Remove and allow to cool slightly before serving.

To Toast Pita

If using the pita bread for a sandwich, slice the bread across the middle. If you want the pita for dipping or spreading, slice all the way around the edge so that you have two flat disks. Cut each half into 12 wedges, so that each pita bread gives you 24 pieces.

To toast the bread, heat a conventional oven to 400°F. On a baking sheet, place as many pita pieces as possible in a single layer. Toast in the oven for 6 minutes, until they are golden brown. Turn the sheet around halfway through the baking if your oven has a hot spot that is toasting some of the pieces faster than others. Repeat with any remaining pita wedges.

93

A *cheerful spring party can draw on goodies from many countries.* **1** *Italian-style Roasted Peppers, yellow and red (page 58), marinated in oil (page 60) and topped with anchovies and barely lavender chive flower buds; also Italian,* **2** *Bread Sticks (page 129) and* **3** *Schiacciata (page 128); first-out-of-the-garden* **4** *cherry tomatoes and* **5** *baby carrots, and from the woods,* **6** *fiddlehead ferns—all of which go well with Middle Eastern visitors,* **7** *Eggplant Moroccan (page 10) and* **8** *Lamb Kabobs (page 269) with cherry tomatoes.* **9** *Fresh Mint Salsa (page 25),* **10** *Guacamole (page 13) and* **11** *blue corn tortilla chips represent Central America.*

savory pastries and shells

I am not a miniaturist like my friend Flo Braker, the superb baker and author of two books, *The Simple Art of Perfect Baking* and *Sweet Miniatures*, but there are times when a tiny tartlet, a shell for a mouthful of a well-seasoned filling, is just what is needed. It was Flo who, at a class I was teaching with James Beard, gave me a version of the recipe for the Cream Cheese Pastry. With her kind permission, I give it to you. It and the Sour Cream Pastry and its variant, Whole-Wheat Pastry, puff up in the baking, making light and airy pastry. The Flaky Tart Dough and the related cheese pastries make more conventional tart shells, with less puff, flakiness and fragility.

These tiny tartlets are really easy to make and can be baked and frozen ahead of time, and it's easier to plunk filling into a shell than to neatly spread it on a canapé. Take your choice.

All can be used for quiche (pages 98–99). The more fragile pastries do well with dollops of spreads, bits of smoked fish topped with sour cream and dill, chives or capers, or fish, chicken or meat salad. Remember, you can mix and match to the limits of your imagination.

While many different kinds of miniature tart pans—ranging in length from 3-inch barquettes (pointy ovals) to 1¾-inch fluted ovals and assortments—can be bought all neatly prepackaged, it is often more convenient to have a goodly number that are the same size. Since the pans are emptied as soon as the shells have partially or fully baked, you can keep producing baking sheet after baking sheet full of these tiny crisps. I wouldn't try to bake more than one sheet at a time. On the other hand, a variety of shapes is fun.

The first time you use the pans they should be thoroughly washed and dried and then wiped out with a paper towel that has been dipped in melted butter. After the first time, simply wipe the pans with paper towels; do not wash. The fat from the pastry will keep them in good shape and they will not need to be greased again. I keep each shape of tiny pan in its own plastic bag, otherwise they seem to roam all over the kitchen, eventually getting lost.

You need about 2 teaspoons of filling for each tartlet—therefore, ⅔ cup of filling will fill twenty-four shells. It will vary between smaller and larger pans and even between the puffy doughs and the flatter ones.

sour cream pastry

One of the light and crisp ones. It is pale in color even when baked. You may want to try this for individual dessert tarts filled with berries on their own or arranged over a layer of crème anglaise or glazed with a little melted jelly.

As a savory tart, try this fully baked with Tropical Shrimp Salad (page 169), Smoked Trout Mousse (page 146), Crunchy Vegetable Dip (page 17) or Chicken Salad (page 263).

To make a **Whole-Wheat Pastry,** *replace a quarter cup of the all-purpose with whole-wheat flour. Consider filling fully baked shells with Green Olivada (page 22), Ham Spread (page 45) or Chicken Liver Mousse (page 149). Top with a sliver of ham or minced parsley.*

Makes 10 ounces pastry

1 cup all-purpose flour
1 teaspoon kosher salt
4 tablespoons cold unsalted butter, cut into small pieces
⅓ cup sour cream

Combine flour and salt in a mixing bowl. Add butter and rub into the flour until mixture resembles coarse meal.

Stir in sour cream until fully blended and mixture comes together into a ball. Cover pastry in plastic wrap and refrigerate for at least 2 hours.

See box for rolling and baking instructions.

cream cheese pastry

Another white and flaky dough. This one is very easy to work with. The thick Taramasalata (page 31), French Olive

Spread (page 22), Rich Shrimp Salad (page 169) or one of the rémoulade sauces (pages 36–37) topped with a little cooked crab meat, a piece of shrimp or a Cod Ball (page 251) would make good mouthfuls.

Makes 12 ounces pastry

4 ounces cream cheese at room temperature (¹/₂ cup)
¹/₂ cup unsalted butter, at room temperature
1 cup all-purpose flour
³/₄ teaspoon kosher salt

Beat cream cheese and butter together in a mixing bowl until smooth and creamy. Add flour and salt and gradually work into the dough until mixture comes together to form a ball.

Cover with plastic wrap and refrigerate for at least 2 hours.

See box for rolling and baking instructions.

flaky tart dough

This is the basic French tart dough, **pâte brisée**. It holds up very well. If you want to fill the fully baked shells several hours before the party, after they have come out of the oven but before unmolding, brush the insides of the shells with a little lightly beaten egg white. Put the baking sheet of shells back in the oven for two minutes. Then remove and unmold. This seals the shells so that they don't get soggy. These are the shells used individually for quiches.

Makes 14 ounces pastry

1¹/₂ cups all-purpose flour
³/₄ teaspoon kosher salt
¹/₂ cup cold unsalted butter, cut into small pieces
1 egg, lightly beaten
1 teaspoon milk

Making Pastry Shells

partially and fully baked

On a lightly floured surface roll out dough to about ¹/₈ inch thick. Cut out pastry shapes to fit your pans and press in pastry using your knuckles. Prick the base of the pastry in each pan twice with a fork and place filled tins on a baking sheet. Re-roll pastry scraps to use up all pastry. Each 2- to 3-inch mold needs about ¹/₂ ounce of pastry per tartlet shell. This means that 1 pound of pastry will make about 32 shells. If you are going to make the quiches (pages 98–102), only partially bake the shells. If you are going to fill the shells with an already cooked or raw mixture, you will need to bake the shells fully.

Preheat oven to 350°F with rack in center. Place shell in the oven and bake for 12 minutes for **partially baked** and 17 minutes for **fully baked** crusts.

Remove from oven; tip baked shells out of pans and transfer to a wire rack to cool completely. The partially baked shells can be filled with any quiche mixture and baked as for quiche recipes (pages 98–102). Fully baked shells can be used immediately, or they can be carefully packed in airtight boxes and kept at room temperature for up to two days. Do not fill until shortly before using. Partially baked shells that are not being used immediately for quiche should be carefully packed in plastic bags and stored in the refrigerator for a week or freezer for up to a month.

Partially baked and frozen or refrigerated shells for use as quiches should be re-placed in tins and allowed to come to room temperature before filling and normal baking. Partially baked and frozen or refrigerated shells to use as containers for precooked mixtures should be placed on a baking sheet (not air-cushioned) in a 350°F oven: from room temperature, the shells take 4 minutes; directly from the refrigerator, 6 minutes; directly from the freezer, 8 minutes.

Parmesan Pastry
¹/₄ teaspoon additional kosher salt
¹/₄ cup grated Parmesan cheese
2 teaspoons additional milk

Cheddar Cheese Pastry
¹/₄ teaspoon additional kosher salt
³/₄ teaspoon dry mustard
¹/₈ teaspoon cayenne pepper
¹/₄ teaspoon caraway seeds, optional
¹/₃ cup grated Cheddar cheese
2 teaspoons additional milk

Combine flour, salt, spices and cheese, if using, in a mixing bowl. Add butter and rub into the flour until mixture resembles coarse meal.

Add beaten egg and milk and gently work mixture together until it forms a ball. Cover pastry in plastic wrap and refrigerate for at least 2 hours.

See box for rolling and baking instructions.

miniature quiches

These savory mouthfuls—to serve hot, warm or cool but not chilly—are a godsend for the cook. The pastry shells can be made well ahead; the fillings can be made a day or so ahead and returned to room temperature before filling the shells for the final baking. The completed quiches can be frozen after baking and being allowed to cool. *Reheat quiches from frozen* in a single layer on a baking sheet (not air-cushioned) for ten minutes at 350°F.

To make miniature quiches with the pastries above in 2- to 3-inch molds, choose a pastry dough—remembering that you will need about ½ ounce of pastry per quiche, so the number of quiches you can make depends on the dough quantity. Multiply or divide the dough or the filling recipes until they match pretty well and you come out with the number of quiches you need. All shells for quiche should be *partially baked* (see box, page 97, for instructions), then frozen or refrigerated if you wish. I allow three per person, but if this is the only thing you are serving—which is fine—you will need at least six per person.

Any of the cooked fillings can be used in most of the pastry cases. The Cream Cheese and Sour Cream pastries work very well with all the fillings and the Whole-Wheat pastry works very well with Salmon and Leek filling. When making a variety of different quiches, any extra amounts of fillings can be mixed together and baked in pastry shells.

miniature anchovy basil cheesecakes

This is not a traditional quiche. Well, I thought, since everybody seems to like cheesecake, why don't I make a little nonsweet one to go with drinks? These can be made ahead, frozen and reheated as needed.

Makes 60

10 ounces cream cheese, at room temperature (1¼ cups)
¼ teaspoon kosher salt
⅛ teaspoon freshly ground black pepper
2 large eggs, plus 1 egg yolk
½ cup plain yogurt
2 medium cloves garlic, smashed, peeled and minced
8 oil-packed anchovy fillets, finely chopped
1 tablespoon chopped fresh basil leaves
60 unbaked tartlet shells

Place cream cheese, salt and pepper in the bowl of an electric mixer and beat until smooth. Add eggs and yolk one at a time, beating well after each addition. Add yogurt and mix until well combined. Stir in remaining ingredients. Let stand for 30 minutes so flavors blend.

Preheat oven to 350°F. Place tartlet shells on a baking sheet (not air-cushioned). Fill each crust with 2 teaspoons of the filling. Bake for 20 minutes. Turn oven off and leave baking sheet in oven for another 10 minutes.

Remove from oven. When cool enough to handle, remove cheesecakes from pans, using the tip of a sharp knife to loosen them if they stick. Place on a rack to finish cooling. Serve warm or at room temperature.

mushroom quiche filling

This is basically a very simple quiche jazzed up with a faintly anise flavor, which blends into the mushrooms, intensifying the flavor rather than concealing it. If like me you are a mushroom hunter, wild mushrooms take this up a definite notch in flavor. You can use fresh farmed shiitake, but I think other store-bought wild or semiwild mushrooms (like oyster mushrooms) are really too expensive to be worth it.

Makes ⅔ cup filling, for 24 quiches

1 tablespoon unsalted butter
3 ounces fresh small domestic mushrooms, wiped clean, trimmed and coarsely chopped by hand
⅓ cup heavy cream
1½ teaspoons Pernod
1 egg
2 teaspoons chopped fresh dill sprigs or fennel fronds
Kosher salt, to taste
Freshly ground black pepper, to taste

Preheat oven to 375°F.
Melt butter in a small skillet over medium heat. Stir in mushrooms and cook for about 2 minutes, or until they just start to give off some liquid. Stir in cream and Pernod and continue to cook for about 2 minutes, or until mixture comes to a boil.

Remove from heat and allow to cool to room temperature.

Lightly beat egg in a small mixing bowl. Stir in mushroom mixture with dill or fennel. Season to taste with salt and pepper.

Fill partially baked pastry shells and bake for 10 minutes. Remove from oven and allow to cool slightly on a wire rack before serving.

tomato-basil quiche filling

More elegant and formal than a pizza, this quiche shares much of pizza's flavor and pleasure.

Since the tomato sauce in this recipe uses only half a can of tomatoes, I often double the recipe or just the Tomato Sauce. What is left of the sauce can be used to top puff pastry, as in Greeks on Air (page 103).

Makes ⅔ cup filling, for 24 quiches

10 medium cherry tomatoes, each cut across into 3 slices
Kosher salt

Tomato Sauce
1 teaspoon olive oil
½ medium onion, peeled and coarsely chopped (½ cup)
½ can (14½-ounce can) Italian plum tomatoes, drained and chopped
¼ teaspoon lemon juice

1 egg, lightly beaten
¼ cup heavy cream
2 tablespoons chopped fresh basil leaves
Freshly ground black pepper, to taste

Place sliced cherry tomatoes in a single layer on a double piece of paper towel. Sprinkle with 1½ tablespoons kosher salt and allow to drain for at least 15 minutes.

Preheat oven to 375°F.

To Make Tomato Sauce. Heat oil in a small skillet over medium heat. Stir in onion and cook, stirring occasionally, for about 10 minutes, or until golden brown. Stir in drained, canned tomatoes. Cover with lid, reduce heat to low and cook, stirring occasionally, for about 10 minutes. Remove lid and cook for 4 minutes longer, or until almost all liquid has evaporated. Stir in lemon juice. Remove from heat and allow to cool to room temperature.

In a small mixing bowl combine egg with cream and basil. Season to taste with salt and pepper. Stir in the Tomato Sauce (or half of it if you have doubled the recipe). Fill partially baked pastry shells with mixture and top each one with a slice of cherry tomato. Bake for 10 minutes.

Remove from oven and allow to cool slightly on a wire rack before serving.

scallion-pea quiche filling

A pretty vegetarian quiche filling. It can even be made in winter if you use the small frozen peas. Try the Parmesan Pastry (page 97) for the shells.

Makes ⅔ cup filling, for 24 quiches

2 tablespoons unsalted butter
1 bunch scallions, white and green parts cut across into ¼-inch slices (about 1 cup)
3 tablespoons water
1 egg, lightly beaten
¼ cup heavy cream
¼ cup very small frozen peas, defrosted in a sieve under warm running water, or tender fresh peas
Kosher salt, to taste
Freshly ground black pepper, to taste
¼ cup grated Parmesan cheese

Preheat oven to 375°F.

Melt butter in a small skillet over medium heat. Stir in scallions and water. Cook, stirring, for about 8 minutes or until scallions are very soft and almost all liquid has evaporated.

Remove from heat and allow to cool slightly.

In a medium mixing bowl combine egg with cream and peas and season to taste with salt and pepper.

Fill partially baked pastry shells with mixture and sprinkle cheese over top. Bake for 10 minutes.

Remove from oven and allow to cool slightly on a wire rack before serving.

99

We have so integrated Italian cooking into our lives that it is nice sometimes to emphasize its integrity. Besides, as this Italian gala will prove, almost everybody loves the food. You don't need to make all of this to have a good party. Think of this as a list of suggestions from which to choose: **1** *Vegetable Brochettes (page 78);* **2** *Tomato Focaccia (page 129);* **3** *Tomato Basil Dipping Sauce (page 27);* **4** *Crostini (page 131) with Chicken Liver Spread (page 132), Softened Juniper Berries (page 132) and sage leaves;* **5** *Sun-Dried Tomatoes cut in pieces and topped with olive slices (page 10);* **6** *Cannellini Beans with Tuna Fish (page 183); country bread;* **7** *Caponata (page 14);* **8** *Mini-Pizzas (page 93);* **9** *Mozzarella in Carrozza (page 243) with* **10** *Anchovy Caper Sauce (page 243); and a platter of figs with thinly sliced prosciutto.*

leek-smoked salmon quiche filling

This is probably the most generally popular of the bite-sized quiches that I do. It certainly stretches a small amount of salmon a long way.

Makes 1 cup filling, for 36 quiches

1 tablespoon unsalted butter
1 medium leek, trimmed and well cleaned, white and very pale yellow-green parts finely chopped (about ¾ cup)
1 egg, lightly beaten
¼ cup heavy cream

Pinch ground nutmeg
Kosher salt, to taste
Freshly ground black pepper, to taste
3 ounces smoked salmon, finely chopped by hand

Preheat oven to 375°F.

Melt butter in a small skillet over medium heat. Add chopped leeks and cook, stirring frequently, for about 5 minutes, or until very soft but not browned. Remove from heat and allow to cool slightly.

In a small mixing bowl combine egg, cream and seasonings. Stir in leeks.

Place about ¾ teaspoon chopped salmon in the base of each partially baked pastry shell. Fill with mixture and bake for 10 minutes. Remove from oven and allow to cool slightly on a wire rack before serving.

You can buy bread sticks for munching on their own or to wrap with prosciutto or thinly sliced cheese. Homemade (page 129) are cheaper, better and variable with different herbs.

puff pastry

Quite good puff pastry can now be bought. This is one of the few pastries used in this book for which I don't give instructions. Most good French cookbooks or a good baking book like Paula Peck's *Fine Art of Baking* will give instructions for puff pastry if you really want to make it. Incidentally, puff pastry defrosts very quickly once it is taken from the freezer—about ten minutes.

greeks on air

The circle of puff pastry makes a crisp and airy little cloud that has a dollop of a faintly Greek-tasting tomato-olive mixture baked on top. These are simple and quite addictive. Allow at least four per person, but while you're at it make the whole recipe—they are sure to get eaten.

You can elevate a Catalan by using a little Romesco Sauce (page 9), a North African with Eggplant Moroccan (10), a Provençale with French Olive Spread (page 22), or use Green Olivada (page 22), Brandade of Sole (page 32) or Sun-Dried Tomato Dip (page 8) in the center of these instead of the sauce in the recipe. You will need about a half cup of any of them for one package of dough. Or use a tiny bit of various dips—if you are making them anyhow for a party—on different circles to have assorted colors and flavors. If you have an oval cutter, it will make a pretty variation as well.

If you like to work ahead, after you roll the dough lightly and cut it out, form the depression in the middle with your finger. You can now either put the formed disks in an airtight package (such as a sealable plastic bag) in the freezer, or fill each depression with your chosen mixture and put the filled circles of dough on a plate or platter in the freezer. When frozen, place in freezer container. They will keep

six months without topping, two weeks with topping. Cook from frozen, as in recipe.

Makes about 50 rounds

½ cup Plum Tomato Sauce (page 27)
2 tablespoons chopped pitted Kalamata olives
Kosher salt, to taste
Freshly ground black pepper, to taste
1 pound to 18 ounces (depending on the size of the package) frozen puff pastry, defrosted (usually 2 sheets)

Combine tomato sauce, olives and salt and pepper. Open out sheets of pastry if folded. On a lightly floured surface, roll each sheet slightly into a shape approximately 10 inches square. Using a 2-inch round cookie cutter with sharp edges—not a glass—cut out rounds of dough, 5 across and 5 down. Make a circular depression in each round with knuckle or fingertip, leaving a rim of untouched dough around the depression. Freeze (see above) or bake. Place on an ungreased baking sheet (not air-cushioned). Preheat oven to 400°F with rack in center. In the center of each dough circle make a heaping ½-teaspoon blob of the tomato-olive mixture. Place baking sheet in oven and bake for 12 minutes. While first batch is baking, repeat with second sheet of dough. Serve hot or warm.

If baking from frozen, put on baking sheet and bake 14 minutes.

These may be reheated in a 325°F oven for 2 to 3 minutes.

pastry straws

Puff pastry straws are a traditional and slightly fancy snack that are very easy to make with store-bought puff pastry. You can also make pastry straws with many other doughs, or just use up your dough trimmings. Choose flavorings from the Optional Flavoring list that follows. I wouldn't use more than two flavorings at a time. A seed and cheese combination is always good.

The straws can be served hot or cold and can be made ahead, frozen and reheated. They are good friends. Allow around four per person.

Wafers *can be made by cutting rolled pastry (not puff pastry) into 1-inch squares and diamonds, seasoning as follows, if desired, and then baking at 350°F for 8 minutes. Use these as nibbles.*

Puff pastry straws can be frozen in plastic containers or bags and then reheated on a parchment-lined baking sheet at 350°F for 4 minutes. Straws made with other pastries can be kept refrigerated for up to a week without freezing in bags or boxes. They are then reheated just like the puff pastry straws.

Makes about 25 to 30 straws

8 to 9 ounces (depending on the size of the package) frozen puff pastry, defrosted (usually 1 sheet)
or
8 ounces pastry (pages 96–97): Sour Cream, Cream Cheese, Parmesan or Cheddar Cheese

(continued)

103

Optional Flavorings
1 to 3 tablespoons grated Parmesan, Cheddar, Gruyère, pecorino or caciocavallo cheeses
¼ to 1 teaspoon caraway, poppy, sesame, celery or anise seeds
Seasoned Salt (page 49)
Sheila's Dry Dunk (page 70)
Other powdered spices such as ground pepper, sweet paprika, cayenne pepper, chili powder or cumin

Egg Wash
1 egg
2 tablespoons water

Preheat oven to 425°F if using puff pastry or 350°F if using other pastry.

To Make Puff Pastry Straws
Place rectangle of pastry on a lightly floured surface, opening if folded. You will need a rectangle about 9½ × 9 inches. If your sheet or piece is smaller, roll out to the proper dimensions. Sprinkle 2 tablespoons of cheese, if using, and/or any additional ingredients in a wide band across the center third of the pastry. Fold one third to the center and sprinkle with remaining tablespoon cheese, if using. Fold other third over to form a new rectangle. With a roll of the pin, seal the visible folded-over edges at each end of the rectangle so that the cheese will not fall out. Then roll from one sealed edge toward the other to form a rectangle about 12 × 8 inches.

To Make Other Pastry Straws
On a lightly floured surface roll out pastry to form a rectangle about ¼ inch thick. Sprinkle the surface with the desired ingredients. Lightly roll the pastry to make the additions adhere to the pastry (it should be about ⅛ inch thick).

Lightly beat the egg and water together with a fork.

To Bake All Straws. Trim the edges of the dough and cut across into ⅓-inch-wide strips. Carefully twist each strip 5 or 6 times to form long curls and place on an ungreased or parchment-lined baking sheet (not air-cushioned) about 1 inch apart, pushing down on the ends of each curl of dough to keep them curled. If necessary, fill two or more baking sheets and cook one at a time. Brush curls with a little of the egg wash and bake for 10 minutes. For regular pastry straws, brush again with egg wash and bake 8 minutes more.

Remove from oven and transfer to a wire rack to cool completely.

pissaladière

One of the delights of the French Riviera is a little strip of an onion-anchovy tart normally served warm and cut into pieces to eat before the first course or as a snack. I have had it made with puff pastry and with bread dough. The bread-dough version is probably more authentic and is certainly easier to pick up in your fingers. The puff pastry version is more gala, more fragile and easier to make if you use store-bought dough. The main recipe uses puff pastry. At the end are instructions for using focaccia dough instead.

While I was working on these, it occurred to me that they would be just as delicious with nontraditional fillings and toppings. Bake yellow bell pepper strips on top of the sun-dried tomato filling or pretty scallions or chives on top of the mushroom filling (when cooked, place a parsley leaf at each crossing of the scallions or chives) and bake the red cabbage filling without toppings and dot after baking with sour cream and chopped dill.

Makes 48 hors d'oeuvre pieces

Onion Filling
6 tablespoons olive oil
2 pounds yellow onions, peeled and coarsely chopped in a food processor (4 cups)
1¼ teaspoons anchovy paste
¼ teaspoon red wine vinegar
Freshly ground black pepper, to taste
or
¼ cup Sun-Dried Tomato Dip (page 8) per strip
or
¼ cup of Mushroom Purée (page 73) recipe
or
¼ cup Sweet and Sour Red Cabbage Strudel Filling (page 214)
1 pound to 18 ounces (depending on the size of the package) frozen puff pastry, defrosted (usually 2 sheets)

Toppings
1 can anchovy fillets in oil, cut lengthwise into thin strips
24 Niçoise olives, pitted and halved
or
A Roasted Yellow Pepper (page 59) cut into strips, or thin strips of scallion or chive about 3 inches long with parsley leaves, or sour cream and chopped dill sprigs
Egg wash of 1 egg yolk with 1 tablespoon cold water

To Prepare Onion Filling. Heat 2 tablespoons oil in a medium skillet over medium heat. Add onions and stir to coat with oil. Reduce heat to very low and cook for about 50 minutes, stirring occasionally so onions do not stick, or until onions are soft and golden brown.

Increase heat to high and cook, stirring constantly, for about 10 minutes, gradually adding the remaining oil so that the onions become slightly darker brown.

Remove from heat and continue to stir for a few

minutes longer, until the onions have cooled slightly. Stir anchovy paste and vinegar into onions seasoned with black pepper.

To Bake. Preheat oven to 425°F.

Cut each sheet of pastry across into 4 strips, each about 3 × 9 inches. Place 4 pastry strips on each of 2 baking sheets (not air-cushioned).

Spread about 2 tablespoons of the onion mixture (or other chosen filling) down the center of each dough strip, leaving about ¼ inch all around the edge. Crisscross anchovy strips (or other topping strips) diagonally across filling, forming 4 crosses along each strip. Arrange 6 olive halves—if using onion filling—equally spaced, on top of each dough strip. Brush the pastry edges with egg wash. Bake one sheet (4 strips) at a time in the center of the oven

for 15 minutes, keeping the other sheet in a cool place.

Remove from oven and allow to cool on a wire rack while baking remaining strips.

To serve, slice each strip across into 6 pieces.

These can be made completely a day ahead and then reheated in a 350°F oven for 5 minutes.

Pissaladière with Basic Focaccia Dough

Use 1 recipe of the dough (page 128) risen for 1 hour. Preheat oven to 350°F. Divide the dough into 4 equal pieces and form each into a long sausage shape. With your fingers flatten each piece into a strip about 14 × 2 inches. Place on a baking sheet (not air-cushioned) that has been sprinkled with 1 tablespoon cornmeal. With your thumb and index finger form

At the Italian end of the French Riviera, they make a delicious strip of crisp pastry with a savory filling and garnish to slice for hors d'oeuvre. The Pissaladière can be made with bread dough as well. Traditionally, it has an onion filling crisscrossed with anchovies, but it can be made in many other ways. Here it is made with Sun-Dried Tomato Dip (page 8) and strips of yellow pepper.

ridges down the edges of each strip. Spread 1 tablespoon of a filling mixture down the center of each strip and top as above. Bake in the center of the oven for 20 minutes.

Remove from oven and finish as above.

To serve, cut off ends and slice each strip across into 10 pieces.

pâte à choux

This is the pastry familiar to most of us in cream puffs and éclairs. By filling the baked puffs with ice cream or pastry cream and topping with melted chocolate, you can achieve nice miniature desserts.

I use the simplest baked version of this dough to make Miniature Choux Puffs (opposite page), warm or cooled. To fill, slice the top off with a serrated knife; add salads, spreads and the thicker dips (see Index) and then topped with the cut-off lids. As a bonus, I follow the basic recipe with a Sunny Tomato Filling (opposite page).

There are two fairly standard variations of cheese puffs: the classic gougère, a Burgundian savory to eat with Kir (page 268) or a glass of wine, and Cheddar and Bacon Puffs, which are only a slight variation of the classic.

These pastries, when baked, can be made up to two weeks ahead of your party and frozen. Allow to cool after baking; put in a plastic freezer bag. When ready to use, preheat the oven to 350°F with the rack in the center; remove as many as desired from the freezer; place on a baking sheet; heat for eight minutes.

Once again, allow three or four of these—of any one kind or assorted—per person.

These doughs can be made into light, crisp **Deep-Fat–Fried Puffs.** Push—with a second spoon —heaping teaspoons of the dough into oil that is a full 375°F (at a lower heat they will not puff properly). Each batch will only take about thirty seconds to puff up and turn a lovely gold. Remove to paper towels to drain. If the fried puffs cool off, they can be reheated on a parchment-lined baking sheet in a 350°F oven with the rack in the center for five minutes.

Eat these as they are or dusted with salt. Do not attempt to stuff; they are too soft.

Miniature Choux Puffs can be made well ahead and filled with any salad or dip that isn't too liquid—here with Sunny Tomato Filling.

miniature choux puffs

These are the basic baked puffs to fill.

Makes 96 miniature puffs

1 cup water
½ cup unsalted butter, cut into ½-inch pieces
½ teaspoon kosher salt
1 cup all-purpose flour
4 large eggs

Place water, butter and salt in a heavy medium saucepan and bring to a simmer over medium heat. When butter has melted, reduce heat to very low. Stir in flour. Whisk until mixture is smooth and shiny and forms a ball around the whisk. Remove from heat.

Beat in the eggs one at a time, making sure each is thoroughly incorporated before adding the next.

Preheat oven to 425°F. Line two baking sheets (not air-cushioned) with parchment paper. Using a pastry bag with a number 8 (plain round ⅝-inch), tip, pipe pâte à choux onto the baking sheets in ½-inch mounds. Bake for 15 minutes. Rotate baking sheets. Turn oven down to 300°F and bake puffs until golden brown and very lightweight, about 20 minutes. Using a skewer, poke a hole in the side of each puff to release steam. Place on a rack to cool.

When choux balls are completely cool, slit them in half horizontally almost all the way through. Scoop out any uncooked dough in the middle.

sunny tomato filling

This is an easy filling to make if you have Sun-Dried Tomato Dip on hand. Since that dip makes a large quantity and keeps well, it is not too improbable. The filling is a golden orange glow.

Makes 2 cups; fills about 60 choux puffs

1 medium yellow bell pepper, stemmed, seeded and cut into 2-inch pieces
1 cup cottage cheese
1 cup Sun-Dried Tomato Dip (page 8)
1 tablespoon water
¼ teaspoon curry powder
¼ teaspoon turmeric
Kosher salt, to taste
Freshly ground black pepper

Place yellow pepper in work bowl of food processor and process until almost smooth, stopping the machine and scraping down the sides of the bowl occasionally. Remove from work bowl and place in a sieve lined with a double piece of cheesecloth. With your hands strain out juice.

Return yellow pepper to food processor and add cottage cheese and Sun-Dried Tomato Dip. Process to combine.

Combine water with curry powder and turmeric in a small bowl. Cook at 100% in a high-wattage oven for 1 minute; 1 minute 30 seconds in a low-wattage oven; or on top of the stove in a very small covered pan over very low heat for 5 minutes. Remove from oven and scrape mixture into mixture in food processor. Process until as smooth as possible. Season to taste with salt and pepper.

Fill each choux puff with about 1½ teaspoons filling.

cheese puffs

This is the Burgundian gougère. It can be energized with a little cayenne pepper. Taste the cheese and decide if you need salt.

If you want cheesier bites, make the cheese puffs and allow to cool; save. When reheating (opposite page), top each one with a half teaspoon of grated Gruyère, squeezing the cheese together a bit to help it stay on. You need a half cup of cheese for a whole recipe. Broil until cheese melts. It will not brown.

To turn cheese puffs into anglicized Cheddar and Bacon Puffs, use Cheddar and crisp bacon.

Makes approximately 50

1 recipe Miniature Choux Puffs
1 cup grated Gruyère or Parmesan cheese
or
1 cup grated Cheddar and
16 thick slices bacon, cut into ¼-inch squares

Preheat oven to 425°F.

If using Cheddar and bacon, cook bacon in a medium sauté pan over medium heat until crisp. Remove bacon with a slotted spoon. Drain.

Stir cheese and bacon, if using, into warm pâte à choux. Line 2 baking sheets (not air-cushioned) with parchment paper. Using a pastry bag with a number 8 (plain round ⅝-inch) tip, pipe dough out in 1¼-inch mounds or drop by rounded tablespoons.

Bake for 15 minutes. Rotate baking sheets. Turn oven down to 300°F and bake until golden brown and lightweight, about 20 minutes. Serve hot or place on a rack to cool. If cooled, refrigerate or freeze, serve as they are, or reheat.

107

miniature biscuits

Biscuits, the American kind, risen and flaky, take well to miniaturization. In that form, they can be used to make attractive sandwiches. The sandwiches can be made ahead of time, or the biscuits can be set out with fillings so that guests can make their own. A basket of Spicy Cheddar Buttermilk Biscuits (opposite page) can be set next to a baked ham on a board with a sharp knife, a wedge of Swiss cheese, a selection of mustards and possibly a crock of Mustard-Anchovy Butter (page 43). I usually surround the ham with some precut slivers and the cheese with some small slices to give people the idea. Encourage guests to make their sandwiches.

Imagine Buckwheat Biscuits (opposite page), more solid than blini, set out with smoked fish and crocks of Horseradish Butter (page 45), Dill Butter (page 42), sour cream and lemon wedges or Jalapeño Cheddar Biscuits (this page), accompanied by any of the cheese or ham spreads (pages 38–45) and a salsa (pages 23–25). Thinly sliced Beef Fillet (page 282) with Green Peppercorn Butter (page 43) would do well on Whole-Wheat Biscuits (see headnote, opposite page). The thicker of the vegetable dips (pages 8–19) would go neatly into Buttermilk Biscuits (this page), possibly with a slice of cheese added, for vegetarian friends.

These sandwiches are particularly good at very informal get-togethers such as those surrounding a sporting event—at home or tailgating.

The recipes can be easily multiplied for large parties or if you want to make extras to freeze for another party.

To make ahead, wrap biscuits airtight and freeze. *To reheat,* heat oven to 350°F with rack in center. Place biscuits on a baking sheet and cook for eight minutes if small or ten minutes if large.

Very cold vegetable shortening can be substituted for butter if desired.

Forming Biscuits

Remove dough from bowl and place on a floured surface. Knead 2 or 3 times. On a floured surface, pat or roll the dough into a ½-inch-thick circle. Using a 1¼-inch or a 1¾-inch cutter, cut out as many biscuits as possible, flouring the cutter frequently to prevent sticking. Gather scraps into a ball, flatten and cut as above.

Place biscuits 1 inch apart on a baking sheet lined with parchment paper.

If a glossy appearance is desired, brush tops with milk or an egg lightly beaten with a little water before baking.

---

cornmeal biscuits

Think of these as a less crumbly cornmeal bread, rather Southern. The jalapeño variations make them more Southwestern.

Makes 52 1¼-inch or 20 1¾-inch biscuits

1½ cups plus 2 tablespoons all-purpose flour
1¼ cups yellow cornmeal
4 teaspoons baking powder
1 tablespoon sugar
1½ teaspoons kosher salt
1 large egg
1 cup plus 1 tablespoon milk
3 tablespoons vegetable oil

Preheat oven to 350°F. Position rack in lower third of oven.

Place dry ingredients in a food processor and pulse to combine. Add remaining ingredients except 1 tablespoon of the milk and process just until combined. Form as in box.

Brush tops of biscuits with milk. Bake for 12 minutes for smaller biscuits, 15 minutes for larger biscuits. Remove from oven and transfer to a wire rack.

Jalapeño or Jalapeño Cheddar Biscuits

Use 4 medium jalapeño peppers, seeded and quartered; if making Jalapeño Cheddar, use ½ pound Cheddar cheese, cut into ½-inch cubes, and 1 teaspoon additional all-purpose flour. Place peppers and cheese and flour, if using, in food processor. Process until finely chopped. Add dry ingredients and finish recipe as above.

---

buttermilk biscuits

Buttermilk usually makes bread and pastries more tender; these are the traditional, melt-in-your-mouth biscuits. If you don't mind vegetable shortening, substituting it for the butter will give you an even more tender texture, if a little less flavor—hey, we pay for everything.

Makes 60

2 cups all-purpose flour
½ teaspoon baking soda
1¼ teaspoons baking powder
¾ teaspoon kosher salt
½ cup plus 2 tablespoons unsalted butter, cut into ½-inch pieces
⅔ cup buttermilk

Preheat oven to 400°F. Position rack in lower third of oven.

Place dry ingredients in a

food processor and pulse a few times to combine. Add butter and pulse until mixture resembles coarse meal. With motor running, pour buttermilk through the feed tube and process just until dough forms into a ball. Form as in box.

Bake for 14 minutes. Remove from oven and transfer biscuits to a rack.

Spicy Cheddar Buttermilk Biscuits

Use ½ teaspoon additional kosher salt, ½ teaspoon sweet paprika, ⅛ teaspoon cayenne pepper and 2 ounces Cheddar cheese (½ cup). Add additional salt and spices with dry ingredients. Add cheese after the butter, processing just until combined.

buckwheat biscuits

These are Blini (page 220) alternatives. Buckwheat flour can be found at health food stores and through mail order sources specializing in baking. Put in a plastic bag and store in the freezer. If you use a cup of all-purpose flour and a cup of whole-wheat flour, you will have a very good **Whole-Wheat Biscuit.**

Makes 48

1 ½ **cups all-purpose flour**
½ **cup buckwheat flour**
2 **tablespoons wheat germ**
2 ½ **teaspoons baking powder**
2 **teaspoons kosher salt**
Freshly ground black pepper, to taste
⅓ **cup unsalted butter, cut into ½-inch pieces**
⅔ **cup milk**

Smoked fish is an easy, if expensive, Ready-Made (page 165) that deserves an interesting bread. The whiteness of sliced sturgeon goes well with the brown of Buckwheat Blini (page 220) or Buckwheat Biscuits. Add a crock of a softened flavored butter (pages 42–45) for sandwich making if you like.

Preheat oven to 400°F with rack positioned in lower third of oven. Place dry ingredients in a food processor and pulse a few times to combine. Add butter and pulse until mixture resembles coarse meal. With motor running, pour milk through the feed tube and process just until dough forms into a ball. Form as in box.

Bake for 14 minutes. Remove from oven and transfer biscuits to a rack.

109

Cheese Puffs with Melted Cheese (page 107), the Burgundian classic gougères.

bread

Rice may be the staff of life to more of the world than wheat flour and its triumphant creation, bread, but not in the world of finger foods and stand-up parties. We need bread to slice and maybe even grill or toast; breads to use for canapés and sandwiches; breads to stuff for sliceable hero sandwiches; bread sticks and also bread that makes a snack on its own, such as focaccia with different toppings or even little pizzas made with bread dough. Miniature brioches and brioche bread for special events like weddings take time but are well worth doing.

We can certainly ask why we should make our own bread when so many good breads can be bought (page 92). There is pleasure for many of us in kneading and baking bread, as well as savings in cost and the wonderful smell of bread baking. More pragmatically, there are many specialty breads we may find it hard to buy and which can give our parties distinction. It is hard to find unsliced loaves for slicing lengthwise and rolling. We need breads like the soda breads (page 114) and Pain de Mie (page 119) to make really attractive, delicious canapés, tea sandwiches and smørrebrød, as they will have a denser texture (better for spreading) and a better flavor.

Besides, it's practical. Bread keeps brilliantly in the freezer. Slice your baked bread into large chunks—enough for one party—and freeze (see Freezing and Defrosting Loaf Breads).

bread baking hints

Some instructions hold true for almost all bread baking and certainly the recipes in this chapter. Instructions that are relevant only to yeast breads are in the box on page 122.

Picking Baking Sheets and Pans

Baking sheets should be of high quality and a good weight so they don't curl with oven heat. Black steel and heavy stainless are both good. Air-cushioned baking sheets, which are made with two layers of metal separated by air, are good for some purposes, such as cookies, but will keep many free-form loaves from cooking properly. Unless air-cushioned baking sheets are called for, do not use them. *Baking pans* can be metal, glass or ceramic. Metal pans will cook your loaves somewhat more slowly than the others. Pan sizes are standard. The only exception is the *Pullman pan,* a loaf-bread pan with a flat top that slides into place. Pullman pans come in many sizes. Recipes are given for one size, or for the Improvised Pullman Pan (see box, page 115), which most of us may be using. If using another size Pullman pan, see Multiplying Recipes.

Preparing Baking Tins, Pans and Sheets

Usually, such pans are either greased with butter or oil or lined with parchment paper so as to keep the food from sticking as it bakes. Follow recipe instructions. For an efficient way to oil pans by spraying, see page 140. When using or making a Pullman pan, grease interior of lid and slides.

Multiplying Recipes, Dividing Dough

Make as many multiples of the dough as you like. Measure the dough by weight or cups in order to see how much should fit in your pan(s). I now advocate a small calculator as well as a scale.

To adjust the dough to the pan when making multiple batches of breads or using smaller pans than those indicated, it is best to divide off the amount of dough you will need for each loaf by weighing out the dough rather than trying to jam it into measuring cups. That way, you will not overhandle the dough and will also get a more accurate result.

If you are using *Pullman pans* (see above) and have pans of sizes other than those listed in the recipes, the general rule is to determine the volume of the pan and to use just over one-third as much dough by volume if working with a yeast dough and two-thirds as much dough by volume if using a soda batter. If you have any question, it is better to use too little dough rather than too much. Too little dough may provide a less than perfectly shaped loaf, but too much dough will cause the top of the pan to stick so you think you will never get the bread out.

Forming the Dough

Soda breads (page 114) and other batter breads should be scraped into the prepared pan(s). It is important to push firmly on the uncooked bread mixture with the scraper and then firmly bang the tin on a counter—covered with a doubled cloth if the pan is glass—to eliminate air bubbles. Once the dough for *yeast breads* (pages 119–122) has been made and has risen, divide as above if the recipe makes more than one loaf or if you have multiplied the recipe. After the dough is divided, form it into balls. Flatten the ball(s), fold the sides under and tuck in each end. Place each piece of dough in a well-oiled pan or form as in recipe; smooth the top with your hand, gently stretching the dough into the corners of the pan. Let rise as recipe directs.

Testing for Doneness

After cooking, turn out of pans or lift from baking sheets. Rap bottom and top of loaf with knuckles. The bread will sound hollow when done. If needed replace loaves sans tins in oven until done. If breads are not meant to be served hot, allow unmolded loaves to cool on racks: do not slice until cool; bread continues cooking as it cools. Focaccias are eaten warm. Loaf breads for slicing, cool.

Baking Times for Multiple Loaves

When baking more loaves at a time than called for in the recipe instructions, baking times will go up about ten minutes for each additional loaf. At the end of the time given in the recipe, test for doneness (above).

Freezing and Defrosting Loaf Breads

One reason to make multiple loaves is that the bread freezes very well. A whole, cooled loaf can be wrapped in plastic wrap and then in aluminum foil. To defrost, remove aluminum foil and allow bread to sit at room temperature for about an hour or until it can be sliced, or wrap in plastic and cook at 100% power in a microwave for 5 minutes. If you think you may be in a hurry when you want to use the defrosted bread or may just want to use a few slices at a time, slice the bread before freezing; separate the slices with pieces of parchment or wax paper and wrap as above.

To defrost: Heat oven to 350°F with rack in center; take out as many slices as you want, seal up the remainder and replace in freezer. Remove paper from slices to be used; place them on a baking sheet; reheat for four to five minutes or until soft but not browned. Use immediately or wrap loosely in a kitchen towel.

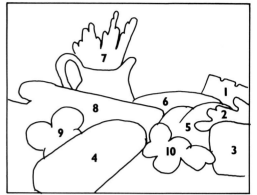

A *variety of breads to use for parties or for every day.* **1** *Pain de Mie (page 119);* **2** *Cheese Straws (page 103);* **3** *Cheese-Filled Focaccia (page 129);* **4** *Brioche Bread (page 132);* **5** *Olivada Focaccia (page 129);* **6** *Herb Focaccia with sage (page 128);* **7** *Bread Sticks (page 129);* **8** *store-bought Italian bread;* **9** *Hamburger Buns (page 125);* **10** *store-bought miniature pitas; Buttermilk Biscuits (page 108).*

soda breads

I want to boast a little. The next two breads are a bit unusual and I think a technical triumph. The problem with making yeast breads even in the machine age is that it takes so long. You can mix and knead with machines and force the dough in the microwave oven (page 122), but rising still takes time, which must be added to baking time.

"What breads," I asked myself, "are quicker?" "Soda breads, quick breads," I answered. The problem with those lovely breads for our purposes is that they are soft and rather porous. They don't make a really satisfactory base for canapés or sandwiches, since they are likely to collapse under the load or leak butters and dressings.

I've come up with a solution. The best white yeast bread normally made for this purpose, Pain de Mie (page 119), is molded into a neat form and a denser texture than it would have if baked free-form or in uncovered loaf pans by being baked in special pans. I have fitted my soda breads into the same pans—Pain de Mie or Pullman pans. The trick works wonderfully. Nobody to whom I have served the bread has guessed the secret until told. They all thought it was "real bread." Using this trick, I am able to get the time for preparing the dough and baking the bread down to one hour.

These pans come in a variety of sizes; however, I have only given dough amounts for one size of pan. This same amount fits in the improvised Pullman pan (see box). To multiply and divide dough for other pans, see page 111.

whole-wheat soda bread

This bread was my starting point and is closely related to the wonderful breads served all over Ireland and in England, thinly sliced and lightly buttered, as an accompaniment to smoked salmon. It is not a bread from which I would remove the crusts—even for canapés for which I would simply slice the bread thinly across the loaf and then cut the slices into four even squares.

Think of this bread with meats, pâtés, smoked fish and cheeses. Canapés (page 116) or Tea Sandwiches (page 118) using it can be made up to three hours ahead and covered with a lightly dampened kitchen towel. The bread will be fine.

Makes 2 pounds, 6 ½ ounces dough (4 cups), or 1 medium loaf; 30 thin slices; 120 canapés

2 ½ cups whole-wheat flour
1 cup all-purpose flour
¼ cup plus 2 tablespoons rolled oats
3 tablespoons wheat germ
1 tablespoon kosher salt
1 ¼ teaspoons baking soda
2 cups plus 2 tablespoons buttermilk
Vegetable oil for greasing pan

Preheat oven to 425°F with rack in lower third of oven. Thoroughly oil the insides, lid and closing elements of a 10 × 3 ½ × 3-inch Pullman pan or an 8 ½ × 4 ½ × 2 ½-inch loaf pan.

Combine dry ingredients in a large bowl. Make a well in the center and pour in the buttermilk. Stir until combined. Dough will be slightly sticky. Press into prepared pan and smooth top. If using a loaf pan, see box for instructions.

In either pan, bake for 15 minutes. Turn the oven down to 350°F.

If using a Pullman pan, continue to bake for 30 minutes.

If using a loaf pan, continue to bake for 45 minutes. Carefully remove weights and baking sheet. Bake for 10 minutes longer if pan is glass, 15 minutes longer if pan is metal.

Turn bread out of pan and place on a rack to cool completely before slicing.

rye soda bread

For most of their lovely smørrebrød, Scandinavians use a densely textured rye bread called limpa. This is not a true limpa, as it is not yeast-raised. If you use milk, you will have a somewhat softer and sweeter bread than if you use water. Some Scandinavian cooks make this a rather sweet bread with a slightly darker color by including molasses. I find the molasses flavor limits the kinds of foods that can be piled on the bread. Since smørrebrød are normally laden with lots of food, the support of the crust is a help and it should not be cut away. I don't cut it away in any case.

Makes 2 ¼ pounds (4 cups) dough, or 1 medium loaf; 30 thin slices; 120 canapés

Vegetable oil for greasing pan
3 cups rye flour
1 ¾ cups all-purpose flour
1 ½ teaspoons baking soda
2 tablespoons kosher salt
1 ¼ teaspoons caraway seeds
1 ½ teaspoons fennel seeds, ground
2 tablespoons melted unsalted butter, cooled to room temperature
1 ¾ cups water or milk

Preheat oven to 425°F with rack in lower third. Thoroughly oil the insides, lid and closing elements of a 10 × 3½ × 3-inch Pullman pan or an 8½ × 4½ × 2½-inch loaf pan.

Combine dry ingredients in a large bowl. Make a well in the center and pour in the butter and water or milk. Stir until combined. Dough will be slightly sticky. Press into prepared pan and smooth top. If using a loaf pan, see box for instructions.

In either pan, bake for 15 minutes. Turn the oven down to 350°F. Continue to bake for 50 minutes.

If using a loaf pan, carefully remove weights and baking sheet. Bake for 10 minutes longer if pan is glass, 15 minutes longer if pan is metal.

Turn bread out of pan and place on a rack to cool completely before slicing.

Improvised Pullman Pan

Use a regular loaf pan in glass or metal that is 8½ × 4½ × 2½ inches and that can contain 6 cups. Oil the bottom of a baking sheet. Place the filled loaf pan in oven, cover with the baking sheet, oiled side down, and weight with a very heavy object, such as a brick. This will not work well with less than 6½ pounds of weight. Do not use full cans for weights, as they may explode. Rocks are fine.

Canapés (page 116) are infinitely variable if you have the patience. A simple and pretty one is made with Pain de Mie (page 119) covered with Watercress Butter (page 43) and topped with overlapping red-rimmed slices of radish. Keep the radish slices in cold water until it's time to serve; the bread can be cut and buttered ahead.

Bread for Small Sandwiches

The best breads for canapés and small sandwiches are Soda Breads (page 114), Pain de Mie (page 119) and the Brioche (pages 132–133).

If removing crusts, slice off from whole loaf with sharp serrated knife. Then slice loaf across or lengthwise (depending on use) into thin slices. Cut into shapes as desired. If using cookie cutters, slice the bread lengthwise for maximum yield. You can pile up unspread or unbuttered bread and cut through about four thin slices at a time. Many people find it easier to spread the bread before cutting it into shapes. Take your spread or butter from the refrigerator before cutting the bread. Use a cookie cutter or sharp-rimmed glass for **round** canapés.

Without any special cutters, **squares** (equal-length sides) and **rectangles** (normally twice as long as wide) and **strips** (rectangles are only a third as long as wide) can be sliced.

You can make **triangles** or **diamonds** by slicing the loaf lengthwise and slicing it on the diagonal into 1½-inch strips. Now cut the strips across to form triangles or diamonds.

Canapés (this page) are open sandwiches of single-bite or two-bite squares, rectangles, circles or fancy shapes of rather thinly sliced, fairly firm bread, usually crustless (sometimes toasted), that won't easily get soggy, break or bend under the weight of its load.

They are slicked with a butter or a spread (pages 42–45) and topped with either a garnish or a slice of some other food, such as smoked salmon or pâté, which may in turn be garnished.

A **tea sandwich** (page 118) normally is two of the rectangular crustless pieces formed into a closed sandwich with a butter, a spread and a thinly sliced vegetable—peeled, seeded, salted and drained cucumbers or peeled tomatoes—or a thinly sliced meat. Both canapés and tea sandwiches get stale easily, so it is a good idea to cover them with a barely damp kitchen towel, or plastic wrap covered with a damp kitchen towel, between the time they are made and the time served. Make up to two hours ahead.

Fancy versions prevalent in the thirties and forties featured ornate patterns made from layering different colored breads and fillings. I always thought they were very messy to eat and a bother to make.

Smørrebrød (opposite page) are substantial Scandinavian open sandwiches normally made with a whole crosswise slice of bread, the crusts left on for greater strength. Smørrebrød make a good informal party on their own with beer and aquavit. For cocktail parties, I often make them with half-slice rectangles for greater manageability, allowing 3 per person.

canapés

See the box: Bread for Small Sandwiches. Italian canapés are discussed in the box on page 131. The bread may be toasted or not. Sometimes it is lightly buttered before toasting. The following are just a few ideas that can be made with recipes from this book. Since I'm not really mad for the fidgety work of making most pretty canapés, I don't suggest as many as you can invent. Those I have suggested require very little work.

The idea is for the bread to be spread with a compound butter (pages 43–45) or cheese spread (pages 39–42) or vegetable or other mousses (see Chapter 4 or the Index). If a butter or cheese spread is used, a slice of a firmer ingredient—vegetable, egg, cooked meat, smoked fish or cheese—is placed on top. Finally, this is usually garnished with a minced herb; a sliver of cooked or uncooked vegetable; smoked, canned or marinated fish; capers; bits of nuts or fruits; slices of Cornichons (page 152) or olives; dollops of chutneys (see Index) or other sauces, such as salsas.

Choose toppings and breads that seem to suit: lighter-tasting or very elegant toppings on the white breads (page 119) and the Brioche Bread (page 132); vegetable, salad and meat toppings on Whole-Wheat Soda Bread (page 114).

Watercress Butter (page 43), radish rounds; Mustard-Anchovy Butter (page 43), Sliced Hard-Boiled Egg (see box, page 88), rolled anchovy garnish; Liptauer without yogurt (page 18), coil of Roasted Pepper (page 58); Scallion Cream Cheese (page 42), slice of smoked salmon, snipped chives; Dill Butter (page 42), cooked shrimp (page 168) halved lengthwise, dill sprigs; Smoked Salmon Cream Cheese (page 39), sliver or roll of smoked salmon with caper in center; Blue Cheese and Port Spread (page 39) topped with walnut half; Mayonnaise (page 32), thin slice avocado, thin slice cherry tomato, finely chopped fresh coriander (cilantro); Prosciutto Spread (page 45), slice of black olive; Minted Butter (page 43), thin slice cucumber, mint sprig; chèvre, thin slice cherry tomato, basil leaf.

Possible Smørrebrød Toppings

These will all do best on Rye Soda Bread (page 114), which is firm and normally not toasted: Herring salads (pages 184–185), Egg Salad and variations (page 88), thinly sliced turkey (page 267), Prosciutto Spread (page 45), Ham Spread (page 45), Liptauer without yogurt (page 18), cheese spreads (pages 39–45), chicken liver preparations (page 132, 149–150), Marinated Anchovies (page 182), fish and seafood salads (page 169) and Steak Tartare (page 275), a favorite garnished just with a little chopped onion and a few capers.

Those catering to vegetarians will need to be a bit less traditional: remember sliced cheeses, eggs, tomatoes (plum tomatoes are less messy to eat), lettuce leaves, herbs, the spreads on pages 72–73 and the vegetarian mousses and pâtés on page 135 as well as asparagus tips (page 70).

Don't forget all the sliced meats, sausages, smoked fish and cheeses you can buy. The Danes wouldn't.

Meat Selections
Mustard-Anchovy Butter (page 43) with Pork Liver Pâté (page 161) and a curl of anchovy; Chicken Salad (page 263) with Watercress Butter (page 43) and a lettuce leaf; sliced roast chicken on Curry Butter (page 43) with a spoonful of chopped Green Pickled Lemons (page 55); Turkey Pâté (page 151) with Sage Butter (page 42) and Cranberry Ketchup (page 267); Roast Loin of Pork (page 286) with Coriander Butter (page 43), Japanese pickled ginger and Plum Chutney (page 150); roast beef with Horseradish Cream Cheese (page 39) or Mustard-Anchovy-Butter (page 43) and a watercress sprig; Beef Fillet (page 282), thinly sliced and rolled on Green Peppercorn Butter (page 43); Chicken Liver Crock with Apples and Onions (page 149) with thin slices of peel-on apples.

Fish Selections
Herrings and smoked fish preparations (pages 184 and 165) are traditional on smørrebrød. Put the salads in lettuce leaves; cover the bread with a compound butter (pages 42–45). Lay out a piece of prepared fish or slices of mousses and pâtés on Curry, Dill or Horseradish Butter (pages 43, 42 and 45), a thin layer of sliced onion and a sprig of an appropriate herb. Spinach and Fish Pâté (page 147) can sit on whole spinach leaves topped with Green Goddess Dressing (page 37); Maître d'Hôtel Butter (page 43) with salmon caviar and chopped chives; Tiny shrimp are traditional piled on bread spread with a plain or compound butter with perhaps a lettuce leaf and garnished with a bit of lemon or dill; Sardine Paste (page 45) goes with filleted sardines, tiny lemon slices and chopped red onion; Horseradish Cream Cheese (page 39) can be topped with Cured Salmon (page 176), a Lemon Twist (page 294), or Dill Butter (page 42), Sweet Mustard Sauce (page 29) and dill sprigs.

This is an absolutely classic canapé made with toasted Pain de Mie or bought white bread that is coated with Mustard-Anchovy Butter (page 43), a slice of Hard-Boiled Egg (page 88) and a rolled-up anchovy.

tea sandwiches

I love afternoon tea, with its finger sandwiches and little tartlets (pages 96–97) or glazed Choux Puffs (page 107) or Whole-Wheat Soda Bread (page 114) thinly sliced, buttered and cut in half. Tea sandwiches were always good for garden parties and wedding receptions at which ladies wore hats, and gloves they didn't want to soil.

I still like tea sandwiches at cocktail parties. In fact, if they are the only hors d'oeuvre, the party can be quite simple to do, especially if you can buy good bread. Remove the crusts from your bread (page 116). Slice it thinly lengthwise. Spread one side of half the slices with a cheese spread (pages 39–42), a meat spread (page 45) or a liver spread (pages 132, 149–150). Top with another slice of bread, even of a different sort, and slice crosswise into rectangles. If using fillings that are not spreads, cover all the slices with a compound butter (pages 43–45). Add a simple filling to half the buttered bread slices and top with another slice, butter down. Cut.

All the sandwiches can now be neatly piled onto plates, covered with a piece of plastic wrap and a damp cloth until the guests arrive (refrigerate if there is more than an hour between making the sandwiches and serving them) and brought to room temperature if necessary, uncovered and served.

The most classic—remember *The Importance of Being Earnest*— are made with peeled and thinly sliced cucumber, Watercress Butter (page 43) or other compound butter (page 43–45), or thinly sliced tomato, or mustard cress on Pain de Mie (opposite page).

Thinly sliced smoked salmon, ham and chicken are the most often used solid fillings, along with sliced hard-boiled eggs and egg salad.

One favorite trick of mine is to put the tomato slices on the buttered bread and then to whir up some chutney in a blender, spread that on the tomatoes and then top with another slice of bread. These are a bit gooey, so it is best to cut the bread up after it is buttered and fill the sandwiches one by one.

Think of James Beard's famous brioche bread rounds spread with mayonnaise—some claim that only commercial mayonnaise will work—sandwiched with a thin slice of onion. The rims of the sandwiches were then thinly spread with mayonnaise and rolled in very finely chopped parsley. A similar trick can be done with whole-wheat bread, a cheese spread and very finely chopped nuts.

yeast breads

There are many more yeast breads than soda breads in the world and in this book. For canapés and tea sandwiches, the most used are Pain de Mie (below) and the brioche breads (pages 132–133). They are not, on their own, my favorite breads, but they are very useful and can undergo many transformations. They are also rather hard to buy, so it is a good idea to know how to make them come party time. They freeze well.

I love the focaccias (pages 126–129) and their relative, the lighter Schiacciata (page 128). They can be used on their own, dipped into sauces or used as a base for sandwiches. They are intimately related to Italian bread, which is good for grilling and toasting as Bruschette and Crostini (see box, page 131). In some areas, an assortment of similar breads can be purchased. If you have a good source of supply, you may still want to read the various suggestions on how to use these breads.

pain de mie

This is the classic French white bread, with a fine texture that makes even slices and is the perfect base for canapés and tea sandwiches. It can also be cut lengthwise and rolled to make things like Cheese Pinwheels (page 201). It usually has its crusts removed before use.

The recipe can be doubled but only in a heavy-duty mixer or by hand. It cannot be doubled in a food processor. If you wish to more than double the recipe, you will have to make it by hand. To figure out how much dough you will need using a pan with a different size from that given below, measure the volume of the pan with water and use 40 percent as much dough by volume.

If you make more dough than your pan needs, there is really no problem, since the dough can be used for Hamburger Buns (page 125), or Fried Bread Puffs (page 125).

Makes I loaf

I cup plus 2 tablespoons milk, lukewarm
I 1/2 packages active dry yeast
2 1/4 teaspoons sugar
2 3/4 cups all-purpose flour
I 1/2 teaspoons kosher salt
I 1/2 tablespoons unsalted butter, cut into small pieces, at room temperature
I tablespoon chopped fresh Italian parsley leaves and I tablespoon chopped fresh tarragon leaves, optional
Vegetable oil for greasing pan

Combine milk, yeast and sugar in bowl of heavy-duty mixer or food processor. Let stand for 5 minutes to proof.

Add 1 cup of the flour and the salt, butter and herbs, if using, and mix or process until smooth. Gradually add 1 1/2 cups of the remaining flour and knead dough (see box, page 122).

Sprinkle a work surface with some of the remaining 1/4 cup flour. Turn dough out and knead a few times until dough is smooth, adding more of the flour

as necessary to make a firm, not sticky dough. Allow dough to rise twice (see box, page 122).

Oil an 8 1/2 × 4 1/2 × 2 1/2-inch loaf pan or a 10 × 3 1/2 × 3-inch Pullman pan very well. Form the dough, place in pan and let rise (see box, page 122). Do not let dough more than double; it should not be near the top of the pan.

Preheat oven to 400°F. If using a loaf pan, see box on page 115 for instructions. Place pan in lower third of oven and turn heat down to 375°F. Bake for 35 minutes if using a glass pan or 40 minutes if using metal. Turn bread out of pan and place directly on oven rack. Bake for 5 minutes longer. Place bread on a rack and cool before slicing.

Remove crust and slice into 1/8-inch-thick slices.

119

*F*ried Bread Boxes filled with sour cream and golden caviar or fillings and toppings of your choice.

Bread Boxes

In the traditional repertoire, these are called bread cases. The fussy part is cutting them out, but that can be done weeks ahead of your party. Tumble them into a large plastic bag, close the bag tightly and freeze. The day of your party, remove the bag(s) from the freezer. Spill the number of boxes that you will need out onto a counter or baking sheet, cover with a kitchen towel, allow to come to room temperature and cook as needed. I usually allow two or three bread boxes per person. These boxes are particularly good for sour cream, fish salads (pages 169, 183–184, 186) and Chicken Salad (page 263), things that are a bit messy to sit on top of bread.

To Form. Remove crusts from unsliced Pain de Mie (page 119), commercial white bread or Brioche (page 132) and cut into 1-inch cubes. With the tip of a paring knife, hollow out the center of each cube, being careful not to tear the sides.

To Bake. Preheat oven to 350°F. Place bread boxes on a baking sheet (not air-cushioned) and brush with melted butter. Bake for 10 minutes.

To Deep-Fat-Fry. Fry until golden brown, turning once, about 40 seconds (see page 236 for specific frying instructions).

Kneading and Raising Yeast Dough

Hand Kneading

Once dough ingredients are combined, rub hands with a little flour. Dust a work surface with flour. Form the dough into a ball. (As you knead, add as little flour as possible.) Push the ball of dough with the heel of your hand to flatten and stretch it. Fold flattened dough in half and turn it one quarter of a circle. Repeat until the sticky, shaggy blob of dough you started with is stretchy and smooth. The whole thing will take four to fifteen minutes. When the dough is sufficiently kneaded, blisters will break on its surface as you push. While most bread doughs, when ready, will spring back when you press a finger into it, focaccia and other soft, oil-rich doughs will not spring back.

Mixer Kneading

Once the dough ingredients are combined, clean the large bowl of the mixer and dust it with a little flour. Using a dough hook, knead the dough at a low speed for four minutes, scraping down the sides of the bowl from time to time. Remove from bowl to floured surface; finish by hand.

Food Processor Kneading

This machine can only be used for recipe sizes given—with the exception of the focaccia, which can be doubled. Other doubled recipes will either clog the machine or not knead well. Combine dough ingredients in food processor and allow to run until dough forms into a ball. Process 1 minute longer.

Raising Dough

(Also see Forcing Dough in a Microwave, below.) Form dough into a ball and put in a lightly greased bowl. Cover with a kitchen towel and let rise in a warm location until doubled in bulk—looking twice as large. If you are uncomfortable determining when dough has doubled, it can be placed in an 8-cup measure so you can watch its progress. Punch dough down—deflate it by pushing your hand into it once or twice. If more than one rising is called for, repeat, including the punching down.

Forcing Dough in Microwave

Prepare dough and place in a glass or ceramic bowl. Cover with a damp sheet of paper towel. Set bowl in a dish 3 inches deep and add warm water to fill the dish almost to the top. Heat at 100% in a high-wattage oven for 1 minute, or for 1 minute 30 seconds in a low-wattage oven. Leave oven door closed for 15 minutes. Rotate the bowl one-quarter turn and heat again in a high-wattage oven for 1 minute, or for 1 minute 30 seconds in a low-wattage oven. Let stand for 15 minutes more. Dough should be doubled in bulk. Do not use method for brioche (too warm) or sourdough breads (not enough flavor).

grilled cheese sandwiches

These are easy, attractive hot hors d'oeuvre which are usually broiled when made in these small sizes. They have the pleasure of childhood familiarity except for the unexpected form as two-bite-long strips. As they can be assembled up to two hours ahead and briefly grilled—two minutes—as needed, they are relatively painless. It is best to make just as many as you want as they are needed; they reheat indifferently. However, they need not be eaten boiling hot.

I allow about three pieces for each guest. Each recipe makes twenty-four sandwiches. These recipes can be multiplied.

Grilled American Cheese Sandwiches are the lunch-counter favorite spiced up with jalapeños. Without the peppers, these should do well with any children present, as should the Grilled Cheddar Cheese Sandwiches. More clearly for adults are the Grilled Mozzarella Sandwiches, the Grilled Blue Cheese Sandwiches and the Grilled Scallion Cream Cheese Sandwiches. The Grilled Reuben Sandwiches are hearty and ideal with beer for a party around a sports event.

Each kind of sandwich will use:
16 ⅛-inch-thick slices Pain de Mie (page 119), or 16 slices firm commercial white bread, crusts removed
6 tablespoons unsalted butter, melted

Grilled American Cheese
24 slices (16 ounces) American cheese, trimmed to make 48 1x3-inch pieces
4 medium jalapeño peppers, seeded through the stem and thinly sliced, optional
12 cherry tomatoes, thinly sliced, optional

12 slices cooked bacon, cut in half crosswise, optional

Grilled Cheddar Cheese

6 ounces Cheddar cheese, finely grated

2 tablespoons Dijon mustard, optional

12 slices cooked bacon, cut in half crosswise, optional

Substitute Mustard-Anchovy Butter (page 43) for the plain butter, if desired

Grilled Mozzarella

6 ounces mozzarella cheese, finely grated

12 cherry tomatoes, thinly sliced, optional

12 fresh basil leaves, optional

Substitute 6 tablespoons olive oil for the butter

Grilled Reuben

6 ounces thinly sliced Swiss cheese, trimmed to make 48 1 x 3-inch pieces

6 ounces thinly sliced corned beef, trimmed to make 48 1 x 3-inch pieces

8 tablespoons sauerkraut

2 tablespoons Dijon mustard

Grilled Blue Cheese

1 cup Blue Cheese and Port Spread (page 39)

Grilled Scallion Cream Cheese

1 cup Scallion Cream Cheese (page 42)

To Assemble and Cook Sandwiches. Preheat broiler. Cut bread slices into thirds (pieces should be about 1 × 3 inches). If using commercial bread, flatten slightly with a rolling pin. Place bread on a large baking sheet (not air-cushioned) and broil until lightly browned, about 2 minutes.

Assemble sandwiches with the toasted side toward the filling. If using fillings other than cheese, place them between two layers of cheese. Mash the sandwiches down slightly with your hand. Brush both sides of the sandwiches generously with butter or oil (according to recipe).

Place sandwiches on the baking sheet. Broil until golden brown on the bottom, about 1 minute 30 seconds. Turn sandwiches over and broil until golden brown on the bottom, about 30 seconds.

Grilled Reuben Sandwiches are one of New York's great inventions. Made in strips, they are easy to eat at a stand-up party or while watching a sports event on television, when the eyes are not on the food.

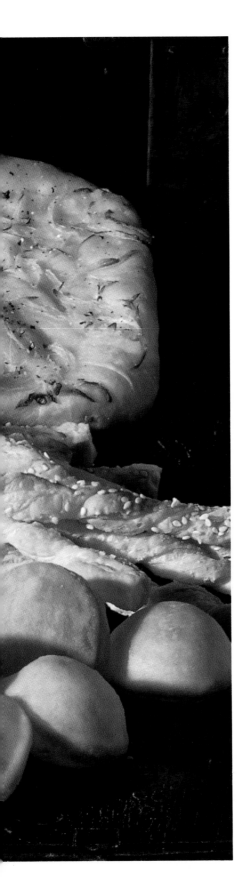

More breads: **1** onion-topped Schiacciata (page 128); **2** Fried Bread Puffs; **3** Miniature Choux Puffs (page 107); **4** Cheese Straws with various toppings (page 103); sliced commercial rye and pumpernickel breads.

hamburger buns

Good girl though I am, I probably wouldn't normally make my own hamburger buns, but for an informal party, particularly one with children, the miniatures are a real godsend. Since they can be made ahead and frozen, you can make some buns on a day when you are making the Pain de Mie in any case. Measure out what you want for your Pullman pan and use the remaining dough for buns. Since each miniature bun uses only a half ounce of dough, even a small amount of leftover dough is worth baking off in this form. A quarter pound of dough, for instance, will make eight little buns—enough for the children? Bake and freeze. Reheat the cooked and frozen buns as needed in an oven set to 350°F for five minutes for miniatures; seven for the regular size.

Hamburger recipes are on pages 279–280.

Makes 50 miniature or 8 regular buns

1 recipe Pain de Mie (page 119)
2 tablespoons poppy or sesame seeds, optional
¼ cup milk, optional

Make dough and let rise twice in bowl. Punch dough down. If making miniature buns, divide into ½-ounce pieces (2 teaspoons). Roll each piece into a ball and press with the palm of your hand to flatten as much as possible. If making regular buns, divide into 3-ounce pieces (⅓ cup). Flatten into a ½-inch-thick disk. Place buns 1 inch apart on a parchment-lined baking sheet. Let rise until doubled in bulk, about 40 minutes.

If desired, brush tops of buns with milk; sprinkle on seeds.

If making miniature buns, preheat oven to 350°F. Bake until golden brown, about 16 minutes. If making regular buns, preheat oven to 400°F. Bake until golden brown, about 20 minutes. Remove from oven to rack and cool before slicing.

Just before serving, preheat broiler. Place buns on baking sheet cut side up and broil until lightly browned, about 1 minute.

fried bread puffs

These crisp delights are another good way to use any leftover Pain de Mie dough. Each quarter pound of dough will make twenty small puffs (forty halves) or eight large puffs (sixteen halves). Two halves per guest is a good allotment. The puffs can be made ahead and halved for filling. Then store them for up to two days in an airtight container in the kitchen or freeze up to one month. Reheat in a 350°F oven for five minutes.

While store-bought mini-pitas can be filled in the same way, you may enjoy the crispness of these crusts. Half of a large puff will take two heaping tablespoons of filling. Each half of a small puff takes a heaping tablespoon. See Fillings in Index for a list of possible fillings or make Salsa Fillings (pages 23–25).

I recipe Pain de Mie (page 119)
Vegetable oil for frying

Make dough and let rise twice in bowl. Punch dough down. Divide dough in half. Roll out dough on a lightly floured surface as thin as possible. Using a 2-inch cutter to make miniature rounds or a 3-inch

cutter to make large rounds, cut out as many circles as possible. Gather scraps into a ball and set aside to rest. Repeat with remaining dough and then with scraps.

Place circles on a baking sheet, cover loosely with a towel and let rise until doubled in bulk, about 40 minutes.

Pour oil in a large skillet to a depth of ¾ inch. See page 236 for heating instructions. Working in batches, place rounds in hot oil and cook for a few seconds on each side, just until light brown. As rounds puff they may turn over once by themselves. Remove with a slotted spatula onto paper towels.

As soon as puffs are cool enough to handle, snip a hole with scissors and cut them in half perpendicular to the seam. If any are doughy inside, pull out excess dough and discard.

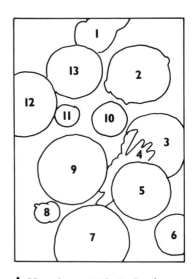

I Ham (page 288), **2** Greek Stuffed Grape Leaves (page 203), **3** Olivada Focaccia (page 129), **4** Puff Pastry Straws (page 103), **5** Sun-Dried Tomato Dip (page 8), **6** Lemon Spiced Olives (page 55), **7** Boiled Shrimp (page 168), **8** mustard, **9** Buttermilk Biscuits (page 108) filled with ham and Cheddar cheese, **11** Parsley and Scallion Dip (page 17), **12** Steamed New Potatoes (page 69) and **13** Pickled Beets (page 89).

focaccia

Focaccia is an Italian peasant loaf that is usually flatish and round, rich with the flavor of olive oil. It is capable of many variations. I also give instructions for baking it in a rectangular pan so that it is easily cut into square portions. Many of these breads can be served on their own or with a dipping sauce (pages 26–29) next to them so that people can dip as they go. Squares of focaccia can also be split in half and filled as sandwiches.

Delicious and crusty, served warm or cold, these are well worth making. I would use a good olive oil, but not by any means the strongest or most expensive. It will be good even with "pure" olive oil.

These recipes can easily be doubled. Divide the dough in half and form each part as instructed in the basic recipe. If possible, bake both loaves on the same oven rack. Otherwise, switch pans halfway through cooking.

Focaccia can be made up to two weeks ahead by partially baking the bread and freezing it. Bake for 35 minutes, remove from oven and cool slightly on a rack. While focaccia is still warm, place it in a plastic bag and seal the bag so that it is airtight. To finish baking, remove the frozen focaccia from the bag and place on a baking sheet (not air-cushioned) in an oven preheated to 350°F for 25 minutes.

Focaccia can be made the day or morning before use. Bake only 40 minutes. Cool on a rack; wrap tightly in plastic wrap. Unwrap, place on a baking sheet and reheat in an oven preheated to 350°F 5 to 6 minutes.

This dough is also used to make Calzones (page 220) and may be varied both in ingredients and in cooking technique to give a wide variety of tastes and textures. It's great fun.

basic focaccia

This is where the whole recipe is written out so that the variations that follow are easy. If you still have any questions, see Bread-Baking Hints (page 111) and Yeast Breads (page 119).

Makes approximately 16 wedges or 24 squares

1 package active dry yeast (¼ ounce)
¾ cup lukewarm (110°F) water
¼ cup olive oil, plus additional oil for greasing pan
2 teaspoons kosher salt
2¼ cups all-purpose flour

Topping
½ teaspoon olive oil
½ teaspoon kosher salt
Freshly ground black pepper

Food Processor Method. Place yeast and water in a food processor and process for a few seconds. Let stand for 5 minutes.

Add olive oil, salt and 1 cup of the flour to the yeast mixture. Process for 30 seconds. Add remaining 1¼ cups flour. Process for 1½ minutes to knead the dough.

Heavy-Duty Mixer Method. Place yeast and water in a mixer fitted with the paddle attachment. Mix a few seconds to blend. Let stand for 5 minutes.

Add olive oil, salt and 1 cup of the flour to the yeast mixture. Mix on low speed until smooth. Replace the paddle with a dough hook. Add remaining 1¼ cups flour. Mix on medium speed for 1½ minutes to knead.

Allow dough to rise once (see box on page 122).

Lightly coat a rolling pin and work surface with olive oil.

To Make a Round. Roll dough into a 10½-inch circle (dough will shrink to about 9½ inches).

Place on an oiled baking sheet (not air-cushioned).

To Make a Rectangle. Oil either an 8 × 11½ × 2-inch or a 7 × 11 × 2-inch baking dish. Roll dough into a rectangle slightly larger than the dish. Place dough in dish.

Allow dough to rise, until doubled. Preheat oven to 400°F. Make small indentations all over dough with a skewer or the handle of a wooden spoon. Gently spread olive oil over top of dough with your fingers. Sprinkle top with salt and pepper. Place pan in lower third of oven and bake 45 minutes.

Remove from oven. Cut into slices and serve hot.

Herb Focaccia
Use ⅓ cup loosely packed fresh sage leaves (½ ounce), OR 2 tablespoons fresh thyme leaves (⅛ ounce) and ¼ teaspoon freshly ground black pepper OR 1 teaspoon fennel seeds. Before processing yeast with water as in basic focaccia recipe, if using sage, place in food processor and process until finely chopped (or chop by hand until very fine, if making in mixer). Add yeast and water and continue recipe. When adding olive oil and 1 cup flour, add thyme and pepper or fennel seeds if using. Finish recipe.

Whole-Wheat Focaccia
Substitute ½ cup whole-wheat flour for that much all-purpose flour in the recipe; use 3 cloves garlic, smashed and peeled, and 1 teaspoon dry rosemary, ground in a spice grinder. Before processing yeast with water as in basic focaccia recipe, place garlic in food processor and process until finely chopped (or chop by hand if using mixer). Add yeast and water and continue with recipe. When adding olive oil and 1 cup all-purpose flour, add the rosemary. Add whole-wheat flour when adding the remaining all-purpose flour. Finish recipe.

schiacciata variation

Both the texture and flavor of schiacciata make it seem like a totally different bread from focaccia. Schiacciata has a lighter, more cakelike texture and a richer, less breadlike taste. After much experimentation, I have found that the only real difference between the two recipes is the abundance of olive oil used in the pan in which the schiacciata must be baked: there is too much oil for it to be a free-form round. Try making a double batch of focaccia dough and bake half as a focaccia and the other half like this variation. You will be amazed by the difference.

1 recipe Basic Focaccia dough (this page)
¼ cup plus 4 teaspoons olive oil
1 small onion (3½ ounces)
½ teaspoon kosher salt
Freshly ground black pepper, to taste

Make the Basic Focaccia dough. When dough has finished its first rising, place 2 tablespoons of the olive oil in a 7 × 11 × 2-inch baking dish. Coat sides and bottom evenly. Roll out dough as above to fit dish; place in dish. Let rise as above until doubled in bulk, about 1½ hours. Do not top with topping ingredients. Instead, thinly slice the onion and cut slices into ½-inch pieces. Toss with 4 teaspoons of the oil.

Gently prick all over top of dough with a fork. Coat top of dough evenly with the remaining 2 tablespoons of oil. Scatter onion mixture over dough. Sprinkle salt and pepper over onions. Bake for 20 minutes instead of as standard. Cover loosely with aluminum foil. Bake for 18 minutes more.

tomato focaccia

This is smashing to look at (see photograph page 26) and is good served with any of the tomato-based dipping sauces, particularly the Spicy Middle Eastern Tomato Sauce (page 27). If you add the tomato paste, the color will be more intense but the flavor will be a little sweeter.

Makes 1 loaf

**Ingredients for Basic Focaccia
   (opposite page), using only
   ¼ cup lukewarm water
¾ cup tomato purée (made
   from whole canned plum
   tomatoes with their fair
   share of liquid)
2 tablespoons tomato paste,
   optional
½ teaspoon additional kosher
   salt
¼ teaspoon additional freshly
   ground black pepper
½ teaspoon celery seeds
2 teaspoons ground cumin
⅛ teaspoon ground cinnamon
⅛ teaspoon ground nutmeg
½ cup additional all-purpose
   flour**

Combine yeast and water as in the basic recipe. Wait 5 minutes. When adding olive oil, add 1 cup tomato purée, the tomato paste, if using, 2½ teaspoons of the kosher salt, ¼ teaspoon of the pepper and remaining spices. Finish recipe, adding all the remaining flour.

olivada focaccia

This bears the same relationship to regular focaccia that squid ink pasta does to normal pasta. Here, the pronounced olive flavor is sensational. Serve with more

Black Olivada (page 22) on the side, with Tomato Basil Dipping Sauce (page 27) or as a sandwich, with sliced mozzarella, or on its own.*

Makes 1 loaf

**Ingredients for Basic Focaccia
   (opposite page), omitting
   olive oil and salt from main
   ingredient list
½ cup Black Olivada
   (page 22)
5 tablespoons additional
   all-purpose flour**

Make basic focaccia recipe, omitting olive oil and salt.

When dough has finished its first rising, punch it down. Knead a small amount of the olivada into the dough. Tear dough into small pieces and place in food processor. Add remaining olivada and additional flour. Process until dough forms into a ball and olivada is completely incorporated.

Roll dough out and let rise as in basic recipe.

Preheat oven to 275°F. Prepare top of dough as in basic recipe. Bake for 40 minutes. Raise heat to 400°F and bake for 25 minutes.

cheese-filled focaccia

This is a splendid recipe but it cannot be baked ahead and it doesn't reheat. If you want to work ahead, use another recipe. The advantage of this recipe is that it is really its own sandwich, a sort of portable fondue. It's good for a small party where you want something unusual and filling. Cut it as soon as it comes from the oven and serve warm.

Makes 1 loaf

**Ingredients for Basic Focaccia
   (opposite page)**

**1 tablespoon additional
   all-purpose flour
6 ounces Gruyère, cut into
   ½-inch cubes**

Make basic recipe through the dough's first rising.

Punch the dough down and divide into two equal pieces. Roll out one piece of the dough. Toss cheese cubes with the additional tablespoon of flour. Press the cubes into the dough, leaving a ½-inch border. Roll out the other half of the dough and place it over the cheese. Pinch edges together to seal. Carefully place in dish or on a baking sheet. Finish recipe.

bread sticks

Since very good bread sticks can be bought, I would make them only to get a distinctive flavor. These are very good. They can be made a few days ahead (up to a week in dry weather) and kept in an airtight container at room temperature. The recipe can be multiplied. Any other of the focaccia doughs would work as well.

It has become rather fashionable to wrap one end of a bread stick with a thin slice of either prosciutto or smoked salmon, which is a convenient way to serve these two things without making canapés.

Makes 32 bread sticks

**1 recipe dough for Herb
   Focaccia (opposite page),
   omitting Topping**

Make the focaccia dough through the dough's first rising. Line two large baking sheets (not air-cushioned) with parchment paper. Punch the dough down and divide into ½-ounce pieces (scant tablespoons). To form bread sticks, first roll dough between

129

the palms of your hands into a cylinder. Place on a work surface and use the flats of your fingers to roll dough evenly until you have a 14-inch length. Place on baking sheet and repeat with remaining dough. Allow dough to rise (this will only take about 15 minutes).

Preheat oven to 300°F. Place baking sheets in oven and bake for 15 minutes. Rotate baking sheets. Raise heat to 400°F and bake for 6 to 8 minutes, until brown on top. Remove from oven and transfer bread sticks to a rack.

An Insalata Caprese Hero is just one example of an easy way to serve diverse groups of ingredients, from those that normally go in salads to those from the deli counter. The bread is flavored with a good oil or a flavorful dressing. The whole thing sits long enough for the flavors to blend and then slices feed a crowd.

heros

Lots of people can be fed rather easily by making hero sandwiches. Some of my favorites are made only with cooked and raw vegetables.

Italian loaves or focaccias are sliced in half horizontally (some of the crumb can be removed) and the cut surfaces sloshed with or dipped in olive oil or a seasoned olive oil such as Bagna Cauda (page 29) or Anchovy Dip (page 29). One of the other dipping sauces (pages 26–29) may be substituted. Spread the bread with one of the mayonnaises (pages 31–38) or an olive dip or spread (pages 21–22), Caponata (page 14) or Roasted Red Pepper Spread (page 14). The bottom half of the spread-flavored bread is then covered with a choice of compact layers of cooked and/or raw

vegetables, thinly sliced cooked meats and cheeses. After the top of the bread is put on, the sandwich is pressed firmly to squash it slightly. It can now be wrapped up tightly and refrigerated for up to a day unless you insist on crisp bread, in which case you'll have to slice it and serve it immediately.

I am not just being lazy when I let the sandwich sit. The French and Italians have been making sandwiches—pan bagna—like this for years.

When ready to serve, hold the sandwich down firmly with the palm of one hand and cut it into 3/4-inch-wide strips. Transfix every small sandwich with a toothpick so that the pieces don't come apart on the serving tray.

By mixing and matching any of the layers below, you can create a hero. Don't add too many layers; people are going to eat these standing up and talking.

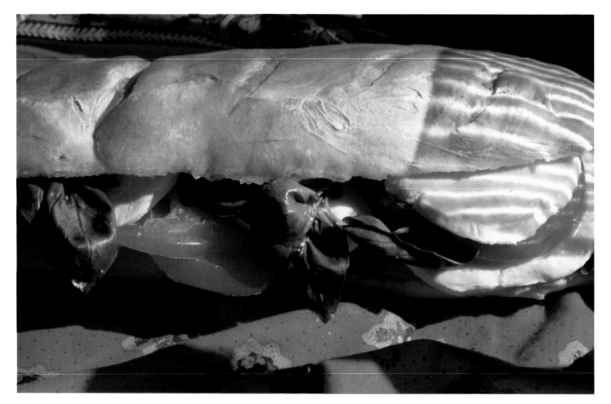

Makes 18 servings

Basics

1 16-inch loaf Italian bread or focaccia, sliced in half

¼ cup olive oil, or a dressing mentioned opposite, or oil from sun-dried tomatoes, if using those

Salt, to taste

Freshly ground pepper, to taste

Layer Choices

¼ pound thinly sliced cold-cut meat, such as salami or ham (about 20 slices), or Roast Loin of Pork (page 286), Roast Turkey (page 267) or Beef Fillet (page 282)

¼ pound thinly sliced firm cheese, such as provolone or Swiss (about 16 slices)

3 ounces reconstituted sun-dried tomatoes (see box, page 10), about 16 pieces

¾ pound Roasted Peppers (page 58), each cut into 6 strips

¼ pound eggplant (skin on), halved and cut in ¼-inch-thick slices (about 6), grilled or roasted (page 82)

¼ pound zucchini, cut in ¼-inch-thick, lengthwise slices, grilled or roasted (page 82)

2 plum tomatoes, cut across into ¼-inch-thick slices, about 14 pieces

1½ ounces red onion, peeled, halved and very thinly sliced

Salt, to taste

Freshly ground pepper, to taste

¼ cup stemmed and coarsely chopped fresh herbs

¼ cup sliced pitted olives

2 hard-boiled eggs (see box, page 88), peeled and sliced

Insalata Caprese Hero

¼ cup olive oil, ¼ cup whole basil leaves, 6 ounces mozzarella in ¼-inch slices (about 7 pieces), 6 ounces tomato in

Italian Canapés

By either simply slicing, toasting, sautéing or grilling slices of peasant bread or slices cut on the diagonal from long, thin bread, the Italians make canapés that keep rather well. Usually the bread is lightly oiled before, after or during cooking.

Crostini can be any kind of canapé of any kind of bread, toasted or not, but the type that gives me particular pleasure is thin, crisp—almost dry—and lightly brushed with olive oil before cooking. They can then be topped with a wide variety of spreads, the Chicken Liver Spread (page 132) being typical. Crostini are often confused with bruschette, which are a specific kind of crostino or canapé.

Bruschette are made only from hearty breads, and after cooking they are usually rubbed with a clove of garlic and topped with a little olive oil, salt and pepper for flavor. The most usual additional topping is peeled, chopped and salted ripe tomato with a bit of basil.

I tend to be iconoclastic and American and use crostini made as below and bruschette in the same way. Crostini are probably a little less messy to eat. Allow two of either per person. The cooking can be done a day ahead. Do not top until an hour or so before serving. Very messy toppings like Bruschette Toppings (page 132) should be spooned on

just before serving, at most 15 minutes ahead of time.

Toppings need to cohere enough to be moundable. Very little garnishing is done. See list page 132.

Crostini

Preheat oven to 350°F. Slice good store-bought Italian bread into ¼-inch-thick slices. Place on a baking sheet (not air-cushioned) and brush tops lightly with olive oil. Bake until edges are light brown and centers are crisp, about 10 minutes, or sauté in a little olive oil or butter until both sides are golden. One loaf Italian bread makes 4 dozen crostini.

Bruschette

Preheat grill or broiler. Slice good store-bought Italian bread slightly on the diagonal, into ½-inch-thick slices. Brush both sides lightly with olive oil. *To Grill.* Grill bread until edges are very dark brown, 10 to 13 minutes on first side, 3 to 6 minutes on second side. Move bread around if there are hot spots on grill to ensure even cooking. *To Broil.* Broil for 1½ minutes on first side, 1 minute on second side.

When bruschette are done, rub each side with a peeled clove of garlic, if desired (optional: infuse the olive oil with garlic), and top with a little more olive oil, salt and pepper. One loaf Italian bread makes about 2 dozen bruschette.

¼-inch slices (about 6 pieces), salt and pepper to taste. Dribble the olive oil evenly on both cut sides of the bread. Lay the basil leaves in an overlapping row along the length of one piece.

Repeat with the cheese and the tomato. Add salt and pepper to taste. Cover with the top piece of bread. Press down hard on the hero so that it sticks together. Slice and toothpick.

chicken liver spread

This is a very classic topping for Crostini (see photograph). The Holland or Dutch gin has a strong juniper berry flavor. If you are topping the crostini with juniper berries, you can substitute the liquid they cooked in for the gin. If you are using the sage leaves as a topping, use them to cook with also. These can be topped simply with freshly ground pepper and finely chopped herbs if you prefer.

If you don't want to stand around making crostini and decorating them, pack the spread into an attractive crock and serve with the crostini on the side and a knife so people can make their own. You can make the spread up to four days ahead. Bring back to room temperature before spreading.

The microwave makes the livers particularly tender. If you do not have a microwave oven, put livers, garlic and oil into the smallest heavy-bottomed pan that will hold them. Cook covered over the lowest heat possible until livers have lost all their red color.

Makes I cup, enough for 16 crostini

¼ cup loosely packed fresh Italian parsley or sage leaves
¼ cup olive oil
½ pound chicken livers, cleaned
I medium clove garlic, smashed, peeled and coarsely chopped
5 anchovy fillets packed in oil, rinsed
Kosher salt, to taste
Freshly ground black pepper, to taste
I teaspoon Holland gin, optional
I recipe Softened Juniper Berries (this page), optional
16 small fresh sage leaves, optional

Place parsley or sage in a food processor and process until finely chopped. Transfer to a small bowl.

Place oil, livers and garlic in a 2½-quart soufflé dish with a tightly fitting lid. Cook, covered, at 100% in a high-wattage microwave oven for 2 minutes. Uncover and stir well. Re-cover and cook for 1 minute. In a low-wattage oven: Cook for 3 minutes. Stir, and cook for 3 minutes more.

Remove from oven and uncover. Scrape mixture into food processor. Add anchovies and process until smooth. Taste and correct seasonings with salt, pepper and gin, if using.

Either scrape mixture into a bowl or spread on crostini. Sprinkle top with the parsley or sage. Garnish each piece, if desired, with 2 or 3 juniper berries and a small sage leaf.

softened juniper berries

Juniper is a very good and underused flavor. The black berries make an unusual garnish when quickly cooked to soften them slightly. Think of them on meat, pâté and smoked fish canapés as well as on liver ones.

48 juniper berries (scant 2 tablespoons; ¼ ounce)
½ cup water

Place juniper berries and water in a small saucepan. Bring to a boil over medium heat. Reduce heat to a simmer. Cover and cook until berries are softened, about 10 minutes. Remove from heat and let stand until cool.

crostini and bruschette toppings

Many of these toppings would not qualify as authentic; but they are very good.

Mushroom Purée (page 73) topped with chopped parsley; Caponata (page 14); French Olive Spread (page 22); Black Olivada (page 22); Green Olivada (page 22); Sun-Dried Tomato Dip (page 8); Eggplant Moroccan (page 10), topped with a few pine nuts; Sardine Paste (page 45), topped with chopped herbs; Taramasalata (page 31), topped with 3 salmon eggs; Sunny Tomato Filling (page 107).

brioche bread

There are hundreds of recipes for brioche. This recipe makes loaves of bread that are sturdy enough for slicing to use toasted or untoasted for canapés and tea sandwiches (pages 116 and 118). If you make them in a regular loaf pan—very good to serve with foie gras or smoked salmon—and want to trim the crusts to make canapés, you will lose lots of brioche. Instead, try making them in Pullman pans (page 111). You will also get a somewhat more compact bread that is easier to spread.

This recipe may be divided and multiplied. To make a double batch, four regular loaves, you will need a heavy-duty mixer with a paddle attachment. A dough hook will not work this quantity of such a sticky dough.

The bread freezes very well if tightly wrapped after cooling in plastic wrap and aluminum foil. Allow to defrost at room temperature.

Makes 2 regular loaves

1½ packages active dry yeast (⅜ ounce)
½ cup warm water (110°F, approximately)
4 cups all-purpose flour
2 teaspoons kosher salt
1 cup melted unsalted butter, plus additional for greasing pans
4 eggs

Egg Wash
(use only if not making in a Pullman pan)
1 egg
2 tablespoons milk

Combine yeast and warm water in the large bowl of an electric mixer or any large bowl if making by hand. Mixing with

the dough hook or by hand, add flour and salt. Reserve 1 tablespoon of the butter and add the remainder to flour mixture with mixer running. Add the eggs one at a time, waiting until each egg is incorporated before adding the next.

Allow dough to rise twice, using the remaining tablespoon butter to coat the bowl (page 111).

Preheat oven to 400°F.

To Make Regular Loaves. See page 111 on forming dough. Use two buttered 8½ × 4½ × 2½-inch loaf pans. Whisk egg wash ingredients together in a small bowl. After dough has risen again, brush tops with egg wash and bake for about 30 minutes, or until the loaves are a deep golden brown and sound hollow when tapped with the knuckles.

To Make Pullman Loaves. See page 111 on forming dough. Use

Crostini (page 131) with Chicken Liver Spread.

two buttered 10 × 3½ × 3-inch Pullman pans. Place pans in lower third of oven. Bake for 35 minutes. Turn bread out of pans and place directly on oven rack. Bake for 5 minutes longer. Turn bread out onto a rack and cool completely before slicing.

Pepper Brioche
Use ¼ cup green, black or pink peppercorns or a combination. If using brine-packed green peppercorns, thoroughly rinse in a sieve under cold running water. If using black or freeze-dried green and/or pink peppercorns, place under a kitchen towel and crack with a heavy pot or coarsely grind in a spice grinder. After bread is knocked down but before it is formed into loaves, thoroughly knead in peppercorns. Form; raise and bake as above.

133

chapter 4

mousses and
pâtés

Pâtés and mousses are invaluable at cocktail parties and buffets, and meat pâtés and mousses can be used as fillings for sandwiches. The main problem with them in the past has been length of preparation, messy and dangerous hot-water baths and prolonged cooking times. Modern appliances—the food processor, blender and microwave oven—have solved these problems. There remains only one: It is necessary to think ahead. Pâtés need to get cold, and in the case of meat pâtés their flavors need to mellow for a day or so. This necessity of making them ahead is a

blessing for the person giving a large party. Vegetable terrines can be made up to two days ahead and fish mousses from one to four days ahead. Meat pâtés and terrines should be made two days ahead—they will keep refrigerated for up to a week.

The many vegetable mousses and terrines in this chapter can be made thoroughly vegetarian by using agar-agar (see box on page 141 for instructions) instead of gelatin. If the dishes are to sit out for a while, it is a good idea in any case, as agar-agar sets up at room temperature while gelatin needs cold. This

Smoked Trout Mousse (page 146) can go with a good biscuit (pages 108–109) or a bread, or be spread on crisp leaves or slices of red pepper or carrots. It can also be an elegant first course at a dinner party.

means that agar-agar–bound dishes will hold their shape better at room temperature. You may want to consider using agar-agar in the smoked fish mousses (pages 144–146). See box on page 141 to substitute agar-agar for gelatin or vice versa. Using the microwave or the stove top is optional. The same box will give you both methods. Agar-agar or gelatin mousse recipes are easily multiplied.

In addition to the vegetable mousses and the gelatin- or agar-agar–set smoked fish mousses (pages 144–146), Spinach Terrine (page 143), Chicken Liver Crock with Apples and Onions (page 149), Veal and Ham Pâté (page 156), Rabbit Pâté (page 157) and Twin Pâtés (page 160) are cooked conventionally or have conventional-oven alternatives in the recipes. All the rest are cooked in the microwave oven, since it cooks your pâtés in anywhere from eleven minutes. See box on page 141 for adapting microwave-cooked pâtés and terrines to a conventional oven.

If you don't have a food processor or a blender to help grind up your ingredients, try to get your butcher or fish person to finely grind the basic ingredient(s) for you, or put them through a meat grinder. Vegetables, raw or cooked, can be put through a meat grinder or finely chopped by hand.

It is very hard to tell just how much of a mousse or pâté guests will eat. Additionally, you will need to serve a whole one unless you are in the lucky position of having leftovers— so servings are given so you know how many of something to make. Pâtés that cut easily into slices have their yields given by the number of servings. Mousses are generally spread by guests onto breads (pages 110–115 and page 119), crackers or vegetables. However, they look much more dramatic if presented whole from a decorative mold. Sadly, guests

will quickly reduce them to a mess. Alternatively, serve small amounts in savory pastry shells (pages 96–97). When slices cannot be given, the yield is given in cups. Allow about three squares of a sliced pâté per person unless it is the only dish served. In that case, allow five. Allow about a quarter cup of unsliceable mousse per person.

If you want to serve any of the dishes in this chapter as a first course, plated, at a dinner party, allow one to two half-inch slices per person. Accompany with good bread and a sauce from Chapter 1.

Many of the mousses and pâtés can also be used as spreads. Balance the amounts with other items. If you have a number of dips and spreads, you may only want one or two spreadable mousse or pâté items. Also balance between fish, meat and vegetable items and keep colors in mind.

Most of these dishes need a good bread. See pages 110–122. Through the chapter are a few recipes for things like Cornichons (page 152) that are good accompaniments to mousses and pâtés.

Good at home or as a truly elegant picnic. The strong colors of the food go well with bright cotton scarves and sunlight. A simpler picnic could have just the terrine, the eggs and either the antipasto or the green beans. The whole array: Lemon Dill Antipasto (page 66); Chinese Pork Terrine (page 153) with oil-cured olives; Gravlax (page 177); Sweet Mustard Sauce (page 29); Marinated Artichokes (page 50); Deviled Eggs (page 88); Insalata Caprese Hero (page 131); daikon radish (page 68); French Olive Spread (page 22); Pissaladière (page 104), classic and with Sun-Dried Tomato filling and yellow pepper strips; haricots verts (page 69).

137

ready-mades

The sine qua non and the most expensive of the bought pâtés is foie gras. The best is bought from a restaurant or store that prepares its own or from a mail-order source that carries what the French call "sous vide," vacuum-packed, pâtés or slices of same made only with whole duck or goose livers. This is only for your nearest and dearest, not the wide world at a large party. Serve with slices of Brioche Bread (page 132) or store-bought. Don't bother with canned foie gras or one of the diluted preparations going under names like "mousse of foie gras." Save your money and make your own liver mousse (pages 149, 161) from cheaper elements.

Charcuteries and other take-out stores often make quite good meat pâtés. Take a leisurely day and go around having tastes and making notes until you find a few that you like. They can be a godsend. Add cornichons from a bottle if you haven't made your own (page 152) and a good mustard or two. Pickled ginger, which can be bought frozen or refrigerated—often, oddly enough, in fish stores—keeps forever if the unopened package is refrigerated. Slivers make good toppings for pâtés and mousses of all kinds. Scallion brushes (page 152) can accompany pâté with a Chinese bottled sauce such as hoisin replacing the mustards.

Vegetable mousses, especially vegetarian ones, are harder to find in stores. Fish ones can be found but are mainly less good than the meat ones, so you might consider making your own.

The homemade chutneys, pickles and relishes cannot truly be replaced, but store-bought substitutions can be made. Look for preserves that are not overly liquid. Consider cutting up any large pieces of fruit into smaller bits. All of these can be puréed to make sauces.

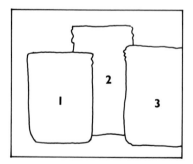

1 *Cornichons (page 152);*
2 *Plum Chutney (page 150) and*
3 *Kalamata Antipasto (page 64)*
are just a few of the goodies you can put up to spark your pâté, your roasted meat or your sandwiches.

138

*M*eat pâtés (pages 151–161) in decorative crusts.

carrot and ginger terrine

This is a brilliantly orange terrine of amazing healthfulness, particularly if you use nonfat fromage blanc. If fromage blanc is unavailable, substitute part-skim ricotta.

Consider serving this with one of the herb and dairy dips (pages 17–18). A crisp cracker (English biscuit) or Whole-Wheat Soda Bread (page 114) would go well.

Makes 4 cups

2 pounds carrots, peeled and cut across into ½-inch slices
I teaspoon turmeric
0.19 ounce agar-agar flakes (¼ cup)
½ cup water
¾ cup vegetable broth
½ cup fromage blanc, or part-skim ricotta
I½ tablespoons grated peeled fresh ginger
2 scallions, thinly sliced
Kosher salt, to taste
Freshly ground black pepper, to taste

Combine carrots and turmeric in a 13 × 9 × 2-inch oval glass or ceramic dish. Cover tightly with microwave plastic wrap and cook at 100% in a high-wattage oven for 15 minutes. Prick plastic to release steam, or steam, covered, on top of stove over low heat with 2 tablespoons of water until tender.

Transfer to a food processor and purée.

Dissolve agar-agar in water as in box on opposite page. Add to carrots along with vegetable broth, fromage blanc and ginger. Process until completely smooth.

Transfer mixture to a bowl and stir in scallions. Season to taste with salt and pepper.

Preparing Molds and Unmolding

Molds, usually for gelatin- or agar-agar–set mousses, are best rinsed with ice water inside and out just before filling with the prepared mixture. Do not dry the mold before filling. Cover mixture with mold lid, plastic wrap or foil. Refrigerate. Incidentally, aluminum bowls make good molds.

Historically, **pans for baked pâtés and terrines** have been lined with fat—bacon or unsalted or blanched sliced fresh lard—or coated with softened butter, buttered paper or lots of oil. While this can be done and in some cases is traditional, today, when we tend to be using smooth glass loaf pans in the microwave oven, it is really not necessary. The pans can be sprayed with vegetable oil or lightly wiped with an oil-drenched piece of paper. Although cooking oil can be purchased in spray cans, the excessive use of plastic or, worse, aerosol, offends the environment. Instead, carefully wash out a spray bottle that is hanging around the house for some other purpose—boiling water followed by lots of cold water is good. Fill the totally clean bottle with rapeseed oil or another oil and happily spray away.

To unmold pâtés and mousses, remove from refrigerator; remove weights and cardboard (see box, page 147), if used; run a knife or spatula around the edge of the pâté, if necessary—some will shrink back enough from the edge so that this is not necessary. Run the hot water until it is as hot as you can get. Select a bowl larger than your mold by a few inches and warm it with the water. Close the drain and fill the bowl with water, allowing the water to spill over and surround the bowl by a couple of inches. This will keep the water hot. Holding the mold or pan by the rim or very top, dip into hot water for about five seconds to loosen. Invert a serving plate over the mold or loaf pan and turn the pan and plate over at the same time. The pâté will drop out onto the plate. If you have no success, dip again. Refrigerate covered if not eating soon.

Prepare mold (a loaf pan works well) with ice water as in box on opposite page. Pour in mixture. Cover with plastic wrap and refrigerate for at least 4 hours.

pickled beet mold

This is really an aspic. It is made with agar-agar and so will hold at room temperature throughout the party. People who would normally rather die than eat beets will try this shiny ruby mold happily. Decorate, as desired, with sour cream and dill sprigs. Serve with a fish such as Cold Cooked Salmon (page 179).

Save extra beet liquid to make Beet Pickled Eggs (page 89).

Makes about 4 cups

- **1 recipe Pickled Beets (page 89)**
- **0.19 ounce agar-agar flakes (¼ cup)**
- **1 teaspoon finely chopped fresh dill sprigs**

Make Pickled Beets through point of pouring spice mixture over beets. Let cool for about an hour.

Working in batches, transfer beets to a blender with a slotted spoon and purée with ½ cup of the pickling liquid. Scrape into a bowl.

Dissolve agar-agar (gelatin) in ½ cup beet pickling liquid as in box on this page. Stir into purée with chopped dill.

Prepare 1½-quart mold with ice water as in box on opposite page. Pour in beet mixture; cover with plastic wrap and allow to set in the refrigerator for at least 3 hours.

Agar-Agar

Agar-agar is a vegetarian gelatin. Besides being vegetarian, it has the advantage of not needing to be cold to retain its firming qualities. It used to be much more popular than it is today. You will probably have to get it in a health food store. It may come in long strips, sheets, flakes or powdered form. To be completely accurate, you have to weigh the agar-agar on a sensitive scale. If you cannot weigh it and you have a coffee or spice grinder, you can grind the agar-agar into a fine powder. Four grams (0.14 ounces) will make about 3¼ teaspoons of powder, which is roughly equivalent to 3 tablespoons of flakes. To substitute gelatin for agar-agar or agar-agar for gelatin, note that 4 grams (0.14 ounces) agar-agar flakes (3 tablespoons) will set up the same amount of liquid as one envelope of gelatin.

To Dissolve Agar-Agar in a Microwave. Combine agar-agar and liquid as called for in recipe in a 2-cup glass measure or bowl. Cook, uncovered, at 100% in a high-wattage oven for 2 minutes or in a low-wattage oven for 3 minutes. If using gelatin, allow it to soak in the liquid for 2 minutes. Cover and cook in a high-wattage oven for 30 seconds or in a low-wattage oven for 1 minute.

To Dissolve Agar-Agar on Top of Stove. Combine agar-agar and liquid in a small saucepan. Stir over low heat until dissolved. If using gelatin, allow it to soak in the liquid for 2 minutes, then proceed as for agar-agar.

Adapting Recipes to the Conventional Oven

To cook meat pâtés in a conventional oven, heat the oven to 375°F with the rack in the center. Put a roasting pan on the rack. Bring some water to boil on top of the stove. Put the filled pâté (loaf) pan in the roasting pan. Pour in water to come halfway up the sides of the pâté pan and cover it with aluminum foil. Cook for 45 minutes. Test temperature at center of pâté with an instant-read thermometer. If it reads 140°F, the pâté is cooked. If not, continue to cook, testing temperature every 10 minutes until 140°F is reached. Very carefully—the water is boiling hot—remove the pâté pan from the oven. Turn off oven and wait until water cools before removing roaster and discarding water.

141

Sweet Potato Terrine is a treat for vegetarians as well as other guests.

sweet potato terrine

This is an extremely easy recipe with an autumn taste and color. Serve with Crisp Vegetable Chips (page 238) or a good bread.

Makes 3 1/2 cups

2 pounds sweet potatoes, peeled and cut into 1-inch pieces (about 6 1/3 cups)
2 medium cloves garlic, smashed, peeled and halved
0.19 ounce agar-agar flakes (1/4 cup)
1 cup vegetable broth
Pinch cinnamon
Pinch nutmeg
Kosher salt, to taste
Freshly ground white pepper, to taste

Combine potatoes with garlic in a 13 × 9 × 2-inch oval glass or ceramic dish. Cover tightly with microwave plastic wrap and cook at 100% in a high-wattage oven for 16 minutes, stirring once during cooking. Prick plastic to release steam, or **steam,** covered, on top of stove until tender.

Transfer to a food processor and process until finely chopped.

Dissolve agar-agar in 1/2 cup vegetable broth as directed in box on page 141. With food processor motor running, pour in dissolved agar-agar with 1/2 cup more vegetable broth. Process until completely smooth. Season to taste with cinnamon, nutmeg, salt and white pepper.

Prepare mold (loaf pan will do) with ice water as in box on page 140. Scrape in mixture. Cover and refrigerate for at least 3 hours.

142

spinach terrine

This is a baked vegetable terrine that is light in texture but firm enough to slice. In Italian it is called a sformato. This recipe is based on the Sformato di Spinaci in the excellent Grande Enciclopedia Illustrata della Gastronomia *put out by Italian Reader's Digest in 1990.*

The uncooked mixture makes a lovely filling to bake at 350°F for ten minutes in partially baked savory pastry shells (see box, page 97). Use two teaspoons of the mixture for each shell. A whole recipe of the mixture will make over eighty filled shells; you might want to consider making half a recipe.

Makes 4 cups, 16 ½-inch slices to serve quartered (64 servings)

5 tablespoons unsalted butter
¼ cup plus 2 teaspoons all-purpose flour (about 1¼ ounces)
2 pounds fresh spinach, stemmed, washed and dried (12 cups)
¼ cup heavy cream
1 cup milk
½ cup grated Parmesan cheese (1½ ounces)
1½ teaspoons kosher salt
⅛ teaspoon nutmeg
Freshly ground black pepper, to taste
2 large eggs, separated
1 egg yolk

Grease an 8½ × 4½ × 2½-inch loaf pan with ½ tablespoon butter. Dust with 2 teaspoons flour.

Place spinach leaves in a 13 × 9 × 2-inch oval glass or ceramic dish. Cover tightly with microwave plastic wrap and cook at 100% in a high-wattage oven for 5 minutes 30 seconds or in a low-wattage oven for 9 minutes. Prick plastic to release steam, or

steam, covered over water until cooked but still bright green.

Remove from oven and uncover. Transfer to a strainer and allow to drain and cool. When cool enough to handle, squeeze out all remaining liquid. Place in a food processor and process until very finely chopped.

Melt 2 tablespoons butter in a medium pan over moderate heat. Stir in spinach and cream. Cook, stirring, for about 5 minutes. Remove from heat and scrape out into a bowl to cool.

Melt remaining butter in same pan over medium heat. Stir in remaining flour and cook, stirring continually, for about 3 minutes. Gradually stir in milk so that there are no lumps and allow to come to a boil. Reduce heat to low and allow to simmer for about 3 minutes, stirring frequently. Remove from heat, stir in spinach mixture with grated cheese, salt, nutmeg and pepper and allow to cool for 5 minutes. Stir in egg yolks.

Preheat oven to 350°F.

Beat egg whites in a clean bowl until stiff peaks form. Gently fold in spinach mixture until just mixed. Pour into prepared loaf pan. Cover with a sheet of buttered foil and bake in a water bath (see box, page 141) for 55 minutes. Remove from oven and allow to cool. Refrigerate, covered, for at least 4 hours or overnight.

Unmold (page 140) and serve whole or slice across in ½-inch slices, which may be quartered to fit on bread.

Making a Collar

It is necessary to shield the outside of the pan with a collar of aluminum foil for some recipes so that the outside doesn't get overcooked. This is perfectly all right, despite what you may have heard about metal in the microwave oven, as long as your pâté is not sitting on a metal surface. If the bottom of your oven is metal or has a metal shelf, put the pâté mold in a larger nonmetal pan to avoid the metal-to-metal contact during cooking. The collar is usually removed partway through the cooking to set the outside. To make a collar, cut a piece of aluminum foil about 28 × 3 inches and wrap it around the sides of the dish. Fold ends together to keep it in place.

Microwave-Oven Wattages

A high-wattage oven is 650 to 700 watts under the old industry standard, and 750 to 800 watts under the new one. A low-wattage oven is 450 to 500 watts under the old standard, and 550 to 600 watts under the new.

thai shrimp terrine

This is a good last-minute recipe, as it can be served warm. If you prefer to work ahead, you can make it up to two days ahead, weight (see box, page 147) after cooling and refrigerate, covered. Unmold and slice across thinly with a very sharp knife. You can get anywhere from 16 to 32 slices, which when quartered will give you 64 or 128 slices, respectively. Serve with squares of green, red or yellow pepper to use instead of bread, or with Asian rice crackers. A blob of Plum Chutney (page 150) or Peanut Dipping Sauce (page 28) on each would be good if you are making them into individual servings. If you are letting the guests manage for themselves, decorate the platter with Scallion Brushes (page 152) and serve the sauce in a bowl.

If you double the amounts of green pepper, celery and onion in the stuffing, the terrine is crunchier and more colorful.

Makes 3 cups

1½ recipes Thai Shrimp Stuffing (page 210), omitting rice paper

Make the stuffing.

Microwave-Oven Method. Spoon the mixture into an 8½ × 4½ × 2½-inch glass or ceramic loaf pan and smooth out surface. Put a collar around the pan (see box, page 143).

Cover with microwave plastic wrap and cook at 100% in a high-wattage oven for 2 minutes. Remove collar, re-cover with plastic wrap and cook for 3 minutes longer. In a low-wattage oven cook with collar and plastic for 11 minutes. Prick plastic to release steam.

Remove from oven and uncover. Allow to stand 15 minutes, loosely covered with a towel. Unmold onto serving plate and allow to cool a little before serving.

Conventional-Oven Method. Preheat oven to 350°F. Scrape mixture into glass, ceramic or Teflon-coated metal loaf pan. Cover with aluminum foil. Bake in a water bath for 40 minutes. Remove from water bath and uncover. Allow to stand 15 minutes loosely covered with a kitchen towel. Unmold onto serving plate and allow to cool a little before serving.

smoked salmon mousse

This beautiful, pastel mousse is light and elegant. You may want to use agar-agar so it holds better when set out, or make a few smaller molds and put a fresh one out as the need arises. I wouldn't leave a mousse with this much cream out too long on a hot day.

Like the Smoked Fish Mousse and Smoked Trout Mousse that follow, this recipe can easily be multiplied or divided. The recipes are very similar but the quantities of ingredients and seasonings have been adjusted for each type of fish.

You need not use the very best salmon for this. In any case, it's a good way to serve a lot of people with a small amount of a costly ingredient.

I like to make this in a decorative ring mold, like a bundt pan or kugelhopf mold. When I unmold it, I fill the hole in the center with Salmon Tartare (page 174) or Parsley and Scallion Dip (page 17) or Herb Dip (page 18) and serve with squares of Whole-Wheat Soda Bread (page 114) or Crostini (page 131). If

you prefer to portion it, place by the spoonful on crostini; on bread; on vegetables such as endive, lettuce or celery or on melba toast. Sprinkle with a few bits of chive, and top, if desired, with a strip of smoked salmon.

Makes 40 hors d'oeuvre servings

3 tablespoons water
1 package unflavored gelatin (¼ ounce)
6½ ounces smoked salmon
3 cups heavy cream
2 tablespoons fresh lemon juice
2½ teaspoons grated onion
2 teaspoons kosher salt
Freshly ground white pepper, to taste
10 drops hot red pepper sauce
¼ cup thin-sliced chives, or if unavailable, scallion greens sliced lengthwise and then across

Garnish
Chives finely snipped
Smoked salmon in thin strips, curled or not, optional

Place the water in a small pan. Add the gelatin and let it sit until absorbed. Place the pan over low heat and stir until the gelatin is dissolved. Set aside to cool to room temperature.

Put the smoked salmon and ½ cup heavy cream in a food processor and process until smooth. Then press the mixture through a fine sieve to get a smooth purée, or purée in a blender.

Whip the remaining 2½ cups cream just until slightly soft peaks form. Beat in the dissolved gelatin. Stir in the lemon juice, onion, salt, pepper, hot red pepper sauce and chives.

Remove about ½ cup of the seasoned whipped cream and stir it into the puréed smoked salmon to lighten the mixture. Fold in the remaining cream. Rinse a 5-cup mold or larger with ice water (see box,

page 140). Spoon in salmon mousse. Refrigerate 1½ hours, or until set.

To serve, unmold (see box, page 140) and garnish with additional chives and smoked salmon, if desired.

smoked fish mousse

This is another fish mousse for molding. You can use smoked whitefish, mackerel, eel, haddock (soaked as in box, page 182), bluefish—that is, any smoked fish that is fatty but also has a soft flesh. You wouldn't want to use sturgeon or sable (black cod) even if they were affordable. See Smoked Fish (box, page 184). Serve as Smoked Salmon Mousse.

Makes 6 cups; serves 24 at cocktails

3 packages unflavored gelatin (¾ ounce)
½ cup cold water
2 tablespoons dry white wine
1 pound boned, skinned smoked fish (2 cups fish pieces)
2 tablespoons fresh lemon juice
Kosher salt
Freshly ground white pepper, to taste
Cayenne pepper, to taste
2 cups heavy cream

Sprinkle the gelatin over the cold water in a measuring cup. Set aside until it is absorbed. Place in a pan of water over low heat until the gelatin is completely dissolved. Set aside until cool. Then stir in the wine.

Place the fish in the work bowl of a food processor;

This molded Smoked Salmon Mousse is one of my favorite starters; it's very elegant. Serve as a first course at a sit-down dinner or think of it as an ultimate spread at a stand-up party. You don't need a fancy mold; a stainless steel bowl will work splendidly. It doesn't require a sauce, but Parsley and Scallion Dip (page 17) goes along dreamily.

(continued)

145

process until it is a rough purée. Stir in the cooled gelatin mixture, lemon juice, ½ teaspoon salt, and white and cayenne pepper to taste. Add more lemon, salt, and peppers as needed, remembering that the intensity will be diluted when you add the cream. Put the mixture in a bowl.

Whip the cream until soft peaks form. Stir some of the cream into the fish to lighten it, then fold in the rest. Prepare a 4- to 6-cup mold with ice water (see box, page 140). Spoon in fish mixture. Tap firmly against the work surface to settle the mixture and eliminate air bubbles.

Chill to set, about 3 hours. Unmold (see box, page 140) to serve.

smoked trout mousse

This is a rather elegant mold that makes a good filling for fully cooked pastry shells (see box, page 97) as well.

Makes 15 servings at a cocktail party

½ pound skinned and boned
    smoked trout, about 2
    whole trout
2½ cups heavy cream
4 teaspoons fresh lemon juice
4 teaspoons prepared
    horseradish, drained in sieve
½ teaspoon kosher salt
½ cup cold water
2 packages gelatin (½ ounce)

Crumble trout into a small saucepan. Add 1½ cups of the cream and stir. Bring to a simmer and cook gently for 10 minutes. Pour mixture into a blender and purée. Pass through a fine sieve into a metal bowl. Stir in lemon juice, horseradish and salt.

Place ½ cup water in a 1-cup glass measure and sprinkle gelatin on top. When gelatin is absorbed into water, place measure in a saucepan of simmering water until gelatin dissolves. Stir into trout mixture.

Whip remaining heavy cream and fold into trout mixture.

Rinse a clean metal bowl or metal mold holding 4 to 6 cups with ice water. Scrape mousse into mold. Chill for 1 hour or, tightly covered, overnight. Unmold (see box, page 140).

salt cod pâté

On page 32 is a nontraditional brandade made with sole for use as a dip. Here a traditional **salt-cod brandade** *is made, nontraditionally, into a pâté. Serve with a flavorful firm bread like Olivada Focaccia (page 129)—nice color contrast—or Bruschette (page 131). Eliminate eggs and baking for plain brandade.*

Makes 42 servings

1 pound cooked baking
    potatoes, peeled (see Note)
1 pound desalinated salt cod
    (see box), cut into 1½-inch
    chunks
2 medium cloves garlic,
    smashed and peeled
6 tablespoons heavy cream
6 tablespoons olive oil
5 large eggs

While potatoes are still warm, pass them through a food mill fitted with the medium disk. Set aside.

Place cod and garlic in a food processor and process until finely chopped. Add potato and 2 tablespoons of the cream and pulse until combined. With the machine running, slowly pour in remaining heavy cream, olive oil

and eggs. Scrape down sides of work bowl. Process until smooth.

Scrape mixture into an 8½ × 4½ × 2½-inch loaf pan. Cover with a paper towel and then wrap tightly with microwave plastic wrap. Cook at 100% in a high-wattage oven for 20 minutes. Prick plastic to release steam.

Remove from oven, uncover and turn out of pan. Trim ends and cut into ½-inch slices. Cut each slice into 6 pieces.

Note: To cook potatoes in a microwave, prick them twice with a fork. Cook at 100% in a high-wattage oven for 11 minutes or in a low-wattage oven for 18 minutes.

Desalinating Salt Cod

Microwave-Oven Method
Rinse 1 pound salt cod under cold running water for 2 minutes. Place in a 14 × 9 × 2-inch oval dish with 6 cups cold water. Cover tightly with microwave plastic wrap. Cook at 100% in a high-wattage oven for 6 minutes. Prick plastic to release steam. Remove from oven and uncover. Drain and rinse with cold water. Repeat soaking process 2 more times. For ½ pound salt cod, place in a 10 × 3-inch round dish, use 3 cups water and cook for 5 minutes. Repeat as above.

Conventional Method
Rinse salt cod under cold running water for 2 minutes. Place in a large bowl and cover with cold water. Cover and refrigerate for 2 days, changing water at least three times a day.

salmon pâté

This salmon pâté is quite different from the smoked fish mousses. It is made with raw fish, which, in combination with the eggs, holds it together when cooked.

Smoked Salmon Cream Cheese (page 39) or Dill Butter (page 42) would be good on the bread if you turn this into canapés (page 116).

Makes about 100 canapés

1½ pounds boneless, skinless salmon, cut into 2-inch chunks
3 large eggs
3 tablespoons fresh lemon juice
1 tablespoon kosher salt
Pinch freshly ground black pepper
1½ cups heavy cream
¾ cup loosely packed fresh dill sprigs, chopped
½ cup snipped or cut fresh chives

Place salmon, eggs, lemon juice, salt and pepper in food processor. Process until smooth, stopping twice to scrape down sides of bowl.

Add cream and process a few seconds, stopping once to scrape down sides of bowl. Stir in dill and chives.

Lightly oil an 8½ × 4½ × 2½-inch glass loaf pan. Scrape salmon mixture into pan. Smooth the top. Cook at 100% in a high-wattage oven for 13 minutes 30 seconds or in a low-wattage oven with a collar (see box, page 143) for 24 minutes.

Remove from oven. Drain off any liquid. Cover and weight (see box). Refrigerate until cold.

Unmold (see box on page 140). Trim ends and cut in ¼-inch-thick slices. Cut each slice into quarters.

spinach and fish pâté

Put some Green Goddess Dressing (page 37) on the bread and another little blob on top of the pâté when serving this as canapés (page 116).

Makes about 50 canapés

¾ pound spinach, stemmed and thoroughly washed
1 pound cod fillet, cut into 2-inch chunks
2 large eggs
1 tablespoon kosher salt
Large pinch ground nutmeg
Pinch cayenne pepper
Pinch freshly ground black pepper
1 cup heavy cream

Steam spinach on top of stove, or place in a 13 × 9 × 2-inch oval dish. Cover tightly with microwave plastic wrap. Cook at 100% in a high-wattage oven for 4 minutes or in a low-wattage oven for 8 minutes. Prick plastic to release steam.

Remove from oven and uncover. When cool enough to handle, squeeze well to remove liquid. Place in food processor.

Add remaining ingredients except cream. Process until very smooth, stopping twice to scrape down sides of bowl. Add cream and process a few seconds, stopping once to scrape down sides of bowl.

Lightly oil an 8½ × 4½ × 2½-inch glass loaf pan. Scrape spinach mixture into pan. Smooth the top. Cook in a high-wattage oven for 10 minutes 30 seconds or in a low-wattage oven with a collar (see box, page 143) for 22 minutes.

Remove from oven. Drain off any liquid. Cover and weight (see box). Refrigerate until cold.

Unmold pâté. Trim off ends. Cut in ¼-inch-thick slices. Cut each slice in half.

Weighting and Chilling Pâtés

After pâtés are cooked, many will need to be weighted and refrigerated. The procedure is the same for all of them no matter what they contain. Cut a heavy piece of cardboard or two pieces if the cardboard is lightweight—to fit inside the top of your pan. Cover the cardboard(s) with a secure layer of aluminum foil. If you can find a brick or knife-honing stone that will fit in the opening, use it. Wrap in foil to keep it from absorbing fat. Or use at least two filled tins that are heavy and will fit in your pan. Make a place in your refrigerator to store the weighted pâté.

After the pâté has come out of the oven, allow it to cool until you can comfortably pick the pan up in your hands. Placing the cooked pâté in front of an open window in cool weather helps. Put the prepared cardboard on top of the pâté, put the weights on top and carefully place in the refrigerator. Fish pâtés will only need to be refrigerated for a few hours or until thoroughly chilled. Meat pâtés should be allowed to chill for at least a day. In two days, the flavor will have fully developed. If you wish to keep the pâtés for a longer time, unmold them and wrap in plastic wrap and then wrap thoroughly in aluminum foil. The fish pâtés will need to be eaten in three to four days. Meat pâtés keep a good week. I have served them after two weeks, but I must be moderate in my recommendations.

147

The Spinach and Fish Pâté (page 147) can go on the vegetables as well as on bread. For ultimate indulgence, consider adding a bowl of Green Goddess Dressing (page 37).

chicken liver mousse

This is a creamy, easily made classic mousse. Another one is Chicken Liver Spread (page 132). Put out bread with the crock of mousse, with a second small crock of butter if you want. Add a bowl of small radishes.

**Makes 3½ cups;
serves about 12**

**12 ounces chicken livers,
    rinsed and trimmed of fat
1 cup milk
2 cups unsalted butter
2 tablespoons brandy or
    Cognac
1 small clove garlic, smashed
    and peeled
2 teaspoons kosher salt
¾ teaspoon freshly ground
    black pepper
Pinch cayenne pepper
Pinch ground nutmeg
Pinch ground allspice**

Place livers in a bowl and pour the milk over them. Allow to stand at room temperature for at least 2 hours. Drain and rinse.

Place ¾ of the butter in a 13 × 9 × 3-inch oval glass or ceramic dish. Cook at 100% in a high-wattage oven for 3 minutes.

Remove from oven and add chicken livers in one layer. Cover tightly with microwave plastic wrap and cook for 2 minutes.

Uncover and stir, then re-cover and cook for 2 minutes longer. Prick plastic to release steam.

Remove from oven and uncover. Pour livers and butter into the work bowl of a food processor.

Place brandy in a very small pan or large, long-handled ladle and place over low heat for about 1 minute. Carefully light brandy with a match and allow to burn for about 1 minute. Blow out the flame and add to the chicken livers with garlic, salt, pepper and spices. Process until smooth. Add remaining butter in small pieces and process until combined.

Pour mixture into a decorative crock. Cover with plastic wrap and refrigerate for at least 3 hours.

chicken liver crock with apples and onions

The apples in here are a mystery ingredient, as they disappear into the purée. You might want to spread this on thin wedges of apple that have been dipped in lemon juice to avoid discoloration instead of on bread.

This recipe can easily be doubled or quadrupled for a large party. Process in batches, if necessary.

**Makes 4½ cups;
serves about 16**

**1 pound chicken livers, rinsed
    and trimmed of fat
¾ cup milk
1¼ cups unsalted butter
1 small onion, peeled and
    thinly sliced (about 1 cup)
1 small green apple, peeled,
    cored and thinly sliced
    (about ¾ cup)
¼ cup Calvados (apple
    brandy) or brandy
¼ cup heavy cream
1½ teaspoons kosher salt
½ teaspoon hot red pepper
    sauce
Freshly ground black pepper**

Place chicken livers in a bowl and pour the milk over them. Allow to stand at room temperature for at least 2 hours. Drain and rinse.

Melt 4 tablespoons butter in a medium skillet over medium heat. Add livers and cook, stirring, for about 4 minutes, or until livers are browned all over and still pink in the center. Remove livers with a slotted spoon to a food processor. Return pan to the heat and stir in onions. Cook over medium heat, stirring frequently, for about 5 minutes, or until softened. Stir in apples and cook for 3 minutes longer, or until slightly soft. Remove from heat and scrape into the work bowl with livers. Return pan to low heat; deglaze pan with Calvados and pour over livers. Add cream, salt, pepper and hot red pepper sauce and process mixture until smooth. Add remaining butter in pieces with the motor running and process until very smooth.

Pour mixture into decorative crock(s). Cover with plastic wrap and refrigerate for at least 3 hours.

Missing Low-Wattage Times

Many pâtés, especially those containing pork, I find problematic in low-wattage ovens. They are ideal for high-wattage ovens (see box, page 143). If you have a lower-power oven, try cooking the pâté for thirty minutes or until an instant-reading thermometer inserted right through the plastic into the pâté reads at least 140°F. If the pâté needs to cook longer, patch hole with a small square of plastic.

149

chopped chicken liver

Chopped chicken liver is as New York as you can get. Put out a bowl with party rounds of rye or crackers. The microwave oven cooks the livers in a particularly creamy, nonbitter way. This is no dish for cholesterol watchers or dieters. Those who don't worry will want to know how to render fat for this dish or others, like confit of duck or goose. Sprinkle the drained rendered fat cracklings on the livers, or serve separately, warmed and dusted with kosher salt.

Makes 2 cups; serves 6 to 8

¼ cup rendered chicken fat, store-bought or made as directed in box
½ pound onion, coarsely chopped (about 2 cups)
2 teaspoons kosher salt, or to taste
¼ teaspoon freshly ground black pepper, or to taste
1 pound chicken livers, connective tissues removed and rinsed (2 cups)
2 hard-boiled eggs

Place fat in an 11 × 8-inch oval dish. Stir in onion, salt and pepper. Cook, uncovered, at 100% in a high-wattage oven for 4 minutes or in a low-wattage oven for 6 minutes.

Remove from oven. Add livers in a single layer. Cover tightly with microwave plastic wrap. Cook in a high-wattage oven for 4 minutes or in a low-wattage oven for 5 minutes. Leaving dish in oven, slash plastic with a knife and stir with spoon put through slit. Patch plastic with a fresh piece of plastic. Cook in a high-wattage oven for 2 minutes more or in a low-wattage oven for 4 minutes more. Prick plastic to release steam.

Remove from oven and uncover. Scrape mixture into bowl of a food processor. Add eggs and pulse to coarsely chop; do not purée. Transfer to a serving bowl. Refrigerate, covered, until chilled, preferably overnight.

Rendering Fat

All kinds of fat (suet) removed from animals can be rendered and most will give you cracklings. The method will be the same as the method for chicken fat.

For rendering fat, you can buy either chicken skin and fat from your butcher or buy a bird (2½ to 3 pounds), pull the fat pockets from the tail end and skin the bird. The bird can then be cut into serving pieces and used for Chicken Salad (page 263). The carcass can be made into stock.

Cut the skin into 1- to 2-inch pieces with a pair of kitchen scissors and have ready a small onion, peeled and quartered, to add to the dish halfway through cooking, if desired.

To Render Fat in the Microwave Oven

Place the skin and fat in a 2½-quart soufflé dish and cook, loosely covered with paper towels. Cook 8 ounces at 100% in a high-wattage oven for 18 minutes or in a low-wattage oven for 30 minutes. Remove carefully from oven when done and let cool slightly.

To Render Fat on Top of the Stove

Simmer with ½ cup of water until water evaporates and fat is rendered. Strain through a fine sieve lined with paper towels. Eight ounces skin and fat yields ¼ cup rendered fat.

plum chutney

This beautiful purple or red chutney is terrific with meat and fish pâtés and terrines. Also consider it on Tea Sandwiches (page 118) and on roast pork (page 286) or Roast Turkey (page 267). To put up, see box, page 56.

Makes 4 cups

Syrup
10 medium cloves garlic, smashed, peeled and cut lengthwise into quarters
1½ hot red peppers, stemmed, seeded, deribbed and cut across into thin slices (1 tablespoon)
1 cup sugar
1 cup red wine vinegar
¼ cup coarsely grated, peeled fresh ginger (2 ounces)
½ teaspoon ground nutmeg
¼ teaspoon ground cinnamon

Plums
2 pounds dark red or purple firm plums (not prune plums), pitted, cut into eight wedges and then cut across into halves, to yield 6 cups
2 tablespoons cornstarch
2 tablespoons water

See box on page 56 for sterilizing jars.

Combine syrup ingredients in a 2½-quart soufflé dish. Cook, uncovered, at 100% in a high-wattage oven for 8 minutes or in a low-wattage oven using a carrousel for 12 minutes.

Remove from oven and stir in plums until well coated. Return to oven and cook in a high-wattage oven for 6 minutes or in a low-wattage oven for 9 minutes, stirring once halfway through cooking.

Combine cornstarch and water in a small bowl and scrape into plum mixture, stirring well. Cook, uncovered, in a high-wattage oven for 2 minutes; in a low-wattage oven for 3.

Remove from oven and allow to stand until room temperature. Ladle into sterilized jars and store tightly covered in the refrigerator.

curried chicken pâté

This is a perfect little crock of pâté to serve when you have unexpected guests, as it takes four minutes to cook and can be served warm. If making ahead, bring to room temperature before serving. Serve bread and a chutney like Plum Chutney (opposite page) if you have it.

Makes 6 servings

**2 medium cloves garlic,
    smashed and peeled**
2 teaspoons curry powder
⅛ teaspoon turmeric
**3 tablespoons melted unsalted
    butter**
**½ pound boneless, skinless
    chicken breast, cut into
    large pieces**
I tablespoon fresh lime juice
I teaspoon kosher salt
**Freshly ground black pepper,
    to taste**
2 tablespoons heavy cream

Place garlic in food processor and process until chopped. Stir spices into butter and place in food processor with all remaining ingredients except cream.

Process until mixture is chopped medium fine. Add cream and process just until well blended.

Scrape into a crock that is 3¼ inches high, with a 3-inch inner diameter. Firmly press mixture into crock to eliminate air bubbles.

Cover tightly with microwave plastic wrap. Cook at 100% in a high-wattage oven for 4 minutes,

6 minutes in a low-wattage oven. Prick plastic to release steam.

Remove from oven and uncover. Serve warm or, if making ahead, refrigerate and bring to room temperature before serving.

chicken and ham terrine

This is another recipe that has the advantage of being able to be served warm—no wait of a night or a couple of days. However, it can also be weighted and chilled (see box, page 147) so that it can be made ahead.

Makes 128 servings

**2 cups fresh bread crumbs
    from about 6 slices white
    bread (5 ounces)**
½ cup chicken broth
**½ cup chopped fresh Italian
    parsley leaves**
1½ teaspoons dried sage
⅛ teaspoon cayenne pepper
**Freshly ground black pepper,
    to taste**
**¾ pound boneless, skinless
    chicken breasts, cut into
    1-inch pieces**
**12 ounces baked ham, rind
    removed, cut into 1-inch
    pieces**
**3 shallots, peeled and roughly
    chopped**
Nonstick vegetable spray

Place bread crumbs, chicken broth, parsley, sage, cayenne and black pepper in a medium bowl and mix well.

Place chicken, ham and shallots in work bowl of food processor. Process until finely chopped. Add reserved bread-crumb mixture and process to combine.

Coat an 8½ × 4½ × 2½-inch glass or ceramic loaf pan with nonstick vegetable spray.

Scrape mixture into pan. Smooth out surface with spatula. Cover tightly with microwave plastic wrap. Cook at 100% in a high-wattage oven for 5 minutes or in a low-wattage oven for 8 minutes. Prick plastic to release steam.

Remove from oven and uncover. Cover lightly with kitchen towel and allow to stand for 10 minutes. Invert onto serving plate.

turkey pâté

This quickly made, inexpensive pâté makes a great many servings because its texture when cooked is very firm. It should be very thinly sliced. Accompany with Cranberry Ketchup (page 267). If serving as a canapé (page 116) use Pepper Brioche (page 133), toasted, or Rye Soda Bread (page 114). Thinly spread bread with Maître d'Hôtel Butter (page 43) or Green Peppercorn Butter (page 43), if using brioche.

Makes 144 servings

**2 pounds raw ground turkey
    or turkey breasts**
**2 scallions, cut into 1-inch
    pieces**
**¾ cup loosely packed fresh
    Italian parsley leaves**
½ cup chicken broth
2 tablespoons heavy cream
**½ teaspoon dried summer
    savory, or 2 teaspoons fresh
    tarragon leaves**
2 teaspoons kosher salt
**Freshly ground black pepper,
    to taste**
Vegetable oil for greasing pan

If using whole turkey breasts, place in food processor and process until coarsely ground. Remove turkey to bowl. Add scallions and parsley to processor and process until

151

coarsely chopped. Add ground turkey, if using, and remaining ingredients. Process until smooth.

Scrape mixture into an oiled 8½ × 4½ × 2½-inch loaf pan. Cover tightly with microwave plastic wrap. Cook at 100% in a high-wattage oven for 12 minutes or in a low-wattage oven for 18 minutes. Prick plastic to release steam.

Remove from oven. Uncover. Cover with a kitchen towel for 10 minutes. Uncover and let stand until cool. Cover and weight (see box, page 147). Refrigerate for 8 to 12 hours. Unmold (see box, page 140). Trim ends and cut across into ⅛-inch-thick slices. Cut each slice into quarters.

Chinese Pork Terrine is a slight twist on a standard and can be garnished with crinkled, oil-cured olives perked up with some chopped roasted red peppers.

Scallion brushes may be used for spreading sauces such as hoisin on pâtés or meats, or simply use them for platter decoration. Trim the root end and cut pieces about 3 inches long. With the scallion lying flat on a cutting board, cut lengthwise slits from either end, leaving about ½ inch in the middle uncut. Place in very cold water and the cut ends will curl.

cornichons

Yes, you can buy perfectly good cornichons, those nonsweetened, tiny, pickled cucumbers with tarragon imported from France. I prefer the flavor of my own as well as the price. Multiply as needed.

Cornichons are a standard French accompaniment for pâté along with mustard, bread and butter. Thin crosswise slices of cornichons make a good topping for canapés (page 116) made with pâté.

Makes 2 cups

1 1/2 cups very small
  cucumbers, from 1 to 3
  inches
2 tablespoons kosher salt, or
  1 1/2 tablespoons coarse or
  pickling salt (do not use sea
  salt or iodized salt)
1 very large or 2 normal
  shallots, peeled and cut
  across into thin slices
  (about 1/4 cup)
1/8 teaspoon white mustard
  seeds
2 cardamom pods, broken to
  remove and keep seeds
6 black peppercorns
5 2 1/2-inch fresh tarragon
  sprigs
1/2 cup or more white wine
  vinegar, tarragon vinegar or
  herb vinegar

See box on page 56 for
sterilizing jars.

Immediately after picking,
remove any stems without
cutting into cucumbers. Place
cucumbers in a sieve under cold
running water and rub with your
fingers to remove any fuzz and
spines. Drain cucumbers and
allow to dry. Thoroughly
combine salt and cucumbers in a
small bowl. Cover tightly with
plastic wrap and refrigerate for
12 to 15 hours. Empty
cucumbers into a sieve and rinse
thoroughly with cold running
water.

In a sterile 1-pint
(16-ounce) glass jar, layer
cucumbers, shallot slices and
spices. When the jar is half full,
stick the tarragon sprigs down
the sides. Finish filling the jar.
Pour on vinegar so that jar is
completely full. Stick a small
knife down the sides of the jar
to release any air bubbles. Screw
on lid. Place in refrigerator for at
least 2 weeks and up to a year.
Turn jars upside down once or
twice.

chinese pork terrine

*Serve with Chinese hot prepared
mustard and Apricot Chutney
(page 161) and Buttermilk
Biscuits (page 108). Make at least
three hours before needed. This
will improve for several days.*

Makes 128 servings

1 1/2 pounds boneless pork loin,
  cut into 1-inch cubes
1 1/2 cups loosely packed fresh
  coriander (cilantro) leaves
6 medium cloves garlic,
  smashed and peeled
3 tablespoons tamari soy sauce
1 1/2 teaspoons Chinese
  five-spice powder
4 ounces water chestnuts,
  finely diced
Freshly ground black pepper

Place pork, coriander and
garlic in work bowl of a food
processor and pulse until finely
chopped. Add soy sauce and
five-spice powder and process
until fully combined.

Scrape into a bowl and stir
in water chestnuts and pepper.
Pack mixture into an
8 1/4 × 4 1/2 × 2 1/2-inch glass or
ceramic loaf pan. Place a collar
around the pan (see box, page
143). Cover tightly with
microwave plastic wrap. Cook at
100% in a high-wattage oven for
5 minutes or in a low-wattage
oven for 8 minutes.

Remove collar, re-cover with
plastic wrap and cook in a
high-wattage oven for 4 minutes
or in a low-wattage oven for 7
minutes. Prick plastic to release
steam.

Remove from oven and
uncover. Allow to stand, loosely
covered with a kitchen towel for
15 minutes. Cover and weight
(see box, page 147). Refrigerate
at least 3 hours, or until chilled.
Slice across 1/4 inch thick;
quarter slices.

pork pâté with tomatoes and pine nuts

*This pâté is rather Italian in
flavor. The Italian paper-packed
tomatoes are the best. If you
cannot find them, drain canned
plum tomatoes and chop coarsely.*

*Put out the mold for guests
to serve themselves. Have a
basket of focaccia chunks—
Tomato (page 129) or Whole-
Wheat (page 128)—Cornmeal
Biscuits (page 108) or Crostini
(page 131).*

Makes 80 cocktail size slices

1 1/2 pounds ground pork
2 cups Italian chopped
  tomatoes, sterile-
  packed in paper carton
6 medium cloves garlic,
  smashed, peeled and finely
  chopped
1/4 cup pine nuts
1 rounded tablespoon anise
  seeds
2 teaspoons dried oregano
2 teaspoons dried thyme
1 teaspoon dried sage
1/2 teaspoon dried summer
  savory
1 tablespoon kosher salt
Several grinds freshly ground
  white pepper
Several grinds freshly ground
  black pepper

Place all ingredients in a
large bowl and mix well. Scrape
into a 1 1/2-quart soufflé dish.
Cover tightly with microwave
plastic wrap. Cook at 100% in a
high-wattage oven for 15
minutes. Prick plastic to release
steam.

Remove from oven and
uncover. Let stand until cool.
Cover and weight (see box, page
147). Refrigerate 8 to 12 hours.
Serve pâté in the mold.

153

santa fe pâté

This is a light-textured pâté. If you like a denser pâté or you have pork shoulder that is very lean, add an additional quarter pound of fatback. The microwave-cooked pâté can be sliced or spread with a knife. Don't be startled if the pâté is reddish; it is the peppers.

Serve with one of the Cornmeal Biscuits (page 108) and a salsa (pages 23–25). This is good with beer.

Makes 20 servings as part of a mixed hors d'oeuvre

1½ red bell peppers (7 ounces each), stemmed, seeded and deribbed and cut into 2-inch chunks (1⅓ cups)
½ pound yellow onion, peeled and cut into 2-inch chunks (2½ cups)
5 medium cloves garlic, smashed and peeled
¾ pound pork shoulder, cut into 2-inch cubes
¾ pound unsalted fatback, cut into 2-inch cubes
3 tablespoons chili powder
2 tablespoons ground cumin
4 teaspoons kosher salt
1 teaspoon dried oregano
1 teaspoon hot red pepper sauce
1 teaspoon ground coriander
½ cup loosely packed fresh Italian parsley leaves
½ pound calves' liver, cleaned
2 tablespoons good beer
1 tablespoon cider vinegar

Place peppers in the work bowl of a food processor. Pulse until finely chopped (it's okay if there are some larger pieces). Remove from the bowl. Do not wash out the bowl.

Place onion and garlic in the processor and pulse until finely chopped. Add pork, fat, seasonings and parsley. Process until combined and meat is chopped. Add liver and process briefly just to combine.

Remove mixture to a large metal bowl. Add beer and vinegar ingredients and reserved peppers. Stir lightly just until incorporated.

Pour mixture into an 8½ × 4½ × 2½-inch glass loaf pan. Cover with paper towels. Cook at 100% in a high-wattage oven for 20 minutes. Carefully discard paper towels.

Remove from oven. When cool, weight the pâté (see page 147) and refrigerate overnight.

pork-pistachio pâté

This is terribly quick (microwave) and very French. Serve with sliced store-bought Italian bread or Whole-Wheat Biscuits (page 109), Dijon mustard and Cornichons (page 152) or store-bought cornichons. Don't bother peeling the skin off of the nuts unless you feel like it. To do so, put between two layers of Turkish towel and rub. Perfect with a robust red wine like a Côtes du Rhône.

Makes 128 servings

1½ pounds pork sausage meat
½ cup cold butter, cut into pieces
4 ounces yellow onion, peeled and cut into quarters
3 medium cloves garlic, smashed, peeled and sliced
2 tablespoon brandy
2½ teaspoons dried thyme
1½ teaspoons dried oregano
1 teaspoon ground fennel seed
¾ teaspoon freshly ground black pepper
Kosher salt, to taste
2 ounces shelled pistachio nuts

Place all ingredients except salt and pistachio nuts in work bowl of food processor and process until smooth. Add salt to taste.

Scrape pâté mixture into a bowl and stir in pistachio nuts. Coat an 8½ × 4½ × 2½-inch glass or ceramic loaf pan with nonstick vegetable spray. Scrape mixture into pan. Smooth out surface with a spatula. Cover tightly with microwave plastic wrap. Cook in a high-wattage oven for 12 minutes or in a low-wattage oven for 15 minutes. Prick plastic to release steam.

Remove from oven and uncover. When cool, weight the pâté (see box, page 147). Refrigerate overnight. Unmold (see box, page 140). Trim ends and slice into ¼-inch slices. Cut each slice into quarters.

Pâté can be enormously various; there is a kind to fit almost any party—or it can be a party—as long as you have a meat eater among your guests. Add a pickle. **1** *Pâté en Croûte (page 156);* **2** *Veal and Ham Pâté (page 156);* **3** *Pork Pâté with Tomatoes and Pine Nuts (page 153);* **4** *Rabbit Pâté (page 157)* and **5** *Cornichons (page 152).*

veal and ham pâté

Conventional-oven-baked and moist enough not to require a hot water bath, this can be easily multiplied.

Makes about 176 half slices

8 ounces thickly sliced slab
   bacon
6 medium cloves garlic,
   smashed and peeled
1 cup packed fresh Italian
   parsley leaves
1¾ pounds ground veal
1 pound 6 ounces slightly fatty
   ham trimmings, cut into
   1-inch chunks
2 tablespoons kosher salt
2 tablespoons pink
   peppercorns

Preheat oven to 400°F with rack in center.

Reserve 2 ounces of the bacon slices and cut the remainder in 1-inch pieces.

Place garlic and parsley in a food processor and process until finely chopped. Add bacon slices, veal and ham. Pulse until coarsely chopped.

Scrape mixture into a large bowl. Stir in salt and peppercorns.

Cut reserved bacon slices into 2¾-inch-long strips. If planning to unmold pâté, place strips along bottom of a 12½ × 4¼ × 3-inch pâté mold at 1½-inch intervals. Pack mixture firmly into mold. If not unmolding pâté, place bacon strips over top.

Bake uncovered until internal temperature reaches 160°F, about 35 minutes.

Let stand until cool. Cover and weight (see box, page 147). Refrigerate at least 8 to 12 hours. Unmold (see box, page 140) if desired. Slice in ⅛-inch slices. Cut each slice in half lengthwise.

pâté en croûte

This is a very handsome presentation that uses special pans. I certainly wouldn't attempt it for a large crowd—too much work, too many pans. Also it is only worth doing when someone is going to see the whole slice of pâté in its golden crust and shimmering aspic.

After the pâté is made and thoroughly chilled, at least twelve hours, you will need to pour a meat aspic—an appropriate meat broth, with or without added gelatin, that will set firmly when cold—through the hole in the crust. Return to refrigerator and allow to set. Slice carefully with a serrated knife.

Pâté Pastry
2 cups flour
5 tablespoons unsalted butter,
   cut into ½-inch pieces
¼ teaspoon kosher salt
1 large egg, lightly beaten
Scant ⅓ cup water

Filling
3 to 3½ cups of mixture
   made for any meat or fowl
   pâté in this chapter that is
   baked in the oven or
   microwave oven

Egg Wash
2 large eggs
1 tablespoon water

Aspic
⅔ cup appropriate broth with
   1 scant package gelatin
   sprinkled on and then
   heated until dissolved

Place flour, salt and butter in a food processor. Pulse until mixture resembles coarse meal. With machine running, pour egg and water through the feed tube. Process just until mixture begins to come together; do not let a ball form.

Press dough together with your hands and wrap in plastic wrap. Refrigerate for two hours.

Preheat oven to 350°F. Butter a 4-cup hinged rectangular mold very well, including the pins that hold the sides together.

Roll out dough to ⅛ to ¼ inches thick. Cut off about one quarter to use for the top. Place the remaining dough in the mold, pressing it into the corners. Trim the overhang to about ¾ inch and cut out a small V at the top of each corner.

Pack the mold with the pâté mixture. Place the dough reserved for the top over the mold and trim it to just fit. Fold the overhang from the bottom crust over the top crust and press them together to seal. Crimp the edges, keeping them away from the rim of the pan to prevent the cooked pâté from sticking. Oil the rim of the pan. Cut a 1-inch round hole in the center of the crust.

Roll out dough scraps and cut out designs for the top if desired. Whisk together egg wash ingredients. Brush over top, being careful not to let it touch sides of pan. Lay designs over top, if using, and brush them with egg wash.

Place mold on a jelly roll pan and bake in the center of the oven until an instant-read thermometer placed inside the vent reaches 150°F, about 55 minutes. Remove from oven. Carefully remove sides of pan. Brush the sides of the pâté with egg wash. Return pâté to oven and bake until sides are golden brown, about 17 minutes.

Remove from oven. Let stand until cool. Refrigerate at least 12 hours. Pour liquid aspic through hole. Return to refrigerator. Pâté will keep up to 10 days. After aspic is set, wrap pâté in aluminum foil.

rabbit pâté

You can substitute chicken for the rabbit, but it won't be as good. Rabbit is widely available frozen. Boning it is a bit of a chore. If it fazes you and the butcher won't do it for you, try another recipe. I like it so much that I give you the recipe both for the microwave oven and a conventional oven. At a cocktail party, let guests serve themselves directly from the mold. Good bread is all that is needed.

Makes 120 servings as an hors d'oeuvre
Makes 12 first-course servings

Pâté
1 whole rabbit (about 3½ pounds), defrosted if frozen
12 ounces bacon, cut into ⅛-inch-thick strips
1 medium clove garlic, smashed and peeled
2 strips orange zest (3½ × 1 inch each)
1 cup Rabbit Broth (see below)
2 teaspoons kosher salt
Scant ¼ teaspoon fresh black pepper (8 grinds)
Pinch each ground cloves, nutmeg, allspice

Rabbit Broth

Makes 1½ cups

Bones from rabbit, chopped up as well as possible
½ cup port
1½ cups water
½ bay leaf
5 medium cloves garlic, smashed and peeled

Bone the rabbit or have the butcher do it for you. Reserve the bones for the broth. Trim rabbit of any silvery membrane covering the meat. You should have about 1½ cups of meat. Set aside.

Make the Rabbit Broth (see recipe below).

Use a 1½-quart glass or ceramic soufflé dish or an

8½ × 4½ × 2½-inch loaf pan or a ceramic specialty mold like that in the photograph, page 155, spraying the inside with vegetable oil (see box, page 140). Using 2 ounces of the bacon, cut strips to fit across the bottom of your dish, placing them 1½ inches apart. Cut another 2 ounces in the same manner, reserving it for the top of the pâté.

If serving the pâté as a first course, reserve the rabbit loins for decoration; if not, include the loins in the pâté mixture. Place meat, remaining 8 ounces bacon, garlic and orange zest in a food processor. Process until smooth. Scrape mixture into a bowl. Add the 1 cup broth and spices. Using your hand with fingers spread, gently fold the mixture up and over itself. Finish each scooping motion by scraping the mixture softly against the side of the bowl. You will notice that the texture changes as the meat absorbs the liquid, getting whiter and more homogenous.

If baking in a conventional oven, preheat to 375°F.

If you have ground all the rabbit meat, scoop the mixture into the mold. Gently pack it into the corners and tamp the mold on your work surface to eliminate air holes.

If you have reserved the loins, pack in half of the mixture. If using a round soufflé dish, arrange the loins in a circle; if using a loaf or other straight pan, line them up parallel to the long sides. Gently pack in the remaining mixture, tamping the mold on the work surface to eliminate air holes. Place reserved bacon slices across the top.

Microwave-Oven Method. Cover the mold tightly with microwave plastic wrap. Cook at 100% in a high-wattage oven for 5 minutes. Prick plastic with a sharp knife and remove the wrap without taking the pâté from the oven.

Cook for another 7 minutes. Remove from oven.

Conventional-Oven Method. Place the mold on a baking sheet and place in oven. Bake for 45 minutes or until an instant thermometer inserted in the middle of the pâté reads 140°F.

Remove the pâté from the oven and cover with a kitchen towel for 10 minutes.

Let stand until cool. Cover, weight and refrigerate (see box, page 147). When cold, uncover and pour over remaining rabbit broth. Re-cover and refrigerate.

To serve as a first course, cut ¾-inch slices or wedges. For hors d'oeuvre, cut ¼-inch pieces and quarter each slice.

rabbit broth

Microwave-Oven Method. Combine broth ingredients in a 2½-quart glass or ceramic dish. Cover tightly with microwave plastic wrap. Cook at 100% in a high-wattage oven for 40 minutes. Prick plastic to release steam. Remove from oven and uncover. Strain and set aside to cool.

Stove-Top Method. Combine broth ingredients in a 2-quart pot and set over high heat. When it comes to the boil, skim off foam and reduce heat to low. Simmer for 1 hour. Strain and set aside to cool.

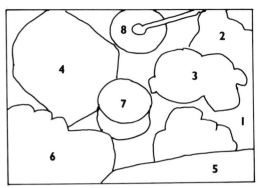

An assortment of pâtés can be given order and made attractive by being presented on a tray or cutting board. Cut store-bought pâtés (buying just as much as you need) or your own **1** Pork-Pistachio Pâté (page 154), **2** Veal and Ham Pâté (page 156) or **3** Pork Pâté with Tomatoes and Pine Nuts (page 153) into serving-size pieces. Set out with store-bought **4** cornichons or your own (page 152), a homemade bread like **5** Whole-Wheat Soda Bread (page 114), **6** French bread and **7** butter in a neat crock, as well as **8** mustard.

twin pâtés

There are times when the party is going to be very large and we need two pâtés of the same type. Here is a splendid recipe for just such a moment worked out for the microwave oven or a conventional oven. If using a low-wattage oven, you can cook only one pâté at a time. These pâtés taste better if allowed to mellow for two or three days after being made, which is probably an advantage if you are preparing for a large party. If you are going to need the loaf pans, unmold the pâtés, wrap them up tightly and refrigerate until needed.

Makes 2 loaves, for a very large party

1/4 cup **Worcestershire sauce**
1/4 cup **brandy**
1 cup **ham bone ends and skin**
1 cup **ham cubes (cooked, smoked ham), cut into 1/4-inch dice (about 4 1/2 ounces)**
4 ounces **unsalted fatback, cubed**
1/4 pound **ham, lean and fat**
2 medium **onions**
1/2 pound **chicken livers (1 cup)**
7 medium **cloves garlic, smashed and peeled**
2 tablespoons **Kosher salt**
1 1/2 teaspoons **freshly ground black pepper**
2 tablespoons **dried thyme**
2 teaspoons **dried oregano**
1 teaspoon each **ground mace, clove, ginger and nutmeg**
2 3/4 pounds **boned pork shoulder, ground**

Microwave-Oven Method. Combine Worcestershire sauce, brandy and ham bone ends and skin in 4-cup measure. Cover tightly with microwave plastic wrap. Cook at 100% in a high-wattage oven 5 minutes or in a low-wattage oven 8 minutes. Prick plastic to release steam.

Remove from oven and uncover. Drain, reserving the liquid and discarding the solids. Pour over cubed ham and fatback.

Place remaining ham, onions, livers, garlic and spices in work bowl of a food processor and pulse until finely chopped but not completely smooth. Put in large bowl with fatback, ham and pork shoulder and mix well.

Divide between two 8 1/2 × 4 1/2 × 2 1/2-inch glass loaf pans. Cover with paper towels and cook in a high-wattage oven for 19 to 21 minutes or until an instant-read thermometer reads 140°F, or cook one pâté in a low-wattage oven for 27 minutes. Remove from oven. Pâté will continue to cook as it stands.

Let stand until cool. Cover, weight and refrigerate (see box, page 147).

Conventional-Oven Method. Combine Worcestershire, brandy, 1 1/4 cups water, ham bone ends and skin in a small saucepan. Bring to a boil over medium-high heat. Reduce heat to low, cover and simmer for 50 minutes. Uncover and simmer for 1 hour.

Preheat oven to 350°F. Assemble pâtés as above. Cover loosely with aluminum foil. Place in a roasting pan lined with newspapers. Pour boiling water in roasting pan so that it comes halfway up sides of loaf pans. Bake for 1 hour, 42 minutes.

chili pâté

The seasoning for this pâté is rather like that of the Santa Fe Pâté (page 154), but this uses beef instead of pork and has beans—sort of like a solid chili. Serve with one of the green salsas (pages 23–25) and tortilla chips.

Makes 104 servings

2 1/4 teaspoons **vegetable oil**
1 3/4 teaspoons **ground cumin**
1/2 teaspoon **red pepper flakes**
1 pound **very lean ground round**
3 ounces **kidney fat, coarsely chopped**
4 medium **cloves garlic, smashed and peeled**
1 small **onion, coarsely chopped**
1 1/2 teaspoons **kosher salt**
Freshly ground **black pepper**
1/3 cup **loosely packed fresh coriander (cilantro) leaves**
1 28-ounce **can plum tomatoes, squeezed and drained thoroughly**
3/4 cup **cooked kidney beans or canned red beans, drained and rinsed**

Stir oil, cumin and red pepper together in a 1-cup glass measure. Cook at 100% in a high-wattage oven for 1 minute 30 seconds, or in a low-wattage oven for 2 minutes 30 seconds. Remove from oven.

Place ground round, fat, garlic, onion, salt, pepper, coriander and reserved spice mixture in a food processor. Process until onion and coriander are finely chopped. Add tomatos and process until just chopped. Scrape mixture into a bowl and stir in beans.

Place mixture in an 8 1/2 × 4 1/2 × 2 1/2-inch loaf pan. Cover tightly with microwave plastic wrap. Cook in a high-wattage oven for 12 minutes or in a low-wattage oven for 18 minutes. Prick plastic to release steam.

Remove from oven and uncover. Cover with a towel for 10 minutes. Uncover and let stand until cool. Cover and weight (see box, page 147). Refrigerate overnight.

Unmold (see box, page 140). Trim ends and cut into 1/4-inch slices. Quarter slices.

pork liver pâté

This is a very Scandinavian pâté. If pork liver is too strong-tasting for you, substitute calves' liver. Serve this with or on Rye Soda Bread (page 114), store-bought limpa bread or any of the Scandinavian crisp, dry breads.

Makes about 110 canapés

¾ pound unsalted fatback, thinly sliced
½ pound pork liver, cut into 2-inch chunks
7 ounces fresh pork fat (can be fatback), cut into 2-inch chunks
1 small onion (4 ounces), peeled and quartered
4½ teaspoons anchovy paste
2 large eggs
⅜ teaspoon ground cloves
¾ teaspoon ground allspice
1½ teaspoons kosher salt
¾ teaspoon freshly ground black pepper
1¾ cups plus 2 tablespoons heavy cream

Line an 8½ × 4½ × 2½-inch glass loaf pan with fatback slices, making sure they do not overlap inside pan. Leave a 2-inch overhang around top of mold.

Place liver, pork fat, onion and anchovy paste in a food processor. Process until liquid. Add eggs and spices. Process until smooth, stopping once to scrape down sides of bowl.

Add cream. Process a few seconds, stopping once to scrape down sides of bowl. Pour liver mixture into a blender. Process a few seconds. Pour into prepared pan. Fold overhanging fatback over top of pâté.

Place pan in a large dish. Cover loosely with paper towels. Cook at 100% in a high-wattage oven for 26 minutes.

Remove from oven. Uncover and let stand until cool. Cover and weight pâté (see box, page 147). Refrigerate overnight.

Unmold (see box, page 140). Trim ends and cut into ¼-inch slices. Cut each slice into quarters.

apricot chutney

The unexpected combination of ingredients—Japanese flavorings, a Mexican root vegetable and dried apricots—in this recipe works very well. It's also convenient to have a chutney that can be made in the middle of the winter, when very little good fresh fruit is available.

Makes 5½ cups

Syrup
⅓ cup tamari soy sauce
⅔ cup mirin
1⅓ cups rice wine vinegar
1 cup sugar
¼ cup peeled and coarsely grated fresh ginger
8 medium cloves garlic, smashed, peeled and chopped
1½ cups jícama, cut into ¼-inch cubes (8 ounces)
⅓ cup Chinese fermented black beans (1 ounce)
2½ teaspoons wasabi paste, or 2 teaspoons wasabi powder mixed with 2½ teaspoons water

Apricots
3½ cups dried apricots, cut into 1-inch pieces (1 pound)
3 tablespoons cornstarch
1 cup (use ¼ cup if making in a low-wattage oven) plus 3 tablespoons water

See box on page 56 for sterilizing jars.

Combine syrup ingredients in a 2½-quart glass or ceramic soufflé dish. Cook, uncovered, at 100% in a high-wattage oven for 8 minutes or in a low-wattage oven on a carrousel for 16 minutes. Stir in apricots and cook, uncovered, in a high-wattage oven for 7 minutes or in a low-wattage oven for 13 minutes.

Combine cornstarch and 3 tablespoons of the water in a small bowl and scrape into apricot mixture, stirring well. Cook, uncovered, in a high-wattage oven for 2 minutes or in a low-wattage oven for 4 minutes.

Remove from oven and stir in remaining 1 cup (¼ cup) water.

Ladle into sterilized jars and store, tightly covered, in the refrigerator.

161

chapter 5

swimmers and sea dwellers

There are vegetarian parties, but the mainstay of other cocktail parties and other informal entertainments is often fish and other seafood. In this chapter, you will find everything from boiled shrimp through seviche and fish tartares to fish cakes, cured fish, marinated fish and fish salads—as simple as tunafish salad, as complex as dilled smoked trout salad. That does not even include the hot seafood dishes such as Grilled Oysters (page 188), Clams with Black Bean Sauce (page 192), brochettes, snails and mussels.

The only thing I have left uncovered is smoking—not cigarettes, but rather hot smoking of fish at home. You cannot really

cold smoke, which is what superb professionals are for. I can only suggest, upon the recommendation of friends who are enthusiasts, that you follow the manufacturer's instructions and experiment with different woods and herbs for flavoring.

Sauces for the watery denizens below are in Chapter 1, and bread and other crusts to serve them on will be found in Chapter 2, except for Swiss Potato Pancakes (page 85), Corn Pancakes (page 85) and Buckwheat Blini and Crêpes (pages 220–221).

Besides the recipes in this chapter, look at those in Chapter 4, the mousses and pâtés (pages 144–147); in Chapter 6, Wrap and Roll, mainly for stuffings; and in Chapter 7, Fear of Frying.

Southwestern Seviche (page 174) is too good to save for a party with plates and forks. Pile portions in small shells (page 97) and set them out for people to slurp and lick up. If you have fancier friends, provide demitasse spoons or seafood forks.

r e a d y - m a d e s

While you will have better taste and texture if you cook your own, cooked and peeled shrimp are readily available, if expensive. A jar of bottled cocktail sauce jazzed up with some horseradish and lemon juice can make a last-minute party. Frozen, inexpensive baby shrimp, called TT in the trade, are available in bags. They are not rich in flavor but are acceptable in salads. Many canned or jarred fish are good helpers: anchovies, sardines, herring, salmon and tuna. Incidentally, many of the herrings can be bought as salads. A little lemon juice, mustard, sour cream or dill—the basic flavor ingredients of the dish—can turn store-bought from ordinary to fresh tasting. I avoid prepared mussels (smoked or otherwise) along with similar oysters and clams. However, if you have a cooperative fish store, clams and oysters on the half shell can be picked up shortly before the party and put out on trays of ice with wedges of lemon and sauces as you choose. This will require cocktail forks and, like many elegant, last-minute solutions, is costly.

There are two other categories of pre-prepared fish dishes, both delicious and both expensive, and about both it is worth knowing quite a good deal to get the best and the best for your money: smoked fish and caviar.

smoked fish

There are many good kinds of commercially smoked fish. They are usually salted to some degree and then cold-smoked to preserve them somewhat. Almost all smoked fish are good on canapés (page 116), Buckwheat Biscuits (page 109), Buckwheat Blini (page 220), Vegetable Confetti Pancakes (page 84), Swiss Potato Pancakes (page 85), Corn Pancakes (page 85) or rolled in Crêpes (page 221). They can then be topped with a bit of lemon, a grind of pepper, an herb sprig or sour cream, yogurt or whipped cream.

Most smoked fish can be made into mousses. See the recipes on pages 144–147 and substitute the fish you want to use. Smoked fish are of two kinds— those that flake and those that can be sliced. The flaky fish are easier to make into mousses; the others will need to be puréed before such use. The mousses can be spread on canapés or spooned into Bread Boxes (page 121), Crisp New Potato Shells (page 241), pastry shells (pages 96–97) or Miniature Choux Puffs (page 107). Some stores may sell acceptable mousses or smoked fish salads.

Some smoked fish can easily be cut into neat thin slices (see box), or they can be bought already sliced—typically salmon, sturgeon and black cod (sable). Whether your fish is bought sliced or is home-sliced, be sure that it is sliced as near to the time of serving as possible. Occasionally, you can buy a whole side of pre-sliced salmon (a large party) that has been vacuum-packed. Small packages of smoked salmon slices are usually dreadful.

Among the flaky fish available smoked are whitefish, eel, trout, bluefish, haddock and herring. These fish are usually easy to skin and fillet. Pieces can be broken off for use on canapés.

Slicing Smoked Fish

Use a filleting knife, which has a thin, flexible blade. Trim off any fins and bony edges and the hard, dry outer surface of the fish. Check for pin bones by running your fingers lengthwise down the fish. Pull bones out with tweezers or needle-nosed pliers.

Hold one hand firmly against the top of the fillet, while holding the knife against the fish, almost parallel to it. Using gentle, even pressure, slowly cut large, flat slices down the length of the fillet. Place the slices beween pieces of plastic wrap as you work to prevent them from drying out or sticking together.

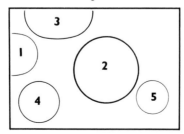

*S*teaming on an iceberg of dry ice an incredibly costly array of caviars: **1** osetra, **2** beluga, **3** salmon roe, **4** sevruga and **5** whitefish.

fish eggs, roes and caviar

All fish have eggs, called roe; that's how we get more fish. Before the eggs are released into the water to be fertilized they are retained inside the fish's body in a sac. The roe in almost all of the sacs are edible. The roe may be gently washed and sieved to separate the eggs from one another, salted (for the American and European market) or salt-and-borax-preserved (European market), sometimes being called caviar. The whole sac of, say, mullet or tuna may be salted and allowed to air-dry for several months making bottarga (Italian), boutargue (Tunisian), poutarque (French), avgotáracho (Greek). The sac becomes very firm and is shaved as thin as truffles. While not quite as expensive as truffles, it is costly indeed. The thin shavings can go on Crostini (page 131) that have been coated with Sweet Potato Aïoli (page 35). The soft roes of various fish—including herring, sole, carp and striped bass—are usually thrown out in America. In Great Britain, they are lightly sautéed in butter and served on croutons.

Caviar is most often thought of as coming from sturgeon, although it may come from any one of a number of fish. The first things to know about caviar are whether it has been dyed and whether it is fresh or has been pasteurized (heated) in a jar or a tin. Undyed is preferable to dyed. Lumpfish caviar is normally dyed and is not good; its dyes bleed onto other foods. Usually, you are looking for eggs that are not broken. You also don't want to see liquid swimming around the eggs in the container. Caviar that is "fresh" is preferable to the pasteu-

rized. Never buy sturgeon caviar that has been frozen. Some salmon caviar can be frozen, depending on the season and the kind of salmon. American golden (whitefish) caviar, Scandinavian bleak (a kind of small whitefish, "löjrom") roe and herring caviar, crisper and firmer, are often frozen. Never freeze any other kind yourself.

Translucent bone spoon with translucent oestra eggs.

Always buy fresh caviar at the last possible moment; your refrigerator isn't cold enough to keep it properly for any length of time.

Sturgeon caviars are priced according to quality. They should never be dyed. They will be better and more expensive "fresh." Then their price will depend on the kind of sturgeon from which they come and the country of origin. The "malossol" on the label is meaningless; it translates to "least salt." Larger sturgeon have larger and more coveted eggs. Beluga is the largest of these fish found in the Caspian and China. Russian or

Iranian from the Caspian will be more expensive, and I prefer it to the Chinese. Also from the Caspian is osetra, which is smaller with smaller eggs, and the smallest with the smallest eggs is sevruga. Sterlet is a smallish fish, used to give a very expensive, golden caviar reserved for royal courts. Sadly, the fish is pretty much extinct. American white sturgeon, Atlantic sturgeon and heckelback give good to very good caviar; white sturgeon is the best. Paddlefish is only a distant relative of a sturgeon, and its caviar is in distant last place. Sturgeon caviars can come in any color from black to gray to brown to greenish black. Color is an accident not an indication of quality.

You are better off downgrading the kind of caviar you are buying rather than its quality. That is to say, buy good sevruga rather than so-so beluga, "fresh" salmon caviar instead of pasteurized beluga, bleak roe or American herring caviar rather than inferior salmon roe. Don't buy lumpfish caviar just to serve caviar.

The better the caviar, the less it needs done to it. Attractive presentations are to serve it in Crisp New Potato Shells (page 241) or Bread Boxes (page 121) with sour cream, or on toast or Buckwheat Blini (page 220). Have lemon wedges for spritzing, but don't indulge in chopped onions or egg. For this usage, I would not buy the very best; I would settle. Save the very best for a small party—perhaps yourself and one loved one.

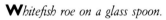

Whitefish roe on a glass spoon.

Pearls of beluga with noncorrosive mother-of-pearl spoon.

Fresh salmon roe with a Japanese wooden spoon.

shrimp

Let's face it: no matter how much cooking we do, no matter what we serve, shrimp will get eaten first and most at any stand-up party except one for a crowd of vegetarians. So before I go on to more amusing fish and seafood recipes, here are the shrimp. Generally, they need to be boiled to be served on their own—in or out of the shell—or to go into salads.

boiled shrimp

Bowls of boiled shrimp are magnets. Putting the shrimp in a different place from the rest of the food is a good method of crowd control—divide and conquer.

Since any number of people no matter how small seem able to eat any number of shrimp no matter how vast, in the interest of financial solvency it is best not to put the shrimp out all at once. Stagger them throughout the time of the party. I'm afraid that to be lavish—even reasonably generous—it is necessary to count on six shrimp per guest. That is just under a quarter of a pound of the best shrimp for dunking at parties—they come between twenty and twenty-four to the pound. If you are having your party out of doors or in a very informal space where a bit of mess will not matter, serve the shrimp in the shell. Shelling slows down consumption.

If the amount of money involved seems poisonous, try serving one of the shrimp salads. The shrimp are bulked out with other things and people will eat less.

It is better to cook shrimp in the shell, even if they are to be shelled. When shelling, try to leave the tail part of the shell on. It's a good handle. The cooking time will be about the same for shelled and unshelled shrimp, if you cannot face the work. Do cook your own shrimp. Fish markets always overcook them, and shrimp taste better if served warm or only refrigerated for a short while. I exempt myself from this rule when cooking a huge amount of shrimp for a large party. 1 pound raw shrimp, about 20–24 pieces = ¾ pound raw shelled = 13 ounces cooked in the shell = 10 ounces cooked and shelled.

No need for an endless variety of sauces. I feel that I do enough work making a large—as opposed to huge—bowl of one or two dips for the shrimp. The best sauces for shrimp dipping are thick enough to stick but not so thick that they cannot be gotten up on that irregular shape. Try Romesco Sauce (page 9) reduced to a purée, Green Goddess Dressing (page 36) and the herb dips (pages 17–18), in addition to the more obvious sauces such as Cocktail Sauce (page 38), Tartar Sauce (page 36), Rémoulade Sauce (page 36), Spicy Rémoulade (page 37), New Orleans Spicy Rémoulade (page 37), and Rémoulade Cocktail Sauce (page 38).

Microwave-Oven Method. When possible, choose a dish that will hold the shrimp in a single layer. Cover the dish tightly with microwave plastic wrap. When cooking large amounts of shrimp that cannot be arranged in a single layer, shake the dish halfway through the cooking time to redistribute them for even cooking.

¼ pound:
High-wattage oven: 1 min.
Low-wattage oven: 1½ min.
½ pound:
High-wattage oven: 2 min.
Low-wattage oven: 2½ min.
¾ pound:
High-wattage oven: 3 to 3½ min.
Low-wattage oven: 4½ min.

1 pound:
High-wattage oven: 4 min.
Low-wattage oven: 7 min.
2 pounds:
High-wattage oven: 5 min. (shelled, 4 min.)
Low-wattage oven: not recommended

Stove-Top Method. *To cook up to three pounds of shrimp:* Bring three times as much water by volume as the volume of the shrimp to a boil. Throw in shrimp. Cover pot. Turn off heat. After 5 minutes, drain shrimp and rinse with cold water.

To cook a huge amount of shrimp—say, the thirty pounds I cooked for a friend's birthday: Use shelled shrimp. Thirty pounds will take forever to peel. Bring a large pot of water to a rolling boil. Add half of the shrimp, or what your largest pot can cope with filled with water and shrimp. Cover; bring back to boil and simmer for 5 minutes. (A whole lot of shrimp will bring the water temperature down so much it has to brought back to the boil.) Remove to a colander using a large skimmer or a sieve as a ladle. Bring water back to a boil. Repeat as often as necessary with remaining shrimp.

all-american shrimp salad

This simple, picnic-style salad is still a delight in our days of seeming sophistication. Serve in a colorful bowl with a plateful of Buttermilk Biscuits (page 108), or spoon into Cream Cheese Pastry shells (page 96). The recipe can be multiplied ad lib.

Makes 4 cups, serving 60 on biscuits or shells, only 16 if plates are used

1 pound peeled cooked shrimp (opposite page) cut into thirds (3 cups), or smaller if going on biscuits
6 hard-boiled eggs (page 88), cut into 1/4-inch dice, or 1/8-inch if for biscuits
2 stalks celery (6 ounces), peeled and cut into 1/4-inch dice (1/2 cup), or 1/8-inch if for biscuits
1 small onion (3 ounces), cut into 1/4-inch dice (1/2 cup), or 1/8-inch if for biscuits
1 teaspoon celery seed
1 1/2 cups commercial mayonnaise
4 teaspoons fresh lemon juice
4 dashes hot red pepper sauce

Combine all ingredients in a medium bowl. Serve or refrigerate covered up to 3 days.

shrimp salad

A similar recipe to the one above, but eggless.

Makes 3 cups, serving 48 on biscuits or shells, only 12 if plates are used

1 pound peeled cooked shrimp (opposite page), cut into thirds (3 cups)
1/2 cup Classic Mayonnaise (page 32), or commercial mayonnaise

1/2 cup sour cream
1 1/2 tablespoons fresh lemon juice
1 1/2 teaspoons dill seed
2 scallions, white and green parts, trimmed and cut across into 1/4-inch slices
1/4 cup chopped fresh dill sprigs
1 teaspoon kosher salt

Combine all ingredients in a medium bowl.

sweet mustard shrimp salad

An unusually zesty shrimp salad.

Makes 6 cups

1 recipe Sweet Mustard Sauce (page 29)
2 pounds peeled cooked shrimp (opposite page), cut in thirds (6 cups)
2 medium red onions, cut into 1/4-inch dice
1 teaspoon kosher salt

Combine all ingredients in large bowl.

rich shrimp salad

Arlene Wanderman represents the Olive Oil Council. This recipe of hers for shrimp salad—almost a dip—is delicious even though it includes no olive oil. I guess a girl can just have enough. This can be made up to two days ahead. The seasonings will get more intense as the shrimp sits covered in the refrigerator. If serving the day you make it, increase the seasonings to taste.

Makes 3 cups

8 ounces cream cheese, at room temperature

1/2 cup plain yogurt
2 tablespoons fresh lemon juice
2 tablespoons finely chopped onion
2 tablespoons snipped fresh dill sprigs
1 teaspoon kosher salt
1/2 teaspoon freshly ground white pepper
1/4 to 1/2 teaspoon ground cumin
1/2 teaspoon cayenne pepper
1/2 to 1 teaspoon hot red pepper sauce
1 pound peeled cooked shrimp, cut into 1/4-inch dice

In bowl of mixer, beat all ingredients except shrimp until smooth. Stir in shrimp. Cover and chill at least 2 hours.

tropical shrimp salad

This is a very fresh-looking and -tasting salad. It can be made up to a day ahead and refrigerated. Do not add the papaya, which can be cut up ahead and tossed in the extra lime juice until just before serving. The enzymes in papaya will make the shrimp mushy. If you have the time, serve by the teaspoon onto Corn Pancakes (page 85), topping each with a fresh coriander leaf.

Makes 3 cups

2 large oranges
Ingredients for Curry Rum Marinade (page 272), substituting vegetable oil for butter and omitting pineapple juice
1 tablespoon additional fresh lime juice
1/2 pound peeled cooked shrimp (opposite page)
1 pound papaya, peeled, seeded and cut into 3/4-inch cubes (1 1/2 cups)

(continued)

169

Working over a bowl to collect the juice, peel the oranges with a paring knife, removing all pith. Cut out each orange section, taking only the fruit and leaving the membrane behind. Place the sections in a medium bowl. Squeeze out the remains to extract all the juice.

Make the Curry Rum Marinade according to the instructions on page 272, adding ⅓ cup of the orange juice in place of the pineapple juice and adding the additional lime juice.

Add the shrimp and papaya to the orange sections. Pour the marinade over and toss to combine.

Microwave-Oven Method.
Wrap each shrimp with a piece of sorrel leaf (or a whole small leaf) and place in a circle around the inside rim of a dinner plate. If they do not all fit in one ring, the remaining few can be arranged in an inner circle. Gently brush with the melted butter.

Cook, uncovered, at 100% in a high-wattage oven for 2 minutes or in a low-wattage oven for 3 minutes, 30 seconds. Serve immediately.

Conventional-Oven Method.
Wrap as above and broil or grill very briefly.

sorrel-wrapped shrimp

To have enough for forty or more guests, you have to make three or four times the shrimp recipe, but all the preparation can be done ahead. Since the shrimp cook for only two minutes, they can be prepared ahead and stuck in the oven to cook as needed. The recipe is based on a langoustine dish tasted at La Bourride, a two-star restaurant in Caen. If you can't find sorrel, substitute large basil leaves. The pink shrimp are beautiful with the herb leaves that are still green as they come from the oven. If these sit cooked for a long time the leaves will darken. Toothpicks are all that are needed for serving.

Makes 25 shrimp

25 medium shrimp (about 10 ounces), peeled and deveined

13 large sorrel leaves, washed, dried and halved down the center vein (or 25 small leaves can be used whole)

1 tablespoon unsalted butter, melted

On a hot summer day, no one needs alcohol, but oh for a cold refreshing pitcher of Lemonade (page 298). Keep accompanying foods light and simple: Steamed Asparagus (page 70), Marinated Grilled Shrimp (page 172) and an aromatic Herb Focaccia (page 128).

lemon marinade

I use this for grilled shrimp. Add a little hot pepper sauce and have a Caribbean-style marinade for fish.

¾ cup fresh lemon juice
1 ¼ cups olive oil
3 medium cloves garlic, smashed, peeled and minced
¼ teaspoon freshly ground black pepper
Kosher salt, to taste

Whisk all ingredients together in a bowl.

marinated grilled shrimp

This is one of my favorite foods for outdoor parties, particularly if there are friends who don't mind dirty fingers and are willing to crunch shrimp shells in their teeth—mine seem happy to do this once they have had the first taste. Repeat as needed.

Makes 30 pieces

30 large shrimp (about 1 ¼ pounds), in the shell
1 ¼ cup Asian or Greek Marinade (page 78) or Lemon Marinade

Remove the feelers from the shrimp. Leaving the shells intact, place each shrimp flat on the work surface. Holding a knife parallel to the surface, slice the shrimp in half evenly, starting at the head and stopping when you reach the tail. Do not cut through the tail. The shrimp will be in two even halves attached at the tail.

Place flesh side down in a shallow dish and cover with marinade. Toss in the marinade to coat thoroughly. Allow to marinate for about 1 hour at room temperature.

Heat grill until coals are very hot. Grill shrimp, shell side down, for about 4 minutes, or until cooked through.

172

raw fish today

It is sad but true that various contemporary realities have impinged on the pleasure that many of us take in what must be, historically, one of the simplest, largest and most pleasurable group of snack foods or hors d'oeuvre: raw fish and other seafood. Pollution has made many of us wary of raw clams and oysters, seviche, sashimi and raw marinated fish such as gravlax.

Upon due consideration, I am giving recipes that use raw fish and seafood because I eat them with pleasure. The one caveat I would enter is that such foods should be bought from really reliable fishmongers who have a good deal of business so that they are constantly turning over their stock. If you are going to fish or dig your own, be careful that the waters and beaches that you are using are safe. A call to local authorities will generally sort the matter out for you.

Where it is possible—not for instance for oysters or clams—I have given instructions for freezing the fish to kill parasites before using. It is ironic that the once proud slogan "fresh fish" is no longer a necessary hallmark of quality. Even the famous green herrings of spring in Holland are now frozen before serving. Where fishing boats go out to sea for weeks at a stretch, it is often preferable to have fish frozen on board rather than having them packed in ice; they are fresher.

Finally, it is up to you to decide what the risks are and whether you want to take them; I'm not giving up oysters on the half shell yet.

Freezing Fish

Freezing Small Pieces of Fish
Cut skinless and boneless fish into ½-inch to 1½-inch cubes, or as needed in final recipe. Line a baking sheet with aluminum foil. Spread fish pieces out all over sheet in a single layer. Cover with plastic wrap and freeze two days. The frozen fish may be kept by removing a single layer to a fresh piece of aluminum foil. Cover tightly with foil before wrapping in plastic wrap. Store flat in freezer. Do not succumb to the temptation to throw the frozen chunks into a freezer bag; they are likely to stick together. To use, remove from freezer and allow to defrost at room temperature for about 30 minutes before marinating—or, as in tartare recipes, grind frozen.

Freezing Whole Fish Fillets
Check the fillets for small pin bones, which run near the thickest part of the fillet starting near the head end. Remove the bones by pulling firmly with a needle-nose pliers or pair of tweezers. Freeze the fillets uncovered on a foil-lined baking sheet until solid, about 12 hours. Remove the fillets and wrap securely in aluminum foil and a layer of plastic wrap. Return to the freezer and keep frozen from 2 days to 4 weeks. The fillets may be marinated frozen as in Cured Salmon and Other Fish (page 176) or defrosted at room temperature about 2½ hours.

fish tartares

These are absolutely delicious spreads or fork foods if there are plates and forks. Mix and match fish and flavorings as you desire, although I have indicated my favorite pairings.

The fish for these dishes is ground frozen with all the remaining ingredients in a food processor. Do not defrost the fish before grinding or you will get a paste. If you want to multiply the recipes, work in batches, removing just enough fish from the freezer for one batch at a time. Putting more in the food processor also results in overprocessed fish.

The tartares will keep, refrigerated, for several hours or overnight. Serve on small individual leaves of Bibb, radicchio or endive, or with Crostini or Bruschette (page 131) or Oven-Fried Potato Chips (page 233).

(continued)

½ pound raw salmon, tuna or swordfish fillets, frozen in 1½-inch chunks (see Freezing Small Pieces of Fish, box, page 173)

Salmon

Makes 1⅓ cups

1 tablespoon olive oil
2 tablespoons fresh lemon juice
1 teaspoon kosher salt
1½ ounces red onion, very coarsely chopped
1½ ounces celery, cut into 1-inch chunks

Tuna

Makes 1 cup

½ teaspoon toasted sesame oil
⅛ teaspoon hot pepper oil
2 tablespoons rice wine vinegar
2 tablespoons tamari soy sauce
1½ medium cloves garlic, smashed and peeled
1 ounce scallion, white and green parts, halved or quartered lengthwise, depending on size and thinly sliced across (can substitute garlic chives)
¼ ounce fresh coriander (cilantro) leaves, chopped

Swordfish

Makes 1¼ cups

1 tablespoon olive oil
2 tablespoons fresh lemon juice
3 medium cloves garlic, smashed and peeled
⅓ cup loosely packed fresh mint leaves
½ teaspoon kosher salt

Place all ingredients (except scallion and coriander if making tuna) in a food processor. Hold food processor firmly in place and process mixture until coarsely chopped. Stir in scallion and coriander for tuna.

pacific overture

Those who prefer can freeze the raw fish (see box, page 173). Freeze fish at least two days before using it.

This seviche with Asian flavors is more aromatic than authentic seviche, less acid and spicy. The mixed colors and textures of the fish and shrimp make it pretty as well. Of course, it isn't necessary to use so many different ingredients. All one kind of fish or shellfish can be used. It is slightly preferable to use firmish fish and shellfish, such as those indicated, rather than soft ones. However, I have made this to acclaim with catfish fillets.

Serve this in scallop or clam shells (see box) with shrimp forks or demitasse spoons or on blue corn tortilla chips.

Makes 4 cups

6 ounces salmon fillet, skinned, boned and cut into ½-inch pieces
4 ounces monkfish fillet, skinned, boned and cut into ½-inch pieces
6 ounces cooked shrimp (page 168), peeled, deveined and cut into ½-inch pieces
¼ cup thinly sliced scallion greens (from 3 scallions)
3 tablespoons soy sauce
3 tablespoons rice wine vinegar
1 tablespoon grated fresh peeled ginger
2 teaspoons mirin
1 teaspoon toasted sesame oil
Freshly ground black pepper, to taste

If using frozen fish, defrost 30 minutes at room temperature.

Combine fish with remaining ingredients and allow to marinate at room temperature for at least 1½ hours before serving.

Cleaning Natural Shells

Scrub saved shells under running water until clean. Fill a large pot with water and add shells (do not overcrowd the pot with shells; if necessary work in more than one batch). Bring to a boil over high heat. Boil at least 10 minutes. Drain shells in a sieve and rinse well with cold water.

southwestern seviche

This traditionally flavored seviche can be made with bay scallops, which saves the work of cutting up large scallops, but it seems a waste of money. If desired, freeze before marinating (see box, page 173). Defrost in marinade in refrigerator. Allow two days ahead for freezing and six hours for defrosting. This permits you to make the seviche ahead.

Serve a tablespoonful in a scallop or clam shell (see box) or a teaspoon on a tortilla chip. This very pretty dish will serve a crowd. Divide or multiply the recipe as need be. If you are not freezing the scallops or fish, don't marinate too far ahead. You can have all the ingredients prepared and then combine when appropriate.

Makes 5 cups; 80 or more servings

1 pound sea scallops, cleaned and cut into ⅓-inch pieces, or same weight of fish cut into similar pieces
12 ounces large cooked shrimp, peeled and cut into quarters
3 medium cloves garlic, smashed, peeled and minced

A *spill of Southwestern Seviche.*

2 ripe medium tomatoes,
 cored and cut into ¼-inch
 dice (1½ cups)
2 medium jalapeño peppers,
 seeded and finely chopped
 (1½ tablespoons)
¼ cup chopped fresh
 coriander (cilantro) leaves
6 tablespoons fresh lime juice
Kosher salt, to taste
Freshly ground black pepper,
 to taste

Line a baking sheet with
aluminum foil. Spread scallops
out all over the sheet in a single
layer. Cover with plastic wrap
and store in freezer overnight.

Remove from freezer and
allow to come to room
temperature for about 30
minutes.

Combine with all remaining
ingredients in a medium bowl
until well mixed. Cover loosely
with plastic wrap and allow to
stand at room temperature for at
least 1 hour before serving.

scallop and pineapple brochettes

*This is a pretty and slightly
tropical dish. If desired, freeze
scallops or fish pieces as in box
on page 173. Defrost at room
temperature for about fifteen
minutes before skewering and
marinating. When skewering fish
or scallops, always skewer across
the grain so that the pieces don't
come apart.*

Makes 24 brochettes

Marinade
¼ cup plus 2 tablespoons
 tamari soy sauce
1½ tablespoons cider vinegar
⅓ teaspoon hot red pepper
 sauce
3 quarter-sized slices fresh
 ginger, peeled and minced
6 medium cloves garlic,
 smashed, peeled and
 minced

1 generous cup fresh
 pineapple, cut into ½-inch
 cubes (about 5½ ounces)
¾ pound bay scallops, or fish
 cut in small pieces

In a 9-inch glass or ceramic
dish, stir together soy, vinegar,
hot red pepper sauce, ginger and
garlic. Let stand at room
temperature for 5 minutes.

On 6-inch wooden or metal
skewers, alternate 3 pineapple
cubes with 2 scallops. (There
should be enough pineapple and
scallops to make 24 brochettes.)
Marinate in soy mixture for 5
minutes, turning skewers over
twice.

Microwave-Oven Method.
Prepare brochettes as above.
Arrange spoke-fashion on a
12-inch round glass or ceramic
platter. Cover tightly with
microwave plastic wrap. Cook at
100% in a high-wattage oven for
1 minute 30 seconds. Uncover
and serve.

Conventional-Oven Method. Broil
3 inches from heat source for 2
minutes on each side. Serve hot
or at room temperature.

175

cured salmon and other fish

Gravlax means cured salmon. The Norwegians sell it in packages. Some specialty stores make it. If you find some you like, buy it. I make my own for fun, to save money, to use fish other than salmon and to be able to flavor the fish as I please.

On the opposite page, I give three different cures. The Classic Gravlax Cure is just what its name says. It is generally used on salmon, which, after curing, can be served with Sweet Mustard Sauce (page 29), as can salmon marinated with the Cinnamon-Sage Cure. This delicious variation on gravlax was Bill Wilkinson's idea when he was at the Campton Place Hotel. I made up the Juniper-Fennel Cure to go with bluefish and found that it did very well on catfish and mackerel as well. You can combine cures and fish at will.

Each cure recipe is enough for a pound and a half of fish. Multiply by the amount of fish you want to cure. If, for instance, you have six pounds of fish, you will need to quadruple the cure recipe. Each pound and a half of fish makes enough to give twenty-five guests several servings as a canapé on Rye Soda Bread (page 114), Buckwheat Biscuits (page 109), Blini (page 220), Swiss Potato Pancakes (page 85) or with melba toast.

For canapés, consider Dill Butter (page 42) to go with classic gravlax, Sage Butter (page 42) to go with cinnamon-sage-cured fish and Maître d'Hôtel Butter (page 43) to go with juniper-fennel cured fish.

The logical garnishes for platters of sliced fish or canapés are dill sprigs, sage leaves or flowers and Softened Juniper Berries (page 132).

The point of curing fish is to give it flavor while at the same time removing excess liquid. The higher the proportion of salt the longer the fish will keep once cured. However, none of these cures is meant to preserve the fish. If you want to keep fish for a longish time, you will have to freeze it or buy cold-smoked fish.

The fish must be made well before your party and will take a fair amount of room in the refrigerator. See times in recipe and be sure to take into account time for freezing the fish (Freezing Whole Fish Fillets, box, page 173) if you wish to do so.

Ideally, you will buy your fish—no matter what the weight—in two equal pieces of pretty much the same shape (for instance, two whole fillets from the same fish). When possible, buy the fish filleted with the skin left on. Even the best fillets of fish will often come with the pin bones left in. These are small bones that march down the thick part of the fillet. You can find them by running your fingers lengthwise along the fish. Remove the bones with a tweezers or needle-nosed pliers.

With a little ingenuity, it has even proved possible to cure a single fillet, although not if the fish is frozen first. Using normal methods, this is not usually feasible, as it is hard to get two evenly sized pieces of fish from one fillet to make the sandwich of fish and cure that is needed in the process.

the cures

Classic Gravlax Cure

Makes ½ cup

¼ cup coarsely chopped fresh dill sprigs
3 tablespoons kosher salt
½ teaspoon freshly ground black pepper
3 tablespoons sugar

Combine ingredients.

Cinnamon-Sage Cure

Makes ¾ cup

3 cinnamon sticks, broken into small pieces
1½ tablespoons whole white peppercorns
3 medium cloves garlic, smashed and peeled
3 tablespoons kosher salt
2 tablespoons sugar
3 tablespoons light brown sugar
6 leaves fresh sage

Grind the whole spices fine in a spice blender. Place the garlic in a food processor. Process until finely chopped. Add the remaining ingredients and the spices and continue blending until the sage is finely chopped and the ingredients are well combined.

Juniper-Fennel Cure

Makes a scant ½ cup

3½ tablespoons juniper berries
1¾ teaspoons anise seed
2 large shallots, peeled
¼ cup fennel fronds
2½ tablespoons kosher salt
⅓ cup light brown sugar
2 teaspoons Holland (Dutch) gin, optional

Grind the whole spices fine in a spice blender. Chop the shallots in a food processor until fine. Add the remaining ingredients and the spices and continue blending to a paste.

Curing the Fish

Multiply fish amount and chosen cure recipe as needed. Each pound and a half of fish will make at least twenty-five finger-food portions.

For Each Recipe Cure
1½ **pounds fish such as salmon, bluefish, mackerel or catfish in two matching (if possible) skin-on fillets (skinless can be used), pin bones removed**

If freezing fish, see Freezing Whole Fish Fillets (box, page 173) and allow extra time for thorough freezing. Start curing frozen fish five days before needed. *If using fresh fish, filleted and pin bones removed,* start curing fish 2 days before serving.

Prepare chosen cure. For each pound and a half of fish to be cured, you will need a recipe of cure. Multiply as needed.

Place a wire rack over a large baking dish and cover with cheesecloth.

Rub equal amounts of the cure mixture on both sides of the fillets and place on cheesecloth, sandwiching the fillets together, skin sides out. If you have a single fillet or got stuck with mismatched ones, rub each with the cure mixture and roll up. Tie with string and place on cheesecloth on rack. However fish is arranged, cover with plastic wrap and refrigerate.

On top of plastic wrap, place a baking sheet. Weight for a day.

After the first day, *if the fillets were frozen,* check to see that the fish is thoroughly defrosted; turn over when it is—not before. *If fish was never frozen,* turn it over. Re-cover the fillets and continue curing: at least 1 day for fish that was not frozen; at least 2 days for fish that was frozen, turning over one more time.

When ready to serve, unwrap the fillets and scrape off all of the cure. Slice on diagonal in ⅛-inch-thick slices, making pieces as large as possible.

---

danish salmon sashimi

This combines traditions, Scandinavian and Japanese. They seem very happy together. Serve on Japanese rice crackers or on toasted canapés of Pain de Mie (page 119). If you want to use frozen fish, cut as in recipe and allow two days for freezing time. Defrosting will go quickly. Marination takes only two hours.

Makes enough to serve 20 as canapés

1½ **pounds skinless salmon fillet, about 6 inches long**

1 teaspoon wasabi powder
2 tablespoons mirin
1 teaspoon sugar
½ teaspoon grated fresh peeled ginger

Using a very sharp knife, cut rectangular slices as thin as possible, beginning at the spine edge and cutting across the grain of the fillet, working toward the belly edge.

If you prefer, at this point, freeze sliced salmon as in Freezing Small Pieces of Fish (see box, page 173). Defrost at room temperature.

Stir together wasabi, mirin, sugar and ginger. Stir in sliced fish. Allow to marinate, covered, in refrigerator for 2 hours.

177

cold cooked salmon

There are many cocktail parties that require a more substantial bit of food, especially toward the end. Particularly in summer, nothing does better and looks more impressive than a large piece of salmon. It is very beautiful with its pink flesh surrounded by edible flowers such as rose petals, nasturtiums or chive flowers. Make sure the flowers have not been sprayed. After the hymn to salmon, I must admit that the same modes of cooking will do equally well with any large fish or fish fillets.

Cold salmon is convenient as well as gala, since it is made ahead and served cold and can be varied by changing the cooking liquid or the sauce. I use plain water to cook in rather than wine, stock or court bouillon. To me the wonderful taste of salmon is more dominant this way. Leftovers are delicious and can be mutated into a rice salad along with the leftover dressing. Chapter 1 is full of sauces you can use with cold salmon, such as the Cucumber Tzatziki (page 17), the salsas (pages 23–25), Spicy Middle Eastern Tomato Sauce (page 27) and any of the mayonnaise-based sauces (pages 31–38). I particularly like Green Goddess Dressing (page 37) and Herb Dip (page 18).

You will notice that I have carefully avoided calling this poached salmon—although that is what the French would do—simply because there are so many good ways to cook the salmon. The most important thing is to cook it gently and evenly so that it cooks through without getting at all dry. If you like it pinky-white throughout, cook it a little longer. To test if it is done to your liking, stick a sharp, thin knife through the flesh toward the bone in the middle of the fish, or if the fish is boneless, into the center of the fillet.

Skin fish while still warm. If skinning a whole fish, take a sharp knife and cut through the skin all along the backbone. With the tip of your knife, tease out the dorsal fin (the one along the backbone) and the backbone. If need be, use your fingers to make sure that all the little bones that extend down from the backbone have been removed. With a pair of scissors, cut through the skin at the tail end of the fish and at the head. Gently pull skin off, working from the backbone side toward the belly flaps and from head to tail. Discard skin. Clean sides of platter with paper towel. Cover the fish with a damp kitchen towel. Refrigerate if not serving within one hour. If refrigerated, remove from refrigerator an hour before serving. You don't have to remove the skin on the bottom side. When you serve the fish, and your guests have worked their way down to the big central bone, simply lift it at the tail end and remove. Continue serving fish.

This dish requires plates and forks . . . no knives.

A *Cold Cooked Salmon is a triumphant party centerpiece; spectacular, surrounded by edible flowers—here, the many colors of peppery nasturtiums and their heart-shaped leaves. Herb flowers—true geraniums, chive, marjoram and sage flowers—can join rose petals, violets and tiger lilies. Use flowers that have never been sprayed.*

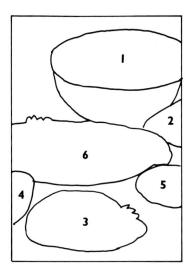

*Scandinavians love seafood feasts. A large bowl or platter of **1 crayfish** on their own would make a party. I would usually substitute a bowl of shrimp as being easier and cheaper, but not if you live where crayfish are readily available. Wash them well; discard any dead ones; half-fill a pot more than four times the volume of the crayfish with water and bring to a boil; plunge in the crayfish; allow to boil until red. Drain in a large colander. The water can be seasoned with red pepper flakes, many sprigs of dill, seaweed, tarragon or basil, as you wish. Add a bowl of Sweet Mustard Sauce (page 29), into which people can dunk their shelled crayfish. Have **2** Rye Soda Bread (page 114) on a board for slicing and a large bowl for shells. Want a more extensive party? Add **3** Smoked Trout Mousse (page 146), **4** Beet and Herring Salad (page 184), **5** Shrimp Salad (page 169) and **6** Gravlax (page 176) to slice thin. If there are real Scandinavians or would-be ones in the crowd, serve ice-cold aquavit in tiny glasses and have large glasses of beer to wash the whole thing down.*

microwave method for salmon

Makes about 24 end-of-cocktail-party servings

2 center-cut salmon fillets, skin on and pin bones removed (together about 3½ pounds)

In a 14 × 11 × 2-inch dish or a 13-inch oval dish arrange 1 of the salmon fillets, skin side down, and top it with the remaining fillet, skin side up and in the opposite direction from the first fillet, so that the salmon is level and will cook evenly.

Cover tightly with microwave plastic wrap. Cook at 100% in a high-wattage oven for 18 to 20 minutes, or until opaque. Prick plastic to release steam.

Remove from oven and uncover. Let stand until cool. Remove the skin from the top fillet carefully.

oven method for salmon

Makes about 30 end-of-cocktail-party servings

7½-pound whole salmon, yielding 4 to 4½ pounds

Preheat oven to 350°F with rack positioned in center of oven. Bring a large pot of water to a boil.

Place salmon in the largest roasting pan that will fit in your oven. Place the fish diagonally across pan. The head and tail can jut out. If salmon is still slightly too large for the pan, cut out two pieces of cardboard,

about 5 × 5 inches. Wrap in aluminum foil. Tuck one under the head and one under the tail so that the boards are partly in the pan to provide support for the fish outside the pan.

Place pan in oven. Carefully pour in boiling water until it comes halfway up sides of pan. Bake for 50 minutes. Very carefully remove pan from oven.

Transfer salmon to a large platter using large, heavy spatulas. Remove skin as directed on page 179. Freeze cooking water to use in a soup.

stove-top method for salmon

Choose your fish based on the length of your fish poacher. Your yield of cooked fish after allowing for the weight of the bones will be about two-thirds of the total weight of the fish. Allow about 2⅓ ounces of the yield per person. Make two or more fish, one at a time, if necessary. Before cooking, put fish on rack in fish poacher; cover with water; remove fish; measure water.

Before cooking fish, bring the measured amount of water (or court bouillon, if you prefer) to a boil in the fish poacher.

Measure the thickness of the fish at its greatest. Put fish in boiling water. Put on lid. Cook the fish for 10 minutes for each inch of thickness. A 2½-inch-thick fish will cook for 25 minutes. As soon as the water sends out steam, reduce heat so fish doesn't boil over.

When fish is cooked, remove from water by lifting rack. Skin as directed on page 179.

miniature tuna melts

Children large and small will love these. Multiply as need be. Yellow rather than white cheddar makes the better color choice.

Makes 24

3 English muffins, split
1½ cups Quintessential Tuna Salad (opposite page)
6 ounces Cheddar cheese, finely grated (1 cup)

Preheat broiler.

Cut the split English muffins into quarters, making 8 pieces from each muffin. Place on a baking sheet (not air-cushioned), cut side up. Broil for 2 minutes.

Place 1 tablespoon tuna salad on each muffin wedge. Top with 2 teaspoons of cheese. Broil until cheese melts and browns, about 2 minutes 45 seconds.

marinated anchovies

The anchovies can be marinated in a variety of ways and used as a garnish, served on bread, tucked into whole-wheat pastry shells (page 96) or served over Roasted Peppers (page 58) or sliced tomatoes. Use your imagination.

Use salted anchovies soaked in water and filleted by running your thumbnail lengthwise along the bone, or use canned anchovy fillets packed in oil. Rinse them under warm water before using.

8 ounces soaked or canned anchovy fillets

Caper Marinade

Makes about 50 pieces

1 tablespoon drained capers
Freshly ground black pepper, to taste
½ cup olive oil
⅓ cup balsamic vinegar

The kids' favorite, Miniature Tuna Melts, made small and open, are a snack anyone could love.

Fennel Marinade

Makes about 50 pieces

2½ ounces trimmed fennel, cut lengthwise into slivers (¾ cup)
Freshly ground black pepper, to taste
¾ cup olive oil
½ cup fresh lemon juice
¼ ounce fennel fronds, chopped (¼ cup)

Roasted Red Pepper Marinade

Makes about 100 pieces

¼ recipe Roasted Peppers (page 59), or 1 7-ounce jar roasted red peppers, drained, cut into ¼-inch strips
4 cloves garlic, smashed, peeled and thinly sliced
1¼ cups olive oil

Lay half of the anchovies in the bottom of a small dish, or if using red peppers, make layers alternating anchovies and red peppers, using half of each.

Sprinkle, according to marinade you are making, either pepper and half of the capers or pepper and half of the fennel or half of the garlic slices over the anchovies. Repeat the layers.

Whisk olive oil with vinegar or lemon juice if used. Pour it over the layers. Refrigerate at least 12 hours.

With Fennel Marinade, sprinkle with fennel fronds.

smoked trout velvet

This certainly can be served with crudités, but I like it spread on Crostini (page 131) or tucked into tartlets made from Sour Cream Pastry (page 96). Top each crostino or filled tartlet with some ground black pepper or a curl of roasted red pepper.

182

Makes 1¼ cups

1 8-ounce whole smoked trout
¼ cup minced celery
¼ cup minced yellow onion
1 tablespoon unsalted butter
¼ teaspoon freshly ground
　black pepper
½ cup plus 2 tablespoons
　heavy cream

Remove the skin, head and tail from the trout. Pull the fillets from the bones very gently, trying to leave even the very fine bones attached to the frame. Transfer the fillets to a mixing bowl. Finely shred the fish with two forks. Check the fish with your fingers to remove fine bones you may have missed. Set the fish aside.

Sauté celery and onion in the butter over medium-low heat until softened, about 5 minutes. Add the vegetables and black pepper to the fish.

Beat the cream in a small bowl until it holds soft peaks. Gently stir the cream into the trout. Refrigerate at least 3 to 4 hours, or 2 days before serving.

cannellini beans with tuna

This is a classic Italian antipasto that works very well in pastry shells (page 96–97), topped with the red onions, chopped, or served out of a bowl.

**Makes 8 servings as antipasto,
or fills 60 pastry shells**

2 16-ounce cans cooked
　cannellini beans, drained
　and rinsed
¼ cup fruity olive oil
¼ cup finely minced fresh
　Italian parsley leaves
Kosher salt, to taste
Freshly ground black pepper,
　to taste
1 12½-ounce can good-quality
　tuna in oil, drained
3 very thin slices peeled red
　onion
2 tablespoons finely minced
　fresh basil leaves, or less
　authentically, fresh dill
　sprigs

In a large bowl, mix together cannellini beans, olive oil, parsley and salt and pepper to taste. Mound on platter.

Break tuna into pieces two layers thick and about 2 inches long. Arrange these in a ring on the outer edges of the mound of beans. Strew red onion slices over beans and tuna. Top with basil. If desired, grind a little more black pepper on top. Serve at room temperature.

quintessential tuna salad

This is the perfect filling for a rye-toast sandwich, or miniature tuna melts. Spoon onto a slice of black radish, daikon or turnip or onto an endive leaf; or use one of the pastry shells on pages 96–97.

Makes 2¼ cups, 40 topping or filling amounts

1 small or ¼ large yellow
　onion (4 ounces)
4 ounces celery, very well
　strung
½ cup commercial
　mayonnaise
2 to 3 tablespoons fresh lemon
　juice
1 12½-ounce can tuna packed
　in water, drained
1½ teaspoon dill seed
Kosher salt, to taste
Freshly ground black pepper,
　to taste

Coarsely chop onion and celery in food processor. Add mayonnaise and process just until combined. Add lemon juice and tuna. Process with 5 to 6 on-off pulses. Remove to a bowl. Stir in dill seed and salt and pepper to taste.

Soaking Dried or Salted Fish

To Soak Salt Fish
See page 146 for rapid soaking of cut pieces of salted fish in microwave oven or conventionally over a longer period of time.

To Soak Smoked Fish
Place the fish in a dish large enough to hold it in one layer. Pour in enough milk (or water if called for) to completely cover the fish. Put a plate or other heavy object over the fish to keep it submerged in the milk. Refrigerate for 24 to 48 hours, until flesh of fish is soft and can be easily pulled away from the bone with your fingers.

Types of Smoked and Salted Fish

There are many types of smoked or salted fish. Those usable direct from the store are discussed on page 165. Those here are soaked to rid them of some of their salt or smoke and then made into various delicious dishes. They are fairly interchangeable between preparations. I have indicated in the recipes those I used to make the dishes. Not all my fish choices are traditional, but they make interesting food.

Smoked herrings, both whole and filleted; kippers, smoked or smoked and frozen; and smoked haddock are soaked overnight, in the refrigerator, covered in milk. Whole salted sardines are available, but tend to be too strong in flavor even after soaking. Salt herrings, while traditional, are often hard for the home cook to find. If you can find them, soak in milk as in box on page 183. Whole salted anchovies should be soaked in water overnight. However, the marinated anchovy recipes (page 182) can be made with canned fillets packed in oil and rinsed. Salt cod is generally not inter-changeable in these recipes.

herring in sweet mustard sauce

I like the sauce so much I have tried it in a great variety of dishes. This is one of my favorites. Use it plain or make a smørrebrød on Rye Soda Bread (page 114) or on store-bought imported rye or pumpernickel.

Makes 2²⁄₃ cups

- **14 ounces soaked, smoked skinless herring fillet (see box, page 183), cut across into ¹⁄₂-inch strips**
- **1 recipe Sweet Mustard Sauce (page 29)**

Stir herring into sauce.

beet and herring salad

This is a version of a standard Scandinavian, German and Russian salad. The beets turn the whole dish a rosy red. Serve with pumpernickel bread or Rye Soda Bread (page 114) or on Belgian endive or small Bibb lettuce leaves. A dollop of sour cream and some extra chives or a sprig of dill on each serving is attractive if you serve the salad out instead of leaving the guests to assemble things for themselves.

I have made this dish with herring out of tins and jars after draining and rinsing the herring, with smoked herring and kippers that have been soaked (page 183), with fresh and raw herring and with salt herrings that have been soaked (page 183). If you use canned beets, no one will know; the pure cook their own—see end of recipe.

Makes 3³⁄₄ cups

- **1 cup sour cream**
- **¹⁄₄ cup red wine vinegar**
- **¹⁄₄ cup sugar**
- **1 tablespoon Dijon mustard**
- **1 tablespoon drained, prepared horseradish**
- **8 ounces small beets, cooked, peeled and cut into ¹⁄₄-inch dice (³⁄₄ cup)**
- **5 ounces soaked smoked herring fillet (see box), cut into ¹⁄₄-inch dice (³⁄₄ cup)**
- **3 hard-boiled eggs (page 88), peeled and cut into ¹⁄₄-inch dice (³⁄₄ cup)**
- **3 ounces peeled and cored Golden Delicious apple, cut into ¹⁄₄-inch dice (³⁄₄ cup)**
- **1 medium onion (5 ounces), finely chopped**
- **1 tablespoon snipped fresh chives (scallion greens sliced lengthwise and then across can be substituted) or dill sprigs**
- **Extra sour cream for garnish, optional**
- **Extra chives or dill sprigs for garnish, optional**

In a medium bowl, whisk together sour cream, vinegar, sugar, mustard and horseradish. Stir in remaining ingredients except chives. Cover and allow flavors to blend in the refrigerator for 1 hour or up to 3 days.

To Cook Beets in the Microwave Oven. Place 8 ounces of beets in a 2¹⁄₂-quart soufflé dish. Cover tightly with microwave plastic wrap. Cook at 100% in a high-wattage oven for 8 minutes or in a low-wattage oven for 12 minutes. Prick plastic to release steam. Place 2¹⁄₂ pounds of beets in a 14-inch oval pan and cook, covered, in a high-wattage oven for 30 minutes or for 45 minutes in a low-wattage oven. Repeat for larger quantities.

To Cook Beets on Stove Top. Bring beets to a boil, covered by water, in a pan with a lid. Reduce water to a simmer and cook for about 1 hour, or until beets are easily pierced with a skewer.

184

This is an interesting variation on Creamed Herring using smoked herring. Alternatively, if you can find frozen herring with its roe packed in brine, soak it for two days in the refrigerator in skim milk; drain and rinse it; lift the fillets and prepare the sauce as in the recipe, adding the puréed roe. Thinly sliced red onions can substitute for white. The herring can also be served in Sweet Mustard Sauce (page 29) with onions and extra dill. As a first course at table, serve it with steamed new potatoes.

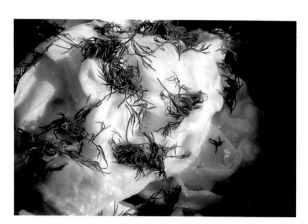

marinated
smoked
herring

While both salt and fresh herring may be marinated, smoked herrings or even kippers or bloaters make a much more interesting dish. Since they are not particularly beautiful, it is best to find a very attractive container and layer the fish and other ingredients in it to marinate. Serve from the container along with small plates and forks or with a good, firm bread such as Rye Soda Bread (page 114). The herring keeps at least two weeks in the refrigerator.

Makes 45 pieces

8 ounces soaked, smoked herring fillet (page 183), cut across into ¹/₂-inch strips

Marinade I
1 large onion (9 ounces), peeled, quartered and sliced very thin (1¹/₂ cups)
2 teaspoons chopped dill sprigs
1¹/₂ teaspoons drained capers
Freshly ground black pepper, to taste
³/₄ cup olive oil
3 tablespoons red wine vinegar

Marinade II
1 large onion (9 ounces), peeled, quartered and sliced very thin (1¹/₂ cups)
1 medium carrot (4 ounces), peeled and cut across into ¹/₈-inch rounds (³/₄ cup)
1 tablespoon coriander seeds
1 small bay leaf
1 cup peanut oil

Use a small container, preferably with a cover, that can go to the table (pretty) at least 2¹/₂ inches deep. Beginning with the onions, layer the ingredients other than liquids so as to end with a top layer of vegetables.

If using Marinade I, whisk olive oil and vinegar together and pour over the herring. If using Marinade II, simply pour oil over layered ingredients. Cover with lid or foil or plastic wrap. Refrigerate at least 12 hours—preferably two days.

creamed
herring

This is the herring of my Russian-family-dominated childhood. I make it myself from salt, smoked or fresh herring. In my childhood, all through the late

fall and winter we would make this dish, using fat, egg-filled herrings. Instead of sour cream, buttermilk would be used, with the eggs whisked in to thicken the sauce.

In summer, we would get salt herring and soak it in milk before proceeding as in this recipe. Serve with toasted, quartered bagel halves, bagel chips or pumpernickel bread. It's messy but delicious. Alternatively, use plates and forks.

Makes 3¹/₂ cups

2 cups sour cream
1 cup buttermilk
1 large onion (8 ounces), quartered and very thinly sliced (1¹/₂ cups)
1 tablespoon fresh lemon juice
¹/₄ teaspoon freshly ground white pepper
7 ounces soaked, smoked herring fillet, cut across into ¹/₂-inch strips (1 cup)
¹/₄ cup chopped dill sprigs, optional

In a medium bowl whisk sour cream and buttermilk together. Stir in onion, lemon juice, pepper and herring. Refrigerate for at least 12 hours.

Just before serving, stir in dill, if desired.

squid salad

Most of us can most readily find squid in the market frozen, in which case it will already be cleaned. If buying whole fresh squid, you will need to buy about one pound. Wash them well. Separate the tentacles from the body, cutting off any of the interior goo that adheres. Carefully wash the tentacles. Wash the body, removing any strange stuff inside, including the stiff quill. If cooking as in this recipe in a microwave oven, you will not need to remove the surface membrane.

The dish can also be prepared on top of the stove over low heat, cooking just until the squid is barely opaque. If cooking this way, pull the thin, light purple membrane from the squid before cooking.

Makes 2 cups

¾ **pound of cleaned squid, whole tentacles and the bodies cut into ¼-inch rings**

Cooking Ingredients
3 ribs celery, peeled, cut crosswise into ⅛-inch slices (about ¾ cup)
¼ **teaspoon Greek oregano**
¼ **teaspoon red pepper flakes, preferably Greek**

Dressing
2 cloves garlic, minced
⅓ **cup coarsely chopped Italian parsley leaves**
1 teaspoon kosher salt
1 tablespoon olive oil
1 tablespoon lemon juice

Mix squid and Cooking Ingredients in large glass or ceramic soufflé dish and cover with plastic wrap or a tightly fitting lid. Cook at 100% in a high-wattage oven for 1 minute. Shake dish, holding lid in place if using. Cook for 1 more minute. Prick plastic, if using, to release steam.

Remove from oven and uncover. Combine Dressing ingredients and mix with warm, cooked squid. This can be made ahead and refrigerated, covered, for 1 or 2 days. Serve at room temperature.

Squid Salad is inexpensive and fresh-tasting. The colors are beautiful if the squid is cooked in a microwave oven. Serve in Fried Bread Puffs (page 125) or in clean shellfish shells (page 174).

186

fishburgers

When making these in quantity, it's easier to make them in the oven than on top of the stove..

I suppose it might be more elegant to call these fishcakes. Indeed, you can substitute a wide variety of fish in the recipe. Salmon is particularly nice, but children are more likely to eat the cod. Serve on Hamburger Buns (page 125) with Tartar Sauce (page 36), ordinary ketchup or Cranberry Ketchup (page 267).

These can be made ahead, refrigerated for up to two days, allowed to come to room temperature and reheated on a baking sheet in a 350°F oven for 3 minutes.

Makes 32

1 scallion, trimmed and cut into 2-inch pieces
¾ pound cod fillet, cut into 2-inch pieces, or salmon or other fish that flakes when cooked
½ medium red bell pepper, cored, deribbed and finely chopped
2 large stalks celery, trimmed, peeled and coarsely chopped
2 tablespoons chopped fresh Italian parsley leaves
¼ teaspoon hot red pepper sauce
2 teaspoons kosher salt
Freshly ground black pepper, to taste
Vegetable oil for frying or greasing baking sheet

Place scallion in a food processor and process until chopped. Add fish and process until finely ground. Scrape fish mixture into a medium bowl. Add remaining ingredients except oil. Use your hand to squeeze the mixture together.

Form the burgers, using a level tablespoon of mixture for each one.

To Sauté. Lightly coat a large skillet with oil. Place over medium-high heat. When skillet is hot, add the burgers. Cook until golden brown, about 1½ minutes per side.

To Bake. Preheat oven to 350°F. Place burgers on a lightly oiled baking sheet (not air-cushioned). Bake for 5 minutes, turning once.

crab cakes

These are the upscale relatives of Fishburgers. The recipe can be multiplied. These are fine with canned crab meat, but if your budget runs to fresh they will be remarkably better. If you are serving them to eat with a fork, they are much better coated with bread crumbs—I have friends who have eaten these this way as finger food. If you are making them into sandwiches, omit the bread crumbs. Use Cornmeal Biscuits (page 108) and a dollop of Tartar Sauce (page 36).

Makes 36

½ pound lump crab meat, picked over for shells, or canned crab meat, drained and rinsed
1½ cups fresh bread crumbs, plus 1 cup for coating, optional
1 scallion, finely chopped
1 tablespoon chopped fresh Italian parsley leaves
1 large egg, lightly beaten
¼ cup commercial mayonnaise
2 teaspoons Dijon mustard
2 teaspoons fresh lemon juice
¼ teaspoon Worcestershire sauce
½ teaspoon kosher salt
Freshly ground black pepper, to taste
Vegetable oil for shallow frying

Combine all ingredients except vegetable oil in a medium bowl. Using 2 teaspoons of the mixture for each, form into ¾-inch-thick patties.

If desired, coat crab cakes in the additional bread crumbs. They may be refrigerated at this point for up to 6 hours.

Working in batches, cook the crab cakes in shallow oil (page 237) until brown on the bottom, about 1 minute. Turn and cook until brown on the other side, about 45 seconds. Drain on paper towels.

spicy crab cakes

Serve these on Jalapeño Cornmeal Biscuits (page 108) and top with Spicy Rémoulade (page 37) or New Orleans Spicy Rémoulade (page 37).

Makes 42

Ingredients for Crab Cakes
2 tablespoons additional fresh bread crumbs
1 additional scallion, finely chopped
½ small green bell pepper, seeded, deribbed and minced
½ to 1 teaspoon hot red pepper sauce

Combine all ingredients in a medium bowl.

Form and cook according to the instructions for Crab Cakes.

187

clams and oysters

Sadly, these cannot be guaranteed safe in today's world whether raw or cooked. Raw, on the half shell, they make one of the world's best finger foods—especially if you can get someone else to do the work of opening them. See suggested sauces for boiled shrimp (page 168) or put out lots of lemon wedges, a pepper mill and thinly sliced Whole-Wheat Soda Bread (page 114), lightly buttered.

angels on horseback

This classic English savory is equally good before dinner or at a party. Allow two to three per person. Multiply as needed. Prepare up to three hours ahead and refrigerate. Broil as needed. For crisper bacon, half-cook the bacon on paper towels in the microwave oven for two minutes, or broil until half-cooked.

Don't throw out the oyster juices. Freeze them and use the next time you make fish soup.

Makes 1 dozen

1 dozen oysters, shucked (see box) and drained of their juice
6 slices lean bacon, about 4 ounces, halved crosswise

Soak 12 wooden toothpicks in water for at least 2 hours. Preheat broiler.

Wrap a half slice of bacon around each oyster and secure closed with a toothpick all the way through the oyster.

Place wrapped oysters on a broiler pan and cook under preheated broiler for 7 minutes, turning once.

Remove from oven and allow to stand for about 3 minutes before serving.

grilled oysters

This is succulent food for an informal outdoor or kitchen party. It's messy to eat. Multiply as needed. Have lots of napkins. Serve cocktail forks or strong toothpicks.

Makes 4 servings

16 large oysters, in the shell, well scrubbed
1/2 cup unsalted butter
Fresh lemon juice

To Grill. Preheat grill until coals are white-hot. Place oysters on the grill curved side down so that as they open the juices do not spill out. Cook for 4 to 6 minutes, or until shells open to about 1/2 inch. Remove from grill with a large spoon to a plate. Open shells completely and place about 1/2 tablespoon butter onto each oyster. Sprinkle a little lemon juice over the oysters and serve.

To Bake. Heat oven to 450°F. Place oysters curved side down on a baking sheet. Cook for 8 to 10 minutes. Remove from sheet with a large spoon. Finish recipe as above.

Opening Oysters in a Microwave

Many dishes call for shucked or opened oysters, and many of us are not very good at doing this with a knife and do not have fish stores friendly enough to do it for us at the last minute. Enter the microwave oven.

Keep the shells to sterilize (page 174) and use as containers another day.

Scrub oysters to remove sand and barnacles. In the smallest microwavable baking dish in which the oysters will fit, stand them on their sides so that the juices will flow into the dish when oysters open. Cover tightly with plastic wrap and cook on high until oysters just begin to open.

6 oysters:
High-wattage oven: 2 min.
Low-wattage oven: 5 min.
12 oysters:
High-wattage oven: 4 min.
Low-wattage oven: 8 min.
24 oysters:
High-wattage oven: 9 min.
Low-wattage oven: not recommended

Prick plastic wrap to allow steam to escape. Remove from oven and remove plastic wrap. Open oysters over a bowl to catch juices. Loosen oysters from shells. Reserve deep shell halves and oysters; discard shallow halves. Strain liquid from bowl and cooking dish through a sieve lined with moistened cheesecloth or a coffee filter.

Clams and Oysters can be grilled or broiled to make a delicious bite at an indoor or outdoor party. Just caution your guests; the shells are very hot.

189

oysters in champagne sauce

This is simple and elegant. You can prepare the oysters and sauce ahead. Pop them in the oven as needed. The Champagne can be replaced by any dry sparkling wine.

I have seen these presented in soup spoons, which are arranged on a tray or platter. It makes things easy for the guests.

Makes 24 oysters

24 oysters in the shell, well scrubbed

1 ½ tablespoons unsalted butter

1 ½ tablespoons flour

½ cup oyster liquid (from opening oysters—see box, page 188)

½ cup dry Champagne

¼ teaspoon ground celery seed

Freshly ground white pepper, to taste

2 cups kosher salt, for broiling oysters

Open the oysters as in box (page 188) and reserve deep shells. Reserve ½ cup of strained cooking liquid.

Microwave Sauce. In a 4-cup glass measure, melt butter, uncovered, at 100% for 2 minutes. Whisk in flour. Cook, uncovered, at 100% in a high-wattage oven for 2 minutes, low-wattage for 3 minutes. Stir in oyster liquid and Champagne. Cook, uncovered, in high-wattage oven for 4 minutes, low-wattage for 6 minutes, stirring twice during cooking.

Stove-Top Sauce. In a small saucepan over very low heat, melt butter; whisk in flour; cook, stirring constantly, for 2 minutes. Stir in liquids. Stirring constantly, bring to a simmer and cook for 5 minutes.

Recipe can be made to this point a few hours ahead.

Preheat broiler with rack at highest level.

Stir seasonings into sauce. Place one oyster in each shell and spoon a little sauce over top of each to coat thoroughly.

Place coarse salt in broiler pan to hold oysters steady. Nestle oysters in shells into salt. Place under broiler until just golden, about 2 minutes.

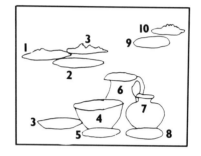

The weather's warm enough for a sundowner out of doors or even a spring wedding. Outdoors need not mean tables. Use what's at hand—a stone wall, a bench. **1** Beet sandwiches on pumpernickel with Crimson Menace (page 19); **2** Canapés (page 116) of radish and Watercress Butter (page 43) on Pain de Mie (page 119); **3** Summer squash filled with Thai Shrimp Stuffing (page 210); **4** Miniature Choux Puffs (page 107) with Sunny Tomato Filling (page 107); **5** radishes; **6** Fruity Iced Tea (page 298); **7** white wine; **8** coriander variation of Fresh Mint Salsa (page 25) in miniature pitas or Fried Bread Puffs (page 125); **9** Crostini (page 131) with Roasted Red Pepper Spread (page 14); **10** Soy-Anise Macadamia Nuts (page 50). If you stuff summer squash with vegetables, it's a vegetarian event.

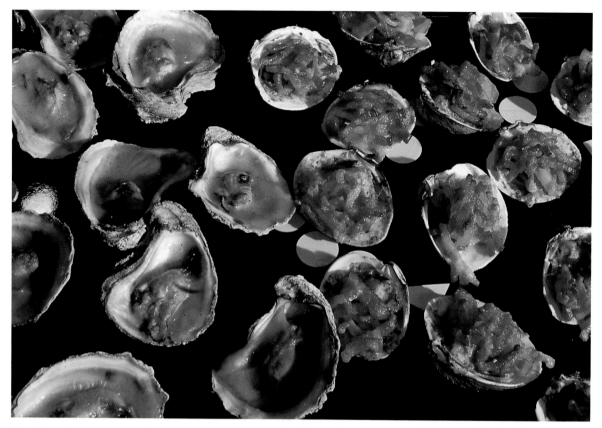

Good as plain oysters or clams, cooked or raw, are as snacks, we sometimes need something a little fancier, maybe even hot. Then it's time to think of Oysters in Champagne Sauce (page 190) or Clams Casino.

clams casino

This is an old-fashioned Italian restaurant dish that everyone still seems to love. Serve with napkins and let clams cool slightly before guests pop them in their mouths. Allow two per person if there is other food. If this is it—and fine that would be—allow six and multiply the recipe.

For crisper bacon, see introduction to Angels on Horseback (page 188).

Makes 24

2 dozen littleneck clams, opened (see box, page 188) and on the half shell
½ cup Maître d'Hôtel Butter (page 43) using half the amount of lemon juice and 2 cloves garlic
12 slices lean bacon, cut across into ¼-inch strips

Preheat broiler.
Loosen clams from their shell and return to the shell. Place about 1 teaspoon of butter over each clam and cover completely with pieces of bacon. Set them on broiler pan and place under preheated broiler for 4 minutes.
Remove from broiler and allow to stand for about 3 minutes before serving.

clams with black beans

I know this is messy. I know it is not a traditional hors d'oeuvre, but I have never seen that stop anybody who likes clams from eating these.

Makes 72

6 dozen littleneck clams (9 pounds), in the shell, scrubbed
½ cup Chinese fermented black beans
10 medium cloves garlic, smashed, peeled and coarsely chopped
½ cup rice wine vinegar
2 tablespoons tamari soy sauce
¾ cup fresh coriander (cilantro) leaves, chopped
2 bunches scallions (white and green parts), cut into 2-inch) pieces (3 cups)

Place all ingredients except coriander and scallions in a large pot. Cook, covered, over high heat, until you hear liquid come to a boil. Shake pot vigorously up and down to toss ingredients. Continue cooking 2 minutes. Add coriander and scallions to pot. Replace lid and shake to combine. Cook until clams open, about 4½ minutes.

seafood skewers

Hot skewered seafood makes a good mouthful. See the Index for other marinades. Mix and match vegetables and fish or shellfish as you like, but choose vegetables that cook quickly as the fish will.

Makes 24 skewers

Dill Marinade (page 194) or Asian Barbecue Sauce (page 77)
12 medium (about 25 per pound) shrimp, shelled, deveined and cut in half crosswise
or
12 medium sea scallops (about 12 ounces), cut in half from top to bottom
or
5 ounces boneless skinless salmon fillet, cut into 1-inch cubes
or
A combination of any two or three
12 small (1½-inch caps) mushrooms, cut in half
1 small red bell pepper (4 ounces), cored, seeded and cut into 1¼-inch dice
Very thin lemon wedges, optional

Soak 24 5-inch skewers in enough cold water to cover for at least 4 hours before skewering the seafood and vegetables.

Make the marinade. Toss the seafood, mushrooms and bell pepper in the marinade until coated and let marinate at room temperature 30 minutes. (If you want to serve the skewers at once, let the seafood and vegetables marinate one hour.)

Spear one piece of seafood between one piece of each vegetable on each skewer. Arrange the skewers in an 8 × 8-inch baking dish. Cover with marinade and refrigerate up to 4 hours.

To Serve. Heat the broiler and place the rack 4 inches from the heat. Arrange the skewers in a single layer on the broiler pan. Broil, rotating the broiler pan once, until the seafood is just cooked through, about 3 minutes. Remove and serve at once, accompanied with lemon wedges, if desired.

snails wrapped in bacon

A real pop-in-the-mouth tidbit that requires little cooking, only thinking ahead to marinate the snails. Multiply the recipe as often as you want. Count on about four pieces per person unless you have very conservative eaters. Cook off as hot ones are needed. Serve with toothpicks.

Makes 30 pieces

2 shallots, about 3 ounces each, peeled and chopped (about ⅓ cup)
2 7-ounce cans large snails, drained and rinsed (about 30 snails)
1 cup white wine
½ teaspoon whole black peppercorns, crushed with the back of a spoon or mortar and pestle
½ pound thinly sliced lean bacon

Combine snails, shallots, wine and peppercorns in a 1-quart bowl and refrigerate overnight.

Cut bacon lengthwise into thirds. Preheat broiler and drain snails, discarding liquid. Wrap each snail in a piece of bacon, tucking the end under the snail to secure. Place on a broiling rack or other ovenproof dish and broil for 4 minutes, or until bacon is crisp and snails are heated through.

Clam Cooking Times

Littleneck clams, the best for eating out of hand, can be prepared on the grill or under the broiler in the same way as oysters (page 188). They will take ten minutes and need to be turned once after three minutes, or they can be opened in the microwave oven.

Cook clams in a single layer, hinge end down in a dish 2 inches deep. Cover tightly with microwave plastic wrap. Clams are cooked as soon as they open; they don't have to gape.

Littlenecks, 8 to 10 per pound

6 clams:
High-wattage oven: 2½ to 3 min.
Low-wattage oven: 4 min.
12 clams:
High-wattage oven: 4 min.
Low-wattage oven: 6 min.
24 clams:
High-wattage oven: 7 min.
Low-wattage oven: 10 min.
48 clams:
High-wattage oven: 11 min.
Low-wattage oven: not recommended

Mussels Cooking Times

Mussels are wonderful to serve hot or cold as snack food. Once they are cooked, just pour them into a large bowl. Show people how to use an empty mussel shell as tweezers to extract the next mussel from its shell. Put out a goodly bowl of Rémoulade Sauce (page 36), Green Goddess Dressing (page 37) or other sauce of your choice. Let them dunk. If you prefer, you can put a little of the sauce in a pastry shell (page 96) and top with a shelled mussel.

When you buy mussels, they should be tightly closed, or when you squeeze them shut they should close tightly and stay that way when the shell halves are pinched together. Discard any that are open and any that feel weirdly heavy; they may contain sand. The best mussels—worth paying extra for—are farmed and come to you very clean. If you cannot get clean mussels and cannot convince the fish person to clean them for you, wash them one by one under cold running water and scrub with a plastic scrubbing pad or a stiff brush. If there is a fibrous beard sticking out of the shell, scrape it off by running the blade of a sharp paring knife along the edge of the shell and giving the beard a sharp tug between your fingers and the knife blade when you get to the sticking point. Unless you are making them ahead to serve cold, wait until the last possible moment to remove the beard.

Always refrigerate mussels until you cook them. Do not refrigerate them covered with water, even if they are already cleaned, as they will lose flavor. Instead, put them in a bowl and cover them lightly with a damp kitchen towel or paper towel.

As you cook the mussels, check to see when they open. Then they are cooked. If they are not open, let them cook a minute or so longer. If one or two fail to open, discard them.

Microwave-Oven Method

Cook mussels (16 to 18 per pound) standing up, hinge end down, in dish just large enough to hold them; cover tightly with microwave plastic wrap or lid.

1 pound mussels (2½-quart soufflé):
High-wattage oven: 3 min.
Low-wattage oven: 6 min.
2 pounds mussels (2½-quart soufflé):
High-wattage oven: 7 min.
Low-wattage oven: 10 min.
4 pounds mussels (5-quart casserole):
High-wattage oven: 15 min.
Low-wattage oven: not recommended

Stove-Top Method

Place scrubbed and bearded mussels in a pot—not aluminum or copper—just large enough to hold them. Add ¼ cup of liquid for each pound of mussels. Cover; bring to a boil; shake from time to time; cook about 8 minutes after boiling begins or until shells are open.

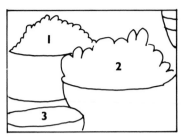

A *simple selection of seafood—cooked, for the leery—can be a party or can be added to one.* **1** *Spicy Popcorn Shrimp (page 242) can be picked up and eaten out of hand like nuts;* **2** *Mussels can be eaten hot, warm or cold using a mussel shell like tweezers to get the meat out. Dip the shelled mussels in a somewhat unusual sauce like* **3** *Spicy Rémoulade (page 37).*

dill marinade

This is also good on lamb or chicken that is broiled plain, or skewered with vegetables and grilled or broiled.

Makes 1 cup

- ½ cup loosely packed fresh dill sprigs
- ¼ cup fresh lemon juice
- 2 teaspoons Dijon mustard
- ¾ teaspoon kosher salt
- ¼ teaspoon freshly ground black pepper
- ⅔ cup olive oil

Combine the dill, lemon juice, mustard, salt and pepper in a blender jar. Blend until the dill is finely chopped. With the motor running, add the oil in a thin steady stream. Process until the oil is incorporated. The marinade can be made up to two days in advance. Store in a tightly covered container in the refrigerator. Shake vigorously before using.

How to Handle Fresh Bay Scallops in the Shell

Some of the world's best scallops—if we can find them—come to us in the shell with their roe attached. They really need no sauce.

If you are able to dig your bay scallops or come by some still in the shell, here's how to handle them.

First make sure the scallops are still alive. It's normal for the shells to be slightly open (gaping shells are a bad sign). See if the scallops close up if you rap on the shell or insert a thin object, like a wooden skewer, into the shell.

Discard any scallop that does not close up at least temporarily. Rinse the scallops under cold water, dislodging any winkles or snails that are attached to the shells. If they feel slick, you may want to scrub the shells with a stiff brush. Rinse again and drain thoroughly.

Conventional-Oven Method
Heat the oven to 450°F. Spread the cleaned scallops out in a heavy roasting pan in a single layer. Roast until the white part of the scallop is cooked through but still slightly translucent, about 12 minutes.

Stove-Top Method
Place scallops in a large skillet (working in batches if necessary). Cover the skillet and heat over medium heat until the scallops have opened and rendered some liquid, about 2 minutes. Reduce the heat to medium-low and continue cooking, covered, until the white part of the scallop is cooked through but still slightly translucent in the center, about 5 minutes.

Grill Method
Place scallops directly on grill over hottest part of the coals until cooked as described above, about 6 minutes.

Save the shells to sterilize (page 174) and use as very pretty containers for seafood salads.

chapter 6

wrap and roll

Rock and roll has nothing on wrap and roll as a worldwide attraction. From Greece and Turkey, Russia and China, Thailand and Vietnam, Mexico and South America, straight through Europe, come more or less spicy mouthfuls of filling wrapped in sliced meats, leaves and a wide variety of doughs. Some are even vegetarian. In their homelands, they may have been large or small. Here, they are all small, one or two mouthfuls each to go straight from fingers to mouth with an occasional stop in a dipping sauce on the way.

By the way, I lay no claim to ultimate authenticity. My Moroccan, Thai and Greek dishes bear a pretty good relationship to the way people in those countries cook, but I am an American working with the ingredients I find, and I like to play with recipes. Don't blame the country, blame me.

Some, like Greek Stuffed Grape Leaves (page 203) or Vietnamese white (uncooked) spring rolls (page 209), are meant to be eaten cold, as are the very American-1940s neat little roll-ups that are sliced to reveal their spirals. Some, such as Beef Empanadas (page 219), Cabbage Rolls (page 207) and miniature mushroom strudels or rolled fallen soufflés, can be served either hot or cold. Others,

Baked Empanadas with Beef Filling (page 219) are delicious and subtle. They don't even need a sauce.

197

however, such as Greek Tyropitta (page 216), cheese-filled phyllo triangles, are meant to be eaten hot.

Don't serve even the hot rolls too hot; people are likely to burn their mouths, particularly when the filling is cheese. Where it is possible, I have explained how to keep things hot or reheat them.

Not everything that is wrapped or rolled shows up in this chapter. Some of them, such as Chinese Eggrolls (page 258), are in Fear of Frying (Chapter 7). In fact, there is a bit of crossover, as some of the dishes in this chapter, like Calzones (page 220) and Vegetarian Spring Rolls (page 211), can be steamed, served uncooked or fried. It's a hard distinction to make. If what you want isn't in this chapter, look in the next one or the Index.

Some of these recipes are more finger work than others in the book, so don't plan to serve more than one or two at any party. If they are hot and special, bring them on later in the party so people don't gorge just on these and ignore the more easily made dips and pâtés. The cook should be applauded, but not killed by overwork.

ready-mades

One of the most useful store-bought rolled finger snacks is one unmentioned in this chapter, sushi. It is unmentioned because it's a lot of finicky work. If you have a nearby Japanese restaurant that makes good sushi, order some small ones that are not messy to eat, usually those with a dark green stripe of nori (toasted sheet seaweed) around the outside. The sushi will need to be picked up at the last minute and kept refrigerated until needed. You don't need a lot of different sushi to make a party.

Other wrapped ready-mades, such as Chinese dumplings, will be discussed in Chapter 7.

One of the better ready-made wrapped snacks is stuffed grape leaves (dolmades), which can be bought canned. Open the can; put the rolls in a bowl large enough to hold them with about an inch and a half of head room. There are about seventeen rolls in an 18-ounce can. Cover the contents of each can with a quarter cup of fresh lemon juice. Tightly cover the bowl with plastic wrap. Shake gently to bathe all of the rolls. Refrigerate for at least one hour or up to one day. Shake the bowl from time to time.

Empanadas come both baked and fried. Crispy Fried Empanadas (page 217) go well with salsas, Fresh Tomatillo (page 23) and Spicy Papaya (page 24).

pigs in blankets

This childhood favorite still pleases grown-ups. You can substitute store-bought puff pastry for the bread dough and even cover the dough with a small piece of thinly sliced or grated cheese before rolling.

Makes 24 pieces

24 cocktail frankfurters (about 8 ounces)
1 cup water
1 10-ounce package store-bought yeast bread or pizza dough
¼ cup Dijon mustard, optional
2 egg yolks beaten with 2 tablespoons water, for egg wash

Place frankfurters and water in a 2½-quart soufflé dish with tightly fitting lid. Cover with lid and cook in a high-power microwave oven at 100% power for 3 minutes, or boil.

Remove from oven and uncover. Drain off liquid and allow to cool completely.

Preheat oven to 400°F.

Roll out dough on a lightly floured surface to a rectangle of about 12×15 inches. Cut crosswise into 6 equal strips, then cut each strip crosswise into quarters. If desired, spread about ½ teaspoon of mustard over each frankfurter. Place one frankfurter across each piece of dough and roll up; seal the end with a little egg wash. Place on a baking sheet lined with parchment paper so that the seam is at the bottom. Repeat with remaining frankfurters and dough. Brush the tops with egg wash and bake in the middle of the oven for 18 minutes.

Remove from oven and cool slightly before serving.

ham roll-ups

These don't even need to be cooked, but they need to be made at least an hour before serving. They can be made up to two days ahead. Like the Smoked Salmon Roll-Ups and Smoked Turkey Roll-Ups that follow, these are quickly made, and you should allow five or six per person early in the party. Multiply as needed.

Makes about 100 pieces

16 slices boiled ham (about 12 ounces), each measuring 6×4 inches
1 cup Horseradish Cream Cheese Spread (page 39)

Lay one slice of ham on work surface and spread with 1 tablespoon of cream cheese mixture all the way to the edges. Roll up ham starting at the shorter end and finish so that the seam is at the bottom. Cover in plastic wrap and refrigerate for at least one hour. Repeat with remaining ham and cream cheese mixture.

Unwrap, trim off both ends and cut across into 6 slices.

smoked salmon roll-ups

The thing here is to get neat slices of salmon; it doesn't have to be the world's finest. Look for thin slices without holes. Use the trimmings to make Smoked Salmon Cream Cheese (page 39). Make up to two days ahead.

Makes 60 pieces

10 slices smoked salmon (about ⅔ pound), each measuring about 3×6 inches

¾ cup Scallion Cream Cheese (page 42)

Lay one slice of salmon out on work surface and trim edges to form more of a rectangle. Spread with 1 tablespoon of cream cheese mixture. Roll up salmon starting with the shorter end and finish so that the seam is at the bottom. Cover with plastic wrap and refrigerate for at least 1 hour. Repeat with remaining salmon and cream cheese mixture.

Unwrap, trim off both ends and cut across into 6 slices.

smoked turkey roll-ups

Again look for thin, even slices. Each roll can be topped with a crosswise slice of pimiento-stuffed green olive, if desired. Make up to two days ahead.

Makes 60 pieces

10 slices smoked turkey (about 10 ounces), each measuring about 5×7 inches
¾ cup Olive Cream Cheese (page 42)

Lay one slice of turkey out on work surface and trim edges to form more of a rectangle. Spread with 1 tablespoon cream cheese mixture. Roll up turkey starting with the shorter end and finish so that the seam is at the bottom. Cover with plastic wrap and refrigerate for at least 1 hour. Repeat with remaining turkey and cream cheese mixture.

Unwrap, trim off both ends and cut across into 6 slices.

cheese pinwheels

This very good and simple recipe is one I remember from my childhood. It's still good and can be prepared up to two days ahead. Broil at the last minute in batches as needed. They are small; multiply recipe as needed to allow three to five per person. The filling can be used as a spread. If you make your own Pain de Mie (page 119), trim the crusts and then slice very thin, lengthwise, you will not have to put rolling pin to bread.

Makes about 96 pinwheel slices

Spicy Cheddar Spread

¹⁄₂ **pound grated sharp Cheddar cheese**

¹⁄₂ **cup unsalted butter, at room temperature, plus 2 tablespoons melted butter**

2 **tablespoons Dijon mustard**

I **tablespoon Worcestershire sauce**

¹⁄₄ **teaspoon cayenne pepper**

Kosher salt, to taste

Freshly ground black pepper, to taste

I **loaf Pain de Mie, crusts removed and loaf sliced lengthwise ¹⁄₈ inch thick, or medium loaf sliced white bread (about 16 slices), crusts removed**

Combine all ingredients except bread and butter in food processor and process until smooth.

If using Pain de Mie, spread slices with enough of the cheese mixture to make a ¹⁄₁₆-inch layer. Roll bread, starting with the long side. Wrap and refrigerate an hour or up to two days.

If using commercial bread, roll one slice of bread at a time with a rolling pin until bread is about ¹⁄₈ inch thick.

Spread about 1¹⁄₂ tablespoons of the cheese mixture on each slice of bread and roll up like a jelly roll. Wrap in plastic wrap and refrigerate as before.

Preheat broiler with rack at top level. Unwrap pinwheels and cut across into ¹⁄₄-inch-thick slices. Line a baking sheet (not air-cushioned) with a piece of parchment paper. Put slices on so they do not touch. Brush with melted butter and place under broiler for about 3 minutes or until browned and bubbling.

Remove from oven and transfer to serving platter.

These children of the thirties and forties, Smoked Salmon Roll-Ups, are still very attractive today for a quick bite.

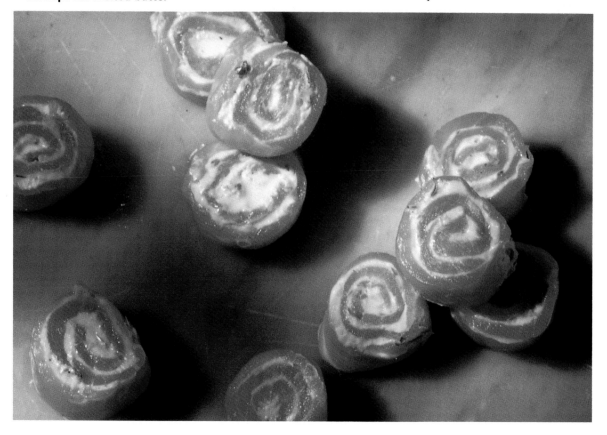

salami roll-ups

This is another snack I can trace back to cocktail parties in the forties. People still seem to love them. Make as many as you want, about three per person, multiplying recipe as needed. You can make these ahead and refrigerate on baking sheets until it is time to broil them. They are easy.

Makes 48 roll-ups

**I recipe Horseradish Cream
  Cheese (page 39)**
**I pound salami, casing
  removed, sliced thin**

Preheat broiler with rack at top, unless making ahead.

Using 1 teaspoon of the cheese mixture for each slice of salami, either spread evenly over the salami and roll up, or place cheese on one side of the salami slice and roll up around the filling. Skewer each roll with a toothpick.

Place rolls in tight rows on a baking sheet so that the toothpicks lean over. Broil for about 5 minutes, or until salami is crisp and cheese starts to bubble. Remove from oven. These can be tossed into a bowl or neatly arranged on a platter.

Mini–Moussaka Rolls, warm bites of eggplant rolled around sauce and filling, not the most beautiful but memorably good.

mini-moussaka rolls

There is a whole group of Middle Eastern, Turkish and Greek eggplant dishes that are layered. Here, I've taken that idea and turned it into a marvelous cocktail bite by rolling instead of layering.

These are more work than the previous recipes, but almost all of it can be done ahead. Prepare up to the final step, bring to room temperature, brush with egg and broil just before serving. They don't need to be piping hot. If you like glossier, crisper rolls, broil and set aside. Just before serving, brush with a second coat of egg wash and broil again. This is a good technique for rescuing ones that have gotten cold.

Unused raw eggplant can be used in Eggplant Moroccan (page 10).

Makes about 75 2-inch rolls

**I large eggplant, about 4
  inches across (about I ¾
  pounds), peeled**
Olive oil
Moussaka Filling (page 76)
**I egg, well beaten with a few
  drops of water**

Try to choose an eggplant that is of even diameter, approximately 4 inches. If the eggplant is thinner on one end, cut off any part that is less than about 4 inches across. Slice eggplant ⅛ inch thick. Heat the oven to 375°F.

Line baking sheets (not air-cushioned) with aluminum foil and brush the foil lightly with olive oil. Arrange as many eggplant slices as will fit in a single layer over the foil and brush the slices lightly with oil. Bake until lightly browned underneath and tender, about 20 minutes. Handling carefully, remove to a plate and cool. Repeat as necessary with the remaining slices.

To Form the Rolls. Place one teaspoon of the filling toward the bottom of each eggplant slice. Roll up each slice, making sure the filling is entirely enclosed. Tuck the ends underneath and arrange the rolls in a lightly oiled 12 × 9-inch baking dish. Bake 12 minutes. Cool to room temperature. (The rolls can be made and refrigerated for up to a day at this point. Bring them to room temperature before continuing.)

Heat the broiler. Brush the rolls very lightly with the beaten egg. Broil 4 inches from heat until warmed through and lightly browned, about 2 minutes.

greek stuffed grape leaves

*You can buy these **dolmades** in cans and doctor them (page 198), but they are much better made at home. These must be made ahead, although they will keep for up to a week. Try to put them in a container that is high rather than broad. The liquid will cover them better that way. Drain, reserving liquid for storage of leftovers; serve cool.*

Makes 50 packages

1 jar grape leaves in brine, rinsed, or home blanched (see box, page 204)

Stuffing (1½ cups)
¼ cup plus 2 tablespoons olive oil
¼ cup finely chopped onion

1 medium clove garlic, smashed, peeled and finely chopped
1½ teaspoons dried mint
½ cup long-grain rice (3 ounces)
2½ cups water
1 teaspoon kosher salt
Freshly ground black pepper, to taste
¾ cup fresh lemon juice

Preheat oven to 350°F.

Heat 2 tablespoons olive oil in a medium pan over moderate heat. Stir in onion and garlic and cook for about 5 minutes or until translucent. Stir in mint and rice and cook for 2 minutes longer. Add ½ cup water and cook, stirring occasionally, for about 4 minutes or until all

liquid has been absorbed. Remove from heat and allow to cool slightly.

Form rolls as in box, page 204, using 1 rounded teaspoon of the rice mixture. Place seam side down in one of two 12 × 8-inch baking dishes.

Divide remaining water and ½ cup of lemon juice between dishes and cover each with foil.

Bake 50 minutes. Remove from oven and allow to stand, covered, until cool. Place in smaller, deep container. Pour over remaining olive oil and lemon juice. Cover and refrigerate for at least 6 hours. Spoon liquid over from time to time.

Ouzo *is an anise-flavored Greek drink related to arak and raki. Once mixed with water, it turns a creamy white. The slightly acrid flavor cuts through olive oil and is a perfect complement to the foods of the Mediterranean basin, as are its yellowish French friends, pastis and Pernod.*

203

Leaves as Wrappers

Many kinds of edible leaves can be filled with a wide variety of stuffings or fillings and then cooked. Stuffed grape leaves will generally require baking in liquid. The other stuffed leaves will usually be steamed (see box, page 210). To test flavor of stuffings, place about a teaspoon of the mixture on a piece of parchment paper and cook either in a high-wattage microwave oven at 100% for 15 seconds, or 30 seconds in a low-wattage oven, or place on a plate in steamer basket and cook for 1 minute.

Grape Leaves

If you have young fresh grape leaves growing, you can *blanch* them in simmering salted water until flexible and then plunge into ice water. Otherwise, buy them packed in brine in jars. Carefully remove from jar and separate as many leaves as you will need. Return remaining leaves to jar and refrigerate. Wash leaves you are using in lots of cold water. If you have the time, soak in cold water for an hour.

To Form Rolls. Work with one leaf at a time. Spread out on work surface and with a small sharp knife remove hard part of center rib and stem end. Overlap the bottom two lobes to fill the gap. Place a rounded teaspoon of the stuffing mixture in the center of the leaf. Fold the sides of the leaf to the center and then roll up the package from the stem end to the tip. Finish with the seam at the bottom and place in baking dish. Repeat with remaining leaves as per recipe.

Napa Cabbage Leaves

Separate the cabbage into individual leaves. *Blanch* the leaves, in groups of 6 or 7, in a large pot of lightly salted boiling water for about 10 seconds. Remove with a wire skimmer to a large bowl of cold water. Repeat with other leaves. When all the leaves are blanched and cooled, drain them thoroughly in a colander.

To Form Rolls. Cut the thick center stalk from each leaf with a paring knife. Cut the leaves into squares approximately 4 × 4 inches. Place each cabbage square on a flat surface with one of its corners toward you. Place a slightly rounded teaspoonful of filling just below the center of the diamond. Fold the point nearest you over the filling. Then fold the two side points over that. Roll the cabbage into a tight cylinder, pressing lightly to squeeze out excess liquid.

Cabbage or Savoy Leaves

Carefully separate cabbage leaves. Cut each leaf in half, removing the center rib. Trim the heavy white sections from each half, leaving a rough square approximately 4½ × 4½ inches. Bring a large pot of salted water to a boil. *Blanch* cabbage for 45 seconds. Drain and immediately place in cold water. When cabbage is cold, drain and pat dry.

To Form Rolls. Place one piece of cabbage leaf outside down on a work surface. Drop a rounded tablespoon of Brandade (page 32) or a level tablespoon of Chinese Pork Terrine, uncooked mixture (page 153) or other loose filling on the top third of the leaf. Fold the top of the leaf over the filling. Fold the sides of the leaf over the filling, then roll up as tight as possible. Repeat with remaining leaves.

Lettuce Leaves

Carefully separate lettuce leaves. Cut each leaf in half, removing the center rib. Trim the heavy white sections from each half, leaving a circle of lettuce approximately 3½ inches in diameter. Set aside; do not blanch.

To Form Rolls. Place piece of fish or teaspoon of selected filling in center of circle. Fold the sides of the circle over the stuffing; roll up. Repeat with remaining leaves.

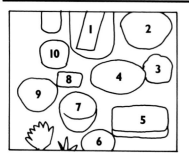

The Greek meze is one of the pleasantest assortments of bites of food to go with **1** ouzo on a warm summer evening. Choose as many of these as delight you and for which you have time: **2** *Squid Salad (page 186);* **3** *Taramasalata (page 31);* **4** *Walnut Dip (page 16);* **5** *Phyllo Packages with Tyropitta (Cheese) Filling (page 216);* **6** *Kalamata olives;* **7** *feta cubes with* **8** *anise seeds into which to dip them;* **9** *Greek Stuffed Grape Leaves (page 203) and* **10** *Macedonian Cheese Dip (page 18). Have some toasted pita (page 93) on hand for scooping.*

205

Greek Stuffed Grape Leaves (page 203) can be made at home with a variety of fillings, or canned ones can be successfully doctored (page 198).

chilean stuffed grape leaves

I was surprised to find that the Chileans make these, but then considering how many wine grapes they have, I guess it's logical. Drain refrigerated rolls, reserving liquid for storage of leftovers; serve cool.

Makes 75 pieces

1½ jars grape leaves in brine, rinsed, or 75 home-blanched grape leaves (box, page 204)

Chilean Beef Stuffing
½ pound lean ground beef
2 teaspoons olive oil
½ cup finely chopped onion
1 medium clove garlic, smashed, peeled and finely chopped
¾ teaspoon ground cumin

2¼ cups beef broth, plus 1¼ cup
½ cup long-grain rice (3 ounces)
2 tablespoons finely chopped fresh Italian parsley leaves
Kosher salt, to taste
Freshly ground black pepper, to taste
or

Lamb-Tomato Stuffing
(page 76, cooking with rice only 8 minutes)
1½ cups lamb or chicken broth

To Make Beef Stuffing. Place beef in a medium skillet over medium heat. Cook, stirring frequently, for about 5 minutes, or until it has lost all its pink color. Remove from heat and allow to drain through a fine strainer.

Heat olive oil in a medium

206

saucepan over medium heat. Stir in onion, garlic and cumin. Cook, stirring frequently, for about 5 minutes, or until onions become translucent. Stir in ¾ cup broth and the rice. Allow mixture to come to a boil. Reduce heat to low and simmer, stirring occasionally, for about 8 minutes, or until almost all the liquid has been absorbed. Remove from heat and stir in reserved beef with parsley. Season to taste with salt and pepper.

Preheat oven to 375°F.

With Either Stuffing. Form rolls as in box on page 204, using 1 rounded teaspoon for each. Place seam side down in an 11 × 7 × 2-inch ovenproof dish to make two layers.

Pour 1½ cups beef or lamb broth over the rolls and cover with foil. Bake for 50 minutes. Remove from oven and allow to cool, covered with foil. As they cool they will absorb more of the liquid. Transfer to a smaller, deeper container so that those on the top layer are now at the bottom of the container. Cover with extra broth as necessary. Refrigerate for at least 2 hours.

salmon wrapped in lettuce leaves

It isn't even necessary to fuss with a fancy filling, as this recipe shows. Serve with Southeast Asian Dipping Sauce (page 28) or Semi-Thai Sauce (page 212).

Makes about 48

4 medium heads Boston lettuce (about 8 ounces each)
1 pound salmon fillet

Prepare lettuce leaves as in box on page 204. Cut salmon

into 1 × 1 × ½-inch squares. Place a square of salmon on each piece of lettuce leaf. Fold edges of leaf pieces over to cover salmon. Steam as for uncooked fillings, page 210.

cabbage or lettuce rolls

Serve warm or cool. These can be made a day ahead with a variety of fillings and refrigerated. No dipping sauce is needed, but I suggest one for each filling. Mix and match to your pleasure. Rolls with cooked fillings need not be steamed. Those with uncooked fillings must be.

Makes about 60 stuffed leaves

1 large, firm head Napa cabbage (about 2 pounds)
or
3 large heads green or Savoy cabbage
or
5 medium heads Boston lettuce (about 8 ounces each)

Separate leaves, blanch (if needed) and form rolls as on page 204.

Steam those made with uncooked fillings as in box on page 210.

suggested fillings for leaves

Cooked
Curry Lamb Stuffing (page 286)—makes 1½ cups
sauce: Cucumber Tzatziki (page 17)
Lamb-Tomato Stuffing (page 76)—makes 1¾ cups
sauce: Spicy Middle Eastern Tomato Sauce (page 27)

Chilean Beef Stuffing (opposite page), its rice fully cooked with extra broth —makes 1¾ cups
sauce: Pacific Tomato Dipping Sauce (page 26)
Minted Rice Stuffing (page 76)—makes 1½ cups
sauce: Romesco Sauce (page 9)
Orzo Filling (page 73)—makes 1½ cups
sauce: Tomato Basil Dipping Sauce (page 27)

Uncooked
Turkey Pâté, uncooked mixture (page 151)
sauce: a mayonnaise (pages 31–38)
Two thirds of Chinese Pork Terrine, uncooked mixture (page 153)—makes 2 cups
sauce: Semi-Thai Sauce (page 212) or Peanut Dipping Sauce (page 28)
Thai Shrimp Stuffing (page 210)—makes 2 cups
sauce: Southeast Asian Dipping Sauce (page 28)
Salt Cod Pâté, uncooked mixture (page 146)
sauce: Tomato Basil Dipping Sauce (page 27)
Cod Ball mixture (page 251)—makes 1½ cups
sauce: Tartar Sauce (page 36), thinned to dipping texture with buttermilk
Smoked Haddock Ball mixture (page 251)—makes 1½ cups
sauce: Pacific Tomato Dipping Sauce (page 26)

rice paper wraps

Rice paper is a perfectly wonderful Thai and Vietnamese ingredient that may take a little hunting down and familiarization. It is used to make the most delicate of spring rolls, lightly dried, uncooked (wrappers, not fillings). The white, uncooked spring rolls have the advantage that they are not meant to be served hot so they cannot get cold. The paper can be used to envelop raw fillings and then steamed, or it can be used to make very delicate fried spring rolls. The competitors to the fried rolls are Chinese Egg Rolls (page 258).

The paper comes stacked in airtight packages. It will keep practically endlessly on the shelf wrapped airtight. If package is opened, rewrap and refrigerate. Use with cooked fillings like Vegetarian Spring Roll Stuffing (page 211) or with uncooked fillings, like a halved shrimp (page 212).

I have found rice paper packaged in 4 × 5-inch rectangular sheets, in 7-inch and 12½-inch diameter circles and in wedge shapes—a quarter of a circle. The circle quarters have been 6¼ inches down a straight side. The larger sheets will need to be cut into smaller pieces before making bite-size rolls. Rice paper can be cut either before or after soaking. The soaking is relatively brief. The rice paper must become thoroughly pliable but must not be allowed to become mushy. The filling is placed on the paper and the paper is rolled up into a neat package. The most familiar shape may be the Spring Roll, but it can also be shaped like the Phyllo Packages (page 215). After rolling, the packages are always allowed to dry for a brief time. If they contain cooked filling, they can be served as is, with a dipping sauce. Those with uncooked fillings need to be steamed or fried (see boxes, page 210).

Rice paper keeps virtually forever on the shelf and requires only a brief wetting before forming into little mouthfuls for steaming and serving on their own or in a spicy sauce. Here, they are filled either with pieces of shrimp and coriander (cilantro) leaves or with Thai Shrimp Stuffing (page 210). Southeast Asian Dipping Sauce (page 28) or Semi-Thai Sauce (page 212) would be good.

208

Making Rice Paper Rolls

To test flavor of uncooked fillings, place about a teaspoon of the mixture on a piece of parchment paper and either cook in a high-wattage microwave oven at 100% for 15 seconds or in a low-wattage oven for 30 seconds, or place paper on a plate in steamer basket and cook for 1 minute.

Make a test of your rice paper. Some are easier to cut before soaking, others after soaking. Try it both ways and proceed as seems best. Working with about 5 sheets of rice paper at a time, soak them in a broad shallow dish of warm water for about 1 to 3 minutes, or until thoroughly pliable. Cut into pieces as below with large, sharp kitchen scissors.

If Using Rice Paper Rectangles

Place one on work surface and cut into 2 strips about 2 × 5 inches, trimming off any excess. Place a rounded teaspoon of the stuffing toward one end and fold up like a flag to form a triangular package. Repeat with other strip, then with remaining rice paper and stuffing.

If Using Rice Paper Rounds or Round Segments

Cut circles that are 7 inches in diameter into quarters, or cut circles that are 12½ inches in diameter into eighths, or cut segments (quarters from 12½-inch circles) in half. For segments from 7-inch circles, use a rounded ½ teaspoon stuffing for each; otherwise use a rounded teaspoon for each. Center the stuffing about ½ inch from the curved side of the rice paper. Fold the curved side over the filling. Fold the sides in over the filling and roll up. Repeat with remaining rice paper and stuffing.

Do not choose fillings that are too wet; they will make your packages soggy. Choose an appropriate sauce. Uncooked and steamed rolls will do better with thin sauces, such as Southeast Asian Dipping Sauce; fried rolls can go with any of the sauces that appeal to you.

Alternatively, these rolls are often served on individual small lettuce leaves.

suggested fillings

Cooked
Vegetarian Spring Roll Stuffing (page 211)—2 cups
Cooked Shrimp and Pork Stuffing (page 211)—2 cups

Uncooked
Turkey Pâté, mixture (page 151)—2 cups
Two-thirds Chinese Pork Terrines, mixture (page 153)—2 cups Thai Shrimp Stuffing (page 210)—2 cups
Shrimp (page 168)

suggested dipping sauces
Peanut Dipping Sauce (page 28)
Southeast Asian Dipping Sauce (page 28)
Semi-Thai Sauce (page 212)
Pacific Tomato Dipping Sauce (page 26)
Japanese Dipping Sauce (page 246)

thai shrimp stuffing

Makes 2 cups filling—fills 48 steamed or fried rice paper packages (see boxes) or 48 steamed Lettuce Leaf rolls or Napa Cabbage rolls (see box)

1 tablespoon unsalted butter
2 medium cloves garlic, smashed, peeled and minced
⅓ cup diced green bell pepper
⅓ cup diced celery
⅓ cup finely chopped onion
¼ teaspoon dried thyme
¼ cup heavy cream
½ teaspoon hot red pepper sauce
2 scallions, finely chopped
1½ teaspoons kosher salt
Freshly ground black pepper, to taste
1 pound large shrimp, peeled and deveined
1½ tablespoons fresh lime juice
½ teaspoon finely chopped lemongrass, optional

Melt butter in a medium pan over medium heat. Stir in garlic, green pepper, celery and onion. Cook, stirring frequently, for about 8 minutes, or until vegetables become translucent and slightly soft. Stir in thyme, cream and hot red pepper sauce and cook for 3 minutes longer.

Remove from heat and stir in scallions. Season to taste with salt and pepper and allow to cool.

Place shrimp in work bowl of food processor and process until very finely chopped (almost smooth). Add to vegetables with lime juice and lemongrass, if using. Stir until thoroughly combined.

Steaming Leaf and Rice Paper Rolls

Either carefully oil the inside bottom of a metal or bamboo steamer insert(s) or basket(s), or very lightly oil a plate that will fit in your steamer insert. You can stack steamer inserts. Bring a quart of water to a boil in the bottom of steamer or in the pan over which the steamer will sit. If using a plate, put insert over water. Working in batches, fill and later refill insert(s) or plate(s) with rolls. Place filled insert(s)—stacked if using more than one—or plate over steam.

Steam leaf rolls, tightly covered, over rapidly boiling water until *Uncooked Filling* is completely cooked, about 10 minutes, or *Cooked Filling* is heated through, about 6 minutes.

Steam rice paper rolls, tightly covered, over rapidly boiling water for 3 minutes.

Drying and Frying Rice Paper Rolls

After the packages have been formed, place them on a plate or baking sheet and cover with a barely damp paper towel. Let stand at least 15 minutes. *Spring rolls with cooked fillings* may be eaten as they are or fried. *Spring rolls with uncooked fillings* must be steamed (opposite box) or fried. They can be rolled a few hours ahead and kept covered at room temperature.

If frying packages, pour enough oil in a heavy nonstick skillet to make a depth of ½ inch (2 cups in a 10-inch skillet). Heat oil to 325°F–350°F (see page 237, for shallow-frying instructions). As you place packages in oil, turn them over immediately. Do not crowd skillet—if packages touch they will stick together. Fry, turning occasionally, until golden brown, about 2 minutes. Remove from oil and drain on paper towels.

Spring rolls can be kept warm in a 150°F oven for up to 3 hours, though they will toughen somewhat. They will stay crisp, however, if kept at room temperature. They can be reheated at 350°F for 5 minutes.

vegetarian spring roll stuffing

Don't be put off by the tofu; this is a vegetarian dish that any guest will eat with pleasure, and it makes a good filling for Egg Rolls (page 258). Slightly modified, it makes a good filling for Chinese Filled Dumplings (page 253). The stuffing can be made and refrigerated up to three days ahead. Make Vegetable Egg Roll Filling (page 257) at the same time to fill rice paper or other doughs and you will use the dark green parts of this Chinese cabbage. The firm white ribs are used in this recipe. The northern Chinese call this bok choy. Don't confuse it with Napa cabbage, which looks like a huge crinkly Belgian endive. Oddly, the Cantonese call that bok choy.

Makes 2 cups filling to fill 48 regular or 96 small fresh or fried rice paper packages (box, page 209) or Chinese Filled Dumplings (page 253)

2 teaspoons vegetable oil
1/2 pound white ribs of bok choy (save leaves for Vegetable Egg Roll Filling, page 257), cut into 1/4-inch cubes (1 1/4 cups)
2 small scallions, trimmed
5 1/2 ounces tofu, squeezed out and crumbled by hand until texture resembles coarse cottage cheese (2/3 cup)
2 1/2 grams dried tree ear mushrooms (2 teaspoons), soaked in 2 cups warm water for 30 minutes, drained and coarsely chopped (about 2 1/2 tablespoons)

7 grams dried shiitake mushrooms (1/4 cup), soaked in 2 cups warm water for 30 minutes, drained and coarsely chopped (about 2 1/2 tablespoons)
1 1/2 ounces bean sprouts, coarsely chopped (1/4 cup)
2 ounces water chestnuts, coarsely chopped (about 5 1/2 tablespoons)
5 tablespoons loosely packed fresh coriander (cilantro) leaves, coarsely chopped
2 medium cloves garlic, smashed, peeled and minced
2 1/2 teaspoons Ginger Juice (page 257)
1 1/2 tablespoons tamari soy sauce or fish sauce (nuac nam)

Heat oil in a small saucepan over medium heat. Add bok choy and sauté until translucent (bok choy should be tender but still crisp). Place in a medium bowl.

Divide white part of scallions from the green. Mince all of the white part. Thinly slice the green part. Use 1/2 in this recipe and reserve the rest for Vegetable Egg Roll Filling.

Add minced and sliced scallion to bok choy with all remaining ingredients. Stir to combine.

Vegetarian Dumpling Filling
Use 1 tablespoon cornstarch and 1 1/2 tablespoons water. Stir cornstarch and water together in a small pan. Place on a flame tamer over medium heat. Stir constantly until mixture becomes very thick. Remove from heat and allow to cool. Using your hand, knead the cornstarch mixture into the filling until well combined.

cooked shrimp and pork stuffing

The work of cooking this can give Asian food a bad name, as the individual ingredients each require separate preparation. You can make it easier on yourself by preparing the ingredients over a day or two. Even the shrimp can be cooked and mixed the day before using.

Makes 2 cups filling; fills 48 regular or 96 small fresh or fried rice paper packages (box, opposite page)

6 ounces peeled, cooked shrimp (see page 168), quartered lengthwise and cut across into 1/4-inch cubes (3/4 cup)
3 ounces Roast Loin of Pork (see page 286), cut into 1/4-inch cubes (1/2 cup)
1 1/4 ounces dry cellophane noodles, covered in water for 20 minutes, drained and cut into 1/2-inch pieces (3/4 cup)
1 1/3 ounces bean sprouts, coarsely chopped
1 1/2 scallions, green part only, thinly sliced across (2 tablespoons)
1/2 cup loosely packed fresh coriander (cilantro) leaves, coarsely chopped
1 teaspoon sugar
1 teaspoon Thai or other fish sauce (nuac nam)

Combine all ingredients in a medium bowl.

semi-thai sauce

Don't put this on a delicate, mild-tasting filling that you want to taste. It will overwhelm it. However, it can make almost anything taste delicious. I have added oil and used it as a salad dressing.

Makes 1 cup

4 medium cloves garlic, smashed and peeled
1 ounce peeled fresh ginger, cut in small pieces
3 tablespoons sugar
2 tablespoons soy sauce
6 tablespoons fresh lime juice
½ cup Thai or other fish sauce (nuac nam)

Place all ingredients in a blender. Process until smooth, stopping once or twice to scrape sides of jar.

shrimp wrapped in rice paper

This is the very easy rice paper version of Salmon Wrapped in Lettuce Leaves (page 207). Salmon can be substituted for shrimp. Serve with Southeast Asian Dipping Sauce (page 28)

Makes 60 pieces

30 4x5-inch rectangles of rice paper, or 7 half rounds (12½ inches in diameter), or 30 segments (from 12½-inch-diameter rounds)
60 fresh coriander (cilantro) leaves
30 large shrimp (about 1¼ pounds), peeled, deveined and cut horizontally in half

Soak rice paper and cut as in box on page 209. Place a coriander leaf ½ inch from end (large end if using a triangle) of a piece of paper. Top with a half shrimp. Fold up as in box. Coriander will be visible through wrap. Continue with remaining shrimp and rice paper. Oil steamer inserts and steam as in box on page 210.

phyllo or strudel leaves

In addition to puff pastry, there is another pastry for which I am not going to give instructions in this book, since there are perfectly adequate commercial alternatives. These are the very thin, almost transparent sheets of dough sold variously as phyllo or strudel. Yes, there are differences between the two types of dough. For our purposes they work interchangeably as would warka, the Moroccan equivalent. The layers of dough are separated by thin brushings of melted butter, oil (sometimes olive) or water, depending on the fillings and forms. All dishes using these doughs are meant to be baked. They can be eaten hot or cool. *They can be frozen before baking and baked from a frozen or defrosted state, or they can be baked and refrigerated and reheated in a 350°F oven for three minutes.* They are very flexible.

Allow your package of dough to defrost at room temperature. It will take about an hour. As you work, keep unused sheets under damp paper towels. Do not allow unbuttered or unoiled sheets to stand for too long or they will dry out. They are not redeemable once they have dried out. Keep wrapped in plastic wrap in refrigerator or freezer.

The pastry can be made into mini-strudels using one greased sheet which is filled and rolled—forming many layers—baked and then sliced into bite-sized servings, or two sheets of pastry can be greased, layered, cut into strips, filled and folded to make typical Greek or Turkish mouthfuls.

Phyllo Packages (page 215) with Tyropitta (Cheese) Filling (page 216) are crisp and savory and are as good at room temperature as hot. They would make a good starting place for a Greek meze party (page 204).

phyllo shells

These are frilly little cups that can be used with any dip, spread or mousse dense enough so that it will not go flying when the crisp shell is bitten. You can also make these in the miniature pans used for pastry shells (page 96). Cut the sheet of dough into two-inch squares and proceed as in recipe checking color of pastry frequently.

The shells can be made up to two days ahead, up to a week if oil is used, and kept at room temperature. If you want to serve them warm or if they need recrisping, reheat in a 350°F oven on parchment-lined baking sheets for three minutes.

Makes 24

6 sheets phyllo dough
1/2 cup melted, unsalted
butter or olive oil

Preheat oven to 375°F with rack in lower third of oven. Have ready enough miniature muffin tins (top diameter of 2 inches) to make 24 shells.

Place one sheet of phyllo dough on a work surface, keeping the rest covered with a damp towel. Cut twelve 3 1/2-inch squares from the sheet, discarding scraps.

Brush one square lightly with butter or oil. Place another square over the first, turned 90° so that the corners do not meet. Brush with butter or oil. Place another square on top, facing the same direction as the first. Brush with butter or oil. Fit the dough into the ungreased muffin tin.

Repeat with remaining dough. Work as quickly as possible, to prevent cut squares from drying out. You can keep cut pastry covered with a damp paper towel while assembling each shell if necessary.

Bake until shells are just beginning to brown, about 10 minutes if butter was used or 7 minutes if olive oil was used. Remove shells from tin and fill, using 1 level tablespoon filling for each.

213

mini-strudels

Consider having a bowl of sour cream for spoonful toppings.

Makes 90 pieces

9 sheets strudel (or phyllo) pastry (about 4½ ounces)
1¼ cups melted unsalted butter
3 cups of a strudel filling or Mushroom Purée (page 73), using ¼ cup per strudel

Preheat oven to 425°F with rack positioned in center.

Keeping all unused pastry sheets under a piece of damp paper towel, lay one sheet of pastry on work surface. Brush generously with melted butter, making sure that the entire surface is covered all the way to the edges. Lay ⅓ cup of the filling (¼ cup if using mushroom) in a thin strip about ½ inch away from the long edge of the pastry closest to you. Fold the ½ inch of buttered pastry over the filling. Continue to roll up the filling in the pastry so that you finish with the seam at the bottom. Place on greased baking sheet (not air-cushioned) and brush with butter. With a skewer or small sharp knife make about 8 pricks down the center of each roll so that air pockets do not form. Bake in the center of the oven for 10 minutes. You can bake several rolls at a time as long as they do not touch.

Remove from oven and allow to cool to room temperature.

With a serrated bread knife cut each roll across on the diagonal into 10 slices and remove either end of the roll.

cabbage strudel fillings

We tend to think of strudels as sweet desserts. The same technique can give us delightful hors d'oeuvre. Cabbage that is thoroughly cooked, down almost to mush, makes perfect fillings, of which there are three here.

All the fillings can be used in puff pastry as a Pissaladière (page 104), using a fourth of the mixture. The sweet and sour variation can also be made in the microwave oven by cooking for the same amount of time, although the sugar, vinegar and raisins should be added ten minutes before the mixture would be done on top of the stove and then cooked for an additional fifteen minutes.

Makes 3 cups

Base
4 tablespoons butter
1 large onion (about 12 ounces), peeled and very thinly sliced (about 2 cups)
2½ pounds green or red cabbage (see variations), cored and very thinly shredded (about 10 cups)
2 cups water
1 tablespoon kosher salt
Freshly ground black pepper, to taste

Paprika Variation
Green cabbage
5 teaspoons sweet paprika
4 teaspoons caraway seeds
3 tablespoons sour cream, optional
1 tablespoon fresh lemon juice

Curry Variation
Green cabbage
4 teaspoons curry powder
4 teaspoons fresh lemon juice

Sweet and Sour Variation
Use red cabbage
Use red onion instead of yellow
1 bay leaf
⅓ cup dark raisins (about 2 ounces)
½ cup packed dark brown sugar
½ cup red wine vinegar
Pinch of ground cloves

Base Instructions
Melt butter in a large heavy skillet over medium heat. If using, stir in paprika or curry powder and cook for 1 minute. Stir in onions and cook, stirring occasionally, for about 4 minutes, or until quite soft. Add cabbage and stir to coat well with butter. Stir in water. Cover with lid and cook over low heat, stirring occasionally, for about 30 minutes. Uncover. If using bay leaf, add it now. Cook uncovered for about 30 minutes longer, stirring frequently so that the cabbage at the bottom of the pan is brought to the top and mixed well. When cabbage is very soft and "melted" and all the liquid has evaporated, remove from heat. Remove bay leaf if used. Proceed with appropriate directions below.

Paprika Instructions
Prepare base. Stir in caraway seeds and allow to cool. Stir in sour cream, if using, and lemon juice. Season to taste with salt and pepper.

Curry Instructions
Prepare base. Allow to cool, then stir in lemon juice and season to taste with salt and pepper.

Sweet and Sour Instructions
While the red cabbage is cooking, place raisins in a small bowl and cover with boiling water. Allow to stand for about 5 minutes and then drain well. Coarsely chop by hand. When base cooking time is finished, stir raisins into cabbage with sugar, vinegar, cloves, salt and pepper.

Cook over medium heat for about 10 minutes. Stir mixture continually so that the liquid can evaporate but take care that the sugar does not cause the mixture to stick and burn. Remove from heat and allow to cool before using.

phyllo packages

These are the Middle Eastern rather than the Middle European form.

Makes 90 pieces

24 sheets strudel (phyllo) pastry (about 12 ounces)
1 1/2 cups olive oil or melted unsalted butter
1 cup Spinach or Tyropitta Filling, or Thai Shrimp Stuffing (page 210), using 1 teaspoon per phyllo package

Preheat oven to 400°F.

Lay one sheet of dough out on work surface and brush generously with olive oil or butter. Lay a second sheet directly over the first and brush with oil or butter. With a long sharp knife trim about 1/4 inch off all the way around the sheets to even them. Cut, crosswise into 8 strips. Place about a teaspoon of the filling at the near short end of each strip. Fold up the packages like a flag to form triangles with the pastry seam at the bottom. Place on ungreased baking sheet (not air-cushioned), about 1/2 inch apart. Repeat with remaining filling and pastry. Brush tops with oil or butter and bake in the center of the oven for 12 minutes, or until golden brown on top.

Remove from oven and allow to cool.

spinach filling I

This is a classic Greek filling for **Spanakopita,** *Phyllo Packages. The amount of salt added will vary depending on the saltiness of your feta. If by any chance you can find sheep's milk feta, use it.*

Makes 2 cups filling

1 1/2 tablespoons olive oil
6 ounces scallions (about 5 scallions), trimmed and cut into 1-inch pieces, with green parts (about 1 cup)
1 pound stemmed spinach leaves, washed and dried (about 6 cups loosely packed)
4 ounces feta cheese, broken into small pieces and rinsed under cold water
1/2 cup packed fresh Italian parsley leaves
1/4 cup packed fresh mint leaves
Kosher salt, to taste
Freshly ground black pepper, to taste

Heat olive oil in a large heavy skillet over medium heat. Add scallions and cook, stirring occasionally, for about 5 minutes, or until they start to become soft. Add about half of the spinach and cook, stirring, until wilted. Add remaining spinach and cover with lid and cook for about 4 minutes, stirring once, or until completely wilted.

Remove from heat and transfer mixture to a strainer set over a bowl. Allow mixture to drain thoroughly for about 5 minutes. Squeeze out any remaining liquid with the back of a large spoon. Transfer mixture to the work bowl of a food processor with feta cheese, parsley and mint. Process until almost smooth. Season with salt and pepper and process to combine. Transfer to a small bowl.

spinach filling II

A nontraditional version of I with a mild licorice taste.

Makes 2 cups filling

1 1/2 tablespoons olive oil
6 ounces scallions (about 5 scallions), trimmed and cut into 1-inch pieces, with green parts (about 1 cup)
1 pound stemmed spinach leaves, washed and dried (about 6 cups loosely packed)
4 ounces feta cheese, broken into small pieces and rinsed under cold water
1/2 cup packed fresh Italian parsley leaves
2 tablespoons grated Parmesan cheese
2 tablespoons ouzo, or Pernod
1/2 teaspoon anise seeds
Kosher salt, to taste
Freshly ground black pepper, to taste

Heat olive oil in a large heavy skillet over medium heat. Add scallions and cook, stirring occasionally, for about 5 minutes, or until they start to become soft. Add about half of the spinach and cook, stirring, until wilted. Add remaining spinach, cover with lid and cook for about 4 minutes, stirring once, or until completely wilted.

Remove from heat and transfer mixture to a strainer set over a bowl. Allow mixture to drain thoroughly for about 5 minutes. Squeeze out any remaining liquid with the back of a large spoon. Transfer mixture to the work bowl of a food processor with feta cheese, parsley, Parmesan, ouzo and anise seeds. Process until almost smooth. Season to taste with salt and pepper and process to combine. Transfer mixture to a small bowl.

215

tyropitta (cheese) filling

On the off chance that your feta is very unsalty, taste this before wrapping in triangles.

Makes 1 cup filling

8 ounces feta cheese, broken into small pieces and rinsed under cold water
¼ cup grated Parmesan cheese (¾ ounce)
½ teaspoon ground nutmeg
¼ teaspoon dried oregano
¼ teaspoon dried thyme
2 egg yolks
Freshly ground black pepper, to taste

Place feta cheese, Parmesan, nutmeg, oregano and thyme in work bowl of food processor. Process until very finely crumbled. Transfer to a medium bowl and stir in egg yolks. Season to taste with pepper.

All *you need to complete this savory picture is a topping, a compound butter, such as Green Peppercorn Butter (page 43), and a sliced vegetable, such as cucumbers, or prosciutto for the Pepper Brioche (page 132). Mini-Strudels with Sweet and Sour Filling (page 214) and Lacy Cheese Cookies (page 58) will get gobbled up on their own. They would make good go-alongs with a dry sherry.*

turnovers

Turnovers are made in almost every part of the world and with almost every kind of dough. They vary in size from meals for a group (coulibiac) to meals for one (Cornish pasties) to those in this chapter that borrow from many areas of the world for mouth-sized snacks. Some are baked and some are fried and some made with noodle dough (**pot stickers,** Chinese Dumplings, page 253) are fried before steaming. The fillings change with the region and the dough. They come from Scandinavia and England, Russia, France, Asia and America, although American ones are often *sweet* rather than savory. You can make sweet ones of your own by using any standard, cooked pie filling or a spoonful of preserves. The best pastries for dessert miniatures are Sour Cream, Cream Cheese and Flaky Tart Dough (pages 96–97).

making turnovers

Classic combinations for savory turnovers would be one of the piroshki fillings (page 218) in puff or piroshki dough. The empanada fillings (pages 219–220) would go in the empanada dough. However, using the doughs and fillings listed below, you can make up your own turnovers. While Calzones (page 220) are also a classic turnover, they have their own recipe because the dough and cooking are so different.

The fillings created especially for turnovers are on the following pages. At the end of the recipe see note for other possible fillings.

Makes about 75 turnovers

**1 ½ cups filling
3 egg yolks mixed with 3 tablespoons cold water for egg wash, if baking**

**Bake-or-Fry Doughs
2 recipes Flaky Tart Dough (page 97) or
2 recipes Parmesan Pastry (page 99) or
2 recipes Cheddar Cheese Pastry (page 97) or
1 recipe Russian Turnover Dough I (page 217) or
2 recipes Russian Turnover Dough II (page 218) or
3 recipes Empanada Dough (page 218)**

**Bake-Only Doughs
3 recipes Sour Cream Pastry (page 96) or
2½ recipes Cream Cheese Pastry (page 96) or
2 packages store-bought puff pastry (about 17¼ ounces each)**

On a lightly floured surface roll out dough to about ⅟₁₆ inch thick. Cut out rounds with a 3-inch round cookie cutter. If not using puff pastry, reroll scraps to use up all the dough.

Place 1 level teaspoon of filling in the center of each round. Lightly brush some egg wash halfway around the edge. Fold the pastry in half to form a turnover, pinch edges together to seal securely.

To Bake. Preheat oven to 350°F, or if using puff pastry, 400°F, with rack in center of oven. Place turnovers on a baking sheet (not air-cushioned) lined with parchment paper. Brush tops lightly with egg wash and bake until golden brown, about 12 minutes. Remove from oven; allow to cool slightly before serving.

To Deep-Fat-Fry. Fry in batches until dark golden brown, about 4 to 5 minutes (see page 236 for specific frying instructions).

To Store and Reheat. The turnovers can be made 1 to 2 days ahead, stored in airtight containers and reheated on a baking sheet in a 350°F oven for 5 minutes. They can also be made 1 week ahead, tightly wrapped and frozen. Reheat as above for 10 minutes.

Alternate fillings
Chicken Liver Piroshki Filling (page 218)
Beef and Pork Piroshki Filling (page 218)
Cheese Blintzes Filling (page 224)
Beef Empanada Filling (page 219)
Pork Empanada Filling (page 220)
Russian Eggplant Dip (page 12)
Cabbage Strudel Fillings (page 214)
Salt Cod Pâté—uncooked mixture (page 146)
Fishburger mixture (page 187)
Crab Cake mixture (page 187)
Cod Balls (page 251)
Smoked Haddock Balls (page 251)
Mushroom Purée (page 73)
Turkey Pâté—uncooked mixture (page 151)

Chilean Beef Stuffing (page 206)
Curry Lamb Stuffing (page 286)
Lamb-Tomato Stuffing (page 76)
Spinach fillings (page 215)
Chinese Pork Terrine— uncooked mixture (page 153)
Thai Shrimp Stuffing (page 210)
Cooked Shrimp and Pork Stuffing (page 211)

russian turnover dough I

*Poland, Ukraine, Russia and many other Central and Eastern European countries make savory turnovers to serve with soup, and there are as many names (**piroshki** may be the best known) as countries. I have often tried to find a strict correlation between name—**pirogen,** for example—and dough or filling, to no avail. All of them, except those made rather fancily in puff pastry, can be fried or baked. This dough, which is yeast-raised, is one of my favorites, but you can use Russian Turnover Dough II (page 218) or any of those listed in Making Turnovers.*

*Jewish knishes use a dough like this but are usually filled with highly seasoned mashed potatoes. A Russian form known as **rastegai** is usually filled with a fish mixture and the dough circle has the filling placed right in the center. Both sides of the dough are brought to the top and pinched together to make an oval with a raised welt going down the center.*

Makes 1¾ pounds

**1 package active dry yeast
¾ cup warm milk
3⅔ to 4 cups all-purpose flour
2 large eggs
1 teaspoon kosher salt
½ cup unsalted butter, at room temperature**

Combine yeast and warm milk in a small bowl. Let stand 5 minutes, or until foamy.

Add ⅔ cup flour and stir well to form a smooth batter. Cover bowl with plastic wrap and let stand about 1½ hours, or until doubled in volume.

Pour batter into food processor or electric mixer. Add eggs and salt and mix well to combine. Add the flour, about a half cup at a time, mixing well with each addition. When mixture forms a dough so that it is beginning to leave the sides of the bowl, add butter and mix well until thoroughly combined. Add remaining flour so that mixture forms a soft dough that is not sticky. Either transfer from food processor to a bowl or leave in electric mixer bowl, cover with plastic wrap and allow to stand in a warm place for at least 1½ hours, or until dough has doubled in volume.

Punch dough down. Divide dough into four portions and wrap each one in plastic wrap. Refrigerate for at least 1 hour so that the dough is easier to handle. Roll out, cut, fill, form and cook as in Making Turnovers (page 217).

russian turnover dough II

This is a very good dough, along with those listed in Making Turnovers (page 217), for those who want a lighter piroshki that doesn't use yeast. It is good with Cheese Blintzes Filling (page 224).

Makes 1 pound

2 cups sifted all-purpose flour
1 teaspoon kosher salt

½ cup unsalted butter, room temperature, cut into ½-inch pieces
5 tablespoons sour cream
1 egg yolk
2 tablespoons ice water

Combine flour and salt in a medium bowl. Add butter and rub into flour with your fingers until mixture resembles coarse meal. Stir in sour cream. Beat egg yolk and water together. Stir into flour mixture to form dough. Wrap dough in plastic wrap and refrigerate for at least an hour.

chicken liver piroshki filling

This is an almost pâté-like filling for Russian Turnover Dough I and II. If you want to give it more punch, use pepper vodka.

Makes 1½ cups

6 tablespoons unsalted butter
1 small onion (4 ounces), chopped
¼ pound mushrooms (caps and stems), coarsely chopped in food processor
½ pound chicken livers, cleaned
1½ tablespoons vodka
½ cup loosely packed fresh Italian parsley leaves, coarsely chopped
1¼ teaspoons kosher salt
Freshly ground black pepper, to taste

Melt 3 tablespoons of the butter in a medium sauté pan over low heat. Add onions and cook until soft. Add remaining 3 tablespoons butter and mushrooms and cook for 2 minutes. Raise heat to medium. Add chicken livers and cook until browned.

Gently heat the vodka in a small saucepan. Ignite with a match and pour over the liver mixture. Reduce heat and allow flame to die naturally. Stir in parsley, salt and pepper. Cook 5 minutes longer.

Scrape mixture into a food processor. Pulse just until finely chopped.

beef and pork piroshki filling

A classic filling for Russian Turnover Dough I and II; see also filling for Pelmenyi (page 256).

Makes 1½ cups

2 tablespoons unsalted butter
1 small onion (4 ounces), chopped
¼ pound lean ground beef
¼ pound lean ground pork
2 tablespoons coarsely chopped dill sprigs
1 teaspoon kosher salt
Freshly ground black pepper, to taste
1 hard-boiled egg (page 88), coarsely chopped

Melt butter in a medium sauté pan over low heat. Add onion, beef and pork. Cook slowly, until meat is no longer pink and onions are soft. Stir in dill, salt and pepper. Cook for 2 minutes. Stir in egg.

empanada dough

Empanadas—or perhaps more correctly, empanaditas (diminutive ones)—are made in almost every Hispanic country with different doughs and fillings. See the two

218

meat fillings that follow. Many
are sweet and made for breakfast,
often using a very flaky dough
like Cream Cheese Pastry (page
96) or Puff Pastry, in which case
they are baked. These can be
baked or fried. Use 1¼ cups of
filling for this amount of dough.
If you like, dust with a hint of
cinnamon after cooking.

Makes 48

1½ cups all-purpose flour
1 teaspoon kosher salt
4 tablespoons cold unsalted
   butter, cut into small pieces
1 egg, lightly beaten
¼ cup ice water

To make the dough,
combine flour and salt in a
mixing bowl. Rub butter into
flour until mixture resembles
coarse crumbs, or lightly
combine in a food processor.

Add eggs and water and
gently work the mixture together
until it forms into a ball; or in a
food processor, just combine.
Cover dough with plastic wrap;
refrigerate for at least 2 hours.

Roll out, cut, fill, form and
cook as in Making Turnovers
(page 217).

*Russian Turnovers can be made
with bought puff pastry as they
are here or with their own special
doughs (pages 217–218). Fillings
vary from Chicken Liver Piroshki
to Beef and Pork Piroshki to
Cheese (page 224).*

beef empanada filling

*To use all of this filling, make
1½ times Empanada Dough.*

Makes 1½ cups

2 teaspoons olive oil
¼ cup finely chopped onion
2 medium cloves garlic,
   smashed, peeled and
   chopped
2 teaspoons finely chopped
   fresh jalapeño pepper
8 ounces ground beef

2 teaspoons kosher salt
1½ teaspoons ground
   cardamom
Freshly ground black pepper,
   to taste
3 canned plum tomatoes,
   drained and crushed
1 hard-boiled egg (see box,
   page 88), finely chopped
2 tablespoons chopped fresh
   coriander (cilantro) leaves
2 teaspoons fresh lime juice

Heat oil in a skillet over
medium heat. Stir in onion and
garlic and cook for about 1
minute. Stir in jalapeño and
ground beef and cook, stirring,
for about 5 minutes, or until
meat has lost all pink color.

Remove from heat and stir
in remaining ingredients.
Transfer to a bowl and allow
mixture to cool completely
before filling empanadas.

pork empanada filling

This fits the Empanada Dough (page 218) perfectly.

Makes 1 cup

1 teaspoon olive oil
1 medium clove garlic, smashed, peeled and minced
8 ounces ground pork
1 teaspoon kosher salt
⅛ teaspoon ground cinnamon
⅛ teaspoon turmeric
⅛ teaspoon ground nutmeg
⅛ teaspoon ground cloves
Freshly ground black pepper, to taste
1 scallion, trimmed and finely chopped (1 tablespoon)

Heat oil in a skillet over medium heat. Add garlic and cook for about 1 minute. Stir in pork, salt and spices. Cook, stirring, for about 6 minutes, or just until pork is cooked through.

Remove from heat, season to taste with pepper and stir in chopped scallion. Transfer mixture to a bowl and allow to cool completely before filling empanadas.

calzones

I first met calzones at the Feast of San Gennaro on New York's streets where booths are set up and Italian street-food specialties are served before, during and after wonderful fireworks. Calzones are a sort of rolled pizza using bread dough. They may be baked or fried. They make terrific miniatures.

Makes 46

1 recipe Basic Focaccia, topping ingredients omitted (page 128)
1¼ cups filling: Italian Cheese Filling or Southwestern Cheese Filling (this page)
Olive oil for brushing baked calzones or vegetable oil for deep-fat frying

When dough has finished its first rising, divide it into three pieces. Wrap two pieces in plastic wrap to keep them from drying out. On a lightly floured surface with a floured rolling pin, roll the dough until you have an approximately 10-inch circle.

Let dough rest while rolling out another piece. Return to the first piece and roll dough to ³⁄₁₆-inch thick. Cut out dough with a 3-inch round cutter. Refrigerate cut rounds as you work. Gather scraps into a ball and let rest before rerolling. Repeat rolling, resting and cutting procedure with remaining dough.

Place 1 slightly rounded teaspoon of filling in the center of a dough round. Fold the dough in half over the filling. Use the tines of a damp fork to seal the edges. Repeat with remaining dough. If frying calzones, refrigerate them as you finish forming them.

To Bake. Place on baking sheets lined with parchment paper. Cover loosely with a kitchen towel and place in a warm place to rise for 20 minutes. Preheat oven to 350°F, with rack positioned in lower third of oven. Brush calzones lightly with olive oil. Bake for 22 minutes.

To Deep-Fat Fry. Allow second rise. Fry in batches until golden brown on the bottom, about 1 minute 15 seconds. Turn and fry until golden on the other side, about 45 seconds (see page 236 for specific frying instructions).

cheese filling

If you make Calzones with the Italian Cheese version, serve a bowl of Tomato Basil Dipping Sauce (page 27). If using Southwestern Cheese version, serve a salsa (pages 23–25).

Makes 1½ cups

½ cup ricotta (4½ ounces)
2 large eggs
5½ ounces mozzarella, cut into ¼-inch cubes (⅔ cup)
2 tablespoons grated Parmesan cheese
½ teaspoon kosher salt
Freshly ground black pepper, to taste

Italian Cheese Filling
1 teaspoon finely chopped fresh Italian parsley leaves
1 tablespoon finely chopped fresh basil leaves, optional

Southwestern Cheese Filling
1 teaspoon finely chopped fresh coriander (cilantro) leaves
1 small garlic clove, smashed, peeled and chopped
½ jalapeño pepper, seeded and minced

In a small bowl, whisk ricotta until smooth. Whisk in eggs. Stir in remaining ingredients.

buckwheat blini

There are two kinds of blini, the Russian, yeast-raised pancakes: white flour and buckwheat. I see almost no point in making the white flour ones; Crêpes (opposite page) or toasted Brioche Bread (page 132) or Pain de Mie (page 119) will make just as good an underpinning for pressed caviar, salmon roe, smoked salmon, eel, trout, whitefish or sturgeon (pages 165–166) or Cured Salmon (page 176). Buckwheat blini, on the other hand, have color and character and are well worth the making, especially as they can be made ahead and reheated. They are even good at room temperature.

To make ahead, store in refrigerator or freezer and reheat: Place on a parchment-lined baking sheet in middle of oven at 350°F: three minutes from refrigerator, six minutes from freezer.

These have a pleasantly sour and yeasty flavor. If you don't like that idea, replace the beer with additional milk. Add the additional milk when the beer would have been added, not when the rest of the milk is added. Blini taste much sourer on their own than when topped with melted butter (brushed on), sour cream and fishiness of your choice.

You may well ask why these appear in Wrap and Roll. Well, when they are a normal size, they are rolled and served with a knife and fork as a first course. Just make the pancakes bigger.

Makes about 40 2-inch blini

½ cup warm milk
I package active dry yeast
Pinch sugar
½ cup buckwheat flour
½ cup all-purpose flour
Large pinch kosher salt
I egg, separated
½ cup beer, at room
  temperature

Combine warm milk, yeast and sugar in a small bowl. Let stand for about 5 minutes, or until foamy.

Combine flours and salt in a larger bowl. Stir in yeast mixture to form a fairly heavy dough. Cover bowl with plastic wrap and allow to stand in a warm place until doubled, about 2½ hours.

Stir in egg yolk and 2

tablespoons of the beer to lighten dough. Whisk in remaining beer a little at a time, until mixture is smooth. In a separate bowl whisk egg white until stiff peaks form. Gently fold into batter until well mixed, being careful not to deflate the whipped whites.

Heat a large nonstick skillet over medium heat. When hot, drop batter into pan by tablespoons, about an inch apart. Allow blini to cook for about 2 minutes, or until large air bubbles appear on the surface. Turn blini over with a metal spatula and cook for 1 minute longer. Remove to a plate and serve, or allow to cool if storing. Repeat with remaining batter.

Nonstick Skillets

Nonstick skillets are a great invention of the modern world, but it is important to buy the best, those made out of heavy metal with a thick layer of nonstick material. Sadly, quality will usually go along with price. These pans make a great difference when making miniature pancakes, since no fat is required—which makes the blini and crêpes a lot pleasanter to pick up with fingers. You will also use these pans for omelets and the Chinese Dumplings (page 253). Buy the largest size that you can find. If you don't have one of these pans, substitute a barely greased griddle or large sauté pan.

---

crêpes

These are the thin, silky French pancakes that, when normal in size, are rolled with a savory filling or in Austria and Hungary, where they are Palatchinken, with melted chocolate or jam.

You can use them flat and top them, or you can fill them, roll them gently and close with a toothpick. Use a rounded teaspoon of filling.

The recipe can be multiplied; crêpes can be frozen—place between layers of wax paper and wrap in plastic wrap. To reheat, place in a single layer on a parchment-lined baking sheet at 350°F for two minutes.

Makes about 35

½ cup cold water
¾ cup cold milk
2 large eggs
½ teaspoon kosher salt
1 cup all-purpose flour
2 tablespoons melted butter,
  cooled

Place water, milk, eggs and salt in blender and run briefly. Add flour and butter. Blend at high speed for 1 minute. Scrape down sides and blend a few seconds more. Cover and refrigerate for at least 2 hours.

Heat one or more large nonstick sauté pans or regular sauté pans lightly brushed with oil over medium-high heat. Drop one tablespoon of batter into the pan. Quickly use the back of a spoon to spread the batter into a thin 4-inch circle. Repeat until pan is full—you can make 4 at a time in a 12-inch pan. Cook until set and tan on the bottom (crêpe should not be evenly browned), about 30 seconds. Turn crêpes with a metal spatula and cook until light brown splotches appear on the bottom, about 20 seconds. Repeat with remaining batter, brushing pan with oil as necessary.

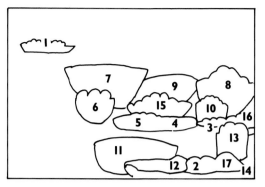

Every once in a while, we need an all-out-elegant party. This one based on black and white would be perfect for a New Year's Eve where the men are in black or white tie and the women are in festive best. Any three or four of these items would do the trick. The whole spread is an entire evening for twenty, but do have bread-and-butter-size plates and forks—remember the formal attire. Caviar (pages 166–167) may be a hallmark of such a party. Tuck it into **1** Crisp New Potato Shells (page 241) with sour cream or **2** Fried Bread Boxes (page 121) or use it to top **3** Swiss Potato Pancakes (page 85). These starches can also go under **4** sliced sturgeon, which would in turn be happy on **5** Buckwheat Biscuits (page 109) or **6** Buckwheat Blini (page 220). Now that you have at least some of the underpinnings on hand, use them as well for **7** Brandade of Sole (page 32), **8** Chicken Salad (page 263), **9** Steak Tartare (page 275), **10** Black Olivada (page 22), **11** Creamed Herring (page 185), **12** Marinated Anchovies with fennel (page 182), **13** Chicken Liver Crock with Apples and Onions (page 149) or **14** Scallion Cream Cheese (page 42). The other goodies come with their own wrapper: **15** Italian Rice Dumplings (page 248); **16** Canapés with Mustard-Anchovy Butter (page 43) and **17** puff pastry Russian Turnovers (pages 217–218).

cheese blintzes filling

As part of the mix-and-match parade, I present in evidence this filling, which does splendidly baked in Russian Turnover Doughs (page 217–218) and can also be used to fill trembling little packages of crêpes called blintzes.

Makes 1½ cups

4 ounces cream cheese, at room temperature
8 ounces large-curd cottage cheese (¾ cup)
2 tablespoons sour cream
2 egg yolks
¼ teaspoon kosher salt
Freshly ground black pepper, to taste
2 tablespoons Dijon mustard, optional (use only if making Russian Turnovers, pages 217–218)

Place cream cheese in a food processor and process until creamy. Add remaining ingredients and process until smooth.

cheese blintzes

Not only are these very good, but they are also very practical, as they can be cooked and held at room temperature, refrigerated, well covered, for up to two days, or frozen (in a single layer and then packed up) for up to two weeks before reheating in batches as needed on a parchment-lined baking sheet (not air-cushioned) at 350°F: four minutes for room temperature, six minutes for refrigerated, or ten minutes for frozen.

Although these are rich, it doesn't seem safe to allow fewer than three per person.

Makes about 35

1 recipe Crêpes (page 221), cooked only on one side
1 recipe Cheese Blintzes Filling

Place crêpes on a work surface, cooked side up. Place a rounded tablespoon of filling in the center. Fold the sides over the filling so that they overlap. Start at one end and fold up the blintz—do not roll tightly.

Heat a large nonstick skillet over medium heat. Working in batches, place blintzes in skillet, seam side down. Cook until browned on the bottom, about 1 minute. Turn over and brown the other side, about 1 minute.

Rolling Italian Omelets and Roulades

Cut Italian omelets **(frittatas)** (pages 226–229) and roulades (opposite page) in half lengthwise before filling and rolling, to produce finger-food-size slices. Also, both are easier to handle if they are also cut in half crosswise. The amount of fillings suggested in the recipes for frittatas and roulades are meant to fill one whole frittata or roulade, which yields sixty slices, but you may decide to fill half a roll with one filling and the other half with a second.

Place the sheet of frittata or roulade on a flat surface with one of the long edges toward you. Coat the entire top of the sheet, except for a half-inch border along the edge nearest you with the appropriate amount of filling. Starting with the uncoated edge, roll the sheet firmly, ending with the crease underneath. The rolls can be wrapped in aluminum foil and refrigerated up to one day.

Bring the rolls to room temperature before serving. Most rolls can also be served warm; check the recipes. To heat rolls, place, still wrapped in foil, in a 350°F oven 10 minutes.

Whether serving room temperature or warm, cut the rolls across into ½-inch slices, using a thin serrated knife.

224

roulades

These are soufflés made to fall on purpose. When cool, they are spread with a filling that has been brought to room temperature, rolled and then cut across to serve cool.

Each filling suggested makes enough to fill one roulade and yield sixty slices. Good combinations:

For Nut Roulade—½ cup Blue Cheese and Port Spread (page 39) with two tablespoons chopped parsley; ¾ cup Liptauer Spread (page 18) without extra yogurt; Sardine Paste (page 45); ¾ cups Horseradish Cream Cheese (page 39).

For Nut Roulade and Spinach Roulade—⅔ cup Mushroom Purée (page 73) with 2 tablespoons Parmesan cheese stirred in.

For Spinach Roulade—1 cup Smoked Trout Mousse (page 146) with 2 tablespoons chopped parsley; 1 cup Brandade of Sole (page 32); 1 cup of Spicy Cheddar Spread (page 201).

spinach roulade

Makes one 15x11-inch roulade, enough for about 60 slices

3½ pounds leaf spinach, stemmed and washed (16 cups packed)
2 egg yolks
¼ cup grated Parmesan cheese (¾ ounce)
3 tablespoons heavy cream
¼ teaspoon ground nutmeg
¼ teaspoon freshly ground black pepper
1 teaspoon kosher salt
6 egg whites

Lightly oil a 15 × 11-inch jelly roll pan. Line with a sheet of wax paper, pressing the paper into the corners. Lightly oil the wax paper. Heat the oven to 375°F.

Place damp spinach in a large nonaluminum pot over medium heat. Cover the pot and steam, stirring once or twice, until the spinach is wilted but still bright green, about 2 minutes. Transfer to a colander and rinse briefly under cold water. Squeeze out as much water as possible with your hands.

Combine the spinach, yolks, Parmesan, heavy cream, nutmeg, salt and pepper in a food processor fitted with the steel blade. Process, scraping the sides of the bowl once or twice, until the spinach is finely chopped and all ingredients are blended. Transfer to a large mixing bowl.

Beat the egg whites in the bowl of an electric mixer until they form stiff peaks. Fold the egg whites into the spinach mixture one-third at a time. Spread the roulade mixture in an even layer into the prepared pan. Bake until the center of the roulade is set, about 8 minutes. Check the roulade halfway through cooking and rotate the pan if the roulade is cooking unevenly.

For fillings see above. To finish, see box.

savory nut roulade

Makes one 15 × 11-inch roulade, enough for about 60 slices

Vegetable oil
¾ cup walnut pieces, chilled
1 teaspoon sugar
1 teaspoon kosher salt
½ teaspoon baking powder
¼ teaspoon freshly ground black pepper
⅛ teaspoon ground nutmeg
3 large eggs, plus one egg white
3 tablespoons heavy cream

Lightly oil a 15 × 11-inch jelly roll pan. Line with a sheet of wax paper, pressing the paper into the corners. Lightly oil the wax paper. Heat the oven to 375°F.

Place the walnuts, sugar, salt, baking powder, pepper and nutmeg in the work bowl of a food processor fitted with the metal blade. Process until finely ground. Transfer to a mixing bowl.

Add the egg yolks and heavy cream to the nut mixture. Stir until well blended.

Beat the egg whites in the bowl of an electric mixer until they form stiff peaks. Fold the egg whites into the nut mixture one-third at a time. Spread the roulade mixture in an even layer into the prepared pan. Bake until the center of the roulade is set, about 8 minutes. Check the roulade halfway through cooking and rotate the pan if the roulade is cooking unevenly.

Remove the pan from the oven and let stand 5 minutes. Turn the roulade out onto a sheet of wax paper. Let stand 5 minutes and carefully peel away the top layer of wax paper. Roll the roulade tightly starting with one of the long sides and let cool completely before continuing.

For fillings, see above. To finish, see box, page 229.

italian omelets

Italian omelets, or **frittatas**, are a particularly useful form of omelet directly related to the Spanish omelet (egg tortilla), especially when made with potatoes. They are thick egg pancakes as good cold as hot—traditional picnic food. They can be cut into squares and served with a dipping sauce (pages 26–29), or filled (see box, page 229).

basic method

The Basic Frittata (Italian omelet) Mix always stays the same. The frittata mixtures can change according to the season, your taste and whatever else you are serving. See page 229 for frittata rolls and a list of fillings. Do not increase cooking time, as the frittatas continue to cook once they are taken out of the oven.

Makes 60 1-inch squares or 60 ½-inch slices

1 recipe of a frittata mixture (pages 226–229)

Basic Frittata Mix
1 to 2 tablespoons olive oil
8 large eggs
2 tablespoons water
2 tablespoons grated Parmesan cheese
2 teaspoons kosher salt
¼ teaspoon freshly ground black pepper

Prepare the frittata mixture of your choice and cool to room temperature. It may be cooked a day or more in advance and refrigerated. Bring to room temperature before using. Preheat the oven to 325°F with the rack in the bottom position. Use the olive oil to grease generously an 11 × 7-inch glass baking dish if cutting into squares or a 15 × 11-inch pan if making rolls. Be sure the sides are well greased.

Combine the eggs, water, Parmesan, salt and pepper in a blender jar. Blend at high speed just until foamy, about 10 seconds, or whisk until foamy. Pour into a mixing bowl and fold in the chosen frittata mixture. Pour into the prepared dish, making sure to distribute the solids evenly.

To Cut into Squares. Bake 15 minutes. Rotate the pan in the oven and continue baking until very lightly browned around the edges and set in the center (firm but not hard to the touch), about 10 minutes, or slightly more for wetter frittata mixtures. Remove from oven.

Let the frittata stand 10 minutes. Cut into quarters with a sharp serrated knife. Remove the pieces to a cutting surface and cut them into 1-inch squares and serve either warm or at room temperature, or make into rolls (page 224) and slice across.

The frittatas can be made a day in advance. After cutting in quarters wrap the pieces separately and store in the refrigerator.

If serving the frittata at room temperature, simply unwrap, cut into 1-inch squares and let come to room temperature. If serving the frittata warm, place unwrapped on a baking sheet in a 350°F oven for 10 minutes.

To Roll. See box, page 224.

spinach and mushroom frittata

Makes enough for one frittata

8-ounce bunch spinach, stemmed
2 tablespoons olive oil
1 small onion (3 ounces), peeled and diced fine
2 medium cloves garlic, smashed, peeled and minced
6 small mushrooms (4 ounces), cut across into ¼-inch slices
2 ripe plum tomatoes (7 ounces), cored and cut into ½-inch dice
Basic Frittata Mix

Wash the spinach leaves in two or three changes of water. Thoroughly dry the leaves, either in a salad spinner or by rolling in several thicknesses of paper towels. Shred the spinach across the leaves into ½-inch-wide strips.

Heat the oil in a large (14-inch) heavy skillet over medium heat. Add the onion

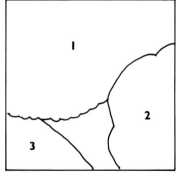

*1 Spinach and Mushroom Frittata can be rolled with a filling (page 229) or it can be cut into squares to moisten with **2** Tomato Basil Dipping Sauce (page 27). Accompany with a crisp like **3** Plantain Chips (page 241), which can also benefit from the sauce.*

226

and garlic. Sauté until the onion is wilted and lightly browned, about 4 minutes. Add the mushrooms. Sauté 3 minutes. Add the tomato and spinach. Reduce the heat to low and stir until the spinach is wilted. Cover the sauté pan and cook 2 minutes. Transfer the mixture to a strainer and squeeze out excess liquid with a wooden spoon.

When the spinach mixture is cool, stir into Basic Frittata Mix and bake as in basic method (page 226).

ratatouille frittata

Makes enough for 1 frittata

- **1 small eggplant (8 ounces), trimmed and peeled**
- **3 teaspoons kosher salt**
- **2 tablespoons olive oil**
- **1 small onion, peeled and diced fine (3/4 cup)**
- **2 medium cloves garlic, smashed, peeled and minced**
- **1 small zucchini (6 ounces) washed, trimmed and cut into 1/2-inch dice (about 1 1/2 cups)**
- **4 plum tomatoes (about 12 ounces), cored and cut into 1/2-inch dice**
- **1/4 cup coarsely chopped fresh basil leaves**
- **Freshly ground black pepper, to taste**
- **Basic Frittata Mix (page 226)**
- **2 tablespoons grated Parmesan cheese**

Cut the eggplant into 1/2-inch dice. Toss it with 2 teaspoons of the salt in a mixing bowl and let stand 10 to 15 minutes. Turn the eggplant into a colander and rinse thoroughly under cold running water. Drain well and squeeze out excess liquid with your hands.

Heat the oil in a heavy medium saucepan over medium heat. Add the onion and garlic. Sauté, stirring occasionally, until the onion is wilted and lightly browned, about 5 minutes. Add the zucchini and continue sautéing just until it begins to brown, about 5 minutes. Stir in the tomato, basil, black pepper and remaining teaspoon salt. Reduce the heat to low, cover the pan and cook 5 minutes. Stir in the eggplant and cook, covered, 5 minutes. Uncover the pan, increase the heat to medium and cook, stirring frequently, until all the excess liquid has evaporated. Turn onto a plate to cool.

When the filling is cool, stir into Basic Frittata Mix, with the additional 2 tablespoons Parmesan, and bake as in basic method (page 226).

broccoli di rabe frittata

Makes enough for 1 frittata

- **1 1/2 pounds broccoli di rabe**
- **2 tablespoons olive oil**
- **3 medium cloves garlic, smashed, peeled and sliced very thin**
- **1/4 teaspoon crushed red pepper**
- **1 1/2 teaspoons kosher salt**
- **1/4 teaspoon freshly ground black pepper**
- **Basic Frittata Mix (page 226)**
- **2 tablespoons grated Parmesan cheese**

Wash and thoroughly dry the broccoli di rabe. Slice thin (about 1/4 inch) all but the very thick ends of the stem. On most bunches this will be about the bottom 2 inches of stem. There should be about 6 cups. Dry the broccoli well, either in a salad spinner or by wrapping in

several layers of paper towels.

Heat the oil in a large heavy skillet over medium heat. Add the garlic and crushed red pepper. Sauté until garlic is fragrant, about 1 minute. Add broccoli—be careful of splattering—and stir until all is bright green and wilted, about 1 minute. Sprinkle the broccoli with the salt and pepper. Reduce the heat to low, cover the pan and cook until the leaves are tender but the stems are still a bit crisp, about 3 minutes.

When the mixture is cool, stir into Basic Frittata Mix, with the additional 2 tablespoons Parmesan cheese, and bake as in basic method (page 226).

potato leek frittata

This is a simple, delicious frittata for serving in squares with a Dipping Sauce (pages 26–29), but it cannot be rolled.

Makes enough for 1 frittata

- **4 tablespoons olive oil**
- **12 ounces small red new potatoes, scrubbed and cut into 1/4-inch dice (about 2 2/3 cups)**
- **4 large leeks, white parts only, trimmed, washed well and cut across into 1/4-inch slices (about 2 1/2 cups)**
- **1 teaspoon minced fresh rosemary**
- **1 1/2 teaspoons kosher salt**
- **1/4 teaspoon freshly ground black pepper**
- **Basic Frittata Mix (page 226)**

Heat 3 tablespoons of the oil in a large sauté pan (nonstick is preferable) over medium heat. Add the potatoes and sauté, stirring frequently, until golden brown, about 12 minutes. Add the remaining tablespoon of oil and the leeks. Sprinkle with the rosemary, salt and pepper and sauté until the leeks are lightly browned and tender, about 5 minutes.

When the mixture is cool, stir into Basic Frittata Mix and bake as in basic method (page 226).

asparagus and pea frittata

A springtime frittata for serving in squares, not rolling.

Makes 60 1-inch squares

8 ounces fresh asparagus
½ cup cooked shelled peas or ½ cup defrosted and drained frozen peas
Basic Frittata Mix (page 226)
2 tablespoons grated Parmesan cheese
2 teaspoons minced fresh thyme leaves

Trim the asparagus ends. If the stalks are more than ¼ inch thick, you should peel them to within an inch of the tip. Slice thin asparagus crosswise into ½-inch lengths and thicker asparagus into ¼-inch lengths, leaving the tips whole. If the asparagus are thick, slice the tips in half lengthwise. Cook the asparagus in a large pot of salted boiling water until tender but still a little crisp, from 1 to 3 minutes (or according to microwave instructions, page 70). Turn into a colander and rinse under cold running water. Shake out excess water and drain the asparagus on a double thickness of paper towels.

Combine the cooked asparagus and the peas in a mixing bowl. Stir into Basic Frittata Mix with the additional Parmesan cheese and the thyme. Bake as in basic method (page 226).

Filled Frittata Rolls for Slicing

Make Spinach and Mushroom (page 226), Broccoli di Rabe (page 228) or Ratatouille (opposite page) frittata. Pour the mix into a 15 × 11-inch pan that has been oiled, lined with aluminum foil and the foil oiled. Bake until set but not firm in the center, about 12 to 13 minutes. Invert the frittata onto wax paper and let stand 10 minutes. Carefully remove the top layer of aluminum foil using a rubber spatula. Roll the frittata into a tight roll while still on the wax paper and let cool completely.

Unroll the frittata. Follow instructions in the box on page 224. The frittata rolls can be refrigerated, tightly wrapped, at this point for up to one day. Use two thirds to three quarters of a cup of rich or strongly seasoned fillings; one cup of milder fillings. All fillings should be at room temperature before spreading.

suggested fillings for frittata rolls

Each makes enough to fill one frittata and yield sixty slices:

Tomato Filling
For Ratatouille, Broccoli di Rabe or Spinach and Mushroom Frittata: Combine ⅔ Plum Tomato Sauce (page 27), ½ cup chopped fresh basil leaves, 1 tablespoon olive oil and 2 cloves garlic, minced, in a small saucepan. Heat to simmering and simmer, uncovered, until very thick, about 10 minutes. Cool completely and stir in ¼ cup grated Parmesan cheese, if desired, before using in room-temperature or warm rolls.

Prosciutto Filling
For Spinach and Mushroom Frittata: Bring ⅓ cup Prosciutto Spread (page 45) to room temperature. Stir in 2 tablespoons finely chopped parsley. Serve at room temperature only.

Olivada Filling
For Ratatouille or Spinach and Mushroom Frittata: ½ cup Black Olivada (page 22). Serve at room temperature only.

Moroccan Eggplant Filling
For Spinach and Mushroom Frittata: 1 cup Eggplant Moroccan (page 10). Serve at room temperature or warm.

Roasted Red Pepper Spread
For Spinach Mushroom or Broccoli di Rabe Frittata: 1 cup Roasted Red Pepper Spread (page 14) (with or without the addition of Olivada). Serve at room temperature only.

chapter 7

fear of frying

The title of this chapter is more than a pun. It is a condition that many otherwise competent cooks share, myself included. In recent years, I have been writing about healthful foods and avoiding saturated fats and so have been able to avoid deep- and shallow-fat frying; my discomfort does not extend to sautéing. However, when it came to a book on party food, it seemed at long last inevitable that I was going to have to conquer my fear and come out of the corner frying.

Incidentally, I am not abandoning healthful cooking, but a fried food from time to time at a party does not seem the end of the world, and the world has supplied us with a vast array of crisply fried mouthfuls.

Even though I have gotten much more comfortable with frying, I wouldn't make more than one fried dish at a time for a big party unless—like Spring Rolls (page 211) or Egg Rolls (page 258)—they can be made ahead and reheated. When something can be fried ahead in calm and reheated when the flurry is on, I tell you how.

There is a difference between shallow-fat frying and deep-fat frying. See pages 236 and

We tend to think of pasta as boiled and sauced. Instead try Fried Ravioli (page 253), first-rate on their own or with one of the tomato dipping sauces (pages 26–27).

237 for an explanation, as well as page 253 for an explanation of the Chinese way of combining shallow frying and steaming of dumplings. The dumpling recipes are on pages 256–257, along with special dipping sauces. There are also dipping sauces for the Japanese Tempura (page 246).

The recipes are listed by the way they are made. I start with two recipes that your guests will swear are fried but aren't and cannot scare even the leeriest and go to things that are fried on their own or just dipped in flour or bread crumbs like Crisp Vegetable Chips (page 238), the thinnest Fried Zucchini (page 240), Spicy Popcorn Shrimp (page 242) and red Fried Onion Rings (page 240). Then I give the things that are dipped in batter before frying, like fritto misto, in Vinegar Batter (page 245), miniature Mozzarella in Carrozza (page 243) and Coconut Fried Shrimp (page 246); the things held together by mixing with a batter, like acras, Cod Balls (page 251), fritters, croquettes and Spicy Chickpea Fritters (page 250) and finally the dough-wrapped crispies.

Everything in this book that is fried is not in this chapter. The Cheese Puffs (page 107) seemed to fit better in the dough chapter, the Spring Rolls (page 211) with the other recipes using rice paper. If you don't find the recipe you want in this chapter, look in the Index.

Once fear is put aside and reasonable caution substituted, and once proper tools are used—such as a thermometer, a wok and a Chinese skimmer (page 236)—you'll find all of these recipes easy. Of course, if you come from the American South or Southwest, it's going to seem easy anyhow.

oven-fried potato chips

If you need lots of chips, this is not the way to go, but if deep-fat frying really panics you and you want the crunch and flavor of homemade, make these. They taste fabulous because you can use the best of fats, and they are practical as they can be reheated for three minutes in a 350°F oven. They can even be made ahead and frozen (imagine frozen potato chips). Just reheat for five minutes instead of three. While you can slice these with a potato peeler, it is much more easily done with a mandoline (see box). The aim is to get the slices as evenly thin as possible without tearing them.

Makes about 125

**1 large baking potato
(10 ounces), peeled**
**¼ cup melted butter or
olive oil**
Vegetable oil for greasing pan
Kosher salt, to taste

Preheat oven to 350°F.
Cut potatoes across into paper-thin slices. Place in a bowl with butter or oil and toss to coat.

Place potato slices in a single layer on well-oiled baking sheets (not air-cushioned). Bake until golden brown, about 12 minutes. If you are baking more than one sheet at a time, it will take a few minutes longer; rotate baking sheets between shelves halfway through cooking.

Transfer chips to paper towels to drain slightly. Sprinkle with salt.

Mandoline

A mandoline is a sort of fancy coleslaw board that is very useful for making very even slices or julienne strips. If you cook a lot or like large parties, it is well worth buying and learning to use. Try to get the store to demonstrate it to you. It's a little tricky until you get the hang of it.

The rectangular metal or wooden frame has various blades for cutting vegetables. It also has a collapsible stand, which can be elevated to keep the mandoline surface at a good incline for slicing. The stand is at the bottom. The top is divided into three sections. On one side of the mandoline there is a handle. Examine the mandoline by putting it top up and parallel to your body with the handle on the side away from you. You can now see that the left section of the top contains a waffle (ripple) blade. The center section has two sharp edges for cutting. The third, or right-hand, section has a flattish piece of metal, along which you will be sliding the food to be cut.

Underneath the mandoline are two levers that are used to lower and raise the right-hand and left-hand sections of the top. To begin, move the left-hand lever so that it is pointing to the center of the mandoline. It will stay in this position unless you wish to make waffled or rippled slices.

Additionally, it has two series of curved, toothed blades that can be used for making matchstick strips. These can be raised or lowered using the lever on the side of the mandoline. The adjacent slide section will need to be raised to get the blades in place and then lowered to achieve the proper strip.

The toothed blades and the ripple blade will be kept down for simple slicing. The height of the slide will determine the thickness of the slices.

Mandolines also come with a box with a hinged lid that can slide up and down the top of the cutting surface. Placing the food in this box and covering it with the lid saves your knuckles from scrapes.

233

ready-mades

There is a vast array of commercially produced fried foods. However, most of these foods are in the chip-and-snack category. Other fried foods do not package well.

A little tasting around will let you know which potato chips you like the best. Although they are very expensive, assorted vegetable chips that are pretty and unusual are now available in bags. Taco chips of various colors are a standby. Pretzels and assortments of Japanese snacks are always usable.

Chinese, Thai and Indian restaurants that provide take-out may be good sources for egg rolls, dumplings, shrimp toast and fritters. Dim Sum (tea lunch) restaurants will have the greatest variety. Try to get the restaurant to make you smaller dumplings than usual. If they don't make small-size egg rolls, cut the egg rolls crosswise into three pieces and serve on toothpicks. You will probably be able to buy sauces as well. To reheat, see similar foods in the recipes in this book.

Attractively arranged, an array of Chinese dumplings from a restaurant can make a good party served up with chopsticks and a collection of sauces, or make your own (pages 252–253).

frying

Frying is the cooking of foods—coated or not—in enough fat so that they are sealed and crisped as they cook, except for some Chinese shallow frying, which is a combined technique used for dumplings where the food sets one firm surface in the fat and then steams, covered, until cooking is completed. Deep-fat frying is generally used when there is quite a lot of food that needs to float free so as not to stick or where the pieces of food are fairly bulky. As food fries, it will generally rise to the surface. Sometimes it will need to be turned so that all sides brown.

deep frying

Select a pan. If you have a gas stove, a large wok, 12 to 14 inches in diameter, with a stand (ring) to hold it securely over the burner is best. A wok can also be used on a wood stove by setting it directly in the hole that appears when one of the round lids over the fire box is removed. In some cases a skillet can be used, which will require less oil. Otherwise, use a large pot or Dutch oven of the same diameter, which will require more oil. In any case, allow enough room in the pan for the oil to bubble up. See opposite page for Shallow-Fat Frying in a skillet. Do not fry in copper; the tin lining cannot withstand the high temperature. If you have a deep-fat fryer, follow the manufacturer's instructions.

If the items you are frying take a minute or more to cook, you can use two or three pans at a time, staggering the batches. Items that cook in a few seconds should be fried one batch at a time in one pan.

Any neutral oil—such as vegetable, canola, safflower, grape seed or peanut—can be used. Place pan over burner and pour in oil to a depth of 2 to 4 inches, just enough to float the items being fried. A wok filled to a depth of 2 inches will take about 6 cups of oil. Turn heat to medium-high. A 12-inch skillet filled 1 inch deep will take about 4½ cups oil.

To ensure good results, use a deep-fat thermometer. Place the thermometer in the oil—it can usually hang securely over the side of the pan. Do not let the thermometer touch the bottom of the pan. If necessary, place a chopstick across the rim of the pan under the head of the thermometer to prop the tip up, preventing it from touching.

If you do not have a thermometer, test the oil by placing a wooden chopstick in the center of the pan. When the oil is hot enough, bubbles will form vigorously around the chopstick from the ambient humidity retained by the wood. This method is not ideal, because it is difficult to monitor the temperature between or during batches.

Normal frying temperature is 375°F. The temperature may vary 5 to 10 degrees in either direction. The temperature should be monitored at all times and heat adjusted as necessary. Oil can get too hot very quickly and takes a long time to cool down. Also, a large batch of food tends to cool the oil. Raise or lower the heat as needed.

There are a few other items to have ready before beginning. A skimmer (particularly a large mesh Chinese one), with its wide shallow basket, is ideal for removing fried food from oil, but a slotted spoon is fine. You will need baking sheets lined with paper towels or brown paper bags (better for the environment) for draining.

Have pot holders nearby. You may want to wear an apron.

When food is prepared, other items are at hand and oil is at the correct temperature, begin frying. When adding items to pan, hold them as close to the oil as possible before easing them in. Foods with stems, such as stuffed peppers can be held by a bit of stem. This prevents splashing hot oil on your hands. Drop in only as many pieces as will float freely in the oil; do not overcrowd or items will not cook properly and oil will cool down. If you have trouble with splashing caused by wet foods, slide the items off an oiled pancake turner or slotted spoon.

Turn pieces over only if instructed to in recipe. In some cases you will need to lift a piece out of the oil slightly with the skimmer to check the color. When desired color is reached, scoop up pieces and transfer them to the lined baking sheet. To keep the fried items warm while you work, place in a 200°F oven.

Check oil temperature, even if using an electric pan. If oil is too hot or too cool, adjust heat and wait until proper temperature is reached. Drop in more pieces and continue in the same manner until all of the items have been fried.

Turn off heat. Leave pan on burner or set aside in a safe place to cool completely. Serve pieces hot or store as recommended in recipe.

When cleaning up, pour

236

cooled oil through a coffee filter into a container with a tightly fitting lid (empty, clean coffee cans are good for this). The strained oil will keep indefinitely at room temperature and can be reused for frying. Do not reuse oil that has been used for frying fish for any other food or the food will taste fishy. Sometimes the fish taste can be cleared from the oil by frying potatoes in it. The potatoes will not be good to eat except as part of fish and chips.

shallow-fat frying

The techniques for shallow-fat frying are basically the same as those for deep-fat frying. The amount of oil needed for shallow frying varies from a thin coating of oil to ½ inch. Heat oil. If oil is deep enough, use a thermometer propped up off the bottom of the pan to check the temperature. If not, use the chopstick method mentioned earlier. Place item(s) in pan; avoid overcrowding. Cook as in recipe.

naked frying

Now that we are getting to real deep-fat frying, it should be noted that there are things that can be fried without any batter or coating of any kind. The only trick, beyond following the basic techniques in Deep Frying (opposite page), is to make sure that you pat the things to be fried thoroughly dry. Resist the temptation to keep vegetables in water. You will get a terrible and dangerous spatter.

It is that spatter that prompts me to caution you strongly as I give you directions for my favorite garnish, *fried herb, celery and spinach leaves.* If you want to try them, wash the herbs well and pluck off attractive sprigs or—as in spinach—individual leaves. Dry the leaves as well as humanly possible. Heat the fat (Deep Frying). Standing well back from the stove, throw two handfuls of leaves into the oil. As soon as it has stopped spitting, advance on the pan and, with a skimmer, remove the leaves to paper to drain. Repeat. The leaves should be crisp and only lightly browned.

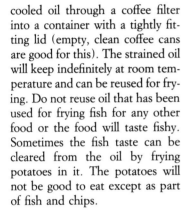

Sage leaves with Sage Potatoes.

sage potatoes

This recipe—impossible to stop eating—from Chef Francesco Antonucci at Remi, a very good Italian restaurant in New York, really had me confused. When I tasted it, I thought it was made with a batter and fried; I couldn't duplicate it. I threw myself on Francesco's mercy and he gave me the recipe, which is neither battered nor fried. It's where I got the idea for the Oven-Fried Potato Chips (page 233). Like them, these can be reheated for three minutes in a 350°F oven, or they can be cooked and frozen and reheated for five minutes. Allow five at least per person and multiply recipe as often as need be. You can have the sheets of potatoes all ready to go in the oven. They need not be eaten hot.

Makes 25

1 large baking potato (about 10 ounces), peeled
¼ cup melted butter or olive oil
25 sage leaves, stems removed
Kosher salt, to taste
Vegetable oil for greasing pan

Preheat oven to 350°F.

Cut potatoes lengthwise into paper-thin slices (this is easily done on a mandoline (see box, page 233). Trim the slices into ovals slightly larger than the sage leaves. Place the ovals in a medium bowl with butter or olive oil and toss to coat.

Place one potato slice on a work surface. Put one sage leaf in center and sprinkle with a little salt. Cover with another potato slice. Place on a well-oiled baking sheet (not air-cushioned). Repeat with remaining potato slices and sage leaves.

Bake until browned on the edges, about 12 minutes. Transfer to a plate lined with paper towels. Sprinkle with additional salt, if desired.

crisp vegetable chips

Here are traditional chips, but so good that they may not even get dipped, made into multicolored delight by using all kinds of vegetables. Of course, you can make regular **potato chips** *the same way.*

The chips can be made up to three days in advance, but don't salt them until they are reheated. Certain vegetable peelers will work fine with this. Choose one that will make very thin chips without tearing the slices.

At the end of the recipe, I give a way of making the chips ahead and reheating them shortly before serving that keeps you away from the fryer in your good clothes.

Vegetable sticks can be made in the same way. Peel the vegetable and cut it in matchstick strips. Think mandoline. Do not bother to reheat.

Makes about 6 cups chips for each vegetable used

1 pound small (3-inch) beets,
white turnips, celery root,
sweet potato, potato or
Jerusalem artichokes,
peeled, or 1 medium
rutabaga (1 pound), pared
and quartered
Vegetable oil for frying
Kosher salt, to taste

Slice the vegetables to the thickness of a penny on either a mandoline (see box, page 233) or with a vegetable peeler. Do not store in cold water. Carefully slip about 20 of the slices into the oil. Fry in 4 inches of oil, stirring with a skimmer to separate (see Deep Frying, page 236), until vegetables are cooked through. Some vegetables will not be crisp at this point and each will be a different color: The turnips should be white with dark brown markings; the celery root, Jerusalem artichokes and sweet potatoes should be dark brown; the beets will be deep purple with golden brown highlights and the rutabagas will be light brown. Repeat with remaining vegetables.

Skim out, drain and let stand until cool and crisp. Sprinkle with salt to taste. The chips can be fried up to three days in advance. Do not salt them. Store in an airtight container at room temperature. Up to 3 hours before serving, heat the chips in a single layer on a baking sheet in a 375°F oven until heated through, about 3 minutes. (The chips will not be crisp at this point.) Drain on paper towels until crisp and salt to taste before serving.

We are all used to potato chips, but all kinds of vegetables can be fried up into thin Crisp Vegetable Chips as varied as autumn leaves. Even potato chips can be turned into a specialty when cooked at home.

fried zucchini

These are absolutely the best if not the most typical of fried zucchini. Instead of being fried after coating with egg and crumbs or battering, these long, very thin, matchstick-sized julienne strips are fried naked to make crisp handfuls. People will eat more than you think. Make in batches as needed or serve cooled or reheated for 1 minute in a 350°F oven. If making in batches, do not succumb to the temptation to keep them in water—they will spatter when fried. Keep them on paper towels and cover with a barely moistened paper towel.

You can use a four-sided grater on the side with the large holes to cut these, but you will get a better result with a mandoline (page 233). Grate lengthwise without peeling. Remove the ends.

If you are using very large—seedy—zucchini, grate or slide through the mandoline, turning on all four sides. Discard the center part with all the seeds and allow about one-third more weight of zucchini when buying to allow for the discards.

Makes 3 cups

Vegetable oil for frying
6 medium zucchini, trimmed, halved and finely shredded
Kosher salt, to taste

In a large skillet, prepare oil for frying (see Deep Frying, page 236).

Add about 1½ cups of zucchini to the oil. Stir. Oil will foam up and bubble vigorously. When bubbles die down and zucchini turn golden brown, skim from oil and drain (page

Crisp finger-licking-good Fried Zucchini in thin ribbons.

236). Repeat with remaining zucchini.

Sprinkle with salt. Serve warm or at room temperature.

fried onion rings

Serve hot or cool, but do not attempt to reheat—the onions get soggy in the oven. If making in batches, have the onions sliced and the seasoned flour prepared, but do not flour the onions until just before frying.

Makes 6 cups

1 cup all-purpose flour
¼ cup kosher salt

1 tablespoon finely ground
black pepper
1 pound red or white onions,
peeled and cut across into
very thin rings
Vegetable oil for frying

Combine flour, salt and pepper in a medium bowl. Add onion rings and toss well to coat evenly with the flour mixture.

Remove about half the onion rings from the flour and shake off any excess flour. Fry, stirring occasionally, until crisp and golden brown, about 5 minutes (see Deep Frying, page 236). Repeat with remaining onion rings.

plantain chips

Recently, I have been very impressed by the restaurants in the Miami area where chefs combine the influence of the recent Cuban immigration with local ingredients and French cooking techniques. Several of the restaurants are making a version of these chips, which can be eaten hot or cold. They are solid enough to hold a bit of grilled fish. I serve them with salsas (pages 23–25), since they will really pick up the somewhat messy mixes.

You don't have to press two slices together—individual slices will work the same way—but the two-slice leaf shape is a nice variation on usual chips and will hold more. If you can only find smallish plantains, buy a little more, as there will be more waste in paring and trimming.

Makes 64 pairs, or 128 slices

2 large green (underripe)
plantains (1½ pounds)
5¾ teaspoons kosher salt
Olive oil for frying

Peel the plantains with a paring knife (the skin does not

peel off like a banana). Slice them on the diagonal, as thin as possible. Lightly sprinkle plantain slices with salt.

Heat a large sauté pan with enough oil to cover the bottom (see Shallow Frying, page 237). If desired, press together the pointed ends of 2 plantain slices to make rabbit ears that overlap by a good ¾ inch at the pointy ends. Repeat with remaining slices. Place 5 of the pairs in the pan. Cook over medium heat until lightly browned on the bottom, about 2 minutes. Carefully turn pieces over with a spatula and cook until lightly browned on the bottom, about 2 minutes. Place on paper towels to drain.

chicken wings

I would be tempted to call these Buffalo wings if I thought that was something specific. Don't reheat these—they get soggy—but feel free to serve at room temperature. Pass a cooling dip such as Herb Dip (page 18) or Green Goddess Dressing (page 37).

Makes 24 pieces

12 chicken wings
Vegetable oil for frying
⅓ cup hot red pepper sauce,
or more, to taste

Remove wing tips and freeze for stock (sharp kitchen scissors are excellent for this). Cut through the triangle of skin at the wing's joint. With your hands, bend the two parts of the wing backwards until the joint pops. Cut through the joint, separating the wing into two pieces.

Working in batches, fry wings until golden brown and cooked through, about 10 minutes (see Deep Frying, page 236).

Place wings in a bowl and toss with pepper sauce.

crisp new
potato shells

These are perfect containers for sour cream and caviar mouthfuls. There is an alternative to deep-fat frying—broiling, which is given below as well. Both of these can be made ahead and reheated in a 350°F oven for 5 minutes.

Allow at least three shells per person. Do not count these as fried food when thinking out your menu, as they are containers made ahead. Good alternates are Bread Boxes (page 121) or Blini (page 220).

Makes 20 to 24 shells

1 pound cooked new potatoes
(page 69)
Vegetable oil for frying, or ½
cup olive oil for broiling

Cut potatoes in half crosswise. Using a melon baller, scoop out flesh, leaving a ⅛-inch-thick shell. The scooped potato flesh can be used for dinner or for Brandade of Sole (page 32) or Salt Cod Pâté (page 146).

To Deep-Fat-Fry. Fry shells for 4 minutes (see Deep Frying, page 236).

To Broil. Preheat broiler. Put olive oil in a small bowl. Quickly dip each shell in the oil, shaking off the excess. Place shells with cut side up on a baking sheet lined with parchment paper. Broil for 10 minutes.

241

*C*risp New Potato Shells (page 241) are a splendid housing for a bit of sour cream and some good salmon roe or for a vegetable salad and a little crumbled goat cheese.

spicy popcorn shrimp

In America, these are most closely related to Cajun popcorn, which is made the same way but with crayfish tails. Shelled crayfish tails can be substituted in this recipe if you have them cheap and fresh and don't mind the work. I decided to make them because of a different delight: In Venice, I was served the tiniest of fresh shrimp in the shell cooked this way. The shells got very crisp and the whole thing could be eaten, shell and all, with a little lemon squeezed on top. This is the closest I could get where I live. If you by any chance can get tiny fresh shrimp in the shell, do try them this way: superb. Incidentally, the Italians would fry in olive oil, not the finest extra-virgin but a good olive oil.

If you have access to fresh whitebait or really small anchovies (bigger ones will have to be filleted with your thumbnail), fry them for 3 to 4 minutes in this seasoned flour.

Makes 6 cups

4 5-ounce packages frozen tiny (bay) shrimp, defrosted
1/2 cup all-purpose flour
2 1/2 teaspoons kosher salt
3/4 teaspoon cayenne pepper
Freshly ground black pepper, to taste
Vegetable oil for frying

Thoroughly dry shrimp with paper towels. Place in a large bowl and toss with all remaining ingredients except oil.

Working in batches, fry shrimp (see Deep Frying, page 236) for 20 seconds.

mozzarella in carrozza

This is a miniaturized version of a traditional dish of Campania, heavenly two-bite pieces crisp over melting cheese and bread seasoned by anchovies. In Naples, it is made with buffalo mozzarella and a peasant bread. For these small pieces I think it is easier to use a conventional loaf bread and a water-packed mozzarella not made with water buffalo milk, as that cooks differently. In any case, serve Anchovy and Caper Sauce on the side.

Occasionally, a light coating can be liquid rather than dry. Here, it is beaten egg. These can be made ahead and reheated in batches, as needed, on a parchment-lined baking sheet in a 350°F oven for 5 minutes. If you invite me to the party, I am likely to eat five, but three should be a normal allowance.

Makes 16 pieces

6 ounces mozzarella cheese, thinly sliced
8 slices firm white bread, crusts removed, Pain de Mie (page 119) or store-bought
8 canned whole anchovies, drained of oil
4 eggs, lightly beaten
Vegetable oil for frying
Anchovy and Caper Sauce (recipe follows)

Divide cheese equally over 4 slices of bread. Place 1 anchovy in each half of the 4 slices over the cheese. Cover each piece with one of the remaining bread slices. Cut each sandwich into quarters.

Just before frying, coat each sandwich in beaten egg. Fry until golden brown, about 2 minutes on each side (see Deep Frying, page 236).

Serve with Anchovy and Caper Sauce.

anchovy and caper sauce

Here is a sauce that you will have to taste to make it to your liking, as anchovies vary markedly in flavor. In addition to using it as a dipping sauce, think of it as a spread for hero sandwiches (page 130).

Makes 1 cup

12 to 14 oil-packed anchovies, drained (not washed)
1/4 cup capers, drained
1 cup packed fresh Italian parsley leaves
1/2 cup olive oil
2 teaspoons white wine vinegar
Freshly ground black pepper, to taste

Combine all ingredients in a blender or food processor and chop finely, or chop solid ingredients with a knife and combine with liquids in a mixing bowl. Allow to stand for at least 30 minutes before serving. Can be made ahead and kept refrigerated for three days. Allow to come to room temperature before serving.

fried mozzarella

As with fried ice cream, a light and brittle crust encloses a soft and succulent interior, but the cheese isn't sweet and it stretches when bitten. Serve a bowl of Tomato Basil Dipping Sauce (page 27) or Anchovy and Caper Sauce (above) for dunking if you wish; the nuggets are really delicious on their own. Don't make them if making Italian Rice Dumplings (suppli al telefono) or Calzones with Cheese Filling.

Some fried foods live in the twilight zone between light coating and battering before frying. They are more fidgety to coat and do not reheat. Have your seasoned flour in one bowl and your beaten eggs in another. The cheese can go through its various coatings up to a half hour before frying. Allow coated cheese to rest in a single layer on parchment paper. Fry as needed. These will not reheat but are fine tepid.

Makes 60

1 pound mozzarella (preferably fresh, packed in water), cut into 3/4-inch cubes
1/2 cup all-purpose flour
1 teaspoon kosher salt
Freshly ground black pepper, to taste
2 large eggs, lightly beaten
1/2 cup dry bread crumbs
Vegetable oil for frying

Allow mozzarella to sit out at room temperature and dry slightly for 30 minutes. Combine flour, salt and pepper in a medium bowl. Add mozzarella and toss to coat. Remove mozzarella from flour and coat in egg. Place bread crumbs on a large plate. Roll cheese cubes in bread crumbs until very well coated.

Working in batches, fry mozzarella just until golden brown, about 10 seconds (see Deep Frying, page 236). Serve hot or warm.

A *heavenly taste of Italy, Mozzarella in Carrozza (page 243) to dip in Anchovy and Caper Sauce (page 243), which can also serve as a dip for chunks of a good, store-bought country bread.*

batter frying

There are many batters for deep-fat frying and many countries use the technique to embellish little bits of food. Tempura batter needs to be handled somewhat differently from the following, so it gets its own recipe (page 246). Beer adds a certain lightness to batter and was a favorite trick of Albert Stockli. Vinegar Batter is particularly nice with sage leaves and vegetables but requires a slightly different technique. Buttermilk Batter is blander and good with seafood.

It is better to sift flour for batters. Mix up to two hours ahead of time. Vinegar batter will need a full two hours refrigerated, covered, before beaten egg whites are added. Whisk batter from time to time to keep it smooth.

Multiply the batter recipes as desired and ingredients to be fried accordingly. To serve, mix and match in a paper-lined basket. Choose a dipping sauce (pages 26–29) if desired.

All batters make 1 cup

To make about 24 pieces

Beer Batter
6 ounces (3/4 cup) light beer
1 cup all-purpose flour
1 1/2 teaspoons kosher salt
1 1/2 teaspoons sweet paprika

Buttermilk Batter
1/2 cup all-purpose flour
1/2 cup buttermilk
2 teaspoons olive oil
1/2 teaspoon kosher salt

Vinegar Batter
2/3 cup all-purpose flour
6 tablespoons white wine vinegar
1 egg, separated
1 tablespoon vegetable oil
Pinch kosher salt

For Vinegar Batter. Combine flour, vinegar, egg yolk, oil and salt in a mixing bowl to form a smooth batter. Cover with plastic wrap and refrigerate for at least 2 hours. Beat egg white until soft peaks form. Fold white into batter gently until completely incorporated.

Selection of: herb leaves with about 1/4 inch of stem attached—sage, lovage, flat-leaf parsley or basil leaves or edible flowers or

Vegetables: red and yellow pepper strips (about 1/2 inch wide), or 1/4-inch-thick slices of green or yellow squash that have been sprinkled generously with salt and allowed to sit to drain for at least 30 minutes, or cauliflower florets that have been blanched like broccoli (page 98) so that they are still a little crunchy or

Seafood: shrimp, shelled tail on, 1 pound; clams or oysters, shucked and dried; medium scallops or large, halved; fish (such as sole), a 6-ounce fillet, halved and center membrane removed, cut on a sharp diagonal into 2 1/2 x 1/2-inch strips

Vegetable oil for frying

Dip herbs, vegetables or seafood in batter so that they are generously coated. Use herb stem or shrimp tail as a handle; other foods go on a slotted spoon. Working in batches, fry in deep fat until golden brown, about 2 minutes on each side (see Deep Frying, page 236).

coconut fried shrimp

This is always successful. A sauce isn't really necessary, but you can put some Plum Chutney (page 150) in a blender and use the result as a sweet and spicy sauce, or use Harissa Sauce (page 28) for the very spice-minded.

This recipe is easily multiplied. Don't serve these first or people will eat too much and they are filling.

Makes about 24

Double recipe Beer Batter (page 245)
2 cups unsweetened, shredded coconut
1 pound uncooked shrimp, peeled, with the tail on
Vegetable oil for frying

Place batter in a medium bowl. Stir 1¼ cups of the coconut into the batter. Add shrimp and stir to coat.

Place remaining coconut on a plate or sheet of parchment paper. Remove shrimp from batter and coat with coconut.

Working in batches, fry shrimp until golden brown, about 40 seconds (see Deep Frying, page 236). Cut one shrimp to make sure it is fully cooked.

tempura

This is very good, but unfortunately last-minute. You may want to save it for an all-tempura party with beer. Put out a bowl of Japanese Dipping Sauce.

Makes about 90 pieces

Batter
1 cup ice water (plus an additional 1½ tablespoons if making shrimp)

2 cups rice flour
½ teaspoon paprika
1 large egg
Vegetable oil for frying

Dipping Choices
Carrots, peeled and cut into long ribbons with a vegetable peeler (1 medium carrot makes about 48 pieces)
Turnips, peeled and sliced into thin rounds (1 medium turnip makes about 24 pieces)
Green beans, cut lengthwise into quarters but left attached at one end (4 ounces green beans make about 24 pieces)
Celery leaves with several sprigs attached (1 head celery will have 2 to 3 pieces)
Shrimp, peeled and deveined (20 to 24 to the pound, with shell on)

Just before ready to cook, place all batter ingredients in a medium bowl. Stir very lightly (chopsticks are good for this) so that batter is barely combined; there should be lumps of flour in batter and around rim of bowl.

Prepare to deep-fat-fry (page 236). Working in batches, dip pieces into batter to coat well. Drop in oil and cook until light brown on the bottom, about 30 seconds. Turn and brown the other side. These do not get deep brown. Serve hot with dipping sauce.

japanese dipping sauce

Ponzu is a standard Japanese sauce for fried foods. I have adapted it for ease of preparation. The original recipe calls for heating the mirin and adding bonito flakes and dried kombu (kelp), a kind of seaweed. That mixture is then allowed to mellow for a month or more. I really like this easily made adaptation, which is good with the Shrimp Balls (page 251) and other semispicy fried foods.

Makes 1 cup

¼ cup mirin
½ cup soy sauce
2 tablespoons Ginger Juice (page 257)
¼ cup rice wine vinegar
2 tablespoons fresh lemon juice

Combine all ingredients in a small bowl.

chiles rellenos

No Mexican is going to recognize these—wrong peppers, wrong cheese—but they are small enough to handle at a stand-up party without a knife and fork and they are puffy and delicious.

Makes about 15 pieces

11 ounces peperoncini (Italian pickled hot peppers) or Greek Salonika peppers
1 cup crumbled feta cheese, drained (4½ ounces)
½ cup shredded mozzarella cheese, preferably fresh (2½ ounces)
¼ teaspoon freshly ground black pepper
4 eggs, separated
⅓ cup all-purpose flour, plus more for dredging
Vegetable oil for frying

Drain the peppers and rinse. Cut a slit along each pepper from stem end to tip. Scrape out the seeds from each pepper, leaving the stem intact. Be careful when working with the peppers not to cut or tear them (other than the one slit), or the filling will leak out during frying. Drain the peppers well on a double thickness of paper towels.

Stir the feta, mozzarella and black pepper in a mixing bowl until well blended. Working with one pepper at a time, form an oval of the cheese mixture roughly the size of the pepper. Carefully fill the pepper with the cheese. The cheese should fill the pepper solidly but not to overflowing. Make sure both sides of the slit meet over the cheese filling. Continue with the remaining peppers. May be prepared ahead and refrigerated to this point.

Beat the egg whites in a mixing bowl with a wire whisk (or in the bowl of an electric mixer) until they form stiff peaks. Stir one third of the whites into the yolks. Sprinkle this mixture with ⅓ cup of the flour and top with the remaining whites. Fold the whites and flour in until no streaks of white remain. A few lumps of flour might remain.

Dredge the filled peppers in flour, making sure all surfaces are coated. Tap off excess flour.

Working in batches, dip the coated peppers in the batter and shallow-fry (page 237), increasing heat slightly after putting peppers in pan. Fry until the underside is dark golden brown, about 4 minutes. Turn and fry until completely browned, another minute or so.

Serve hot with a salsa (pages 23–25), if desired.

Melting and mildly spicy, miniaturized Chiles Rellenos can be the star of any party. Bring them on after the opening acts so people don't eat too many.

247

Italian Rice Dumplings (Suppli al Telefono) are an addictive snack.

italian rice dumplings

Leftover risotto is too good to waste. In its home, Italy's Po valley, leftovers are turned into fried dumplings called **suppli al telefono**. If you have leftover risotto, feel free to use it, but you don't have to make a risotto to turn out these delicious snacks. Suppli are telephone wires, which is what the cheese will look like if you tear these in two. Reheated, they will not make the wires, but they will still be delicious. Serve with Tomato Basil Dipping Sauce (page 27), if desired.

Makes 45 pieces

1 ½ tablespoons olive oil
2 tablespoons finely chopped
    onion
1 cup short-grain rice
    (7 ounces)
2 ½ cups water
2 ½ teaspoons kosher salt
3 tablespoons grated
    Parmesan cheese
Freshly ground black pepper,
    to taste
1 egg, plus 1 egg yolk
1 cup grated mozzarella
    cheese (4 ounces)
1 tablespoon chopped fresh
    Italian parsley leaves
1 ½ cups fresh bread crumbs
    (about 3¾ ounces)
Vegetable oil for frying

Heat oil in medium saucepan over medium heat. Add onion and sauté for about 5 minutes, or until softened but not browned.

Stir in rice, water and 1½ teaspoons kosher salt. Bring the mixture to a boil over medium heat. Cover with lid, reduce heat and simmer for 10 minutes.

Remove from heat and stir in Parmesan and pepper.

Transfer mixture to a bowl and allow to cool.

Lightly beat egg and yolk together in a small bowl. Stir into rice with mozzarella and parsley. Form into small balls using about 1 tablespoon of mixture for each ball. Gently roll between your hands then roll balls in bread crumbs so that they are coated evenly. Fry immediately or keep in a single layer on parchment paper for up to an hour.

Working in batches, fry balls until golden brown, about 3 minutes (see Deep Frying, page 236).

These can be fried ahead and refrigerated, then reheated for 5 minutes on a baking sheet in a preheated 350°F oven.

caribbean vegetable fritters

Christophines (*also called chayotes and mirlitons*) *are often cooked and turned into fritters, called* **acras,** *in the French Caribbean islands. They are served with a hot dipping sauce such as Harissa Sauce (page 28).*

Makes 36 pieces

4 christophines

Fritter Batter
1 envelope active dry yeast
¼ cup warm water
2 cups sifted all-purpose flour
½ cup minced onion (3 ounces)
4 medium cloves garlic, smashed, peeled and minced
3 tablespoons minced fresh Italian parsley leaves
2 teaspoons crumbled dry thyme
1 tablespoon kosher salt

½ to 1½ teaspoons cayenne pepper
1½ cups water
2 whole eggs, beaten lightly

Vegetable oil for frying

Cook christophines.

Microwave-Oven Method. Prick christophines four times with a fork. Set on paper toweling in a high-wattage oven. Cook, uncovered, at 100% power for 15 minutes. Remove from oven.

Discard the soft white heart. Scoop out all of the flesh and mash with a fork. Drain, then squeeze dry between doubled paper towels.

Stove-Top Method. Cut christophines in half lengthwise. Cook cut side down in a steamer over boiling water for 40 minutes, or until flesh is easily pierced with the tip of a sharp knife.

To Make the Batter. Dissolve yeast in the warm water. In a large bowl, combine flour, onion, garlic, parsley, thyme, salt and cayenne to taste. Slowly stir in more water, as necessary, to make a fairly thick batter. Add eggs and stir just to combine. Cover loosely with a damp kitchen towel and put in a warm place for 4 to 5 hours. Stir in christophines.

Final Preparation. Fry one teaspoon batter until golden, about 1½ to 2 minutes (see Deep Frying, page 236). Drain and taste for seasoning, adjusting with additional cayenne, if desired. Working in batches, fry remaining batter. If desired, the fritters may be fried several hours in advance and recrisped in a 400°F oven for 5 to 7 minutes, or until heated through and crisp.

corn fritters

These slightly sweet, all-American fritters are delicious. Serve with Plum Tomato Sauce (page 27), Tartar Sauce (page 36) or Cranberry Ketchup (page 267).

Makes 25 to 30 fritters

4 ears fresh corn, shucked and silk removed
2 tablespoons sugar
2 teaspoons kosher salt
Pinch sweet paprika
Freshly ground black pepper
3 eggs, separated
¼ cup sifted all-purpose flour
½ teaspoon baking powder
3 cups vegetable oil

Score corn through the middle of each kernel with a sharp knife. Grate corn from cob or cut kernels from cob with a very sharp knife (do not cut so deeply as to include part of the cob). Put kernels in a 4-cup glass or ceramic bowl. Mash slightly with a potato masher until a milky liquid is exuded. Add sugar, salt, paprika and pepper. Cover tightly with microwave plastic wrap. Cook at 100% in a high-wattage oven for 1 minute; low-wattage for 1 minute and 30 seconds. Prick plastic to release steam. Uncover and stir.

Add egg yolks, flour and baking powder; stir just to combine. Beat egg whites until stiff. Fold into corn mixture.

Fry by tablespoonfuls until fritters are golden brown (see Deep Frying, page 236). Drain.

249

cod fritters

*Salt cod is popular in much of the world. In the Antilles, it is used to make these crisp balls, called **acras**. I like them with an atypical sauce—preferably spicy—such as Spicy Middle Eastern Tomato Sauce (page 27).*

Makes about 36 pieces

Salt Cod Mixture
1/3 **pound desalinated salt cod (box, page 146)**
5 **chives, sliced thin**
1/3 **cup minced onion**
3 **medium cloves garlic, smashed, peeled and minced**
1/2 **cup thinly sliced green onion, green and white parts**
1/2 **teaspoon dried thyme**

To Prepare the Cod. Shred the salt cod with a knife or in a mortar. Combine with remaining ingredients. Set aside.

Batter
1 1/2 **cups sifted all-purpose flour**
3/4 **cup milk**
1/4 **cup melted, unsalted butter**
2 **large eggs, lightly beaten**
1 1/2 **teaspoons kosher salt**
1/2 **teaspoon cayenne pepper**
10 **drops hot red pepper sauce**
1/2 **teaspoon freshly ground black pepper**
Vegetable oil for frying

To Make the Batter. In a large bowl, make a well in the center of the flour. Pour milk and melted butter into center of well. Stir together until well combined. Add eggs, salt, cayenne, pepper sauce and black pepper. Beat until well mixed. Set aside for one hour.

Final Preparation. Combine salt cod mixture with batter. Deep-fry 1 teaspoon batter for

spicy chickpea fritters

*These are a version of **pakora**, a spicy Indian fritter, to be munched on its own or served with a cooling sauce such as Herb Dip (page 18). They can be made ahead and kept for up to two hours at room temperature and reheated on a parchment-lined baking sheet at 350°F for four minutes, or made up to a month ahead, wrapped airtight and frozen. Reheat as above for ten minutes.*

Makes about 16 pakoras

1 1/2 **cups chickpea flour**
1 **teaspoon kosher salt**
1 **teaspoon curry powder**
1 **teaspoon ground cumin**
1/4 **teaspoon cayenne pepper**
1/2 **teaspoon baking powder**
1 **fresh jalapeño pepper, stemmed, seeded, deribbed and minced**

1/2 **cup loosely packed fresh coriander (cilantro) leaves, chopped**
2/3 **cup plus 2 tablespoons cold water**
Vegetable oil for frying

Combine all ingredients except water and oil in a medium bowl. Add the water slowly, stirring constantly, until dry ingredients are moistened. Do not overmix; a few remaining lumps won't matter. Cover and let the batter rest at room temperature for 2 to 3 hours. The batter may be refrigerated up to one day.

For each fritter use a rounded tablespoon of batter. Starting as close to the oil as possible, push the batter off the tablespoon with a second spoon; this helps the fritter retain its shape. Working in small batches, fry until golden brown, about 3 minutes (see Deep Frying, page 236).

about 2 minutes (see Deep Frying, page 236). Drain and taste for seasoning, adjusting if necessary. Working in batches, fry remaining batter. Serve immediately or recrisp as for Caribbean Vegetable Fritters (page 249).

cod balls

Americans made as much use of salt cod as the French and Italians, and this is their version of acras. You can substitute fresh cod in the recipe. Serve with Tartar Sauce (page 36), Green Goddess Dressing (page 37) or one of the cocktail sauces (page 38). The raw mixture can be made ahead, formed and frozen for up to two weeks. Allow to come to room temperature before frying.

Makes about 45

1/2 pound desalinated salt cod
   (box, page 146), finely
   chopped with a knife, or
   fresh cod
3/4 cup dry bread crumbs
6 tablespoons finely chopped
   onion
1/2 cup heavy cream
2 egg yolks
4 drops hot red pepper sauce
Several grinds black pepper
2 tablespoons finely chopped
   green bell pepper, optional
Vegetable oil for frying

Stir all ingredients together in a medium bowl. Form into balls, using a rounded teaspoon for each.

Fry until golden brown, about 15 seconds (see Deep Frying, page 236). You can reheat these on a baking sheet in the bottom third of a 350°F oven for 6 minutes.

Smoked Haddock Balls.
Substitute soaked smoked haddock (see box, page 183) for cod and use 6 tablespoons additional bread crumbs and 1/2 teaspoon kosher salt. Place in a food processor and pulse until finely chopped. Scrape into a medium bowl and continue as for Cod Balls.

shrimp toast

Almost anybody who eats at Chinese restaurants has had shrimp toast. It is easy to make at home, and there are many ways to avoid frying it at the last minute. There is only one method that absolutely will not work, and that is to assemble the shrimp toasts and freeze them uncooked (the bread gets soggy).

Here are the ways to make these ahead: Fry a couple of hours ahead; reheat on a baking sheet 350°F, for five minutes; drain. Or make filling (decrease chili paste to one teaspoon); assemble triangles; store airtight and refrigerate up to a day ahead; fry just before serving. Or fry ahead and refrigerate in airtight container for a day and a night; reheat in a 350°F oven for seven minutes; drain.

*The well-chilled Shrimp Mixture can be fried up into tasty little **Shrimp Balls** on their own. Cook in batches. Push the mixture by slightly rounded teaspoons into hot fat. Cook briefly—about thirty seconds—until golden brown. By the time the last balls in the batch go into the fat, the first will need to come out. You will get about four dozen balls. If you make them ahead, you can reheat them from room temperature on a baking sheet in the bottom third of a 350°F oven for five minutes, or from frozen in seven minutes.*

You can also use this mixture to fill Chinese Dumplings (page 253). It will fill about a hundred dumplings, or about twice the dough recipe.

Makes 40

Shrimp Mixture
1/4 pound cooked and cleaned
   shrimp (page 168)
2 ounces raw unsalted pork
   fat, coarsely chopped
2 large scallions, white part
   chopped, green part sliced
   across into thin rings (keep
   green and white separate)
1 teaspoon kosher salt
1 1/2 teaspoons cornstarch
2 large eggs
1 1/2 teaspoons Chinese chili
   paste with garlic
10 slices firm white bread,
   crusts removed
5 tablespoons sesame seeds
Vegetable oil for frying

Place shrimp, pork fat, white part of scallion, salt, cornstarch and eggs in a food processor. Process until very smooth, stopping to scrape down sides of bowl.

Scrape mixture into a small bowl. Stir in chili paste and 2 tablespoons scallion rings. Refrigerate until cold.

Place 2 tablespoons (1 ounce) of the shrimp mixture on each slice bread. Spread it out so that the mixture touches the edges of the bread, but is slightly mounded in the center.

Using a serrated knife, cut the slices diagonally into triangles. Coat each one lightly in sesame seeds. Deep-fat-fry (page 236) in batches, shrimp side down. Fry until golden brown on the bottom, about 20 seconds. Turn and cook until the other side is golden brown, about 10 seconds. Serve hot.

251

filled dumplings

It is particularly pleasurable to bite through a crisp crust into a juicy filling, a pleasure compounded by a quick dunk into a spicy sauce—not you, the dumpling. There are nonfried dumplings, such as Calzones (page 220) and Russian Dumplings (piroshki) (pages 217–218). Some of those can be fried as well. Here we have the dough-filled tidbits that are too messy to eat without knife, fork and plate unless fried, and fry I do. There are also the rice-paper-wrapped Spring Rolls (pages 210–212), which can be fried, and the Egg Rolls (page 258), which are always fried. See also page 234 to use store-bought and restaurant-prepared dumplings.

Many parts of the world have discovered how much food can be made with a very small amount of expensive ingredients by wrapping it in a dough. Many of these foods, such as Ravioli and Pelmenyi, are most usually poached or, as in the case of Chinese Dumplings, steamed. They can also be deep-fat-fried or combined-cooked, as is done with the Chinese Dumplings, pot stickers.

It was interesting to discover that the dough for Pelmenyi, a Russian Dumpling, and Chinese Dumplings is the same, although the method of kneading differs, which makes no effective difference. The important difference is the way the dough is rolled and formed plus, most of all, the flavor. If all this seems like too much work, you can use store-bought Italian pasta sheets or, for the Chinese Dumplings, store-bought egg roll wrappers. Cut to size and proceed with forming (page 234).

You can use many fillings either in the classic Italian Egg Pasta or in the Non-Egg Pasta. Fried Ravioli are good with Cheese Filling (page 220), Spinach Fillings I and II (page 215), Tyropitta (Cheese) Filling (page 216), or Cheese Blintzes Filling (page 224). Thai Shrimp Stuffing (page 210) would be another good choice for Chinese Dumplings. The Chicken Liver Piroshki Filling (page 218) and the Beef or Pork Empanada Fillings (pages 219–220) do well in Pelmenyi.

You can use many different dipping sauces as well. Pelmenyi and Chinese Dumplings are often just sprinkled with a little bit of white vinegar. The Chinese Dumplings are good with a few drops of chili oil on them, or set out a chosen dipping sauce, such as Chinese Dipping Sauce (page 257), Japanese Dipping Sauce (page 246), Peanut Dipping Sauce (page 28), Southeast Asian Dipping Sauce (page 28), Semi-Thai Sauce (page 212) or Pacific Tomato Dipping Sauce (page 26), along with cruets of the vinegar and the chili oil. The standards are in the recipes.

These are some of the first hors d'oeuvre to disappear from a tray, basket or bowl. Allow as many as four or five per person, especially if they are the only hot bites. In any case, these recipes make quite a few pieces and can easily be multiplied, although they take some work until you get used to doing them. On the other hand, they can be *frozen* uncooked by putting them in a single layer on a parchment-lined baking sheet. Once frozen, they can be tumbled into a plastic bag. When it's time to cook, take as many dumplings from the bag as you need; let them come to room temperature in a single layer and cook.

I don't find that anybody minds eating these when they have cooled off. To reheat Chinese Dumplings or Pelmenyi, see page 253. To reheat Fried Ravioli, place on a parchment-lined baking sheet in a 350°F oven for 4 minutes.

Makes about 75

Egg Pasta
6 large egg yolks
2 whole large eggs
2 teaspoons olive oil
3 cups all-purpose flour
¼ cup water, if needed

Beat the egg yolks, eggs and olive oil in a small bowl. Place 2½ cups of the flour in a food processor. With motor running, pour the eggs and oil through the feed tube. Process until a stiff dough forms. If dough is too wet, add 3 to 4 more tablespoons flour. If too dry, add the water.

Remove dough to a lightly floured board. Knead, adding 3 to 4 tablespoons more flour as necessary, until dough is very smooth and elastic. Either cover dough with a damp kitchen towel and let rest at room temperature for 30 minutes or wrap in plastic and keep refrigerated up to 24 hours, letting dough return to room temperature before using.

Non-Egg Pasta
2 cups sifted all-purpose flour
½ teaspoon kosher salt
¾ cup water

Place flour and salt in a food processor and pulse a few times to combine and aerate. With machine running, pour in water in a thin stream. Dough will form very small kernels and some will begin to collect into a ball. Turn dough out onto a floured work surface and knead just until smooth. Form into a flattish round. Wrap in a kitchen towel and refrigerate 1 to 2 hours.

¾ cup Filling (3 cups for Pelmenyi)

See Rolling Pasta (opposite page).

To Form Pasta

To Form Ravioli and Pelmenyi. Have ready filling, rolled pasta sheets, a circular cutter or a pastry crimper, a pizza wheel or sharp knife, two pastry brushes and a small bowl of water.

To Make Squares. Place one sheet of dough on a work surface. Trim to 10½ × 3 inches. Use one of the brushes to brush the cornmeal off the pasta.

To Make Square Ravioli. Place a rounded ¼ teaspoon of filling on the pasta, spacing the mounds of filling ½ inch from the edge and 1½ inches apart. Lightly brush the pasta with water along the edges and in between the portions of filling. Place a second sheet of pasta over the filling. Press it gently with the sides of your hands to remove any air bubbles and to seal. With the cutter, cut the pasta between the lumps of filling to form 1½-inch square ravioli. Repeat with the remaining pasta and filling, placing finished ravioli on a baking sheet and covering with a damp kitchen towel.

To Make Rounds. Brush cornmeal from pasta sheets as you use them. Use a 2-inch round cutter, preferably with crimped edges. Cut out rounds from the pasta sheets, staggering the cuts to get as many as possible. Keep cut rounds covered with a damp cloth as you work. Lightly brush water around the edges of each round.

To Make Round Ravioli. Place a rounded ¼ teaspoon filling in the center of half of the rounds. Cover each of the filled rounds with one of the unfilled ones. Press the edges together to seal.

To Make Pelmenyi. Use Non-Egg Pasta and 1½ teaspoons of filling and form as ravioli. To make Chinese Dumplings, see below.

To Form Chinese Dumplings

There are many traditional shapes for these dumplings, which are actually easier to form with the homemade dough, as it sticks together, but which can be made with 2½-inch circles cut with a circular cutter from egg roll skins. The easiest just puts a half teaspoon of filling in a line down the middle of the circle, stopping ¼-inch from each end. Gather up the two edges of the dough parallel to the line of filling. Press these edges together along 1½ inches in the middle. Fry and then steam (right) bottom down. To make the traditional pot sticker shape, put the filling in a blob in the center of the dough. Hold ⅓ of the edge of the circle flat between your thumbs and next fingers. Keeping your thumbs in place, raise the front of the dough straight up (do not fold over). Make pleats in the remaining dough by gathering in a little of the slack dough at a time from each side of the rear of the circle with the second finger and any other fingers you need holding the dough. Pinch each pleat as it is formed against the front edge. It is much like gathering a full skirt into a waistband. When you have used up all the dough in pleats, gently turn the pleated band forward toward the flat center to make a crescent.

Those wishing illustrations and more detailed instructions may want to consult Barbara Tropp's excellent book *The Modern Art of Chinese Cooking.*

To Cook Ravioli

In batches, deep-fry (page 236) ravioli until light brown on the bottom. Turn and fry until light brown on the other side. The Italians would use olive oil, not the finest extra-virgin but a good one. If made ahead, reheat from room temperature on a baking sheet in the bottom third of a 350°F oven for 4 minutes.

To Fry Chinese Dumplings and Pelmenyi

Shallow-fry (page 237) in ⅛ inch oil (about ⅓ cup) in a single layer in a large nonstick skillet until lightly but evenly brown on one side—less than a minute. Holding a pot lid slightly smaller than the skillet over the dumplings, carefully pour off most of the oil and discard. Return pan to heat. Pour on ⅓ cup water. Cover pan. As soon as you see steam, reduce heat to low and cook for 2 minutes. If made ahead, reheat from room temperature in a steamer over boiling water 2 minutes.

rolling pasta

Machine Rolling

Divide the dough into sixths, keeping the unused pieces covered with a damp kitchen towel while you work. Sprinkle a baking sheet with cornmeal. Take one piece of dough and flatten with your hands into a round disk. With machine set on 5, run the disk through the machine. Fold the dough in half. Turn it one quarter turn, so that the folded edge is facing you. Run it through the machine again. Repeat the folding and turning process three or four times. Change the setting to 4. Continue running the dough through the machine, folding and turning each time until the dough is silky smooth. Change the setting to 3. Run the dough through the machine; the dough will get much longer at this point, so have your hand ready to catch

A *springtime feast. See photographs, pages 94–95 and 170–171.*

the front end as it comes out and catch the back with the other hand when it comes out. Flip the dough over, so that the end that went in first now goes in last. Continue in this manner until the dough is roughly 17 × 4 inches. Place the pasta on the baking sheet. Sprinkle cornmeal over the top. Repeat with remaining dough pieces, placing cornmeal between each layer. Cover with a damp kitchen towel when not using.

Hand Rolling

Pasta dough will be much easier to roll by hand if it is allowed to rest before and during the rolling. Make pasta according to directions on page 252. Allow the dough to rest under a bowl for 15 to 30 minutes. Cut the dough into sixths, or 2-ounce pieces, and place them under a lightly floured kitchen towel. Choose a heavy rolling pin and roll a dough ball out until it begins to spring back noticeably. (This is the gluten at work; resting will relax the gluten, making the dough easier to roll.) Place that piece under the towel and continue with the other pieces. Allow all the dough pieces to rest 5 to 10 minutes before rolling again.

Flour the pasta sheets lightly or sprinkle with cornmeal if necessary to prevent them from sticking together. Continue until the sheets are the desired thickness. While dough for noodles should be thin enough to easily read magazine print through, for ravioli and other filled pasta for frying it should be somewhat thicker.

Rolling Chinese Dumpling Wrappers

These instructions are for Non-Egg Pasta, which is what many Chinese use for delicate dumplings. Other Chinese use Egg Pasta, rolling it somewhat thinner than it would be rolled for ravioli. Since I do not recommend boiling or steaming Chinese Dumplings for use as finger food, I find that the egg dough doesn't work as well with the cooking method used, but you can try it.

You will only get 54 dumplings with this method. If you would rather, roll as for other pastas. There is a major advantage to the Chinese method: The edges of each disk of dough are thinner than the center so that when the dumplings are formed and two edges of dough are joined, the made dumpling has less, better-cooked dough at the edges.

For the Chinese method, divide dough in half. Roll each piece between your hands or on a floured surface into a snake that is just under 1 inch in diameter and about 13 inches long. Cover with a slightly dampened kitchen towel. Let rest 20 minutes. After relaxing, the snakes will be about 14 inches long.

Pinch off ½-inch pieces of dough, replacing under towel as you work. Each snake will make about 28 pieces. Roll each piece into a ball. Re-cover with towel as they are made and let rest 20 minutes.

The Chinese typically use a small, short rolling pin about the size of a relay runner's baton. They can be bought in Chinese shops. You can make one yourself by cutting off an 8-inch piece of 1½-inch-diameter dowel and sanding the ends until they are rounded, or use the narrowest rolling pin you can buy.

Work with one dough ball at a time. Flatten ball into a circle with palm of hand. Hold dough with one hand and rotate it as you roll dough with rolling pin, using a circular motion to move around the edge of the dough and flattening it into a 2½-inch circle that is a good bit thinner at the edge than in the middle.

255

sausage and clam filling

This makes good ravioli. If you can't get sweet Italian sausage, use the same amount of ground pork, half fat and half lean, and season with a little salt, pepper and ground fennel seed. You can buy the clams already shucked or even use canned minced clams. You will drain the clams for this filling, but you will need to retain the clam juice if making the Chinese Pork and Clam Filling, which follows. These are very nice with Tomato Basil Dipping Sauce (page 27).

Makes ¾ cup

6 ounces sweet Italian sausage
**6 clams, shucked, reserving
    clam liquid, and minced**
2 tablespoons minced scallion
**⅛ teaspoon freshly ground
    black pepper**

Place the sausages in a small, heavy skillet. Pour in enough water to coat the bottom of the pan. Heat over medium heat until the water is steaming. Cover the skillet. Cook the sausages, turning occasionally, until no trace of pink remains in the center, about 15 minutes. Remove to paper towels to drain. When cool, remove the casings and crumble the meat fine, or chop with a knife; put in a small bowl. Stir in remaining ingredients.

chinese pork and clam filling

This filling is a good illustration of the difference seasoning makes. The ingredients are almost the same as for the Italian filling (left), but the taste is totally different and more appropriate for Chinese Dumplings.

Makes ¾ cup

**Ingredients for Sausage and
    Clam Filling (this page),
    substituting ground pork
    (half lean and half fat) for
    the Italian sausage**
**Ingredients for Semi-Thai
    Sauce (page 212), omitting
    Thai or other fish sauce**
**2 tablespoons chopped fresh
    coriander (cilantro) leaves**

Drain and reserve the juice from the shucked clams; you should have about ½ cup. Make the Semi-Thai Sauce according to the recipe, adding the clam juice in place of the nuac nam. Stir in the coriander. Set aside.

Heat a small skillet to warm over medium heat. Add the ground pork. Cook, pushing the meat into the pan with the back of a spoon to separate it, until no traces of pink remain. Do not let it brown. Place pork in a small bowl and stir in clams, scallions and pepper.

Add 6 tablespoons of the sauce to the pork mixture. Use your hand to knead the liquid into the mixture. Use the remaining sauce for dipping.

pelmenyi filling

Originally, pelmenyi were a Siberian specialty made at the end of the summer with meat from animals too expensive to winter over. The little filled dough pockets were left outside the dwelling to freeze. When they were wanted, a block was hacked off and they were poached either in broth or water. Freshly made, the pelmenyi can be shallow-fried (page 237) and sprinkled with white vinegar. Accompany with a bowl of sour cream topped with chopped dill for dipping.

The pelmenyi can be served as part of a soup or stew by poaching them in chicken broth and serving with the gizzards, dill and sour cream.

While pelmenyi use smaller circles of dough (page 253) than the other dumplings, they take more filling.

You can make **Siberian Meatballs** *from the filling mixture by deep frying (page 236) in batches, using two teaspoons of filling for each and pushing them into the fat and cooking for thirty to forty seconds, or until golden brown and when one cut open shows no pink. You will make about fifty-four meatballs. You can make them ahead and reheat on a baking sheet in the bottom third of a 350°F oven for six minutes. Serve with Spicy Middle Eastern Tomato Sauce (page 27).*

**Makes 2¼ cups, filling about
72 dough rounds**

½ pound ground beef
**½ pound ground pork, half
    fat, half lean**
**⅓ pound finely minced onion
    (about ⅔ cup)**
1 teaspoon water
1 teaspoon kosher salt
**Freshly ground black pepper,
    to taste**

Lightly mix beef, pork and onion together. Add water, salt, and pepper and mix just until combined. Test seasoning by sautéing a small patty on top of the stove.

vegetable egg roll filling

I have seen an endless variety of fillings for egg rolls but few that are actually vegetarian. If you make this on the day that you make Spring Rolls (page 211), you can use the greens from the bok choy and the leftover bit of scallion. If not, substitute spinach or kale for the bok choy. The scallion should be no problem.

Makes 1⅓ cups, to fill 64 to 128 Miniature Egg Rolls

Greens from 1 medium-sized bok choy (3.2 ounces), cut across into thin strips, then coarsely chopped
¼ cup water
2 large eggs
2 tablespoons Ginger Juice (this page)
1 tablespoon toasted sesame oil
1 medium clove garlic, smashed, peeled and minced
¼ cup packed peeled and grated carrot (1¼ ounces)
¼ cup packed peeled and grated daikon radish (1½ ounces)
1½ ounces drained, canned straw mushrooms, cut into ⅛-inch cubes
1 small scallion, green part only, thinly sliced
1 teaspoon Chinese chili paste with garlic
1 tablespoon tamari soy sauce

Place bok choy and water in a small saucepan over medium heat. Cook until completely wilted. Drain.

Lightly whisk the eggs with the ginger juice.

In a small nonstick skillet over low heat, cook and stir sesame oil and garlic, about 30 seconds. Stir in carrot and continue to cook for 1 minute. Stir in daikon and cook another 1½ minutes. Stir in mushrooms and scallions and cook 30 seconds. Stir in bok choy, chili paste and tamari. Allow to heat briefly.

Pour egg mixture into pot and raise the heat to medium. Allow to cook for 2 minutes, scraping the sides and bottom of the pan as you stir, until you get a soft scrambled-egg-like mixture and see no separate liquid. Let cool.

ginger juice

This is a first-rate Chinese trick that I learned only recently. It is a good way to keep the flavor of ginger virtually indefinitely (refrigerated in a closed container), although the juice will darken and the flavor will get a little weaker with age. The ginger juice can be added to soups or any other dish where you want the flavor of ginger but may not want to bite a piece.

Makes 1⅓ cups

½ pound fresh ginger, trimmed, peeled and sliced thin (6 ounces)
⅔ cup water

Place ginger and water in a blender. Blend until a smooth paste forms, stopping several times to scrape down sides of jar. Cut two 9-inch squares of cheesecloth. Put one on top of the other. Dampen and wring out and place in sieve over storage container. Pour in ginger mixture. Gather up ends of cheesecloth and wring out all the liquid from the ginger. Discard very dry pulp. Refrigerate. Stir well before using.

chinese dipping sauce

This is a simple all-purpose sauce for fried egg rolls and Chinese Dumplings (page 253). Those who like hot food can use up to twice as much chili paste. Those who want a milder sauce can use Japanese Dipping Sauce (page 246).

Makes 1 scant cup

¾ cup dark Chinese soy sauce with molasses
1 tablespoon Chinese chili paste with garlic
¾ teaspoon sugar

Whisk all ingredients together in a small bowl.

257

Restaurant egg rolls are adequate but nowhere near as good as Miniature Egg Rolls you make.

miniature egg rolls

Everybody seems to like egg rolls. If it's easier, you can make full-sized ones; let them cool and cut them across into pieces to be reheated. I happen to like miniatures, which can be popped into the mouth whole, or at the very most, in two bites; there is less mess. You can make two different sizes of miniatures, depending on the size dough with which you start, the way you fold it (two different ways) and the amount of filling used. Egg roll skins (sometimes called wonton wrappers) can be bought in two sizes—3-inch squares and 8½-inch squares—or you can use the Non-Egg Pasta (page 252) and cut it to the size needed.

Sliced or whole, the egg rolls can be reheated on a baking sheet in the bottom third of a 375°F oven for 6 minutes.

Makes 64 to 96, depending on size

64 3x3-inch egg roll skins (only if making smaller miniatures) or between 6 and 8 8½x8½-inch egg roll skins, depending on the size egg roll you are making (see below)
1 recipe Vegetable Egg Roll Filling (page 257) or 1⅓ cups Spring Roll fillings (pages 210–212)
Vegetable oil for frying

Have ready two damp kitchen towels, a small bowl of water, a paper towel and a well-oiled baking sheet. Cut skins or Non-Egg Pasta as desired (see below). As you are working, keep pieces covered with one of the damp towels. Place one piece of dough on a work surface. Dip corner of paper towel in water and gently rub it on inside edge of dough to moisten. Fill and roll as below. Transfer to an oiled baking sheet and cover with a damp towel.

To Make Larger Miniatures
Cut large egg roll skins into nine equal squares or pasta into 3-inch squares, or use small skins. Place 1 teaspoon of filling in top third of a cut skin. Fold top over filling. Fold sides in over filling, pressing dough together below filling. Roll up egg roll so that seam side is down. Repeat with remaining skins.

To Make Smaller Miniatures—Squares or Rectangles
If using large egg roll skins, cut into 16 equal squares, or trim small skins to 2 × 2-inch squares, or cut Non-Egg Pasta into 2-inch squares. Use ½ teaspoon filling. Either fold as above, or diagonally cut each 2-inch square of egg roll or wonton skin into 2 triangles. Place ½ teaspoon of filling in center of a triangle.

258

With the long edge facing you, take the two near corners and fold them up over the filling so that they meet the top corner. Press edges to seal.

Repeat with remaining skins.

To Cook Egg Rolls. In a large skillet, add enough oil to make a depth of 1 inch. Heat oil. Working in batches, fry egg rolls until brown (see Deep Frying, page 236). Serve hot.

scallion pancakes

These are work and should be tried only by the cook who likes working with dough and will be interested by the technique—an early form of puff pastry—of making layered pastry by working with oiled hands and surfaces rather than with flour.

These are fatty and filling. Allow about two wedges per person. Since these take some time to cook, it is a good idea to make them early in the day, cut them into wedges and then reheat on a parchment-lined baking sheet in the bottom third of the oven at 350°F for 3 minutes. To minimize last-day work, note that the dough can be made ahead and refrigerated. This is a messy dough to work with, so roll up your sleeves and take off any jewelry before beginning.

These are formed to make thick Peking pancakes. Thinner Cantonese ones can be made by using smaller pieces of dough and coiling the rolled dough into a flat mat. Serve with an ample amount of Chinese Dipping Sauce (page 257).

Makes 48 pieces

3 cups unbleached flour
1½ cups cold water
2 tablespoons vegetable oil

1 cup thinly sliced scallions, green part only
4 teaspoons toasted sesame oil
Additional vegetable oil for forming and cooking

Place flour, water and oil in a large bowl. Use your hand to combine ingredients; mixture will be like a sticky biscuit dough. Cover the bowl with a damp towel. Let rest 20 minutes.

To knead dough, make a fist and use your knuckles to lift the dough from the bottom of the bowl and push it against the sides of the bowl, allowing the dough to fall back on itself. Continue kneading, cleaning the sides of the bowl as you work, until the dough starts to pull away from the sides and begins to blister. Cover and let rest for 20 minutes.

Knead the dough again. With each kneading, the dough will become smoother and more elastic. Cover and let rest for another 20 minutes. At this point, the dough can be refrigerated overnight. Wrap dough in oiled plastic wrap. Wrap in second layer of wrap. Let come to room temperature before continuing.

Coat a work surface, a rolling pin (a long thin one of equal width is best) and your hands with oil; be extremely generous, but do not make great pools of oil. Place the dough on oiled surface and coat hands with oil. Roll dough into one long rope that measures 21 × 2½ inches. Continue to oil the work surface, particularly if you are working on wood.

Divide dough into 4 equal pieces. Fill a large dish with oil to a depth of 1 inch, greasing the sides as well.

Work with one dough piece at a time. Roll into a rough square, about 14 inches wide, pushing the dough out from the center. You may want to start by pressing the dough out with your

fingers. Do not worry if dough tears slightly; overlap and press. Sprinkle 5 tablespoons of scallions onto the dough, leaving a ¼-inch border on all sides. Sprinkle lightly with 1 teaspoon of sesame oil. Gently and rather loosely roll up dough. Twist the roll using a similar motion to that for wringing out laundry. Coat your hands with oil as necessary.

Taking one end of the twisted roll, coil and twist it into the palm. Tuck the end of the roll into the center of the coil. It should resemble a turban. Place in greased dish.

Continue in the same fashion with the other pieces of dough, being careful not to let the coils touch one another. Let rest 15 minutes.

Scoop a coil up from the oil and tighten it slightly. Place on the oiled work surface and gently flatten with the palm of your hand until you form an 8-inch disk, being careful not to burst any air bubbles. You will not need the rolling pin to do this.

Heat ¼ cup oil in a large nonstick skillet over medium heat. Pick up one of the pancakes and place in the oil, being careful not to let it fold onto itself. Immediately turn the heat to low and cover the pan. It is important to reduce the heat quickly. If you have an electric stove, you may want to move the pan to a second burner.

Let cook until golden brown on the bottom, about 4 minutes. Turn the pancake over, re-cover and let cook until golden brown on the other side, about 12 minutes. Remove from pan and drain on a paper-towel-lined plate. Continue in the same manner with the remaining coils, adding oil to the pan as needed.

With scissors, cut each pancake into quarters and then cut each quarter into three wedges.

chapter 8

bird and beast

Yes, you're right, you have seen both bird and beast in this book before, and for a full list of recipes look under the meat of your choice in the Index.

Here you will find things such as Chicken Salad (page 263), Yakitori and Saté (pages 272–273) using a variety of meats, Mahogany Quail with Peppercorns (page 264), Marinated Chicken Wings (page 264) and a whole turkey (page 267) for guests to hack at at parties needing more substantial food, along with other roasted meats that, as well as

going to the table whole, can be sliced cold and put on biscuits (pages 108–109) and soda breads (pages 114–115). There are meats for grilling at informal outdoor parties.

There are raw meats like Steak Tartare (page 275), Lamb Tartare (kibbeh) (pages 276–277) and Carpaccio (page 274); and grilled meats like flank steak (page 273), to slice thin and serve with a sauce, or Fajitas (page 274). There are a whole poached fillet to slice and put on bread (page 282), Marinated Lamb Riblets (page 283), miniature

Add some Crudités (page 67) and Herb Dip (page 18) or Russian Eggplant Dip (page 12) for a gala based on Mahogany Quail with Peppercorns (page 264), dressed up with some orange sections and zest and a dish of Seasoned Salt (page 49) for dipping, and Baked Empanadas (page 218).

hamburgers stuffed with ketchup, a whole ham and Stroganoff meatballs.

If you have a carnivorous crowd, you will probably need two or more meat dishes, one of which can come from this chapter. Allow at least six pieces of meat stuff per guest.

When allotting meat from a roast, think of two to three ounces of meat—not bone—as a serving.

Look as well for some interesting accompaniments to meats.

ready-mades

This is one area in which there is a vast array of purchasable alternatives. Indeed, a whole party can be organized around bought sausages just by adding a few good breads, mustards, butter, cornichons and olives. A few of the many sausages that can be bought are salami, Hungarian and Italian; coppa; French saucisson sec, sometimes coated in herbs; chorizo (the hard kind) and spicy sopressata.

Smoked birds such as turkey and chicken are good, whole or sliced. Tongue, roast beef, prosciutto and other hams can all be bought sliced.

Logical accompaniments are cheeses, fruits and fresh or pickled vegetables.

Think also of small pieces of take-out fried chicken and barbecued ribs, American or Chinese.

A reminder that a party need take little work beyond intelligent shopping. Here, a roundup of sausages of different textures and tastes. Add bread, mustard, pickles and cheese if you want. Bring on a slightly coarse red wine and make an occasion out of it. With a little ambition, add some spiced olives (pages 53–55), a vegetable antipasto (pages 54–55) or Marinated Artichokes (page 50) to make a full evening.

barbecued cocktail franks

Quick and easy franks from a package cooked in bottled sauce will be scarfed up by even the sophisticated as long as you don't apologize. If you cannot find cocktail franks, cut regular franks into one-inch pieces.

Makes about 50 pieces

1 pound cocktail franks
1 cup commercial barbecue sauce

Combine franks and barbecue sauce in a 9-inch pie plate. Cover tightly with microwave plastic wrap. Cook at 100% in a high-wattage oven for 6 minutes or in a low-wattage oven for 9 minutes. Prick plastic to release steam.

Remove from oven and uncover. Serve warm.

chicken salad

Good in childhood, good at picnics, this can be just as welcome at a stand-up party on plates with a fork, or tucked into Choux Puffs (page 107) or spooned into pastry shells (pages 96–97). More ambitiously, consider it as part of a Smørrebrød (page 117).

Makes 5 cups

4 half chicken breasts (4 ounces each), poached (see box) and cut into 1/4-inch dice (5 cups)
1 medium onion (5 ounces), finely chopped (3/4 cup)
1 cup commercial mayonnaise
1 cup snipped chives
5 tablespoons caraway seeds
Kosher salt, to taste
Extra caraway seeds to sprinkle on top

Combine all ingredients, including still-warm chicken, in a medium bowl. Refrigerate until cold.

Poaching Chicken Breasts

Cooked chicken is a valuable commodity for the salad and to cut into cubes that can be impaled on a toothpick and served with a dipping sauce (pages 26–29), with Herb Dip (page 18) or with a saucer of Sheila's Dry Dunk (page 70) or Seasoned Salt (page 49). The cubes can be dipped in the last two before serving if you prefer. Two half chicken breasts cut into 1-inch cubes will make a cup.

Use skinned, boned and split chicken breasts, each half breast weighing about 4 ounces.

Stove-Top Method
Bring a pot of water or chicken broth to a boil. Reduce heat to a simmer. Add chicken. Let water return to a simmer. Cook for 12 minutes.

Microwave-Oven Method
Place chicken in a dish just large enough to hold it in a single layer. Cover tightly with microwave plastic wrap. Cook at 100% for time specified below. Prick plastic to release steam.

1 half breast:
High-wattage oven: 2 min., 30 sec.
Low-wattage oven: 3 min.
2 half breasts:
High-wattage oven: 3 min., 30 sec.
Low-wattage oven: 4 min.
4 half breasts:
High-wattage oven: 5 min.
Low-wattage oven: 7 to 8 min. on a wind-up carrousel or turning the dish once
6 half breasts:
High-wattage oven: 6 min.
Low-wattage oven: not recommended
8 half breasts, with 1/4 cup chicken broth:
High-wattage oven: 8 min.
Low-wattage oven: not recommended

marinated chicken wings

These are messy, but people still seem to like them. Since they can be made by the panful, it's an easy recipe to multiply, which makes a lot of sense if you are using the barbecue sauce. Remember lots of paper napkins and places to discard the bones.

Makes 24 pieces

12 chicken wings
1/2 recipe Saté Marinade (page 273), or 1/8 recipe Quick Barbecue Sauce (page 282)

Remove wing tips and freeze for stock (sharp kitchen scissors are excellent for this). Cut through the triangle of skin at the wing's joint. With your hands, bend the two parts of the wing backward until the joint pops. Cut through the joint, separating the wing into two pieces.

Place wing pieces in a dish large enough to hold them in one layer. Add marinade and toss to coat. Refrigerate at least 2 hours and preferably overnight.

To Broil. Preheat broiler. Place chicken on a baking sheet and broil until dark brown and cooked through, about 5 minutes per side.

To Grill. Heat grill. Grill until dark brown and cooked through, about 8 to 9 minutes per side.

fried quail

Quail are lovely for cocktail parties because you can cut them into quarters with a large scissors. If you're feeling fancy, cut out the backbone. This will give pieces that are just the right size to be held in the fingers. There's always a little bone sticking out

somewhere to use as a handle. *Obviously, if you buy them frozen, they will need to be defrosted overnight in the refrigerator. My dear friend Stephen Spector taught me about deep-frying quail; he had a quail farm. The seasonings are mine. Multiply as often as desired, especially as these can be reheated.*

Makes 16 pieces

1 1/2 tablespoons kosher salt
1 tablespoon ground cumin
1/4 teaspoon freshly ground black pepper
3 cups vegetable oil
4 quail, quartered
8 small wedges lemon
Fresh coriander (cilantro) sprigs for garnish, optional

Combine seasonings and rub well into all sides of quail pieces. Allow to marinate 30 minutes.

Working in batches, fry quail (see Deep Frying, page 236). These can be reheated on a baking pan, in a 350°F oven for 3 minutes.

Serve with lemon wedges and coriander, if using.

marinated grilled quail

For those who don't like deep-fat frying, this recipe provides for broiling or grilling. A wet marinade does better with these methods. The marinade can be used for chicken pieces as well.

Makes 48 pieces

Marinade
1 cup safflower oil
1 1/4 teaspoons chopped fresh Italian parsley leaves
1 1/2 teaspoons kosher salt
2 medium cloves garlic, smashed, peeled and chopped

1 scant teaspoon dried thyme
A few needles rosemary
1 tablespoon Stone's ginger wine, or Ginger Juice (page 257)
1 tablespoon red wine vinegar
3 grinds black pepper
12 small quail, quartered

Combine marinade ingredients in a bowl large enough to hold all the quail. Mix in quail. Cover and marinate in refrigerator overnight. Mix from time to time.

Before cooking, heat grill or broiler and allow quail to come to room temperature.

Cook quail pieces on grill, bone side down (under broiler, bone side up), not touching, for 2 minutes. With tongs, turn over and cook 3 minutes, or until browned. These can be reheated on a baking pan in a 350°F oven for 3 minutes.

mahogany quail with peppercorns

This is a recipe that Mark Militello of Mark's Place restaurant in the Miami area gave to me. Even though my Fried Quail are equally good, I like this so much I often do it instead.

Makes 20 pieces

Marinade
6 tablespoons water
5 tablespoons tamari soy sauce
4 teaspoons grated tangerine zest
5 tablespoons fresh tangerine juice
4 teaspoons grated peeled fresh ginger
4 medium cloves garlic, smashed, peeled and minced
3/4 teaspoon sugar

½ teaspoon Chinese five-spice
  powder
3 jalapeño peppers, stemmed,
  seeded, deribbed and
  minced

5 quail, quartered
1¼ teaspoons Szechuan
  peppercorns
1¼ teaspoons dried green
  peppercorns
1¼ teaspoons pink
  peppercorns
Kosher salt, to taste
Peanut oil for frying

Combine marinade
ingredients in a medium bowl.
Add quail and marinate
overnight.

In a dry sauté pan, lightly
toast peppercorns over medium
heat, about 5 minutes. Coarsely
grind peppercorns in a spice
mill. Combine pepper and salt
and place in a flat dish.

Remove quail from
marinade (reserve) and pat it

dry. Place enough oil to make a
depth of 2 inches in a medium
pot. Heat oil to 375°F. Place 4
quail pieces in pot, skin side
down, and fry until they turn the
color of mahogany. Remove from
oil and drain on paper towels.
Repeat with remaining quail.

Lightly dip each side of the
quail pieces in the pepper
mixture. Serve hot, using the
reserved marinade, which you
have boiled, as a dipping sauce.

These can be reheated on a
baking pan in a 350°F oven for
3 minutes.

*Chicken Salad (page 263) is a
summer favorite that is often
ignored in favor of fancier hors
d'oeuvre when people would
really prefer this piled into Crisp
New Potato Shells (page 241),
Pâte à Choux (page 106) or Fried
Bread Boxes (page 121).*

1 Roast Turkey, to be sliced thin and served on **2** Pepper Brioche (page 132) with a semitraditional **3** Cranberry Cassis Mold (page 268), can turn a sympathetic group of foods—all red or golden—into a holiday extravaganza. Spread **4** Sweet Potato Aïoli (page 35) on it or dunk. These **5** red pepper strips (page 68) can also be sprinkled with **6** Seasoned Salt (page 49) that also goes on **7** Beet Pickled Eggs (page 89). Add more **8** red pistachios with shells; **9** Mini-Strudels with Sweet and Sour Cabbage Filling (page 214); **10** Sante Fe Pâté (page 154); **11** Lacy Cheese Cookies (page 58); **12** Liptauer Cheese (page 18); **13** Fresh Mint Salsa (page 25) and **14** radishes. This buffet will feed thirty. Subtract dishes until you get to a comfortable assortment in terms of work and people to be served.

roasting turkey

Turkey is convenient at any large party for sandwiches or for guests to pick at. Even a stand-up event can be made a holiday festivity with a roast turkey, Cornmeal Biscuits (page 108) and one of the cranberry recipes (pages 267–268). Another time, serve with Sage Mayonnaise (page 274) or Green Goddess Dressing (page 37).

Order your turkey ahead and see if an unfrozen, natural—no self-basting treatment—one can be had. Remove the wing tips and add to the giblets and neck and freeze for stock or gravy. Keep the livers separate.

All times are for untrussed turkeys cooked in a shallow roasting pan at 500°F or over—as hot as your oven will go—with the rack set in the bottom third of the oven. Turkeys are presumed to be at room temperature. If a thin slice of unsalted fatback or lard is available, set it under the bird, which should be breast-side-up. Slide the turkey into the oven— legs first. After fifteen minutes move the turkey around with a wooden spatula so that it doesn't stick. Repeat, moving the bird around about every twenty minutes. If the bird seems to be getting too dark before it is cooked through, cover it with a tent of aluminum foil.

Your kitchen will be smoky and your oven a mess, but you will have the best and quickest turkey of your life.

cranberry ketchup

We tend to think of ketchup as something made with tomatoes that we buy in a bottle. In the past it has been made with all sorts of fruits and vegetables, particularly mushrooms. Tart cranberries, available in winter, make a ketchup that is particularly good with bird. Think of all those sandwiches of leftovers, or use it to baste a duck.

Makes 6 cups

3 pounds fresh cranberries (if using frozen, allow to defrost at room temperature) (about 13½ cups)
1 pound sugar (4 cups)
1 cup white vinegar
1½ ounces grated peeled fresh ginger (about 3 tablespoons)
1 teaspoon ground cinnamon
½ teaspoon freshly ground black pepper
¼ teaspoon ground allspice
⅛ teaspoon ground cloves

See box page 56 for sterilizing jars.

Combine all ingredients in a 5-quart casserole with tightly fitting lid. Cook, covered, at 100% in a high-wattage oven for 30 minutes, 50 minutes in a low-wattage oven, stirring occasionally.

Remove from oven and uncover. Pass mixture through a food mill fitted with a fine disk. Allow to cool.

Ladle into sterilized jars and store, tightly covered, in the refrigerator.

Roasting Turkey

WEIGHT	STUFFED	UNSTUFFED
9 to 10 pounds	1 hour 45 minutes	1 hour 15 minutes
12 pounds	1 hour 50 minutes	1 hour 20 minutes
15 pounds	2 to 2½ hours	2 hours
20 pounds	3½ hours	3 hours

A *flavorful stick full of spicy meat for nibbling, Chicken Saté (page 272).*

cranberry cassis mold

When a stand-up party is masquerading as Christmas or Thanksgiving, add this rich garnet-colored jelly, which slips out of the mold easily. If you like things rather sweet, add an extra quarter cup of sugar. By the way, you may want to have the kind out of a can for children.

Cassis is a lightly sweetened black-currant syrup from Burgundy. An alcoholic version is often used with wine in Kir or with soda as a summer cooler. Similar non-alcoholic syrups are made in Germany, Switzerland, Poland and Czechoslovakia. All will work.

Makes 1 mold

- **1½ cups Sirop de Cassis (not liqueur or juice)**
- **½ cup water**
- **¾ cup sugar**
- **2 12-ounce packages cranberries, rinsed (7 cups)**

Microwave-oven Method.
Combine all ingredients in a 2½-quart soufflé dish with a tightly fitting lid. Cook, covered, at 100% in a high-wattage oven for 10 minutes or in a low-wattage oven for 15 minutes.

Uncover and stir well. Cook, uncovered, in a high-wattage oven for 10 minutes or in a low-wattage oven for 21 minutes. Remove from oven.

Stove-Top Method. Combine Sirop de Cassis, water and sugar in an 8- to 9-inch saucepan. Bring just to a gentle boil over medium heat. Stir in cranberries and slowly bring back to a boil (mixture is heavy and can scorch easily). Reduce heat and simmer for 10 minutes, stirring only two or three times (stirring too often will break cranberries).

To Finish. Carefully remove pan from heat (mixture is extremely hot). Allow to cool for 5 minutes.

Rinse a 7-cup metal bowl or mold with ice water. Pour in cranberry mixture. Cover with plastic wrap and refrigerate overnight.

Just before serving, dip mold into a bowl of hot water for a few seconds and jiggle slightly to loosen. Invert onto a serving platter or into the well of a dinner plate.

268

skewered things

Stringing almost any kind of meat on a skewer is a relatively unmessy way of serving it at a stand-up party. You can even broil or grill skewered chunks of a sausage that has been parboiled, such as kielbasa, to dunk in mustard. If you are grilling your skewers, be sure to put a metal grid or piece of screen on top of the grill to keep these little skewers from falling in. You can grease the metal with an oil-soaked piece of brown paper.

Meats for skewers can be cut into cubes for kabobs or in strips for winding down the skewer (see box, page 273). Meats, vegetables and fruits for skewers are usually soaked in a marinade to give them flavor and to tenderize the meats. Before using any leftover marinade as a dipping sauce, you must boil it to kill any bacteria.

kabobs

Kabobs are popular skewers of cubed meat—or occasionally ground meat—that can be miniaturized to make substantial party snacks. They can be broiled, but if you have an outdoor grill going, consider cooking them on it. Get the look and taste you like by simply mixing and matching marinades, vegetables and fruit. I particularly like the Curry Rum Marinade with chicken and pineapple, the Greek Marinade with lamb, scallions and cherry tomatoes and the Peachy Marinade with lamb or pork and papaya.

Makes about 20 skewers

Greek Marinade (page 78), Curry Marinade (page 272), Curry Rum Marinade (page 272), Peachy Marinade (page 272), barbecue sauce or marinade of your choice from Index
1 pound boneless, skinless chicken breast
or
1 pound lean lamb
or
1 pound well-trimmed pork tenderloin
or
1 pound beef round, cut into ½-inch cubes

One 8-ounce zucchini, trimmed and cut into ½-inch cubes
or
10 ounces small (2-inch) mushrooms, cut into quarters
or
3 red bell peppers, cored, seeded and cut into ½-inch cubes
or
20 small cherry tomatoes
or
4 scallions, cut into 1-inch lengths
or
1 large pineapple, peeled, cored and cut into ½-inch cubes
or
1 ripe papaya, peeled, seeded and cut into ½-inch cubes
or
A combination of the above

If broiling, soak 24 6-inch skewers (see box); *if grilling,* use small metal skewers.

Alternate two pieces of meat and two pieces of vegetable or fruit on each skewer. Arrange the skewers in an 8 × 8-inch baking dish. Pour marinade over skewers and turn them so that each is well coated.

Marinate at room temperature for 5 hours or

269

overnight in the refrigerator (bring to room temperature before continuing). If you are in a hurry, an hour of marination at room temperature will probably be enough, particularly for chicken.

Either heat grill until coals are white hot or heat the broiler with the rack 4 inches from the heat. If broiling, arrange the skewers in a single layer on the broiler pan. *For chicken,* grill or broil until just cooked through, about 3 minutes, rotating the pan once if broiling. *For lamb, pork or beef,* cook about 5 minutes, rotating the pan once if broiling. You may want to stop and cut into the meat to check the doneness; pork should not be pink, but cook other meats to the degree of doneness you prefer.

A*n outdoor party from the grill for hearty eaters:* **1** *Sliced Grilled Flank Steak (page 273);* **2** *sliced tomatoes;* **3** *Bruschette (page 131);* **4** *a crock of mustard;* **5** *grilled portobello mushrooms (page 82) for slicing along with* **6** *ramps (page 83) and baby eggplant (page 82);* **7** *Chicken Saté (page 272) to coat with* **8** *Peanut Dipping Sauce (page 28). It can all—except the saté and sauce—be piled onto a split Focaccia (page 128) brushed with olive oil for scrumptious, mouth-stretching sandwiches.*

curry marinade

The guava paste gives this a slightly musky, tropical flavor.

Makes 1 cup

½ cup fresh orange juice
6 tablespoons guava paste
 (4½ ounces) (available at
 Hispanic markets)
¼ cup Dijon mustard
1 tablespoon curry powder

Combine all ingredients in a blender and blend until smooth. The marinade can be made up to 3 days before using.

curry rum marinade

This is spicier than the Curry Marinade and very good indeed.

Makes about ¾ cup

2 teaspoons unsalted butter
1 tablespoon curry powder
⅓ cup dark rum
2 tablespoons molasses
⅓ cup pineapple juice
3 tablespoons fresh lime juice
1 tablespoon kosher salt
1 teaspoon minced fresh hot
 green pepper

Heat the butter in a small saucepan over low heat until it foams. Stir in the curry powder and cook until fragrant, about 2 minutes. Mix the rum and molasses together and add to the saucepan. Using a long kitchen match, carefully ignite the rum and shake the pan until the flames subside. Stir in the pineapple juice, lime juice, salt and hot pepper. Cool to room temperature.

peachy marinade

In the box on page 303, see my recipe, made every summer, for peach purée. If making this in summer, use pieces of underripe peaches on the skewer.

Makes 1⅓ cups

1½ teaspoons ground cumin
1 teaspoon ground cardamom
¼ teaspoon ground cinnamon
2 tablespoons vegetable oil
1 cup peach purée or nectar
2 tablespoons fresh lemon
 juice
1 tablespoon honey
½ teaspoon hot red pepper
 sauce
2 tablespoons sherry

Combine spices and oil in a small pan and cook, stirring, over low heat for about 4 minutes. Remove from heat.

Stir in peach nectar, lemon juice, honey, hot pepper sauce, and sherry.

chicken, beef or pork saté or yakitori

Depending on the part of the East, these skewers with waves of meat undulating up them will be called saté or yakitori. Choose your name, your meat and your dipping sauce: Southeast Asian Dipping Sauce (page 28), Peanut Dipping Sauce (page 28), Pacific Tomato Dipping Sauce (page 26) or Asian Marinade (page 78) or a dipping sauce (see Index) from another part of the world if you are trying another kind of marinade. If there is leftover marinade, it can be used as a dipping sauce, but it will have to be brought to a boil before use.

All of the marinade recipes that follow make enough for about twenty brochettes.

Makes 20 to 24 brochettes

1 pound boneless, skinless
 chicken breasts
 or
1 pound well-trimmed flank
 steak
 or
1¼ pounds trimmed pork
 tenderloin, cut into ¾-inch
 cubes
**Saté Marinade, or Yakitori
 Marinade (opposite page) or
 ½ recipe Asian Barbecue
 Sauce (page 77)**

Soak 24 6-inch wooden skewers (see box, page 269).

For chicken or beef, make into strips and thread on skewers as directed in box. If using the pork cubes, spear 2 cubes on each skewer.

Place skewers in a shallow dish. Pour marinade over skewers and turn them so that each is well coated.

Marinate at room temperature for 5 hours or overnight in the refrigerator (bring to room temperature before continuing). If you are in a hurry, an hour of marination at room temperature will probably be enough, particularly for chicken.

Heat the broiler with the rack 4 inches from the heat. Carefully arrange as many of the skewers as will fit in a single layer on the broiler pan. For chicken and pork, broil until just cooked through—about 3 and 4 minutes, respectively. For beef, cook until medium, about 2½ minutes. Repeat with the remaining skewers if necessary.

Strips of Meat for Skewers

For Chicken
Separate breast halves, removing the connecting cartilage and any bits of fat. Gently pull off the loins; each one will be its own brochette. Put the breasts in the freezer for 3 minutes to firm up so they will slice more easily. Cut each half breast into ½-inch-wide strips, following the grain of the meat; you should get 4 to 6 pieces from each half.

Lay 6 strips on a piece of plastic wrap or wax paper on a stable surface. Make sure each piece is lying straight. Cover with a second piece of wrap or paper. Using a heavy flat object such as a cleaver, pound each strip to ¼-inch thick. After each whack, feel the chicken (your hand is more sensitive than your eye) to see how even the pounding is. You want long, narrow pieces, so push the long way rather than to the sides. Repeat with remaining strips.

For Beef
First, trim the meat of all exterior fat. Chill the meat, uncovered, in the coldest part of the refrigerator for 30 minutes to an hour. With a sharp thin-bladed slicing knife, carve into very thin slices on a slight bias (about a 70-degree angle).

To Skewer the Meat
Thread 1 chicken or beef slice onto each skewer in a wave, or S pattern, making more than one curve if possible, and making sure both ends are on the same side of the skewer.

saté marinade

Very good, and it is close to being a standard.

Makes about 1½ cups

⅓ cup vegetable oil
⅓ cup packed fresh coriander (cilantro), stems included
¼ cup fresh lime juice
¼ cup tamari soy sauce
6 slices (¼-inch) peeled fresh ginger (1 ounce)
8 medium cloves garlic, smashed and peeled
1½ tablespoons sugar
1 tablespoon ground cumin
1 small whole dry red chili pepper

Combine all ingredients in blender and blend until the coriander and chili are finely chopped. The marinade can be made up to two days in advance. Bring to room temperature and stir well before using.

yakitori marinade

As this is thinner than the marinade above, you will need less of it to coat the skewers.

Makes about ¾ cup

⅓ cup tamari soy sauce
¼ cup mirin
2 tablespoons light brown sugar
1 tablespoon rice wine vinegar
1 medium clove garlic, smashed and peeled
¼ teaspoon grated peeled fresh ginger

Combine all ingredients in blender and blend at medium speed until the sugar is dissolved. The marinade can be made up to 3 days in advance and stored, covered, in the refrigerator.

grilled flank steak

This is particularly good for an outdoor party. When the meat is cooked, slice it across the grain in thin diagonal strips. Then cut each strip into two pieces. Surround with Grilled Vegetables (page 77), add some sliced tomatoes and onions, put out a salsa (pages 23–25) and a crock of mustard and have miniature biscuits (pages 108–109) and/or Whole-Wheat Soda Bread (page 114) or bought Italian bread on hand. You'll be surprised how many people are happy to use their fingers.

1 flank steak (about 1¾ pounds)
2 teaspoons kosher salt
Freshly ground black pepper, to taste
¼ cup olive oil

Sprinkle steak on both sides with salt and pepper. Coat with oil and allow to stand at room temperature for at least an hour, turning at least once.

Preheat grill until coals are white-hot. Grill meat for about 10 minutes on each side for medium-rare. The length of time for grilling meat may differ according to the heat of your grill.

Remove meat from grill and allow to stand for about 5 minutes before slicing. To slice meat, see box.

273

fajitas

One of my assistants, Lee Ann Cox, is from Texas and has very clear ideas about how this adaptation of Mexican food should be served. She puts out all the components in separate dishes and lets people build their own. This can be a whole party with beer. Put out the sliced grilled meat, tortillas (always wheat), grilled strips of onion and green pepper (page 77), grated Cheddar or Jack cheese, Guacamole (page 13), salsa (pages 23–25) and sour cream. Texans would serve refried beans on the side as well as sliced chicken (see box, page 273), marinated and grilled just like the fajitas.

For more manageable snacks, place a piece of folded over meat on a tortilla chip and top with salsa and a drop of sour cream.

I prefer to use skirt steak when I can get it, but flank is quite acceptable.

Makes 36 to 44 slices, depending on type of meat used

1 pound skirt or flank steak, trimmed of all surface fat
½ cup fresh lime juice
8 or 9 large cloves garlic, smashed and peeled
4 serrano or jalapeño peppers, seeded and coarsely chopped

If using skirt steak, cut meat along the grain into 3-inch squares. If using flank steak, cut in half lengthwise. To slice meat, see box, page 273.

Place remaining ingredients in a blender and blend until smooth. Rub the mixture into the meat on all sides. Allow to marinate for 2 hours at room temperature or overnight in the refrigerator (let come to room temperature before continuing).

To Grill. Grill skirt steak for 3 minutes, turning pieces once, or flank steak for 2 minutes, turning once.

To Broil. Broil skirt steak for 2 minutes, 30 seconds, turning once, or flank steak for 1 minute, 30 seconds, without turning.

carpaccio

Raw meat is probably as caveman as we get in normal eating habits. Yet it turns up in some of the world's most sophisticated dishes. Carpaccio seems to be the invention of Harry's Bar in Venice, which has a penchant for naming things after artists as in the Bellini (page 303). There the thin slices of beef are overlapped to coat a plate, and a sauce much like the Sage Mayonnaise is artistically scribbled on top. The cheese is optional. Here, I turn the whole thing into manageable little rolls for snacking and give a choice of two sauces.

Makes about 40

2½ pounds shell steak, 3 inches thick, trimmed of all fat and bone (1¼ pounds)
½ recipe Anchovy and Caper Sauce (page 243), or 1 recipe Sage Mayonnaise (this page)
½ cup coarsely shredded Parmesan cheese
40 endive leaves, optional

Place meat in freezer until very firm but not frozen, 2 to 3 hours.

Cut meat lengthwise into ⅛-inch-thick slices. Cut each slice crosswise into quarters. Place 1 piece of the meat between 2 large pieces of plastic wrap. Using the flat side of a meat pounder or the bottom of a heavy glass, start in the center and push the meat outward into a rectangle, as if you were rolling dough with a rolling pin. Continue with remaining pieces.

Place ½ teaspoon sauce in the center of each piece. Spread the sauce out, leaving a ¼-inch border. Sprinkle ½ teaspoon of the cheese over the sauce on each. Loosely roll up each slice lengthwise.

To make up to 1½ hours ahead, place rolls in a glass or ceramic dish in a single layer. Brush very lightly with olive oil. Cover with plastic wrap directly touching meat. Refrigerate. Remove from refrigerator 30 minutes before serving. If using endive, separate leaves and place in a bowl of cold water.

Either secure the rolls with a toothpick placed at an angle or place each roll on an endive leaf.

sage mayonnaise

This is perfect with Carpaccio but would do well with sliced Turkey (page 267) or Roast Loin of Pork (page 286).

Makes ½ cup

½ cup Classic Mayonnaise (page 32) or other mayonnaise (pages 31–38)
1½ tablespoons loosely packed fresh sage leaves
2 teaspoons brandy

Place mayonnaise in a food processor. With the motor running, add the sage and brandy and process until well combined.

As long as there are meat eaters, this rosy, poached Beef Fillet (page 282) will be welcomed sliced onto Whole-Wheat Soda Bread (page 114) that is spread with Green Peppercorn Butter (page 43) or mustard.

steak tartare

This is a well-known hangover cure—say, for a New Year's Day feed. It's very popular at any time. Serve with store-bought party rye or with homemade Whole-Wheat or Rye Soda Bread (page 114), or put large spoonfuls on individual leaves of Bibb lettuce or large basil leaves.

Elegant restaurants used to purée meat by skewering one end of the whole fillet to a cutting board. Then with a thin-edged silver spoon they would scrape the meat from any tendon or sinews. This was done instead of grinding the meat. It is still important to grind the meat as close to the time of serving as possible. If you and the butcher are not close, grind the meat at home, after cutting very lean meat in cubes, by putting once through a meat grinder or coarsely grinding in batches with on-off pulses in a food processor.

Once this is made, serve within two hours. Multiply as need be.

Makes 3 cups

3 egg yolks
¹/₄ cup olive oil
2 tablespoons Dijon mustard
1 tablespoon Worcestershire sauce
2 teaspoons red wine vinegar
2 teaspoons chopped anchovies, rinsed under cold water and any bones removed
1 pound very lean ground beef
1 small onion (about 3 ounces), peeled and finely minced (about ¹/₂ cup)
2 tablespoons capers, rinsed and drained
Kosher salt, to taste
Freshly ground black pepper

In a small bowl combine yolks, oil, mustard, Worcestershire, vinegar and anchovies.

Place beef in a medium bowl with onion and capers. Pour over egg mixture and season to taste with salt and pepper. Lightly toss together just until thoroughly combined. Do not overmix. Serve immediately or refrigerate, covered with plastic wrap, for up to 2 hours.

lamb tartare

A *surprising and welcome taste for many will be Fried Kibbeh served with toasted pita (page 93) and some Spicy Middle Eastern Tomato Sauce (page 27).*

In the Middle East, raw lamb is ground, spiced and combined with soaked cracked wheat and sometimes eaten raw as **kibbeh** **nayé** *just as we eat Steak Tartare. Serve it with a dish of small Bibb or other lettuce leaves, as well as a bowl of finely sliced scallions and one of lemon wedges. Guests use a leaf held between the thumb and first two*

fingers of the right hand to pick up some of the meat mixture, which is then sprinkled with the sliced scallions and dribbled with lemon juice. You can make the small portions up ahead.

According to my friend Paul

Levy, the Laotians make a similar dish searingly hot using toasted ground rice in the place of bulgur. I think I will leave that to purists.

Makes 4 ½ cups

1 cup bulgur wheat (cracked wheat)
3 cups boiling water
1 large onion (about 10 ounces), peeled and cut into ½-inch pieces (3 ⅓ cups)
10 ounces very lean ground lamb
2 teaspoons kosher salt
½ teaspoon ground allspice
Freshly ground black pepper, to taste
Bibb lettuce leaves
Finely sliced scallions, white and green
Lemon wedges

Soak bulgur in boiling water in a bowl for about 5 minutes. Strain through a fine sieve and squeeze out any remaining water. Allow to cool.

Place onion in work bowl of food processor and process until as smooth as possible, stopping the machine and scraping down the sides of the bowl occasionally. Add lamb and seasonings and process until mixture becomes very smooth like a paste. Add cooled bulgur and process until smooth again. If you find you get a smoother result, make this by adding all the ingredients in small amounts to a blender until all is smooth.

Scrape into serving dish and refrigerate until ready to serve. Serve with Bibb lettuce leaves, chopped scallions and lemon wedges.

fried kibbeh

Those who wouldn't eat raw meat on a bet can serve these equally savory and traditional bites. You

can serve these on wedges of pita (page 93) or in individual pitas if you can buy them, along with Eggplant Moroccan (page 10) or Spicy Middle Eastern Tomato Sauce (page 27).

Forming kibbeh in the traditional manner is not as intimidating as some books and a few grandmothers make it out to be. The method is not suitable for the small sizes that make these snacks, but you might want to try it so as to stuff the hollow oval with a second mixture or to form kibbeh to put on a skewer for grilling. Take a little kibbeh, traditionally described as the size of a walnut, of mixture in a dampened hand and form it into a rough oval. With the thumb or first finger of the other hand, equally wet, push a hole lengthwise into the oval. Don't press too tightly but smooth gently. Withdraw your finger.

Makes about 45 pieces

1 cup bulgur wheat (cracked wheat)
3 cups boiling water
1 small onion (about 5 ounces), peeled and cut into ½-inch pieces (1 ⅔ cups)
½ pound very lean ground lamb
1 ½ teaspoons kosher salt
¼ teaspoon ground allspice
Vegetable oil for frying, optional

Soak bulgur in boiling water in a bowl for about 5 minutes. Strain through a fine sieve and squeeze out any remaining water. Allow to cool.

Place onion in work bowl of food processor and process until as smooth as possible, stopping the machine and scraping down the sides of the bowl occasionally. Add lamb and seasonings and process until mixture becomes very smooth, like a paste. Add cooled bulgur and process until smooth again.

Form lamb mixture into

277

small patties, using 1 tablespoon for each one.

To Broil. Preheat broiler and generously coat a baking sheet (not air-cushioned) with vegetable oil. Place patties on sheet about ¼ inch apart. Broil for 5 minutes. Remove from oven and loosen from pan with metal spatula.

To Fry. Work in batches and fry patties until golden brown, about 2 to 3 minutes (see Deep Frying, page 236).

Cinnamon Pine Nut Kibbeh

Use ¼ teaspoon ground cinnamon and 6 tablespoons pine nuts. Add cinnamon with other seasonings. Before forming into patties, stir in pine nuts. Finish as above.

koftah

Koftah is usually made with lamb or beef. Sometimes it is fried as a meatball or the mixture is formed around a soaked skewer and then either grilled or fried. It is different from the fried Kibbeh, as it has no bulgur, although it is sometimes made with rice. The small patties or meatballs can be poached in liquid (a sauce), sautéed or fried. The fried or sautéed ones can be served with room temperature Spicy Middle Eastern Tomato Sauce (page 27) or Cucumber Tzatziki (page 17) as a dipping sauce. Alternatively, the meat can be poached in the tomato sauce. Consider adding some chopped Lemon Pickles or Green Pickled Lemons (page 54) to the sauce. If sautéing before simmering, reduce cooking time by a minute. To hold, see Buffet Meatballs (this page).

More authentically, this is made with fattier meat—about an eighth fat—and the seasonings are much greater. For this amount of

meat, you can add a teaspoon of finely chopped fresh mint (¼ teaspoon dried) or coriander leaves, a pinch of chopped marjoram, ½ teaspoon ground cumin and ground hot pepper (hot paprika) to taste.

Makes about 50 meatballs

- **1 ¼ pounds lean ground lamb**
- **¼ cup finely chopped onion (1 ½ ounces)**
- **¼ cup chopped fresh Italian parsley leaves**
- **2 tablespoons chopped fresh coriander (cilantro) leaves**
- **¼ teaspoon dried marjoram**
- **2 teaspoons ground cumin**
- **2 teaspoons kosher salt**
- **Freshly ground black pepper, to taste**
- **Vegetable oil for frying, optional**
- **Spicy Middle Eastern Tomato Sauce (page 27), optional**

Combine all ingredients except oil in a bowl until thoroughly incorporated. Form into small balls using about 1 tablespoon of the mixture.

Either sauté in a nonstick skillet over medium to high heat for about 3 minutes, turning once **or** working in batches, fry for about 1 minute (see Deep Frying, page 236) **or** poach in Spicy Middle Eastern Tomato Sauce (page 27) in a deep skillet over medium heat for 5 minutes.

buffet meatballs

Koftah in sauce or Stroganoff Meatballs can be put on a buffet and kept warm in a chafing dish or out-of-use fondue pot—with small bread-and-butter plates and forks available. The meatballs can be made ahead on the day of the party, as can the sauce. Keep them separate at room temperature. Combine and reheat for three minutes to serve. Toothpicks are helpful for the meatballs if there are no plates or breads to put them on, but I have messed some outfits disastrously this way.

stroganoff meatballs

Beef Stroganoff is a luxurious semi-Russian dish that was a great favorite of cocktail parties in the 1950s. It should be made with expensive fillet of beef cut in ¼-inch thick strips or thin slices that are briefly sautéed and then briefly simmered in the sauce. Unfortunately, it was almost never good. In exchange, I offer these meatballs, which are good. To serve, see Buffet Meatballs (this page).

Makes about 70 meatballs

Meatballs
- **⅓ pound fresh mushrooms, stems removed, caps trimmed and quartered (about 1 ½ cups)**
- **⅓ pound peeled yellow onion, cut into 2-inch chunks (about 1 ½ cups)**
- **1 ½ pounds ground chuck**
- **2 ½ teaspoons sweet paprika**
- **1 tablespoon Worcestershire sauce**

½ teaspoon dry mustard
2 teaspoons kosher salt
Freshly ground black pepper,
   to taste

Sauce
1 cup sour cream (8 ounces)
1 cup chicken broth
1 tablespoon cornstarch
   dissolved in 2 tablespoons
   cold water
Kosher salt, to taste
Freshly ground black pepper,
   to taste
¼ cup packed chopped fresh
   dill sprigs (½ ounce)

Place mushrooms and onions in a food processor and pulse until coarsely chopped. Scrape into a medium bowl and stir in ground beef and seasonings. Shape into teaspoon-sized meatballs.

Arrange half the meatballs in an 11 × 8 × 2-inch dish, leaving a small space between

each meatball. Cover tightly with microwave plastic wrap. Cook at 100% in a high-wattage oven for 2 minutes 30 seconds. Prick plastic to release steam. Uncover and transfer meatballs to a plate, reserving liquid. Repeat with remaining uncooked meatballs.

Combine sauce ingredients except dill in a 4-cup glass measure. Add reserved meatball cooking liquid. Cook, uncovered, for 4 minutes, 30 seconds, stirring twice. Remove from oven and stir in dill. Adjust seasoning, pour over meatballs and serve warm.

No child and few adults can refuse these Miniature Hamburgers on Hamburger Buns (page 125), especially as the hamburgers can be varied in so many ways, from basic to sophisticated.

miniature hamburgers

Hamburgers are a great American favorite and are liked at informal parties by children and adults, particularly on Hamburger Buns (page 125) made in an appropriate size. If you don't feel up to making buns, quarter bought buns and use them. The meat mixture can be varied with seasonings, the burgers can be stuffed—nice for children so they don't make a mess—and topped. Have fun. Allow two to three burgers per person unless they are the main attraction at a football party or the main feed for kids. Then I would go up to four per person. The recipe can be endlessly multiplied. It's easier than you think, since you can broil entire pans of the burgers

rather than having to watch them on top of the stove.

Pick appropriate toppings from bottled ketchup, relish out of a jar and sliced onion to Cranberry Ketchup (page 267) and Pepper Relish (page 280). Olivada Hamburgers could be topped with slices of cherry tomatoes and a basil leaf. Other good toppings are Romesco Sauce (page 9), Eggplant Moroccan (page 10), salsas (pages 23–25), Tartar Sauce (page 36), one of the rémoulades (pages 37–38), Green Goddess Dressing (page 37) or one of the cheese spreads (pages 39–42).

Makes 24

1½ pounds ground beef
1½ ounces minced onion
  (4 tablespoons)
2¼ teaspoons kosher salt
Freshly ground black pepper,
  to taste

To Assemble Mixture. Place all ingredients in a medium bowl. Using your fingers, gently pinch the onions and seasonings into the meat until they are evenly distributed. Do not compact the meat.

To Form Hamburgers. Divide hamburger mixture into 1-ounce portions (scant 2 tablespoons each). Lightly roll each piece into a ball. Pat the balls into ½-inch-thick disks; do not tightly compact the meat. Moisten your fingers slightly with water and smooth out the edges of the patties.

Hamburgers may be made ahead up to this point. To freeze, stack between pieces of plastic wrap or parchment and place in an airtight container or bag. To refrigerate, lay hamburgers flat on a piece of parchment; when ready to cook, place an oiled jelly roll pan upside down over the parchment, invert the pan and remove the paper—do not cook on a cold baking sheet.

To Cook. Preheat broiler. Place hamburgers on lightly oiled jelly roll pans. If cooking from room temperature, broil for 2 minutes 30 seconds; if cooking from refrigerator, broil for 3 minutes 30 seconds; if cooking from frozen, broil for 5 minutes 30 seconds.

Southwestern Hamburgers
Use ¾ teaspoon additional kosher salt, 2 large cloves garlic, smashed and peeled, 1 tablespoon drained prepared horseradish, 2 tablespoons minced green pepper, 2 tablespoons minced scallion and 1½ teaspoons minced, seeded jalapeño pepper, optional.

Sprinkle salt over garlic cloves and mince very fine, pressing them into salt with the flat of the knife from time to time until they form a paste.

Assemble as above, adding the garlic paste and all remaining ingredients. Form and cook as above.

Green Peppercorn Hamburgers
Use 2 tablespoons green peppercorns packed in brine, drained and rinsed, and 2 tablespoons Dijon mustard.

Mash peppercorns between your fingers. Assemble as above, adding peppercorns and mustard. Form and cook as above.

Olivada Hamburgers
Use ¾ teaspoon additional kosher salt, 2 large cloves garlic, smashed and peeled, 2 tablespoons Black Olivada (page 22) or commercial and 1½ teaspoons minced anchovies.

Mince garlic with salt, as in Southwestern Variation. Assemble as above, adding garlic paste and all remaining ingredients. Form and cook as above.

Stuffed Burgers
Use ¼ cup finely grated Cheddar (1½ ounces) OR ¼ cup blue cheese (3 ounces) OR ¼ cup ketchup. Assemble and form basic ingredients as above. Make a well in the center of a ball with your little finger. Press your finger around the outside of the well to make it as large as possible. Place ½ teaspoon of the desired filling in the center and pinch the meat around it to form a seal. Repeat with remaining balls. Form and cook as above.

pepper relish

This is perfect with hamburgers and Ham (page 288). To store on the shelf instead of the refrigerator, see box, page 56.

Makes 3½ cups

3 bell peppers (one each red, yellow and green, about 8 ounces each), stemmed, seeded, deribbed and cut into 2-inch chunks (about 4½ cups)
6 ounces yellow onion, peeled and cut into 2-inch chunks (about 2 cups)
1 cup cider vinegar
½ cup maple syrup
1½ teaspoons dry mustard
½ teaspoon hot red pepper flakes, or 3 small dried red peppers
1 tablespoon kosher salt
1 tablespoon finely chopped peeled fresh ginger (about 6 quarter-sized pieces)
4 medium cloves garlic, smashed, peeled and minced
2 teaspoons cardamom seeds
2 teaspoons black mustard seed

See box on page 56 for sterilizing jars.

Place peppers and onions in the work bowl of a food

processor. Pulse on and off until finely chopped but not puréed or mushy (a few larger pieces are fine).

Scrape into a 2½-quart soufflé dish. Add remaining ingredients and stir to combine. Cover tightly with microwave plastic wrap. Cook at 100% in a high-wattage oven for 4 minutes or in a low-wattage oven for 6 minutes, or until vegetables are cooked but firm. Leaving dish in oven, prick plastic with the tip of a sharp knife; uncover and stir. Cook, uncovered, in a high-wattage oven for 2 minutes

longer, or until liquid reduces to create a relish, or in a low-wattage oven for 3 minutes for a slightly crunchy relish or 4 minutes for a softer one.

Remove from oven. Ladle into sterilized jars and store tightly covered in the refrigerator.

Marinated Lamb Riblets (page 283), a cheap and delectable chew.

beef fillet on french bread

Beef fillet (tenderloin) poaches evenly to an unimagined tenderness in a microwave oven so that thin slices can easily be eaten on slices of bread. Add mustard, a compound butter or horseradish as you choose. If you don't have good—unsalted—beef broth, use water. Save the resulting beef broth to use another time. The beef doesn't have to be sliced and assembled in the kitchen. It can be put out and sliced as desired. Leftovers—if there are any—can be sautéed and used in a main course salad.

If you don't use a micro-wave oven, bring broth to a boil; place deep roasting pan in a 350°F oven. Pour in broth; slip in meat; cook about twelve minutes or until done to your liking.

Makes 140 pieces

2 pounds beef tenderloin, trimmed of any fat, about 10 inches long
3 1/2 cups unsalted beef broth or water
5 medium cloves garlic, smashed, peeled and coarsely chopped
1/4 teaspoon freshly ground black pepper
French baguettes
Watercress Butter (page 43) or Dijon mustard

Cut the beef tenderloin into quarters lengthwise and place in a single layer in a 13 × 9 × 2-inch glass or ceramic oval dish. Add remaining ingredients. Cover tightly with microwave plastic wrap. Cook at 100% in a high-wattage oven for 4 minutes or in a low-wattage oven for 6 minutes. Prick plastic to release steam.

Remove from oven and uncover. Rearrange the pieces of beef so that the outside ones are now towards the center. Re-cover and cook in a high-wattage oven for 3 minutes more or in a low-wattage oven for 7 minutes more. Prick plastic to release steam and uncover. Let beef cool in broth for about an hour, or until room temperature.

Remove beef to a cutting board and cut each piece across into about 35 very thin slices, using a very sharp knife. Strain broth into a small container and reserve for another use. Discard garlic. Cut bread into thin slices, spread with butter or mustard and place slice of beef on each.

barbecued ribs

Spectacularly messy and always good, particularly for children out of doors. These can be made instead with Asian Marinade (page 78) or Asian Barbecue Sauce (page 77). Make sure your butcher trims the bone so that the ribs can be easily cut apart. If it's easier, cook the ribs ahead, cut apart and then reheat briefly under broiler or on grill.

Makes 13 ribs

1 rack pork ribs, 3 to 3 1/2 pounds
Cold water
4 cups Quick Barbecue Sauce (this page)

Microwave-Oven Method. Place ribs in a single layer in a 14 × 11 × 2-inch glass or ceramic dish. Pour 1 cup water over the ribs and tightly cover with microwave plastic wrap. Cook at 100% in a high-wattage oven for 20 minutes, turning ribs once, or in a low-wattage oven for 35 minutes, turning once. Prick plastic to release steam.

Remove from oven and uncover. Drain off water.

Stove-Top Method. Place ribs in a pan large enough to hold them comfortably and cover with water. Bring to a boil over medium heat. Reduce heat to low and simmer, uncovered, for 15 minutes. Remove from the heat and drain off water.

To Finish. Place ribs in a single layer in a shallow dish. Add sauce and toss until well coated. Marinate at room temperature for about 3 hours or overnight in the refrigerator.

To Grill. Allow ribs to come to room temperature if refrigerated. Heat grill until coals are very hot. Remove ribs from marinade and grill for about 20 minutes on each side, brushing frequently with the barbecue sauce.

To Broil. Proceed as for grilling, cooking ribs under heated broiler about 15 minutes to a side, turning once.

quick barbecue sauce

Yes, you can use bottled barbecue sauce, but I hate liquid smoke. This is so quick and easy it seems a shame to pay a premium for commercial. If you're big on spice, add two minced or puréed hot peppers.

Makes 4 cups

8 medium cloves garlic, smashed, peeled and sliced
3/4 cup water, if cooking on top of the stove
1 large can tomato purée (1 pound 13 ounces)
1/2 cup dark molasses
3 tablespoons Dijon mustard
3/4 cup cider vinegar
2 tablespoons chili powder
Kosher salt, to taste
1/4 teaspoon hot red pepper sauce, or to taste

Microwave-Oven Method.
Combine all ingredients except
salt and pepper sauce in an
8-cup glass measure. Cook,
uncovered, at 100% in a
high-wattage oven for 10 minutes
or in a low-wattage oven for 20
minutes.

Remove from oven and stir
in remaining ingredients. Allow
to cool to room temperature and
use, or store, covered, in 1-cup
containers in the refrigerator or
freezer.

Stove-Top Method. Combine
garlic and water in a medium
saucepan and bring to a boil
over medium heat. Reduce heat
to very low and simmer for 10
minutes, until garlic is soft. Stir
in remaining ingredients except
salt and pepper sauce. Increase
heat to medium; bring to a boil.
Reduce heat and simmer about 5
minutes. Stir in the remaining
ingredients.

Remove from heat. Allow
sauce to cool to room
temperature and use, or store,
covered, in 1-cup containers in
the refrigerater or freezer.

marinated lamb riblets

*I love these and love the size just
large enough to put in my mouth
and chew and suck. Getting rid
of the bone is a problem in
tact—behind the napkin.*

*To reheat, cover dish with
plastic wrap and place in
high-wattage microwave oven for
three minutes, or place in dish
with lid in center of regular oven
heated to 350°F for eight minutes.*

Makes 25 to 30 pieces

**3 racks of lamb ribs (left from
  rib chops) weighing about
  ¾ pounds each, each rack
  cut across the bones into 3
  strips**

Marinade
3 tablespoons soy sauce
1 tablespoon hoisin sauce
**7 medium cloves garlic,
  smashed, peeled and
  chopped**
1 tablespoon dry vermouth
Pinch dry mustard
**Pinch Chinese five-spice
  powder**
**½ scallion, trimmed and
  sliced into ¼-inch rounds
  (⅛ cup)**
2 teaspoons rice wine vinegar
1 teaspoon tarragon vinegar

With a sharp knife, cut
between the ribs of the 9 strips
(3 per rack) to divide them into
riblets.

Mix marinade ingredients
together. Add riblets and stir to
coat them well. Let riblets
marinate for at least 3 hours, or
refrigerated overnight, turning
them occasionally in the
marinade.

Preheat oven to 375°F while
riblets come to room temperature if they have been
refrigerated.

Place riblets, separated, on a
roasting or jelly roll pan. Bake
for 35 to 50 minutes, depending
on meatiness of ribs, basting
every 10 minutes. Remove from
oven and pour off fat. Transfer
ribs to serving platter. Deglaze
pan and pour the liquid over the
ribs.

Serve hot with plenty of
napkins—these are succulent but
greasy.

lamb chops

*I do look around me at the real
world to see what people are
doing. It's not always something I
would do or feel that I can
afford. That said, these baby lamb
chops have become popular on the
posh party circuit. Have those
frilly little paper holders for the
bones on hand. Multiply as*

*needed and money allows—two
to three per person, especially if
the party is replacing dinner.*

Makes 12

**12 small rib lamb chops (about
  1½ pounds total), trimmed
  as below**
Kosher salt, to taste
**Freshly ground black pepper,
  to taste**

Have your butcher "French"
the chops. This is done by
removing the fat around the
outside of the meat and scraping
the bone of all meat and fat.
There is a small section of meat
near the bone connected by a
membrane, which should also be
removed, leaving a round of lean
meat about 1¾ × 2 inches. The
bone should be cut to about 2½
inches longer than the meat. Ask
the butcher to include a few
pieces of the trimmed fat.

Rub the fat over your pan
or grill to prevent sticking.

To Pan-Cook. Heat a large skillet
(do not use a nonstick one) over
medium-high heat until quite
hot. Add as many chops as will
fit without crowding. Cook
about 2½ minutes per side.
Repeat with remaining chops.

To clean pan, deglaze with a
little water.

To Broil. Preheat broiler. Place a
jelly roll pan under the broiler
for 5 minutes to heat. Place
chops on pan and broil for
about 2 minutes per side.

To Grill. Heat grill. Grill for 2
to 3 minutes per side, moving
the chops around from time to
time if you have hot spots on
your grill.

Sprinkle with salt and
pepper and serve hot.

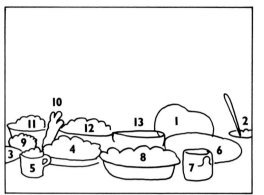

Cold winter days invite robust foods. You can make an assortment based around a **1** Ham (page 288) or **2** a block of Cheddar to which you can add a cheese scoop for charm. Put out **3** Olivada Focaccia (page 129) or **4** Buttermilk (page 108) or other biscuits along with **5** mustard so people can make their own sandwiches. Optional others are **6** Steamed New Potatoes (page 69) to go in **7** Parsley and Scallion Dip (page 17); **8** Greek Stuffed Grape Leaves (page 203); **9** Lemon Spiced Olives (page 55); **10** Puff Pastry Straws (page 103) and **11** Sun-Dried Tomato Dip (page 8) for potatoes or sandwiches, the favorite, **12** Boiled Shrimp (page 168) to dip in everything and **13** a splash of tart Pickled Beets (page 89).

curry lamb stuffing

This stuffing is usable in so many different foods it seemed best to give it on its own. See Stuffed Miniature Vegetables (page 72) and Leaves as Wrappers (box, page 204). It can also be sautéed as meatballs.

Makes 1½ cups

½ pound ground lamb
1 small onion, finely diced (about ⅓ cup)
1 small clove garlic, smashed, peeled and minced
1½ teaspoons curry powder
⅛ teaspoon cayenne pepper
2 tablespoons long-grain rice
½ cup chicken broth, or water
¾ teaspoons kosher salt
⅛ teaspoon freshly ground black pepper
1½ tablespoons plain yogurt
1 scallion, trimmed and sliced
1½ teaspoons fresh lemon juice

Crumble the lamb into a large saucepan. Place over medium heat and sauté, stirring, until no trace of pink remains. Stir in the onion, garlic, curry powder and cayenne pepper. Sauté until the lamb is browned and the onion is tender, about 10 minutes. Stir in the rice and add the broth, salt and pepper. Heat to simmering, cover the pan and cook until the rice is tender and the liquid is absorbed, about 15 minutes.

Check occasionally and adjust the heat if necessary. If the liquid is evaporated before the rice is tender, add a little water or broth.

Remove the pan from the heat and stir in the yogurt, scallions and lemon juice.

roast loin of pork

For years, this has been my favorite economy roast. You buy it boned and rolled by the butcher. It is the kind of meat you can buy by the inch. Ask the butcher to include the bones. When the meat cools—not stone cold—this can be sliced extremely thinly, about eight slices per inch. Each slice can be halved or quartered for miniature sandwiches made with Biscuits (pages 108–109). Top with a sauce. See list for Hamburgers (page 280) and think of mustard and the olive dips (pages 21–22).

The Spicy Chinese Variation can be used in dishes calling for Chinese barbecued pork, or it can be served on a biscuit with some of the sauce and a little Chinese mustard.

Each 6-inch amount of roast yields 48 slices that may be quartered for sandwiches, making 192 pieces

1 pork loin, boned and rolled

Use 1 times the following amounts for every 6 inches of roast:
3 medium cloves garlic, smashed, peeled and slivered lengthwise
Fresh or dried rosemary
Kosher salt
Freshly ground black pepper

¾ cup red wine

Use the point of a small knife to make small incisions toward the center all around the roast. Insert the slivers of garlic. Pat rosemary, lots of salt, and freshly ground pepper onto the roast.

Preheat oven to 500°F with the rack positioned in lower third of oven. If you have the pork bones, place them in the center of a roasting pan and use

as a rack. Place pork over bones or in pan. No matter what the length of the roast, leave it in the oven for 50 minutes. As long as the meat reaches an internal temperature of 140°F at the center, don't worry if it is slightly pink. The traditional worst crime against pork is cooking it to a dry and dusty death.

You can place the bones back in the oven for 15 minutes longer to crisp them. Cut them apart and serve them with the roast if you have the kind of guests that don't mind using their fingers, or save the bones to crisp up the following day for a private orgy.

Transfer pork to a platter. Pour fat from pan. Add any pork juices that have accumulated on platter and wine to pan. Place over high heat and stir vigorously, scraping up browned bits from the bottom of the pan. Makes about ½ cup sauce.

Spicy Chinese Pork
Omit all ingredients from above except pork. Use 1¼ ounces peeled fresh ginger, cut in small pieces, 2 medium cloves garlic, smashed, peeled and chopped, ¼ cup dark Chinese soy sauce or tamari soy, 2 tablespoons malt syrup or molasses, 2 tablespoons chili paste with garlic, 1 tablespoon toasted sesame oil and 1 tablespoon rice wine vinegar.

The day before cooking combine all ingredients. Place in a dish just large enough to hold the meat. Add the pork, turn it in the marinade to coat all sides and refrigerate overnight. Place pork in pan and reserve marinade. Roast as above. Deglaze pan as above, using ¼ cup water and reserved marinade in place of the wine. Boil sauce for a couple minutes to kill any bacteria from marinade.

286

zucchini bread and butter pickles

These are good to make when the garden has more zucchini than you can possible imagine. Serve with any roast meat or hamburgers. To put up for shelf storage, see page 56.

Makes 4 pint (16-ounce) jars

3 pounds zucchini (6 to 8 ounces each), cut into ½-inch rounds with a ripple potato slicer, with ripple blade of mandoline or with a food processor (about 12 cups)

¾ cup thinly sliced onion (about 3 ounces)

2 medium cloves garlic, smashed and peeled

3 tablespoons kosher salt

3 cups ice cubes

2 tablespoons black mustard seed, or yellow mustard seed

2 cups white vinegar

1½ cups sugar

3 2 x ½-inch pieces orange zest

1 teaspoon dill seed

1 teaspoon ground cumin

See box on page 56 for sterilizing jars.

Combine zucchini, onion, garlic and salt in a large bowl. Add ice cubes and stir to combine. Let stand for 3 hours.

Drain zucchini, discard liquid and reserve zucchini mixture.

Place mustard seeds in a 5-quart casserole dish. Cook, uncovered, at 100% in a high-wattage oven for 2 minutes or in a low-wattage oven for 3 minutes, 30 seconds. Remove from oven and stir in vinegar,

Roast Loin of Pork is one of my standbys. A wreath of rosemary seems very appropriate.

sugar, zest, dill seed and cumin. Stir well and cook, uncovered, in a high-wattage oven for 6 minutes or in a low-wattage oven for 10 minutes.

Remove from oven. Add zucchini mixture and stir to combine. Cover tightly with lid or microwave plastic wrap. Cook in a high-wattage oven for 12 minutes or in a low-wattage oven for 16 minutes. Prick plastic, if using, to release steam.

Remove from oven. Divide zucchini among sterilized jars, making sure they are covered with liquid.

All you must make are the Buttermilk Biscuits (page 108). The cheese, mustard and ham can all be bought, or cook your ham.

cooking ham

Adding a whole or half ham to an array of foods is an easy way to turn a cocktail meal into a whole meal. Complement with a large wedge of cheese (page 49), mustard, biscuits (pages 108–109) and

288

Otherwise ham must be cooked or heated. The best way is to poach the ham to warm it and keep it moist, and then bake it. It is slow but requires little attention.

Find a pot large enough to hold the ham covered by an inch of water. A whole, boned, smoked ham will require a large brazier roughly 13 × 7 inches. You can also use a stock pot by turning the ham on end. The trick is to heat the ham very gently in liquid that simmers but never boils; this maximizes juiciness and minimizes shrinkage. Then the ham is removed to a roasting pan and the final cooking is done. The ham can be left in the warming liquid with the heat turned off for up to two hours before final cooking. The final cooking can be done at least two hours before serving; you want it warm, not hot. Cover with aluminum foil while holding.

The liquid you use will depend on availability and affluence. As you replace liquid that evaporates from the warming liquid, use water. The amount of liquid needed will depend on the size of the ham. About one third of the original amount of liquid should be flavored. Choices are ruby Port, cream sherry or sweet white wine. For a whole ham, supplement or replace wine with the onions, six cloves and garlic. Add sugar if you like very sweet ham.

After the ham has cooked in the oven, you can quickly glaze it by turning the oven heat up as high as it gets, peeling back any skin, scoring any fat and coating the surface with brown sugar mixed to a paste with some of the pan juices and mustard, if desired.

When the ham is cooked, remove from the pan. Allow to cool for thirty minutes. If boneless, cut in half lengthwise. Turn each half on cut side. Slice as thinly as possible. If making biscuit sandwiches, cut slices into appropriately sized pieces.

a chutney (pages 150, 161), Pepper Relish (page 280) or Zucchini Bread and Butter Pickles (page 287). Ham can come boned or bone in. Unless you are a good carver or trust the resourcefulness of your guests, boned is easier to manage. If you have a really good butcher shop, you may be able to get them to cook the ham for you and then slice and reassemble it.

The following is a guideline.

5½ pounds boned smoked ham

Warming Liquid
24 cups (6 quarts) water, or 35 cups (8¾ quarts) if no wine is used
11 cups cream sherry, Port or sweet white wine
Optional: 2 halved onions, 1 cup sugar, 10 cloves garlic, 6 cloves
18 cups (4½ quarts) water during cooking time

Baking Liquid
1½ cups extra wine as above, or unsweetened pineapple juice

Glaze
1 cup dark brown sugar
¼ cup Dijon mustard or honey mustard, optional

Place ham in large pot. Add Warming Liquid ingredients. Over medium-low heat, uncovered, bring to a simmer. Add water as needed, a few cups at a time, to keep ham covered. Cook until an instant-read thermometer inserted into the thickest part of the meat reads 140°F., about 4 hours.

Either turn off heat and leave in water until finishing, or remove immediately to a roasting pan. Heat oven to 350°F. Pour Baking Liquid into pan. Place pan in oven. Tent meat with aluminum foil. Cook for about 45 minutes. If glazing, remove pan from oven and foil from ham. Raise oven heat to maximum. Remove any skin; score any fat. Combine sugar with enough of pan juices to make a paste. Stir in mustard, if using. Spread ham with paste. Return to oven 5 to 10 minutes, or until glaze is cooked.

The warming liquid can be reduced by boiling and used as soup stock.

chapter 9

down the hatch

There is no party without something to drink, even if it's only pitchers of cold water. A small party or just a few friends can probably be taken care of by whatever you normally keep on hand. Your house is not a bar. A bottle of white wine in the refrigerator, a bottle of red wine on the table, some sodas and some fruit juice are all that's really needed, and that should take care of the children, too.

Remember, it's your party and there are no rigid rules even when the party gets large. Do, however, have lots of cocktail napkins—paper is fine—and twice as many glasses as guests. People tend to abandon glasses and plates, if there are any, as they wander. With a double supply of either I am saved hectic mid-party washing and simply run a couple of dishwasher loads after the party is over.

The easiest way to serve is to limit the offerings of liquors by thrusting a filled glass at guests as they enter and asking if that is all right. Nobody is ever insulted by Champagne, or failing that, a good bubbly such as the less expensive Italian prosecco. If lots of bubbly is

Summer-day Lemonade (page 298).

available via a waiter or a table with glasses and large plastic planters filled with ice right next to the entrance, I cut down on the complication of everybody wanting a different kind of drink as well as the overall liquor consumption. Pitchers of mixed drinks are a reasonable alternative. I do have the standard brands available, just in case. Today, I have two kinds of bottled water, a fizzy and a flat, available along with well-chilled juices for the healthier or dieting friends.

Years ago, when I realized how expensive it is to rent glasses, I went to a restaurant supply house and bought many dozens of a tulip-shaped Champagne glass that I stick in an out-of-the-way corner until it is time for a big party. Then I use the same glass for everything. Out of doors, near a pool or on a stone terrace, plastic glasses are a good idea.

Depending on the number of people, I set up one or two more refueling stations at far parts of the room or in separate rooms to get people moving around and avoid waterhole crush. Separating food from drink is another way to minimize elephant-stampede syndrome.

It's hard to know exactly how much to have on hand, but I always allow extra, figuring that another party will come along. Your child's college friends will drink more beer than you can imagine; small children may gulp milk or spurn it in favor of sodas and juice; but there are norms for the average party.

Champagne or bubbly wine drinks (pages 302–303) are very festive and bring out some of the world's loveliest glasses. Come summer, ripe fruit—a peeled peach, thoroughly cored strawberries—plunge into oversize glasses filled to the brim with bubbles.

Lemons garnish many drinks as well as foods. The peel can be made into **1** a long spiral by using a vegetable peeler all around a lemon or **2** short pieces for slipping into drinks or, more usually for food, into **3** little matchsticks of zest, which can be cut across for **4** tiny cubes. Before lemons are sliced, a channeler or zester can be run along the lemon lengthwise to make stripes. When the lemon is cut, the slices will be **5** scalloped. Slices of lemon or lime **6** can have a slit cut halfway through them. Then they can be slipped over the edge of a drink glass, or the slice can be twisted to create a decorative curl.

Unless the party is to be endless, something I try to avoid at all costs, a bottle of bubbly or still wine should cope with three to four people, meaning that a case is enough for about forty people. Each bottle of wine contains about twenty-five fluid ounces. Since a wineglass should never be filled to full—three to four ounces is about right—you will get six to eight glasses per bottle. If the bubbly is to be diluted with a fruit purée or other mixer, one bottle will provide eight to ten drinks. A pitcher of Bloody Marys (page 305) should be enough for twenty drinks of ten repeat offenders. I usually add the vodka to the drinks individually so that I will have some uncontaminated mix for nonliquor people.

I try to buy half bottles of vermouth ever since I gave an aged bottle to a martini-making friend only to find to my horror that it had maderized—turned a nasty, musty gold. I didn't even know dry vermouth went bad. This brings me to the subject of martinis. I never try to make a martini for anyone. They always have their own formula. I supply the makings: a small glass pitcher, ice cubes, a good gin and a dry French vermouth. On the side, I have small dishes with cocktail olives—I'm told that the smallest green Spanish olives are the best—pickled baby onions and thin lemon twists made pithless by using a potato peeler. The guests are on their own unless on a very rare day there is a bartender.

A basic bar stock is one Scotch, one vodka, one gin, one bourbon, one light rum and one dark rum.

Obligatory mixers are orange juice, cranberry juice, tomato juice, diet sodas, cola, tonic and club soda or seltzer.

Specialty parties will skew the drink mix, although the bubbly rules seem to hold true for all of them. If the party isn't too large and

you are having a rather Italian event—whether it be as simple as sliced sausages, cheese and olives or as lavish as that on page 101—you may want to have a tasting of Italian red wines. Six or seven different wines should do the trick. Talk to your wine seller, or have some fun trying different wines for a few weeks before the party. A party of Greek meze (page 204) calls for a good bottle of ouzo, which will cloud mysteriously in the glass with ice and water; but there are increasingly good, not resinated, wines coming from Greece these days and you might want to try to find some. Russian parties (page 41) and caviar will demand vodka, which can be frozen in a block of ice for drama, as can a bottle of aquavit to go with a Scandinavian spread.

In addition to the visible sources of ice—for self-serve or chilling wine—there needs to be a hidden resource. At this time, your bathtub is your best friend. Put the wine to be cooled, the sodas and the beer in the tub, neck up. Fill the tub with crushed ice about two hours before the party and cover that with cubes. A normal tub will take two to three 40-pound bags of crushed ice and one of cubes, available from ice-suppliers. The cubes can be skimmed off the top for making drinks. Bags of ice from the corner store will be only five pounds each. You will need a lot.

Larger ice cubes will melt more slowly than smaller ones, but smaller ones will dilute drinks more quickly—good or bad depending on your point of view.

If you live in a place where you can get ice delivered, it is well worth the expense. If you have to send someone to the store, make sure that the store will have enough ice for you by calling a good week before the party and then reminding them the day before. Con a friend or relative into making the ice run about two and a half hours before the party is set to begin. The only way out of the ice dilemma is provided when nature is obliging. If the party is in the chill of winter, you can simply set your wine out of doors or even in the snow if there is any. The alcohol should protect the wine from turning to ice for several degrees below freezing, but not much more. In summer, if your party is near a cool brook or pond, tie strings firmly around the bottle necks and lower them into the water.

A block of ice in a punch bowl is an old-fashioned and still intelligent way of keeping a largish quantity of a mixed drink cold during a party. The chunk of ice will melt less than an equivalent amount of ice cubes. If possible keep the mixers, mixed concoctions you make, juices and sodas cold in the fridge or bathtub along with the wine. While having crushed ice is advisable for some drinks, a good blender is probably more useful.

Remember that fresh juices make an enormous difference in drinks with alcohol as well as without. Some time spent with a juicer making up pitchers of lemon, lime and orange juice will vastly improve your party. Fruit garnishes can be prepared ahead as well: wedges and slices of citrus fruits, lemon peel thinly removed from the fruit with a potato peeler before the juice is made and any oddities like cucumber strips for Pimm's Cup that are required by what you plan to serve.

This chapter is not a drink manual—teetotal or otherwise. There are plenty of those around for you to consult. I give here only recipes for badly abused drinks like iced tea and Bloody Mary or things that I thought might not readily come to mind that I like. Brewing coffee and making tea are practically as personal skills as making a martini. Suffice it to note that many gatherings require them and cups, saucers, spoons, pitchers for various milks from skim to cream (depending on diet and habit) and sugar—cubes, loose, colored or flavored (fantasy is possible here)—and artificial sweeteners and lemon slices.

Cucumber provides crudités for dunking in dips and can be peeled and cut into sticks. If the skin has not been waxed (it will look dull and when you run a fingernail along it no wax will peel off), you can make attractive rounds or ovals by scoring the skin before slicing across or on the diagonal. Score the skin either with the sharp tines of a fork or by running a zester or channeler down the length of the cucumber. An attractive non-canapé is made with a blob of Quintessential Tuna Salad (page 183) on a cucumber slice.

296

ready-mades

In a sense, this is an almost entirely ready-made category, since few of us are making Champagne, other wines or liquor at home, nor do we make flavorings such as Worcestershire sauce, hot red pepper sauce or horseradish.

Sodas—acceptable—and juices often come under the heading of ready-mades. Generally, I much prefer home-squeezed juices and never use bottled lemon or lime juice. I make an exception for tomato juice, which is a lot of work, and cranberry juice, which I have never even thought of making. Frozen juices are less to be desired than fresh in a refrigerated container, though not if made from concentrate. Often a bottled juice can be perked up with a little lemon juice. It's the acid that dies in preserving processes.

Pre-made drink mixes are mostly unpleasant, and instant lemonade and iced teas hardly seem worth the money. Oddly enough, the dried, package mixes such as "sour" mixes are often better than the liquid ones. I have found the very fancy bottled juice mixes for combining with bubbly wine overly expensive and easily replaced by semi-homemade alternatives (see recipes). Frozen fruits, unsweetened, and canned fruits—in juice, not syrup—can be kept on the shelf to enliven many drinks.

If you find orzata (orgeat), a slightly almond-flavored sugar syrup named for the barley from which it was at one time made) on store shelves, it can replace simple syrup as can cane sugar syrup, available in some places.

Many drink garnishes, such as olives and pickled onions, are off-the-shelf staples. If you keep your offerings simple, you won't need ready-mades.

Feta cheese cubed and dipped in anise seeds is one way to customize cheese and add flavor, particularly at a large party. See Ready-Mades (pages 14–16) for other cheeses, other dips.

297

lemonade

Nothing is as refreshing as lemonade or prettier gleaming through a glass pitcher. Make a lot of lemon juice and multiply the recipe as often as you want using simple syrup. I usually slice a lemon thinly and add the slices to the pitcher.

Makes 2 cups

6 tablespoons fresh lemon juice, from about 3 lemons
1 ⅓ cups cold water
3 tablespoons cooled Simple Syrup I (page 300)

Combine all ingredients in a pitcher and allow to chill in the refrigerator for at least 2 hours. Serve over ice.

fruity iced tea

This is a virtually perfect hot-weather drink. If you entertain a lot of dieters, don't add the sugar. Instead, serve a small pitcher of Simple Syrup II (page 300) on the side.

I dislike Long Island Iced Tea which seems a way to get people sick on an ungodly assortment of liquors. However, this real iced tea can have American whiskey added, as in the variation, for a good drink.

Makes 10 cups

8 cups water
3 tablespoons plus 1 teaspoon loose tea
¼ cup tightly packed fresh mint leaves
1 ¼ cups sugar
1 ½ cups strained fresh orange juice
½ cup strained fresh lemon juice
Fresh mint leaves, for garnish
1 orange, thinly sliced, each slice cut halfway across

In a large pot (do not use aluminum, iron or copper), heat water until it just comes to the boil. Stir in tea, mint and sugar. Boil for 3 minutes.

Immediately strain tea through a fine sieve. Stir in juices. Let cool to room temperature. Place tea in one large pitcher or divide between two smaller pitchers. Fill pitchers or glasses with ice and serve. Garnish each glass with a sprig of mint and a slice of orange.

Whiskey Iced Tea
Makes 10 servings. Use ½ recipe Fruity Iced Tea and 1¼ cups bourbon or blended whiskey. Whisk together and serve over ice.

raspberry fruit punch

Here is a really good, nonalcoholic drink that is as satisfying to adults as to children. This adult particularly likes the ginger variation made with ginger beer; it's festively fizzy, stretches the raspberry purée and is very refreshing. There is a rum variation for those who want a "real" drink.

If you don't have time to make the raspberry purée, try substituting raspberry syrup, called himbeersaft in German and sirop de framboise in French. Don't add any simple syrup until you have tasted; the raspberry syrup has sugar in it. In a simpler variation, add ginger beer or club soda to the raspberry syrup and serve over ice.

Makes 8 servings (6 cups)

8 ounces raspberry or strawberry Fruit Purée (see box, page 303)
3 cups pineapple juice
2 cups fresh orange juice

2 tablespoons plus 2 teaspoons fresh lemon juice
½ cup Simple Syrup I (page 300)

Whisk all ingredients together in a bowl or pitcher. Serve over ice.

Ginger Fruit Punch
Make as above and whisk in 4 cups ginger beer. Makes 10 cups or 14 servings.

Rum Fruit Punch
Make as above and whisk in 2 cups light rum. Makes 7 cups or 10 servings.

curried yogurt drink

Not all cold drinks are sweet. This variation on a Middle Eastern favorite is a good complement to spicy foods. You can use lowfat yogurt if you prefer.

Makes 8 servings

4 cups plain yogurt
1 teaspoon kosher salt
4 teaspoons curry powder
4 cups ice water

In a bowl, whisk yogurt, salt and curry powder until smooth. Slowly whisk in ice water. Divide among 8 glasses with 4 to 5 ice cubes in each glass.

Certain parties seem to call for classic setups for drinks, Scotch and other alcohol in decanters, soda in a charger bottle and appropriate rocks and highball glasses. Less formally, the whole thing can be done with bottles of liquor and soda and all-purpose wineglasses. Ice will still be a must.

simple syrup I

One of the pleasantest gentilities of iced tea in a European restaurant is having it accompanied by a little pitcher of simple syrup. That way there is no desperate stirring to get the granular sugar to dissolve in the cold liquid. Simple syrup is also one of the tricks of the bartender's trade. It keeps virtually indefinitely in the refrigerator and can be used to make sorbets.

Makes 6 cups

4 cups sugar
4 cups water

Put sugar and water into a deep, non-tin-lined pot. Have on hand a pastry brush and some water to wash down sides of the pan should crystals form. Stir over very low heat, letting the sugar dissolve before allowing the mixture to come to a boil. Once the mixture boils, cover and let it continue cooking for 3 to 5 minutes. Remove from heat and cool.

Simple Syrup II
Follow the directions above, using 3 cups water and 6 cups sugar. Makes 5½ cups.

shandygaff

This is an old-fashioned pub drink. It sounds awful, but it's excellent and reduces the alcohol per drink by half.

Makes 8 servings

4 12-ounce bottles of ale
4 12-ounce bottles of ginger beer

Gently mix the ale and the ginger beer. Pour into 8 glasses. Serve immediately.

horse's neck

When I was a little girl and wanted to be grown up, Horse's Necks and Shirley Temples were the drinks we were given. It was clear that we were really being given ginger ale, but the names and the presentations made us feel very sophisticated. The Shirley Temple varies from the Horse's Neck in omitting the sugar cubes and using orange slices for garnish instead of lemon peel. In my day, they added maraschino cherries, but that's another tale.

Makes 8 servings

8 lemons
8 large or 16 small sugar cubes
2 teaspoons nonalcoholic grenadine
6 cups ginger ale

Using a vegetable peeler, start at the top of one lemon and remove zest in a spiral around the lemon, so that you end with one long coiled strip of zest. Repeat with remaining lemons.

Place one large or two small sugar cubes in eight tall glasses. Pour ¼ teaspoon grenadine over each sugar cube.

Place one lemon strip in each glass so that it coils up the sides. Hang the end of the strip over the edge of the glass to hold it in place.

Fill the glass with ice. Pour 6 ounces of ginger ale over ice in each glass and serve.

One of America's all-time favorites, Crab Cakes (page 187), shrunk to two-bite size and plopped in an appropriate bread—Cornmeal Biscuits (page 108), maybe in the Jalapeño variation—and gilded with the traditional Tartar Sauce (page 36), unless you want to pick a Spicy Rémoulade (page 37).

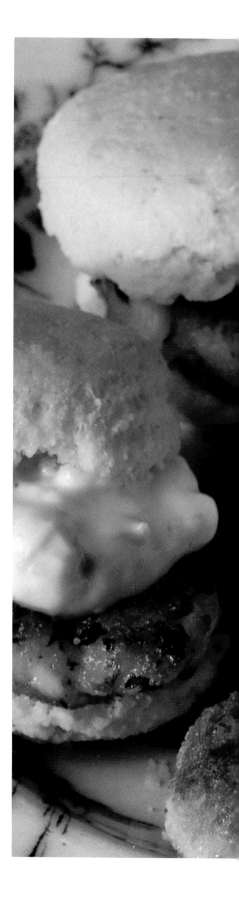

A *classic Champagne canapé, Pain de Mie (page 119) with a butter and almost transparent slices of good smoked salmon.*

champagne drinks

There is nothing more festive than a bubbly drink enlivened by a fruit purée, a juice or another liquor. Generally, you can use a less expensive bubbly wine than you would serve on its own, but taste and make sure you would be willing to drink it. Many of these drinks dilute the bubbly and so reduce the alcohol content of the drinks and the cost.

At a large party, I make these in pitchers—but not too much at a time, as the bubbly will go flat. Make sure that the purées and juices are well chilled before you begin. Don't try and overfill the pitchers, because these drinks foam up. Have a long, thin spoon like a drink muddler or an iced tea spoon on hand for stirring.

In some of these drinks, I add a little simple syrup; it depends on the sweetness of the fruit. Make the drink without simple syrup, taste and add syrup as desired.

For a smaller group, you may want to pour individual drinks or let people mix their own. Since a 750-milliliter bottle of bubbly contains a little more than three cups and you will want to allow about three ounces, or eight servings, per bottle, divide the other ingredients by eight to get a per-drink amount.

Paradis
I first tasted this at Eden Roc at the Hôtel du Cap on Cap d'Antibes. It is the most luxurious drink I know.

Makes 8 to 10 servings

- 1 bottle Champagne or sparkling wine
- 1 cup raspberry purée (see box)
- 2 tablespoons Simple Syrup I (page 300), optional

302

Strawberry Foam

Makes 8 to 10 servings

1 bottle Champagne or
    sparkling wine
1 cup strawberry purée
    (see box)
2 tablespoons Simple Syrup I
    (page 300), optional

Peach (Bellini)

*This is the classic from Harry's Bar
of Venice, where it is made only
with white peaches.*

Makes 8 to 10 servings

1 bottle Champagne or
    sparkling wine
1 cup peach purée (see box)
2 tablespoons Simple Syrup I
    (page 300), optional

Pear (Tintoretto)

Makes 8 to 10 servings

1 bottle Champagne or
    sparkling wine
1 cup pear purée (see box)
2 tablespoons Simple Syrup I
    (page 300)

Cranberry Crater

Makes 12 servings

1 bottle Champagne or
    sparkling wine
3 cups cranberry nectar
1 teaspoon Cointreau or
    Grand Marnier

Orange (Mimosa)

*At Harry's Bar, they add a little
fresh tangerine juice. I like this with
blood orange juice if it's available.*

Makes 8 to 10 servings

1 bottle Champagne or
    sparkling wine
1 cup orange juice

Cassis (Kir Royale)

Makes 8 to 10 servings

1 bottle Champagne or
    sparkling wine
½ cup plus 2 tablespoons
    cassis liqueur

Pernod (Death in the Afternoon)

*I really thought I had invented this
drink one winter afternoon about
1960, when I served Pernod with
Champagne, which just shows how
careful one must be. According to
Sardi's Bar Guide, Hemingway
was fond of Pernod and often said
that it "tastes like the tears of
remorse." The drink "Death in the
Afternoon" was invented for
Hemingway one afternoon in Paris
in the early 1930s by Harry Mac
Elhone of Harry's New York Bar,
when young Ernest came in after a
particularly grueling boxing match
in a Paris gym.*

Makes 8 to 10 servings

1 bottle Champagne or
    sparkling wine
¼ cup plus 2 tablespoons
    Pernod

Pear Liqueur

Makes 10 servings

1 bottle Champagne or
    sparkling wine
2 cups pear nectar
1 cup pear eau de vie
    (unsweetened pear liqueur,
    often called "poire")

Apricot Brandy

Makes 8 to 10 servings

1 bottle Champagne or
    sparkline wine
2 cups apricot nectar
1 cup apricot brandy

French 75

*There is some argument as to how
this is properly made. Whatever the
recipe, this is only as good as the
Champagne and Cognac used. It's
not as odd a combination as it
sounds like. Brandy was once used
to fill up the Champagne bottles
after the sediment formed by
fermenting Champagne in the
bottles was removed, degorged. This
is my way of making the drink, but
watch out—it's strong. If you're
uncertain of the crowd, mix these
one by one—an ounce of Cognac
to three of Champagne.*

Makes 8 to 10 servings

1 bottle Champagne or
    sparkling wine
1 cup Cognac

Black Velvet

*This is a pub classic and wonderful
with cold oysters or smoked
salmon. Think of it at brunch time,
or very late after the theater or
opera. Pour the two elements at the
same time and stir gently. A
creamy head will form.*

Makes 8 to 10 servings

1 bottle Champagne or
    sparkling wine
4 12-ounce bottles stout

Gently stir together
Champagne or other dry bubbly
and additional ingredients in a
large pitcher. Pour into glasses
and serve immediately.

Fruit Purées

Unless you have fruit
that is fresh, ripe and
in-season, unsweetened
frozen fruit will be as good
as fresh. Pear purée can be
made from drained
unsweetened canned pears.

If using fresh fruit, peel
and core as necessary. If
using frozen fruit, place in a
bowl over another bowl half
filled with warm water, until
defrosted.

Place fruit in a blender
and process until smooth,
stopping once or twice to
scrape sides of jar. If fruit
has seeds (raspberries and
strawberries), pass the purée
through a fine mesh sieve.

1 cup (4 ounces) raspberries	= ¼ cup purée
1 cup (5 ounces) strawberries	= scant ½ cup purée
1 cup (5 ounces) sliced peaches	= scant ½ cup purée
1 cup (8 ounces) pears	= scant ¾ cup purée

coffee granita

Granita di Caffé is just the thing you want to spoon or slurp up with a short straw on a hot day in an Italian trattoria sitting out of doors under colorful umbrellas. This version with Kahlúa makes a good summer version of Irish coffee. Try it instead of dessert at a small party. Top with whipped cream for real indulgence.

Makes 8 servings

¹/₂ cup instant espresso
¹/₂ cup sugar
4 cups warm water
1 to 2 cups Kahlúa or other coffee liqueur
Whipped cream, optional

Dissolve the espresso and sugar with the warm water. Pour into ice cube trays, preferably metal, and freeze.

Place the frozen cubes in a food processor and pulse until ice is well chopped but not slushy. Divide into 8 glasses and pour 1 to 2 ounces of Kahlúa over each. Top with whipped cream if desired.

lime daiquiri

This is Cuba's gift to the world and Hemingway's other great favorite. Triple Sec and Cointreau are interchangeable, lightly citrus, sweet liqueurs that are often used in fruit-juice-based drinks instead of simple syrup.

Makes 8 servings

1 cup fresh lime juice
1¹/₂ cups light rum
¹/₃ cup Simple Syrup I (page 300) or Triple Sec
Cracked ice

Whisk all ingredients except ice in a bowl. Half fill glasses with ice and fill with mixture.

rum punch

At first glance this looks very much like the daiquiri above. However, the difference in rum and proportions makes it a totally different drink. This is the simplest and, to me, best of the traditional tropical punches. If you look at Raspberry Fruit Punch (page 298) you will see another one.

Makes 8 servings

2 cups dark rum
2 cups fresh lime juice
1 cup Simple Syrup I (page 300)
Cracked ice
¹/₂ teaspoon nutmeg

Whisk rum, lime juice and simple syrup in a pitcher; refrigerate. Fill glasses with ice and pour in punch. Sprinkle each drink with a pinch of nutmeg.

honey bourbon sour

A version of this virtually addictive drink was developed several years ago by Michael Whiteman for a restaurant with which he was consulting.

Makes 8 servings

¹/₂ cup honey
1¹/₂ cups fresh lemon juice
2 cups bourbon

Have ready two good-sized pitchers. In one, combine honey and lemon juice and mix well. Stir in bourbon. This can be done ahead and refrigerated. Before serving, add 4 cups ice cubes to the second pitcher. Pour in chilled drink mixture. Pour drinks and ice back and forth between pitchers three or

four times. Glasses can be garnished with orange slices if desired.

papaya slush

This is a divine taste of the tropics and will delight the nonalcohol drinkers if the rum is omitted. The fruit and drink mixture can be made ahead and refrigerated. Multiply as desired, but don't try to make a bigger batch of the finished drinks at one time—too difficult in the food processor.

Makes 5 servings

1 ripe papaya (about 1 pound)
¹/₂ cup sour cream
¹/₂ cup dark brown sugar
¹/₃ cup fresh lemon juice
¹/₂ cup orange juice
³/₄ cup dark rum
3 cups ice cubes

Halve and seed the papaya and scoop out its flesh. Purée in a blender. Add sour cream, brown sugar, juices and rum to the blender and combine. Refrigerate.

Just before serving, put ice in the work bowl of a food processor and pulse until the ice is the consistency of chunky snow. Pour in liquid mixture and pulse, just to combine. Pour into 5 glasses and serve immediately.

mango rum milk shake

Although this is a lighter drink than the papaya, it tastes as rich.

It can be made ahead but may thicken in the refrigerator. Thin with a little additional milk or by shaking with some extra crushed ice.

304

Makes 5 servings

½ cup ice cubes (2¾ ounces)
1 cup Mango Purée (below)
¼ Simple Syrup II (page 300)
½ cup milk
½ cup light rum

Wrap ice cubes in a clean, smooth towel and smash with a hammer or the bottom of a sturdy pot. Put ice, purée, syrup, milk and rum into blender and process until smooth. Pour into 5 glasses with 4 or 5 ice cubes in each.

Mango Lime Shake
Use ⅓ cup of Simple Syrup II, substitute 3 ounces of lime juice for the milk and use dark rum instead of light. Garnish with sprigs of mint.

mango purée

Makes 2 cups

2 mangoes (about 11 ounces each)
2 tablespoons lemon juice

Peel and slice mangoes into cubes. Put into blender and purée with lemon juice.

margarita

Margaritas are Mexican versions of daiquiris. They are often briefly shaken with the cracked ice and then strained over cubes into a glass, the rim of which has been crusted with coarse salt. To salt the rim of a glass, dip the rim of the inverted glass in water and then in a saucer of kosher salt.

Makes 8 servings

1 cup fresh lime juice
1½ cups tequila
⅔ cup Triple Sec
Cracked ice

Whisk all ingredients except ice in a bowl. Half fill glasses with ice and fill with mixture.

eggnog

This is rich, but it's an insignia of holidays. Sadly, in today's world it's important to have cooked eggs in your eggnog. Make some of this without liquor for children. Serve into cups in small amounts.

Makes 8½ cups, about 22 3-ounce servings

6 large egg yolks
6 to 8 tablespoons sugar
4 cups milk
1 cup brandy or rum, or ½ cup of each
1 cup heavy cream
Nutmeg, preferably freshly grated

Whisk yolks and sugar together in a medium saucepan. Whisk in 2 cups of the milk. Place pan on a flame diffuser over medium-high heat (if you don't have a flame diffuser, you will have to work over very low heat or in a double boiler and it will take much longer). Have remaining 2 cups milk nearby.

Cook egg mixture, stirring constantly until it coats the back of a spoon and begins to form little bubbles all over the top, about 140°F to 145°F. Remove from heat and immediately stir in cold milk to cool the mixture down.

Pour into a metal bowl and refrigerate until cold. Stir in brandy. Whip the cream until soft peaks form. Fold the whipped cream into the egg mixture. Pour into a pretty bowl and lightly sprinkle the top with nutmeg.

bloody mary

Although there are recipes for Bloody Mary in every drink book, I include my own because it's a drink I like with brunch and at the end of a hard day, but I don't like it made with mixes—they never taste right to me. I like my drink mildly spicy. You can up the amount of hot red pepper sauce if you like a hotter drink. I like lemon juice, but you can use lime juice—too sweet for me. A Virgin Mary omits the vodka. The recipe makes six cups of mix without vodka. A nice variation is to use bottled clam and tomato juice in place of the tomato juice.

If you prefer, make as much mix as you like and add an ounce to an ounce and a half of vodka to each drink. At home, I don't garnish each glass; if you like, a small stalk of celery or a wedge of lemon can go in each glass.

Makes 8 servings

5¾ cups good-quality tomato juice
2 tablespoons prepared horseradish (do not drain)
1 to 2 teaspoons hot red pepper sauce
¼ cup Worcestershire sauce
½ to ¾ cup fresh lemon juice
⅛ teaspoon freshly ground black pepper
1 to 1½ cups vodka

Whisk all ingredients together in a bowl or pitcher. Serve over ice.

INDEX

Page numbers in **boldface** refer to photographs. Green dots (●) following page numbers refer to vegetarian recipes.